Introduction to Engineering and Technology

Introduction to Engineering and Technology

W. Lionel Craver, Jr.
Darrell C. Schroder
Anthony J. Tarquin

The University of Texas at El Paso

HOLT, RINEHART AND WINSTON, INC.

New York   Chicago   San Francisco   Philadelphia
Montreal   Toronto   London   Sydney   Tokyo

Library of Congress Cataloging-in-Publication Data

Craver, W. Lionel.
  Introduction to engineering and technology

  Includes index.
  1. Engineering.   2. Engineering mathematics.
I. Schroder, Darrell C.   II. Tarquin, Anthony J.
III. Title.
TA147.C73   1988   620   86-14251

ISBN 0-03-009729-0

Requests for permission to make copies of any part of the
work should be mailed to:
Permissions
Holt, Rinehart and Winston, Inc.
111 Fifth Avenue
New York, NY 10003

Printed in the United States of America

8   9   0   1   039   9   8   7   6   5   4   3   2   1

Holt, Rinehart and Winston, Inc.
The Dryden Press
Saunders College Publishing

To Becky Craver and Virginia Tarquinio,
and to the memory of Paula Schroder

Preface

This text is directed toward acquainting freshman college students with engineering and technology. By providing these young men and women with some review of their high school science and mathematics along with concise capsules of important engineering and technology courses, it demonstrates how their current knowledge will dramatically expand in subsequent studies. We find that this process of "building bridges of knowledge" also builds the student's level of confidence to meet the exciting challenge of being a member of a technical profession.

While our primary motivation in writing this textbook was to introduce students to their future profession, we also took into consideration the motivations and concerns of the college administration and faculty: students who are academically prepared and highly motivated naturally perform better in the classroom. The time and place to make certain that this preparatory process is intact is their introductory technical course.

There are, of course, many ways to accomplish this process of sequencing information to inform and enhance the student's desire to reach for a technical career. From our combined teaching experience, we know that this text needs a valuable instructional element called *flexibility*. We each have areas of interest that we think are most important. When teaching freshmen we therefore pick and choose corresponding chapters which match our individual areas of specialization. Instructors will find that each chapter does, in fact, stand by itself, thus allowing them to choose only those chapters deemed appropriate for the course in question, with little risk of confusing the student. While we are each tempted to offer our own recommendations for alternate sequences of topical chapters, we know that creative instructors are in a better position to tailor the chapter sequencing to meet their needs, and more importantly, the needs of their students.

Having presented the overall philosophy of this book, let us now look at the specifics. The material in this text ranges from a review for the high school graduate to new material for virtually any incoming freshman student. We adopted the philosophy that this text should preview what lies ahead in the engineering and technology curricula. It was recognized in doing so that some of the subject matter in this book will be covered in subsequent courses in greater detail. It is our hope that the brief introductions provided here will serve some students by improving their abilities to understand technical topics, while giving creative students the drive to "plow ahead" into more challenging technical subject matter.

Every chapter begins with a list of its objectives, and concludes with a summary of objectives achieved. Each specific objective is associated with a single section in the chapter. To the greatest extent possible, the chapter sections have been written to stand alone. Thus, even within a chapter, an instructor can skip sections as desired without preventing the understanding of subsequent sections. In as much as we feel that proof of understanding is the ability to work problems, each chapter concludes with several exercises. In addition, there are numerous solved examples in nearly every section of the book. for students who want even more examples, a supplementary example section containing additional solved problems is included in each chapter. We have tried to write clearly, concisely, and in an interesting manner. We thus hope that both the student and the instructor will find this text enjoyable to use and easy to understand.

Although breadth of coverage is emphasized in this book, there is a sufficient amount of depth in each subject area to allow an instructor to teach a course with whatever amount of rigor is desired. We also encourage instructors to reach beyond the book's content and bring to the classroom vivid examples from their own professional engineering experiences that reinforce specific assignments. We are hopeful that this work, in combination with the instructor's creative classroom enthusiasm, will contribute to the technical student's lifetime of learning. if, as a result of using this book, a student decides strongly on a career in engineering or technology, it will have served its purpose.

L. C.
D. S.
A. T.
El Paso, Texas

Contents

Introduction to Engineering and Technology

CHAPTER 1

Introduction

Technology has been a major cultural determinant in the past and promises to play an even more important role in shaping our society in the future. Increasingly, in almost every aspect of human endeavor, the opportunities and constraints are being dictated by the technologies available. Newly available technologies can provide rewarding opportunities for those capable and willing to embark on associated careers, but changes in technologies can also decisively signal the end of careers for those unwilling or unable to change. The very essence of our society is more and more driven by developments and implementations of various technologies.

Objective: The objective of this chapter is to describe the relationships among technology, science, and engineering; outline how technology has come to have such an effect on us and what can reasonably be expected in the future; and discuss some aspects of a career associated with technology.

Criteria: After completing this chapter, you should be able to do the following:

- **1.1** Differentiate among the terms *technology*, *science*, and *engineering*, and list five major events in the historical development of technology.
- **1.2** List five different areas where technology is likely to cause dramatic changes in our society.
- **1.3** List the members of a technical group and describe the roles or job functions typical of each.
- **1.4** Describe, in general terms, the personal attributes of many successful engineers, engineering technologists, technicians, and craftspersons.
- **1.5** List at least three reasons why professional ethics is of importance to a person pursuing a technology-related career.

■ **1.6** List several types of learning resources for continuing a technical education and list a possible provider for each resource.

▲ 1.1 Historical Overview of the Development of Technology

The terms *science, technology,* and *engineering* are often used with a degree of interchangeability and confusion. In simplest terms *science* addresses the "why" of things, *technology* deals with the "how" of things, and *engineering* is the profession that takes these "hows" and "whys" and uses this knowledge to economically produce something useful.

More specifically, the Engineering Council for Professional Development defined engineering as the "profession in which a knowledge of the mathematical and natural sciences gained by study, experience, and practice is applied with judgment to develop ways to utilize economically the materials and forces of nature for the benefit of mankind."

The interrelationships among science, engineering, and technology are complex and historically are surprising. We think of the discoveries from science as directing and determining the resulting technologies. This is generally true, but there are numerous examples where technology has preceded the resulting scientific areas of inquiry, examples such as: powered flight, which led to aerodynamics; gunnery, which preceded ballistics; and the steam engine, which led to the study of thermodynamics.

The history of technology begins with the skills and knowledge needed to produce the primitive stone tools that were developed by the earliest humans. By the end of the Paleolithic (Old Stone Age) Period, available technologies included, in addition to stone tools, the use of fire, spears and spear throwers, the bow and arrow, oil lamps, pigments, mortars and pestles, and bone sewing needles.

During the Neolithic Period, much effort was directed toward the stabilization of food supplies by domestication of plants and animals. Land was cleared for cultivation and improvements were made in the stone tools. The crafts of pottery, weaving, basket making, and construction of simple shelters were developed.

The development of the animal-drawn plow in the fourth millennium B.C. marked the beginning of the third major period of technological advancement. Since animals were now used for cultivation, the separate endeavors of animal husbandry and plant cultivation merged. Techniques for fallowing, irrigation, and flood control were developed. Writing evolved during this period, the concept of a political state was developed, large-scale organized warfare became common, and copper and bronze metallurgy was first practiced.

The ability to make and use metals, which developed during the bronze age, produced relatively rapid changes in society. This period saw substantial advances in building technology including the construction of the pyramids, and the development of the horse-drawn two-wheeled chariot, a development that dramatically changed warfare.

By the end of the second millennium B.C., technology produced higher furnace temperatures, which allowed the refining of iron. Whereas copper and bronze were cast, iron came from the furnace as a red-hot plastic mass that was then shaped by forging. The ability to use iron in the production of tools and weapons resulted in much better, more durable instruments.

The Greeks, mastering the column and beam structure, produced major advances in architecture and also developed the catapult, which allowed military forces to attack fortified positions more effectively. They also coined the term *architekton* — which we would consider a mixture of the disciplines of engineering and architecture. Although these technologies remained generally separated from the scientific tradition being developed by the Greek philosophers, a school of scientist/engineers evolved in Alexandria and developed expertise in mechanical and pneumatic devices.

Roman engineers made extensive use of the arch, which had been developed much earlier, in their construction projects. Variations of the arch were used to construct vaults and domes, and all of these technologies were used in the construction of aqueducts, roads, reservoirs, and various military fortifications. Roman engineers were also familiar with water-wheels and associated gearing and used them in the construction of mills.

The light ox-drawn plow was appropriate for cultivation of the light soils found in the Middle East and Mediterranean areas, but could not effectively till the heavy, wet soils of the Northern European plain. The need for a better tillage instrument spurred the development of a much heavier plow that used a vertical coulter, horizontal plowshare, moldboard, and to provide the increased power necessary, teams of four, six, or eight animals were yoked in pairs. The heavy plow changed cultivation to a community effort — due to the number of animals required and the larger land areas that could be tilled. This was a factor leading to the feudal system of medieval Europe. Improved agricultural productive capacity also freed many people to pursue various arts and crafts, which led in turn to numerous advances in many fields.

Technological advances of this period included the horseshoe and collar, windmills for corn grinding and water pumping, waterwheels used for sawmills, hammermills, and stamping mills, and water-driven bellows used with blast furnaces. The increased blast-furnace capabilities made it much easier and cheaper to produce iron, which resulted in wider usage of this most desirable material. Architectural advances, including the development of the flying buttress, led to construction of much higher, lighter, and stronger buildings.

Illustration 1.1 Sophisticated mass transit systems such as the one shown here are excellent examples of engineering accomplishments. (Courtesy Washington Metropolitan Transit Authority)

A major military advance of this period was the introduction of firearms in the fourteenth century. This and the catapult spelled the end of castles. By the middle of the sixteenth century English founders were producing guns from iron rather than bronze, thereby decreasing their cost. Widespread use of heavy ordnance resulted in polygonal and star-shaped fortifications. These increased the length of the ramparts on which guns could be mounted, and also resulted in effective shot deflection angles. The handgun made the long-bow obsolete and the musket made the infantry once again a decisive military force. The sailing ship was fortified, and it, too, became a formidable military instrument.

Naval power transformed Europe into a center of world power. Commerce made possible by control of the seas became increasingly profitable, and cultural life flourished. One of the major advances was the development

Illustration 1.2 *The design of the extravehicular mobility unit shown here required considerable creativity and imagination because of the unusual constraints. (Courtesy National Aeronautics and Space Administration)*

of movable type and the printed book. The profitability of businesses related to technology and industry was widely recognized and promoted extensive interest in these areas. Even in the sixteenth century, however, indiscreet application of technology caused problems. The widespread smelting of iron required vast supplies of timber, as did the construction of ships. This resulted in a rapid deforesting of Europe, and particularly England. The search for minerals led to increasingly deep mine shafts that had to be constantly pumped to remove infiltrating water. Animals were used initially, but the need for more powerful pumps was evident.

The present period of technological advancement began in the eighteenth century. Darby produced cast iron in a blast furnace charged with iron ore and coke, and Newcomen invented the steam engine, which was effectively used to pump water from the mine shafts. These two developments marked the beginning of the Industrial Revolution. Watt and Wilkinson dramatically improved the steam engine, making it a practical source for powering vast numbers of soon-to-to-developed industrial devices including spinning and weaving machinery, and a wide variety of mills and factories. The combination of sufficient food supplies and abundant power led to the growth of large cities where industrial civilization as we know it developed.

The Industrial Revolution gave rise to the profession of engineering. Prior to this time, persons functioning as engineers were trained by an apprenticeship system in the same way as artisans and craftsmen. In the 1740s, the British government opened a military academy at Woolwich where subjects like mathematics, statics, gunnery, and fortification design were taught. In the late eighteenth century the term ''civil engineer'' was widely used to distinguish between those involved in civil projects — as opposed to the ''military engineer.''

Established universities were often reluctant to initiate programs of study in technical areas, so it was the newly created universities that were first to offer engineering studies. Two of the first of these were the Ecole Polytechnique in Paris and the University of London.

A number of inventions occurred during the nineteenth century which allowed the conversion of energy into large amounts of usable power. A variety of improvements were made in steam engines, allowing them to be more widely used, not only as stationary power sources, but also to power railroads, steamships, and the ''horseless carriage.'' The second half of the nineteenth century saw the development of the internal combustion engine. Otto invented and marketed a 4-cycle gas engine, and Rudolf Diesel produced, in 1897, an engine in which high pressure produced the needed heat for combustion.

Michael Faraday and Joseph Henry discovered the principle of electromagnetic induction about 1831. A series of discoveries and inventions followed — including the telegraph, the electric dynamo and motor, the incandescent lamp, the electric street-trolley railway, the telephone, and the central generating plant. Most principles necessary for modern bulk power transmission and utilization were developed by Nikola Tesla who in 1888 demonstrated the first successful alternating-current induction motor. Marconi demonstrated many principles of radio transmission about 1896.

Bessemer and Kelley are credited with developing processes that allowed large amounts of steel to be made cheaply. Once steel was readily available it was used in a myriad of applications including the construction of industrial machines and tools, and also became a principal building material that allowed the construction of skyscrapers and larger and better bridges. The availability of steel also allowed the construction of high-powered, long-range weapons and superior armor.

The availability of lightweight and reasonably reliable internal-combustion engines spawned the automobile industry, which then helped create the petroleum industry. The early 1900s also saw the development of the airplane, which later became a dominant force in military warfare.

Technological advances of the twentieth century were closely linked to warfare. World War I saw widespread use of long-range artillery, machine guns, poison gas, submarines, torpedoes, tanks, aircraft, and radio communications. In World War II, additional weaponry introduced included aircraft carriers, radar, sonar, ballistic missiles, the atomic bomb, and limited use of jet aircraft.

The second half of the twentieth century has produced what some call an explosion in technology. Nuclear energy has become widely used, although for a variety of reasons, the full potential of this source of energy has not been fully developed. Much has been accomplished in medicine—

Illustration 1.3 This agile six-legged robot is designed to walk on uneven terrain and step over obstacles while maintaining a stable payload platform. (Courtesy Odetics, Inc.)

including development of additional vaccines for prevention of disease, additional antibiotics and other drugs for treating illness, and the ability to successfully transplant organs.

Much of the new technology has directly or indirectly resulted from the technological gains made in electronic and computer circuit design. The development of the transistor, followed by a series of discoveries that allowed fabrication of increasingly complex circuits in smaller and smaller packages, has made it economically feasible to build devices with tremendous computational and control capabilities. The gains made in other technical areas would not be possible without the computers and other electronic devices now routinely used to explore the unknown.

But from the viewpoint of the future, the most spectacular technological achievements of this period will almost certainly be the beginnings of the exploration of space and the ability to modify life forms through gene splicing and other techniques.

▲ 1.2 The Future Challenge of Technology

Man's ability to discover and invent seems more and more to lack constraint. We have lived through a period when the wildest dreams of science fiction writers have become reality. We can communicate on a world-wide basis, we have the machines to sustain life for indeterminate periods, we build computers and robots that can duplicate many of the basic functions of human beings. In fact, a large number of tasks formerly done by humans are now accomplished by machines which do the work faster, better, and often cheaper. There is presently no reason to expect an abatement of these trends.

Many would argue that the various technological advances have far outpaced the societal and political systems that attempt to manage their impacts. One reason for the rise of a large middle class in America was the efficient manufacture of goods, which resulted in wide availability of jobs with relatively high salaries. Recently we have seen much of this manufacturing moved overseas to where the cost of production is significantly lower, a move that has caused the loss of hundreds of thousands of jobs.

As economic forces continue to dictate how we produce the goods we consume, many predict that much of the manufacturing will again be done in America. Most believe, however, that it will be done in increasingly automated facilities requiring fewer and fewer humans. Our society is clearly changing from one based on manufacturing to one based on services. Recent surveys have noted that an increasing percentage of new jobs are in the service area, many at or near the minimum-wage level. Some suggest a trend toward a two-tiered society with a relatively small number of highly trained and paid professionals at the top, a much smaller middle class than at present, and a relatively large number of lower-paid service

Illustration 1.4 *This beet harvester employs a unique design that features an elevating wheel that carries the beets from the grab rolls to the truck conveyor, (Courtesy Deere & Company)*

workers at the bottom. The political ramifications of such a society with a large number of people desiring many material things and not having sufficient earning power to buy them may be less than desirable.

It is almost universally agreed that new technologies will continue to develop, displacing old ones. The dominant concern is how to manage and direct this motion. The mechanisms presently available to determine who will benefit from new technologies, and who will suffer, leave much to be desired.

▲ 1.3 The Technical Group

The development of any new idea or technology into something useful requires the efforts of a number of people. Although no two products will be developed in the same way, some generalizations can be made about the people who comprise the technical group responsible for a product's development and the services they perform.

Generally, the process starts with a scientist whose job is to search for new knowledge. By inspiration, perseverance, and occasionally by accident, a new phenomenon or concept emerges. The engineer then attempts to apply this information to a present or anticipated problem. The engineer must be able to identify the problem being solved and the economic aspects of the product's development and marketing. The most brilliantly conceived and developed product will be useless if the consumer cannot perceive a need for it.

Assisting both the engineer and scientist are the craftsperson, technician, and technologist. A *craftsperson* typically displays a high degree of manual skill. This person's job is to use available tools and materials plus a significant amount of imagination to produce what are often the more visually pleasing aspects of a product. A craftsperson might, for example, make the master molds used to produce the plastic cases for a new electronic product. This work normally requires good physical dexterity and is learned largely through practice. The work is repetitive and requires little management of others.

The *technician* is responsible for maintaining, setting up, and operating the equipment involved. Generally, the technician is supervised by an engineer or scientist. A technician may conduct experiments designed by engineers and do a routine analysis of the resulting data, but the responsibility for both the completion of the task and the interpretation of the results rests with the supervising engineer or scientist.

Following detailed plans, the technician builds the prototype devices and tests them. Many smaller companies whose work volume and technological level do not justify an engineering staff employ technicians who assume some of the job functions of an engineer. The term *nondegreed engineer* is often used to describe such people, although the use of this term is discouraged by professional groups. In large companies a technician may occasionally supervise other technicians. Sometimes a technician may be trained on the job, but usually a two-year, college-level training program with additional work in post–high school courses like mathematics and English and a program of study in a chosen technical area are required.

A *technologist* usually applies engineering principles to the production, construction, or operation of an engineering product. In terms of theoretical or abstract thinking, a technologist lies between the technician who implements and the engineer who designs. A technologist usually holds a four-year B.S. degree in engineering technology and will have studied many of the same subjects that an engineer has. But close inspection of the technologist's curriculum usually shows that the level of mathematics is somewhat lower than that of an engineer; that is, although many courses in engineering and technology programs will have the same or similar titles, the level of the mathematics used will often be considerably lower in the technology programs.

From a company's standpoint, a technologist can be an extremely valuable person. A technologist typically can be employed at a somewhat lower salary than an engineer and in some instances can be used in lieu of an

Illustration 1.5 Artist's conception of space station design. (Courtesy National Aeronautics and Space Administration)

engineer. Perhaps the differences between a technologist and an engineer are less apparent than for any other two positions in the technological group. The degrees earned and their mathematical and modeling skills clearly distinguish the two, but the differentiation based on duties performed often becomes indistinct.

No single category in a technical development and production group can be considered the most important. Such a group must be carefully assembled and managed so that each person contributes to the group's overall goals. Specific tasks must be assigned so that the designated person can perform the desired task. It is both economically wasteful and frustrating to assign highly trained people to jobs they consider trivial. Conversely, to assign tasks beyond the capabilities of the individuals involved is equally inefficient.

▲ 1.4 Becoming an Engineer, Engineering Technologist, or Technician

One of the most important choices a person must make is that of career, for there can be few fates worse than going to work for a lifetime to a job that is disliked. At the same time, career changes, when they involve years of education in a new specialty, must be considered carefully and may be difficult or even impossible to achieve. An often recurring question emerges: How do I know that I will like a career in engineering? There is no simple answer to this question. The following paragraphs summarize some important considerations that should be reviewed before embarking on an engineering career. The attributes discussed are based on generalizations that may indicate success, but their absence certainly does not preclude success in properly motivated individuals.

What Type of Person Becomes a Good Engineer or Engineering Technologist?

There is no simple answer to the question of what type of person makes a good engineer. Engineering is diverse, and the range of needed talents is broad. Most successful engineers compile good academic records in both high school and college, particularly in mathematics and the physical sciences. Often, as students, they participated in extracurricular activities like science or mathematics fairs and various academic competitions. These students were and are interested in how things work. They often completed optional or extra credit projects and showed imagination or creativity in their work.

Such students usually are disciplined and able to stick with a project until it is completed. These qualities must be present to succeed in the professional programs of study. Virtually without exception, successful engineers can recall a period in their lives, usually while they were in college, when they questioned the value of what they were doing but decided to continue their studies and to obtain an engineering degree.

Often engineers' hobbies are closely related to their choice of discipline within engineering. The high school student who rebuilds a car, repairs a lawn mower, or simply likes to fix mechanical things may well become a civil or mechanical engineer. A student who has his or her own computer system and enjoys writing different programs for it may well go into computer engineering or computer science. The lack of money and a place to do such things may preclude many high school students from such activities, but even an interest in some area as evidenced by reading books or magazines about it can be a good indicator. We tend to do best those things that captivate and hold our interest.

What Type of Person Becomes a Good Technician or Craftsperson?

Some of the same characteristics needed for an engineering career are needed for a career as a technician or craftsperson. An interest in technology is especially essential. As students, successful technicians and craftspersons probably had a keen interest in building and assembling things and in trying to figure out how things work and how to improve the way things work. Most certainly they always had a facility for spatial visualization.

Prospective technicians and craftspersons probably enjoy mathematics, such as algebra and geometry, and are not bored with repetitive mathematical calculations. Often they like using computers, but also are interested in the inner workings of the computer and the peripheral devices.

Many technicians and craftspersons have an artistic bent. They are able to create aesthetically pleasing physical designs. Another characteristic needed is perseverance, the ability to keep trying until the job is completed.

Job Availability

The jobs available to engineers and the number of students in the nation's universities studying to become engineers vary for a number of reasons. The demand for engineering graduates is tied to economic conditions in the country and, to an increasing extent, in the world. In periods of growth and high profitability, companies are willing to hire substantial numbers of engineers who will presumably create additional products and thereby generate more profit. But in periods of economic recession, the demand for engineering skills diminishes, as fewer products are prepared for entry into the marketplace. Research and development costs seldom return immediate profits to a company, and so financially strapped companies concerned with short-term goals are often tempted to cut back these efforts. Although usually a poor management practice, such cutbacks obviously affect the engineering job market. Mass layoffs of engineers are extremely rare, but the rate of replacing professional personnel does decrease during business recessions.

News stories about the great demand for engineers do raise enrollments, especially of freshmen at engineering colleges. The starting salaries of new engineers are substantially above those of many other professions, and so a perceived or real scarcity of engineers tends to bring freshmen who were previously undecided into engineering programs. Similarly, when the demand for engineers drops, so too do engineering enrollments.

Although the demand for engineers is somewhat cyclic, jobs have always been available for good students. Obviously, during periods when the relative demand for engineers is down, the students with the best academic credentials have the widest selection of job opportunities, and those who barely maintained a sufficient grade point average to graduate may have difficulty finding a good job.

Since most engineering projects are accomplished by the technical group, the engineer, the engineering technologist, the technician, and the craftsperson, the demand for all of these professionals rises and falls together. Therefore, this discussion of job availability applies to all of the technical group.

Federal government policies and programs also affect the job market.

Substantial increases in defense spending almost certainly mean that defense contractors will increase their staffs. Major efforts like constructing an interstate highway system, putting people on the moon, or cleaning up the environment may result in many job openings in a specialized area.

For the long term, there is every reason to believe that the technical professions will continue to offer attractive opportunities to capable individuals. Our society is changing, and the direction of this change will benefit the engineering profession. Production workers with little training and few skills were at one time highly paid for their work on assembly lines, but they have recently seen their salaries remain relatively constant or in some cases even decrease. In many cases, the jobs that seemed so easy to get and desirable have vanished owing to foreign competition or increasingly automated production plants.

▲ 1.5 Professional Ethics and Responsibilities

Like other professional groups, engineers and technicians often find that their technical ability and expertise are beyond those of the people paying for their services or those who will ultimately be affected by them. Such circumstances require a level of professional performance significantly above that expected in many occupations. A multitude of pressures may require the product or service to be cheaper or of lower overall quality, and such pressures must be balanced by the desire to provide as much safety, value, and quality as possible.

In order to help individuals achieve a reasonable balance in their technical work, most professional groups have adopted codes of ethics. These lists of rules are necessarily written in general terms and must be interpreted in order to be applied to specific situations, but they are very useful in helping members to establish minimum standards of behavior.

The various codes of ethics are enforced to some extent by boards or review panels, which are maintained by most of the professional groups. It is the job of these boards to review questionable conduct by any member. Generally, the most severe penalty that can be imposed is withdrawal of membership in the organization, but the embarrassment of a public investigation can be a very powerful motivator.

There is increasing pressure from the federal government and also many state governments to license practitioners in various professions. The licensing process often requires proof of some minimum level of education and a demonstrated ability to pass qualifying examinations. Also associated with this process are quasi-judicial boards which may revoke a license to practice for severe breaches of appropriate conduct.

The importance of developing a good image and public trust should not be underestimated. Virtually all efforts that provide advances in technology are intimately connected with the governing process both as a source of

Illustration 1.6 *The large main memory of a supercomputer. (Courtesy Cray Research, Inc.)*

funding and through a multitude of regulations enforced by many different agencies. Without strong public support, major projects cannot be accomplished.

▲ 1.6 Career Learning

In any field of endeavor, whether it is plumbing, manufacturing, or medicine, the necessity to keep learning never ends. This is because the discovery of new knowledge is inevitable. This is especially true in the areas of science and technology where new knowledge is emerging at an ever increasing rate. Technical people can keep abreast of new developments in their profession through a rather extensive network of learning opportunities shown in Table 1.1.

TABLE 1.1 Summary of Continuing Education Activities

Learning Resource	Provider
College Courses (regular)	College/Universities
Short Courses	College/Universities
	Professional Societies
	Private Companies
Conferences	Professional Societies
Seminars	College/Universities
	Professional Groups
Journals	Technical Societies
Public Domain Materials	College/Universities
	Government Agencies
Company Training Programs	Private Companies
Expositions	Trade Associations
Self-teaching, Media-based	College/Universities
Materials	Technical Societies
—Audiotape	Private Companies
—Videotape	
—Slide/Tape	
—Computer-based	
Public TV	College/Universities

Traditional college courses will continue to be one of the primary sources for in-depth learning of technical information. In addition to the usual daytime courses, many institutions offer graduate-level courses at night, on weekends, and through telecommunications at company sites. Many of these courses are also available on videotape for rent or purchase.

Short courses (generally one to five days) are an increasingly important source of information for graduates of engineering and technology programs because they are timely, very specific, and involve limited loss of work time. Technical courses available through continuing education departments at universities generally range in cost from $100 to $700 depending upon the length of the course and where it is taught. Their main objective is educating the audience in a relatively narrow subject area.

Conferences are meetings of people who are knowledgeable in well-defined technical areas where state-of-the-art information is exchanged. Such conferences usually involve presentations by individuals who are knowledgeable in topics of considerable current interest. Conferences are frequently the forum for the outlet of recent research results and therefore, are particularly important for people working in fields where technology is advancing most rapidly. Satellite technology has made conference proceedings available to participants at sites far removed from the actual event.

Seminars are similar to short courses except that the primary function of a seminar is information exchange rather than education of the audience.

Journals are the primary outlet for research results at both the basic and applied levels. Journals span the spectrum from those that publish highly theoretical articles intended for persons with Ph.D. degrees to those that publish articles based on actual operating experiences and are therefore directed toward technicians and plant operators. Virtually all technical societies publish and distribute a journal as part of the organization's membership fees.

Public domain materials are available from a variety of sources including professional associations, consumer-oriented government agencies, special-interest groups, and a number of local, county, state, and federal agencies.

Company-sponsored training programs are becoming increasingly popular as industries strive to keep their employees abreast of technological developments. These programs can be on-site with in-house personnel conducting most or all of the training or outside specialists can be brought to the plant. Alternatively, many companies pay for their employees to attend off-site training experiences that range from short courses to advanced degree programs. Technical or trade schools also provide training in many different areas for operators and technicians.

Expositions are displays of hardware, software, and equipment that might be of interest to professionals in a given field. Expositions are frequently held in conjunction with seminars and conferences to increase the attractiveness of the event to a wider range of professionals.

Self-teaching, media-based materials are available from a number of sources, especially technical societies and private companies. With the escalating demands on the time of professional people, videotape and computer-based modes of learning are certain to become more widespread in the immediate future.

Although the full potential for education through *public television* has not been fully exploited, credit for college-level courses can be obtained through public TV in many cities in the United States. As tuition and other college costs increase, this medium is likely to play a more important role in professional education activities.

● CHAPTER SUMMARY

The chapter began with a historical overview of the development of technology, then moved to future challenges for technology. The concept of a technical group was developed, the responsibilities of each member were outlined, and personal attributes of the different technical people were discussed.

The ethical responsibilities of technical professionals were introduced, and the necessity for career learning was described.

2

Careers in Technical Fields

In the past few decades the growth in technology has been rapid. Technical knowledge has burgeoned and necessary technical skills have increased as new areas of specialization in engineering and technology have evolved. New technologies and new disciplines are appearing. Today we still have mechanical engineers and electrical technicians, but we also have biomedical engineers and robotics technicians, terms not known fifty years ago. This chapter will present an overview of careers in technical fields and a discussion of some of the labels used.

Engineers, technologists, technicians, and craftspersons are labeled not only by the discipline of their education, but also by their work specialization. In this chapter the technical disciplines will be described and the different types of work performed by the technical people will be discussed.

Objective: The objective of this chapter is to introduce and describe the disciplines, or fields, and types of work, or functions, of the professionals in technical fields.

Criteria: After completing this chapter, you should be able to do the following.

■ **2.1** Identify the major engineering disciplines and the technical areas of concern spanned by each discipline.

■ **2.2** Describe the types of work or technical functions performed by members of the technical group.

▲ 2.1 The Technical Disciplines

Members of the technical group to be considered here include engineers, engineering technologists, technicians, and craftspersons, all of whom are professionals. Formal education is usually necessary for entrance into a profession, and the **engineering** disciplines discussed herein are the most common ones recognized by the technical professions. **Technology** programs provide education in these disciplines and confer degrees with various titles. A list of technology degrees is shown at the end of this section.

Civil Engineering

Civil engineering is one of the oldest engineering disciplines and is perhaps the one most necessary to maintain our society in its present form. Civil engineering is broad in scope and is often divided into subdisciplines, one of the largest being structural engineering. Structural engineers design and supervise the construction of buildings, bridges, tunnels, dams, and many other public and private facilities. Architects depend on structural engineers to make sure that their aesthetically pleasing designs will have structural integrity and will function as intended under the actual load conditions. A closely related area is soil mechanics, a second recognized area of civil engineering. Soil engineers provide the proper foundations for structures so that they can withstand time or disasters. Exciting challenges for structural and soil engineers include the design and construction of tall buildings, offshore platforms, and earthquake-resistant structures.

Transportation engineers plan and supervise the construction of systems used to move people and materials. An example of their creative ability is the interstate highway system, which has made travel by automobile, especially near large metropolitan areas, safer, faster, and more convenient. The need for reliable, economic mass transit and rapid transit systems will occupy transportation engineers for decades to come.

Another branch of civil engineering, urban and municipal engineering, is concerned with the planning and orderly growth of cities. It is much less expensive to plan for urban growth and provide needed facilities than to attempt to rectify existing problems caused by poor planning or the lack of an overall plan of development. Traffic congestion problems are an example. Once business and residential areas are established and connecting roads have been built, it becomes extremely expensive to modify the roads to carry additional traffic. But a well-designed municipal plan anticipates such growth and the future demands of the transportation system and ensures that appropriate facilities are available when needed.

Environmental engineers are concerned with the availability, treatment, and distribution of pure water and the appropriate disposal of gaseous, liquid, and solid wastes. In the United States, disease outbreaks that can be traced to public water supplies are virtually unknown. No matter

Illustration 2.1 *Jack-up type offshore drilling rig. (Courtesy Exxon USA)*

where one travels, the availability of pure water can be taken for granted. Lakes and rivers, which in the not-too-distant past contained virtually no marine life and, in extreme cases, were so polluted that they occasionally would catch fire, again support fish — and fishermen. Although pollution is a continuing problem and concern, there has been significant progress in cleaning up the environment. Still, many challenges remain for environmental engineers in the disposal of toxic materials and radioactive wastes, the removal of pollutants from the air around cities and industrial complexes, and the development of better and more economical treatment systems to recycle waste water and reclaim lakes.

Electrical Engineering

Electrical engineering accounts for the largest number of practicing engineers. This field is diverse, in both the types of problems addressed and the backgrounds of the engineers involved. The Institute of Electrical and Electronic Engineers, the professional society for this discipline, recognizes approximately thirty subdivisions or specializations within electrical engineering.

Electrical engineers generally are concerned with three areas: energy, information, and materials. Electrical engineers in the energy area influence the production of electrical energy, its transportation and distribution, and its utilization.

Many of the engineers in the information area work on the design and application of computers, and many develop various types of systems and carry out the tasks associated with the establishment of the communication networks that provide the convenient and timely exchange of data and information on which our society is so dependent.

Electrical engineers working in the materials area improve existing materials or develop new ones. From them come the technologies to produce integrated circuits, improvements in electrical insulating materials,

Illustration 2.2 High energy laser beam director. (Courtesy United States Navy)

and materials needed to produce cheaper, more efficient, and better energy conversion devices like motors, generators, and electromechanical actuators.

Additional innovation is possible in many of the areas in which electrical engineers work. The performance-to-cost ratio of computer systems continues to improve, and, as costs decrease, a wide variety of new products and applications become economically possible. One area in which this will be particularly noticeable is automotive electronics. Very complex navigation systems will solve the problem of finding one's way in unfamiliar areas. Radar collision-avoidance systems will make travel by automobile safer. Additional improvements will be made in automotive engine control and electrical systems to make them simpler, better, and cheaper.

Much remains to be done in improving the ways in which information is stored, retrieved, and utilized. Electrical engineers will be at the forefront of this effort. The communication networks of the future will be more complex and have greater capability than current ones but will be relatively cheaper and easier to use. World-wide access to a virtually unlimited supply of information will be technically possible.

Other areas of investigation, like artificial intelligence and the development of expert systems, hold much promise, and expectations are currently high, but a great deal of fundamental understanding is lacking and work remains to make such concepts fully useful.

As in other engineering disciplines, the body of knowledge currently available is sufficient to keep electrical engineers busy for many years, and there is no reason to expect the flow of new discoveries and inventions to stop.

Mechanical Engineering

Mechanical engineering is also a very diverse engineering discipline. Because mechanical engineers work in industries that involve mechanical elements, structures, and energy processes, they work in practically all industries.

Energy is one of the topics closely associated with mechanical engineers, as they are concerned with the generation and transformation of useful forms of energy and power. Some mechanical engineers design machines that produce power such as internal combustion engines, jet engines, and gas and steam turbines. In this time of energy awareness, mechanical engineers are developing alternative sources of energy such as solar collectors, solar ponds, wind turbines, biomass conversion systems, and ocean gradients.

The automotive industry is a large employer of mechanical engineers involved in research, design, and manufacturing. Mechanical engineers work to make automobiles more efficient, less polluting, and safer.

The aerospace industry is dependent on large numbers of mechanical

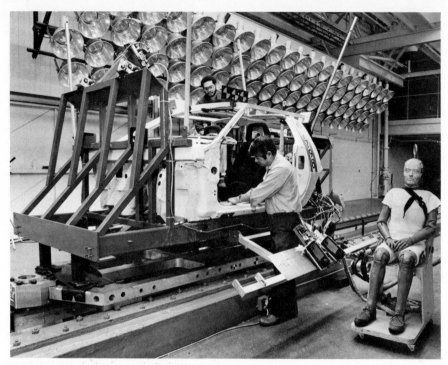

Illustration 2.3 An anthropomorphic dummy with impact sled. (Courtesy General Motors Safety Research Development Laboratory)

engineers to develop, design, and manufacture the structures, propulsion systems, control systems, and life and comfort support systems in airplanes, space vehicles, and defense systems.

The heating, ventilating, and air-conditioning systems in buildings and all forms of transportation are designed by mechanical engineers. Because refrigeration and environmental control have become so important to our way of life, mechanical engineers are working to improve the old systems and develop new ones.

Manufacturing requires mechanical engineers in all areas to select or design equipment and machines and supervise the arrangement and operation of the manufacturing operations. These engineers are researching and developing computer-aided manufacturing and incorporating robots into the manufacturing process.

Metallurgical Engineering and Materials Science

Most of the engineering breakthroughs since 1960 have been enabled, at least in part, by the availability of appropriate materials. In this context, such materials include not only metals but also polymers and ceramics. The metallurgical engineer's job is primarily to provide the materials needed by other engineering disciplines. Metallurgical engineering can be divided into two areas. The first is extractive metallurgy and concerns the location, evaluation, and mining of ore deposits. Such engineers also improve methods of concentrating the ore and producing basic metals and other materials.

The second branch of metallurgy is the selection or development of appropriate materials and the fabrication of metals, alloys, and other materials into various products. This branch is often called the materials area of metallurgical engineering. The development of high-strength, lightweight materials has contributed significantly to the United States' success in space exploration. This area of metallurgy will become even more important when plans for habitation of the moon and the planets are implemented.

Mining and Geological Engineering

Geological engineers combine their engineering problem-solving ability and an understanding of geology. Their job is to locate new mineral deposits and develop economical methods for their removal. Mining engineers are directly responsible for the design and construction of mines and for transportation systems used to move the ore from the mines to the processing facilities.

Naval Architecture and Marine Engineering

Naval architecture and marine engineers design, construct, and test various categories of ships. The backgrounds of such engineers need to be broad, for a ship at sea is much like a floating city, with similar requirements. Civil, mechanical, and electrical engineering problems all must be resolved by marine engineers.

Nuclear Engineering

A nuclear engineer uses fundamental engineering concepts to harness the energies released by nuclear reactions. This discipline is one in which there remains considerable interest, but it currently is suffering to some extent because of the public's disenchantment with nuclear energy. Serious issues have been raised concerning both the economics of nuclear energy and its safety. It is clear, however, that at some time the world's reserves of fossil fuels will be depleted, that other sources of energy must be found, and that nuclear fusion will be among them.

Aside from tasks relating to the production of energy, nuclear engineers also are employed in a wide range of jobs that utilize radioactivity for purposes other than the production of power. These areas include medical applications and the use of isotopes as a means of tracing material move-

Illustration 2.4 Nuclear power plant. (Courtesy El Paso Electric Co.)

ment in a host of biological, chemical, physical, and engineering applications.

Chemical Engineering

Chemical engineers are involved in all aspects of the production of chemical-based products from various raw materials. The largest concentration of chemical engineers is found in the petroleum industry, which manufactures products ranging from asphalt to sophisticated plastics. Chemical engineers design the processes, control systems, and plants necessary for safely, efficiently, and economically converting material from one form into another. Because of their extensive background in chemistry, many chemical engineers also work on air and water pollution control.

Petroleum Engineering

A major source of energy and raw materials is petroleum. The petroleum engineer deals with many problems, from locating petroleum deposits to manufacturing and delivering petroleum-based products. The training of a petroleum engineer is broad and includes civil, mechanical, chemical, and electrical engineering as well as geology and chemistry.

Agricultural Engineering

Agricultural engineers work on engineering problems related to the production and availability of food and fiber. The body of knowledge required lies between agriculture and engineering. Many aspects of agricultural engineering are similar to mechanical engineering in that they use energy and machines to accomplish some given task. Partly because of the efforts of agricultural engineers, the farming industry in the United States is the most efficient in the world in the amount of food produced. The reliable production of sufficient amounts of food to feed the world population continues to be a significant problem with which, either directly or indirectly, agricultural engineers shall be struggling for many years.

Architectural Engineering

Architectural engineering is closely related to civil engineering. An architectural engineer is concerned with the structural design, materials, and methods necessary to construct both artistically pleasing and functional structures. Another closely related area is architecture. There is a substantial overlap between the two disciplines, but architects spend more time designing the creative or artistic aspects of buildings, whereas architectural engineers are more concerned with their structural designs, safety, and construction.

Bioengineering

Bioengineering is a relatively new and expanding area concerned with applying engineering principles to biological systems. This area normally requires training in the sciences, typically biology, and in engineering, usually mechanical or electrical. This extended training often means advanced degrees, and so those planning to enter this area should contemplate one or more degrees beyond the B.S. level. Tools developed by other engineering disciplines have enabled bioengineers to sense, measure, and analyze much more complex biological systems than were previously possible. Society currently holds great expectations, and is willing to pay, for improvements in the quality and duration of life, through research efforts in medicine and particularly bioengineering.

Ceramic Engineering

Ceramic materials are nonmetallic, inorganic materials that can be exposed to high operating temperatures. Ceramic engineers use such materials to resolve various engineering problems. The performance of many engineering products can be improved if they are lighter or stronger or can operate

Illustration 2.5 Chemical refinery. (Courtesy Texaco, Inc.)

Illustration 2.6 Hillside combine with automatic leveling. (Courtesy Deere & Company)

at higher temperatures. Ceramic materials often provide attractive alternatives to metals or alloys. Ceramic permanent magnets are now widely used in electrical motors and offer savings in manufacturing costs as well as improved efficiency. Ceramics are also widely used in sealing high-temperature rotating members. Their use in various types of engines and turbines promises an improved efficiency and a longer service life.

Industrial Engineering

Industrial engineers develop the most efficient methods of production. Their training is broad in scope and may include elements of virtually any other engineering discipline or branch of science. An industrial engineer organizes people, equipment, and plant layout so as to produce the most efficient facility or process possible. Such engineers are concerned not only with costs but also with the quality of both the raw materials and the finished product. As manufacturing plants become more automated, industrial engineers will rely more on computers for process control, in addition to their more traditional uses for inventory management, economic analy-

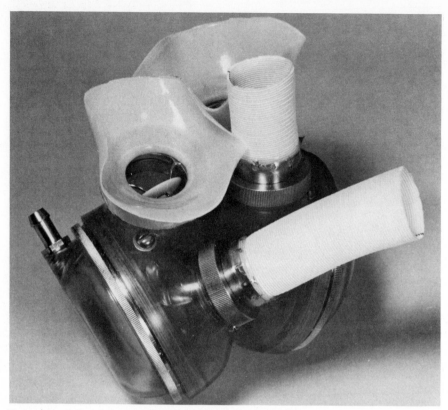

Illustration 2.7 (above and facing page) The artificial heart combines the expertise of the medical and engineering professions. (Courtesy the Milton Hershey Medical Center, The Pennsylvania State University)

sis, optimization, and the like. Likewise, the use of robots in manufacturing is a rapidly growing area of industrial engineering.

Aeronautical and Aerospace Engineering

Aeronautical engineers are concerned with flight in the atmosphere, and aerospace engineers are concerned with flight in space. Both disciplines rely heavily on the older disciplines of civil and mechanical engineering. The design of the airframes for airplanes, rockets, and missiles is a specialized application of structural engineering in which care must be taken to ensure that the design is as light as possible and is also sufficiently strong. Many skills from mechanical engineering are utilized in designing propulsion and control systems, to provide the maximum performance and reliability and the minimum weight.

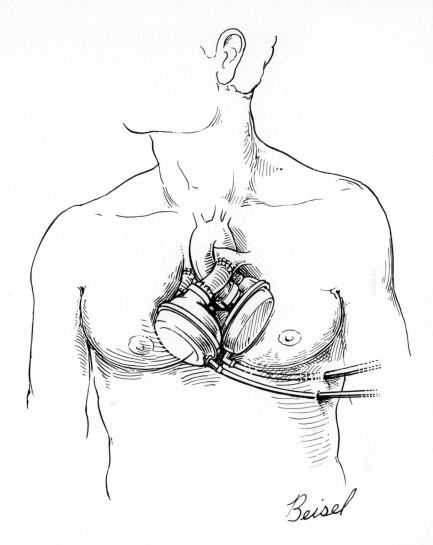

Beisel

Table 2.1 shows some of the various degrees offered in Engineering Technology programs. This information is taken from *Accredited Programs Leading to Degrees in Engineering and Technology, 1987*, Accreditation Board for Engineering and Technology, 345 East 47th Street, New York, NY 10014-2397. Many programs offer both Associate degrees, for two-year courses of study, and Bachelor's degrees, for four-year courses of study.

From our brief descriptions of the various technical disciplines, you can see that there is considerable overlap among them. Despite their training in a particular curriculum, engineers, technologists, technicians, and craftsmen often work on problems outside their specialty. Indeed, problems often are solved by teams of technical professionals from different disciplines.

Illustration 2.8 Industrial robot. (Courtesy Unimation, Inc.)

The selection of a discipline at the beginning of one's career is important, but those contemplating a technical career should also be aware that the approaches learned and the skills developed in solving problems are more important to the beginning engineer than is the knowledge acquired in a specific discipline. In time, the technologies available will change, and the details learned earlier will become obsolete. Thus engineers, technologists, technicians, and craftsmen must constantly be learning throughout their professional careers. At the rate that technologies are currently changing in most disciplines those who learn nothing new will find themselves obsolete in less than five years.

The beginner must learn a broad range of concepts based on mathematics and science and then learn how to apply these principles to specific problems. The professional then must keep up to date on the most recent advances.

TABLE 2.1 Degree Programs in Engineering Technology

Program	Type of Degree Awarded (A, Associate Degree) (B, Bachelor's Degree)
Aeronautical Engineering Technology	A, B
Aerospace Engineering Technology	B
Agricultural Engineering Technology	B
Air Conditioning and Refrigeration Engineering Technology	A, B
Aircraft Engineering Technology	B
Apparel Engineering Technology	A, B
Architectural and Building Construction Technology	A, B
Architectural Drafting and Design Technology	A
Architectural Engineering Technology	A, B
Architectural Technology	A, B
Automotive Engineering Technology	A, B
Biomedical Engineering Technology	A, B
Biomedical Equipment Engineering Technology	A
Chemical Engineering Technology	A
Civil Engineering Technology	A, B
Civil Surveying Engineering Technology	A
Computer Drafting and Design Technology	A, B
Computer Engineering Technology	A, B
Computer Systems Engineering Technology	A, B
Construction Engineering Technology	A, B
Construction Management Technology	B
Controls Systems Technology	A, B
Drafting and Design Engineering Technology	A, B
Electrical and Electronics Engineering Technology	A, B
Electrical Engineering Technology	A, B
Electrical Power Engineering Technology	A, B
Electromechanical Engineering Technology	A, B
Electronics Engineering Technology	A, B
Environmental Engineering Technology	A, B
Fire Protection and Safety Technology	A, B
Highway Engineering Technology	A
Industrial Engineering Technology	A, B
Instrument Engineering Technology	A
Manufacturing Engineering Technology	A, B
Manufacturing Processes Technology	B
Manufacturing Systems Technology	B
Mechanical Design Technology	A, B
Mechanical Drafting and Design Engineering Technology	A, B
Mechanical Engineering Technology	A, B
Mechanical Power Technology	A, B
Mechanical Technology	A, B
Metallurgical Engineering Technology	A, B
Mining Engineering Technology	A, B
Nuclear Engineering Technology	A
Petroleum Technology	A, B
Plastics Engineering Technology	B
Public Works Engineering Technology	A, B
Solar Engineering Technology	A, B
Structural Engineering Technology	A, B
Surveying Engineering Technology	A
Textile Engineering Technology	A, B
Welding Technology	B

Illustration 2.9 Space shuttle Atlantis. (Courtesy National Aeronautics and Space Administration)

▲ 2.2 Types of Technical Work

No matter which technical discipline one chooses, the types of work available in that discipline are many. In this section the types of work, or primary functions or activities performed by technical people, have been divided into the following specific areas: research, development, design, production, plant operation, technical sales, and management.

Research

Scientists are supposed to discover new information, and engineers are supposed to convert these discoveries into something useful to society. Actually, many research engineers function as scientists, in that their principal job is to seek new information. Conversely, many scientists are also interested in the commercial applications of their discoveries. Thus most of the current research is carried out by teams that include scientists, research engineers, and a wide variety of technically oriented individuals.

Most of the successful research engineers have a keen imagination and use creative approaches to resolve problems. They are thorough and observant, often noting important details that have escaped others. Patience and self-discipline are also important because most breakthroughs result only after a great deal of frustration and failure. Research engineers typically have strong academic records, and many hold advanced degrees in a specialized area.

Development

The term *development* implies making a new discovery or invention into something practical. That is, if such a discovery is to serve a useful purpose, it must be made to work. Furthermore, it must work not only in a research laboratory supervised by highly trained individuals but also when placed in the hands of the consumer who may well have little or no technical training or aptitude.

Although cost is always a consideration, it becomes particularly important to the development engineer. The goal is usually a working product that can be marketed at a profit. The final selling price can greatly affect the product's acceptance. As an example, the technical knowledge required to build microwave ovens has been available since just after World War II. In 1960, microwave ovens were commercially available, but their cost then was considerably more than $1000. Development engineers thus had to reduce this to $300 or $400 before many consumers would buy them. And now, because of their wide acceptance and mass production, microwave ovens are available for less than $100. Development engineers and others were responsible for making them functional and economically practical for the consuming public.

Research and development are closely related. Many organizations recognize this by having single research and development departments. For a company to remain competitive, the sale of its products must generate enough revenue to justify the initial costs of research and development.

The management of research and development groups can be difficult, for before beginning research and development, it is difficult to predict the result of these efforts and even harder to predict whether or not a useful and salable product will emerge. A great deal of money can be made or lost as the result of such predictions.

Design

After the development has been completed, the designers take over. Their job is to modify a working device — which presumably is marketable — as necessary so that it can be mass-produced. Designers must be imaginative and practical and must constantly address the issue of cost. They must understand the device being designed and the manufacturing processes required, including the capabilities of the machines and the people involved. Many design engineers' decisions are intuitive and in some cases depend more on experience than on training.

Design engineers possess many of the attributes of research and development engineers, but they must be more practical. Typically, their educa-

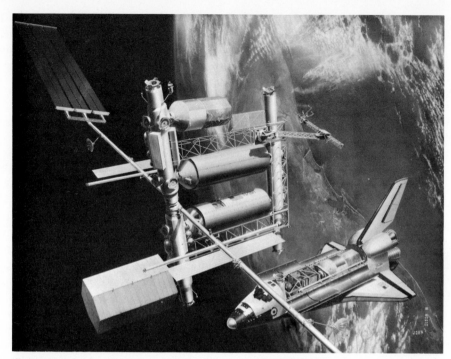

Illustration 2.10 Artist's conception of the design of a space operations center. The cylinders, with connecting passageways, would serve as the command control center, living quarters, and laboratory. (Courtesy National Aeronautics and Space Administration)

tions are less specialized but broader in scope. Most good designers will also be more familiar with economic principles, management, and interpersonal skills than are research and development engineers.

Production

Following the detailed plans of the designers, production engineers oversee the construction of the item. Production engineers must be conscious of costs and must schedule production so that the components are available when needed and the project progresses smoothly.

Production engineers must have a great deal of management ability and be good at visualizing the sequential steps necessary for completing a project. They must also be able to resolve any practical problems not anticipated by the design engineers, while minimizing costs and time delays.

Plant Operation

The operation of complex plants often requires specialized training. Because of engineers' broad education, they can quickly learn the detailed information needed to operate such plants. Plant engineers are usually confronted with problems ranging from controlling ongoing processes to scheduling and completing their maintenance. Plant engineers must understand the processes involved and the equipment used and must be able to deal effectively with the people working at all levels in the plant.

Technical Sales

The financial success or failure of any company depends on its selling the products it makes. Most consumer products are marketed through mass media advertising campaigns. The consumer typically has a good idea of what the product is and how it operates before deciding to buy. But in regard to high-technology items, the potential customer normally has identified a problem or at least an area needing improvement. In one way or another, the sales engineer becomes aware of this problem and attempts to convince the potential customer that a particular product is needed.

But the process is more complicated than just detailing the virtues of a product. Often the potential customer does not fully understand what the problem is or how the product will solve it. This lack of understanding may be general, but more often it involves highly technical matters with which the customer is inadequately prepared to deal. In this situation, the sales engineer must be both a teacher and a salesperson.

Many products sold by sales engineers are custom tailored to the customer's specific needs. Thus the sales engineer must understand both the problem and the product well enough to suggest an appropriate solution. Sales engineers also function as design engineers. For example, modern computer systems are highly technical products typically sold by sales engineers. Many alternative configurations are possible for a given computer system, and the sales engineer must match a specific configuration to a given need. How well the engineer is able to do this often determines the success in selling the product represented.

Sales engineers must also be familiar with the operation of the product they are selling. They must understand the potential consumer's problem and the implications of various solutions. Finally, sales engineers must work well with other people. No matter how good the technical solution to a problem is, unless the sales engineer can convince the customer of the benefits to be derived from the product being bought, a sale will seldom be made.

Management

The basic goals of company managers are similar, regardless of the particular product or service that the company provides. The manager's job is to organize and direct the company in such a way that its resources can best be used to make a desired product that can be sold at a profit.

TABLE 2.2 A Sample of Employment Opportunities for Engineers, Technologists, and Technicians

Type of Organization	Representative Job Title	Representative Function
Defense Contractor	Project Manager	Supervises all engineers, technologists, and technicians working on radar system
Automobile Manufacturer	Test Engineer	Evaluates effectiveness of air bag development systems through crash tests and computer simulations
Aircraft Company	Hydraulic Engineer	Designs and tests hydraulic systems for brakes on aircraft
Oil Company	Reservoir Technologist	Evaluates effectiveness of enhanced oil recovery through CO_2 injection
Large Bank	Computer Technician	Sets up, diagnoses, and maintains computer systems
Any U.S. City	Water Treatment Plant Superintendent	Determines type and concentration of disinfectant, checks clarity, odor and bacterial content of product water, and evaluates new chemicals to minimize cost of treatment
Pulp and Paper Company	Laboratory Technician	Conducts chemical testing on process liquids and wastewater flows
State Highway Dept.	Supervising Resident Engineer	Oversees highway construction projects in accordance with plans and specifications
U.S. Gov't. Research Laboratory	Project Engineer	Designs and tests bomb detonation devices

Engineers are trained to use available resources to create things, a skill that managers must also possess. Managers must, as well, understand financial matters and the long-range implications of their decisions. Engineers learn these skills when they move into positions, such as project engineers, in which they must not only assume technical responsibility but also manage budgets and other resources to accomplish a specific engineering task. There is a trend to employ more and more technically trained individuals as key executives in various companies.

▲ 2.3 Employment Opportunities

From the discussion in the previous section of this chapter, the wide-ranging nature of the engineering profession should be quite evident. One of the most exciting benefits associated with involvement in engineering and engineering technology is not only the abundance of jobs available to the professional but also their variety. It can safely be stated that engineers and engineering technologists are involved to a significant extent in almost every aspect of human civilization.

While it would obviously not be feasible to identify all of the organizations where technical people might be employed or possible to describe all of the types of jobs they perform, the reader can obtain a feel for the variety of opportunities available to professionals in the engineering-related disciplines by referring to Table 2.2. The table shows a sampling of the employment opportunities available to engineers, engineering technologists, and engineering technicians. The left column lists some of the typical employers of technical people while the center and right columns show representative job titles and functions, respectively. Obviously, the effects of engineering related activities are ubiquitous.

● CHAPTER SUMMARY

This chapter briefly described many of the technical disciplines in which engineering degrees are offered, and a table showed various degrees offered in engineering technology programs. The different types of work performed by technical people was then discussed.

3

Numbers

Extensive mathematical skills are, not surprisingly, a prerequisite for persons expecting to enter a technical profession, and thus an understanding of "number language" is essential. In this chapter, we shall discuss some of the procedures for interpreting and manipulating numbers.

Objective: The objective of this chapter is to introduce the fundamentals of recording and manipulating numerical information.

Criteria: After completing this chapter, you should be able to do the following:

- **3.1** Define significant figures and determine the number of significant figures in a decimal number.
- **3.2** Convert a number from decimal to scientific notation while maintaining the correct number of significant figures.
- **3.3** Define precision and accuracy, and determine the possible range of values from a stated precision or accuracy.
- **3.4** From a graphic representation of a measuring device, record the indicated reading in accordance with accepted data-recording procedures.
- **3.5** Define systematic and random error, and correct a reading containing a systematic error, given information for determining the correction factor.
- **3.6** Round a given number to a specified number of significant figures.
- **3.7** Add, subtract, multiply, or divide specified numbers and express the answer to the proper number of significant figures.

TABLE 3.1 Significant Figures Determination

Item		Number of Significant Figures
a.	576	3
b.	21	2
c.	33.619	5
d.	34.02	4
e.	6.320	4
f.	970.00	5
g.	0.0216	3
h.	0.0210	3
i.	0.02100	4
j.	0.0003	1
k.	600	1, 2, or 3
l.	8320	3 or 4

▲ 3.1 Significant Figures

In the same way that letters are used to form words for oral and written communication, engineers, technologists, technicians, and scientists use numbers. Because numbers, like words, must convey information accurately, certain guidelines have been established regarding their use. A *significant figure* is a number that conveys information in accordance with rules established to prevent misleading its user. As the degree of correctness of the information to be reported is increased, so is the number of significant figures that are reported. That is, the number 12.3632 provides more information than does the number 12.3 and, therefore, contains more significant figures. The former number would obviously be interpreted as being more exact than the latter.

The number of significant figures contained in a number is equal to the number of digits it contains, with the exception of zeros that are placed at the beginning or end of the number solely for the purpose of locating the decimal point (i.e., establishing the relative size of the number). Table 3.1 contains several numbers with their corresponding number of significant figures. Note that the zeros in items e and f are significant figures because they are *not* necessary for locating the decimal point. In items g, h, i, and j, the zeros at the beginning of the numbers are ignored (as beginning zeros always are), as their only purpose is to establish the size of the number. Items k and l are ambiguous because it is not known whether the ending zeros are merely for locating the decimal point or whether the resulting measurement takes account of the zeros in those positions. The next section describes a method of reporting numbers in which this ambiguity is eliminated.

Supplementary Example 3.3
Problems p3.1 – p3.3

TABLE 3.2 Conversion from Decimal to Scientific Notation

Column 1 Decimal Notation	Column 2 Number of Significant Figures	Column 3 Scientific Notation
a. 7321	4	7.321×10^3
b. 66.1839	6	6.61839×10^1
c. 0.0076	2	7.6×10^{-3}
d. 0.1900	4	1.900×10^{-1}
e. 243.00	5	2.4300×10^2
f. 3200	2	3.2×10^3
g. 3200	3	3.20×10^3
h. 3200	4	3.200×10^3

▲ 3.2 Scientific Notation

Scientific notation is a method of reporting numbers that indicates exactly and reliably the number of significant figures involved. The procedure for expressing a number in scientific notation has three steps:

1. Locate the decimal point so that a number between 1 and 10 is obtained.
2. Record all digits that are significant figures.
3. Multiply by the appropriate power of 10 so that the correct magnitude is obtained.

Table 3.2 shows how numbers expressed in decimal notation can be converted into an equivalent scientific notation format, while maintaining the correct number of significant figures. Items f, g, and h show that the number 3200 in decimal notation may contain either 2, 3, or 4 significant figures, as shown in columns 1 and 2. The use of scientific notation, however, eliminates all doubt in this regard, as shown in column 3.

Calculators and computers usually display large numbers in scientific notation. The letter E is usually used in place of the power of 10. Thus, the number 3.642×10^2 can also be represented as 3.642 E2.

Problems p3.4–p3.6

▲ 3.3 Precision and Accuracy

When data are obtained through some type of measurement, several factors can affect their precision and accuracy. *Precision* is defined as the reproducibility of a reading or analytical method when the procedure is repeated on the same sample under exactly the same conditions. *Accuracy* is defined as the extent to which the indicated reading represents the true or correct value. Clearly, the two are not the same, as it is possible to have a precise value that is not necessarily accurate. When using an instrument to collect data, therefore, both its precision and accuracy are important with respect to correctness of the reading obtained.

Precision and accuracy are usually reported as a value plus or minus ($\pm$) a number, such as 7.92 ± 0.03. The number following the $\pm$ sign can be used to determine the range of values that are equally representative of the indicated value. Thus, the number 7.92 ± 0.03 represents the numbers ranging from 7.89 to 7.95. The range of values associated with a stated precision or accuracy can also be indicated as a percentage of the given number. For example, an instrument's accuracy might be stated as ± 1.0 percent of the full-scale reading. If the full-scale reading were 150 volts, all readings obtained could be expected to be within ± 1.5 volts of the true value (i.e., 150 volts $\times$ 0.01 = 1.5 volts).

Example 3.1: Find the range of values associated with the following measurements:

a. 531 ± 4
b. 0.052 ± 0.001
c. 6623 ± 1025

Solution: The range of values is obtained by adding and subtracting the possible variation from the indicated value. Thus,

a. Range = $531 - 4$ to $531 + 4 = 527$ to 535
b. Range = $0.052 - 0.001$ to $0.052 + 0.001 = 0.051$ to 0.053
c. Range = $6623 - 1025$ to $6623 + 1025 = 5598$ to 7648

Supplementary Example 3.4
Problems p3.7 – p3.11

▲ 3.4 Recording Data from Instruments

Because most of the data that engineers need must be obtained from some type of measurement, guidelines governing the acquisition of such data have been established. A measurement made with any type of instrument is limited by its precision and accuracy. In general, a manufacturer will not graduate an instrument to a greater extent than is warranted by its accuracy. For example, it would be meaningless for a meter to have divisions of 0.01 units if its accuracy were only ± 1 unit, because there would clearly be no advantage to such an exact reading when it is not very accurate. For this reason, an instrument's accuracy can be presumed to be $\pm$ one-half of the smallest division of the scale.

Figure 3.1 *Recording data from instruments.*

When taking data from instruments, it is standard practice to record numbers until one doubtful (i.e., estimated) figure has been obtained. The doubtful digit is considered to be significant. Because the last figure recorded is an estimated number, it is customary to provide the range within which the true reading is likely to be. In accordance with what was stated previously, this range is assumed to be ± one-half of the smallest division of the device being read. The meter shown in Figure 3.1, for example, should be read as 4.6 ± 0.5. Because the first digit after the decimal point (i.e., the 6) had to be estimated, no further recording of numbers is justifiable.

This procedure assumes that the instrument's accuracy is greater than its precision (i.e., its readability). If it is known that this is not the case, the number following the ± sign should be the accuracy. If, for example, the meter in Figure 3.1 is known to have an accuracy of ± 1, the reading should be recorded as 4.6 ± 1, not 4.6 ± 0.5.

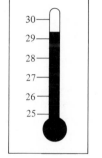

Figure 3.2 Thermometer for example 3.2.

Example 3.2: Record the temperature from the thermometer shown in Figure 3.2 in accordance with accepted data-recording procedures.

Solution: The temperature should be recorded as 29.3 ± 0.5, as the 3 had to be estimated and one-half of the smallest division is 0.5 (i.e., one-half × 1.0).

Problems p3.12 – p3.15

▲ 3.5 Systematic and Random Errors

Whenever an instrument is used for making a measurement, the value obtained will be different from the true value because of errors inherent in the acquisition of the data. The types of errors commonly made when recording data from measurements are classified as systematic and random errors.

A *systematic error* (also known as a consistent or cumulative error) is a divergence from the true value and can usually be eliminated by applying an appropriate correction factor. Examples of systematic errors are an instrument that is out of calibration by a known amount, a steel measuring tape that is too long or too short because the air temperature was different from the air temperature when the tape was calibrated, or readings taken from the wrong scale of a multiscale device. When data are collected under conditions that are known to cause a systematic error, an appropriate correction factor can be used to eliminate it. For example, if a 3-m rule were known to be 0.3 m too short, a length measured as 12 m would be corrected to 10.8 m. Similarly, if a thermometer were known to yield temperature readings too low by 0.2°C, a reading of 4.8°C would be corrected to 5.0°C.

A *random error* (also called an accidental error) is unforeseeable and is usually beyond the control of the data taker. Random errors, unlike systematic errors, tend to be associated with the measuring device's precision and accuracy. Because such errors occur randomly, they tend to cancel each other when a series of readings are taken. For example, if 1000 people were asked to record the reading shown on the meter in Figure 3.3, most would record a value of 13. A few would record the value as 14. If the number of people who recorded a 12 were equal to the number of people who recorded a 14 (and this is likely to be the case), these "erroneous" readings would balance each other, and a "correct" result of 13 would be obtained.

Figure 3.3 Estimating meter readings.

Problems p3.16 – p3.19

▲ 3.6 Rounding of Numbers

When working with numbers, it often is necessary to decrease the number of significant figures so that the number will be recorded in accordance with the aforementioned rules. The process of dropping digits from a number so that it will contain only those digits that are considered to be significant is called *rounding*. This text will use the simplest of the standard rounding procedures. If the number to be dropped is 5 or higher, the preceding digit should be increased by 1. On the other hand, if the number to be dropped is 4 or less, the digit should simply be dropped without changing the preceding digit. Examples of rounding are shown in Table 3.3.

TABLE 3.3 Examples of Rounding of Numbers

Original Number	Significant Figures Desired	Rounded Number
651.321	5	651.32
9.367	3	9.37
0.04185	3	0.0419
73.24763	4	73.25

Other methods of rounding use this same procedure unless the number to be dropped is a 5, in which case one procedure raises the preceding number if it is odd and leaves it the same if it is even. In most cases, the procedure used for rounding will make little difference in the final results as long as the same method is used consistently.

Problems p3.20 – p3.23

▲ 3.7 Arithmetic Operations and Significant Figures

When arithmetic operations are performed on numbers generated according to the guidelines outlined in the preceding sections, it becomes necessary to establish additional rules regarding the retention of significant figures in the answers obtained from the operations. Although rules have been established for virtually every mathematical operation, we shall limit our discussion here to the most common transactions of addition, subtraction, multiplication, and division. The most common rules governing the retention of significant figures following these operations can be summarized as follows:

1. When adding and subtracting numbers, the answer should be rounded to the left-most column that contains a doubtful figure (recall that all readings contain only one doubtful figure and it is significant). Thus, when adding the following numbers, the answer should be rounded to column f, as it is the first column from the left that contains a doubtful figure.

$$\begin{array}{l} \text{Column: abcd efgh} \\ \quad\quad 95.331 \\ \quad\quad\ \ 0.0613 \\ \underline{5321.17} \\ 5416.5623 = 5416.56 \end{array}$$

2. When multiplying and dividing numbers, the answer should contain the same number of significant figures as is contained in the number with the fewest significant figures entering the calculation. Thus, if a number with seven significant figures is multiplied or divided by a number that has only two, the product or quotient should be rounded to two significant figures.

   These multiplication and division rules do not apply when exact conversion factors or whole discrete numbers enter the calculations. For example, the number of bolts required for assembling six bicycles that require 8 bolts apiece would be 48, not 50. Discrete numbers and exact conversion factors, in essence, contain an unlimited number of significant figures, and so the final result is controlled by the other numbers in the calculation.

Supplementary Example 3.5
Problems p3.24 – p3.32

● CHAPTER SUMMARY

This chapter introduced some of the accepted procedures for recording and manipulating data. We defined a significant figure as a number that conveys useful information, and we discussed the use of scientific notation for recording significant figures as a way of avoiding ambiguity in recorded numbers. The differences between precision and accuracy and systematic and random error were presented, along with the proper procedure for recording readings from measuring devices. Finally, we considered the proper recording of significant figures after various mathematical operations have been performed.

Supplementary Examples

Example 3.3: Determine the number of significant figures in each of the following numbers: 63.290; 4.9273 × 10⁻³; 960 000; 7.305 00 E3.

Solution: The number of significant figures associated with the given numbers are as follows:

Number	Number of Significant Figures
63.290	5
4.9273 × 10⁻³	5
960 000	2, 3, 4, 5, or 6 (ambiguous)
7.305 00 E3	6

Example 3.4: A measurement has been recorded as 45.2 ± 1.3 percent. Determine the range of values associated with this reading to the proper number of significant figures.

Solution: This problem requires multiplying two numbers followed by adding and subtracting two numbers. The proper number of significant figures must be carried through each step. Thus,

$$\text{Numerical error} = 45.2 \times 0.013$$
$$= 0.5876$$
$$= 0.59 \text{ (rounded to two significant figures)}$$

Range: 45.2   45.2
       − 0.59   + 0.59
       44.61 = 44.6   45.79 = 45.8

∴ Range = 44.6 to 45.8

Example 3.5: Add the following numbers and express the answer to the correct number of significant figures: 1.4620, 536.1, 1.43 × 10³, 7.321 E-1.

Solution: The first step is to convert all numbers into decimal notation, paying attention to the number of significant digits involved:

$$
\begin{array}{ll}
1.4620 & \\
536.1 & \\
1430 & \text{(only three significant figures)} \\
\underline{0.7321} & \\
1968.2941 = 1970 &
\end{array}
$$

Comment: The answer was rounded to the first column that contained a doubtful figure. In this case, because the 3 in the number 1430 is a doubtful number, the answer could not be carried beyond that column.

▲ Problems

p3.1   Determine the number of significant figures in each of the following numbers:
(a) 46.73   (b) 9.2   (c) 586.21
(d) 979.003   (e) 702.19   (f) 1.9007

p3.2   Determine the number of significant figures in each of the following numbers:
(a) 63.20   (b) 0.315   (c) 0.0021
(d) 0.0200   (e) 0.000 90   (f) 63.960
(g) 690   (h) 1.30   (i) 10 000

p3.3   Determine the number of significant figures in each of the following:
(a) 4.391×10^3 (b) 6.8300×10^2 (c) 1.0000×10^{-2}
(d) 3.19 E3   (e) 8.0314 E-1   (f) 2.1 E6

p3.4   Convert the following numbers from decimal into scientific notation:
(a) 69.38   (b) 78 634   (c) 0.003 29
(d) 569.30   (e) 0.093 700   (f) 2963.020

p3.5   Convert the following numbers from decimal into scientific notation (assume that all numbers shown are significant):
(a) 3562   (b) 0.256   (c) 0.031 77   (d) 56 000
(e) 921.310   (f) 00.901   (g) 29.30   (h) 2.781

p3.6   Convert the following numbers from scientific into decimal notation:
(a) 4.631×10^2 (b) 8.9313×10^{-1} (c) 2.300×10^1
(d) $1.329\ 66 \times 10^{-3}$ (e) 5.1900×10^{-3} (f) 7.3191 E3
(g) 5.0020 E-2   (h) 9.9631 E4

p3.7   An engineering instructor stated that in order for a student to earn a grade of B, the student's average must be 84.5 ± 5.0. What are the maximum and minimum averages that would result in a B grade?

p3.8   An electrical technician was told that the batteries in a portable conductivity meter should have a voltage of 9.0 ± 0.3 volts. What are the maximum and minimum voltages that the technician would consider acceptable?

p3.9   The accuracy of a certain chemical test is listed as 3.0 mg/L. If a result of 93 mg/L is obtained from one sample, the true value is likely to lie between what values?

p3.10   The accuracy of a piece of equipment is listed as ± 0.6 percent of full scale. If the full-scale reading is 54, what will be the range of values associated with a full-scale reading?

p3.11   A quality control engineer measured the diameters of randomly selected ball bearings and obtained the following results (in cm): 2.13, 2.20, 2.17, 2.31, 1.99, 2.07, and 2.30. Which bearings would she have rejected if only those with diameters of 2.00 ± 0.12 cm were considered acceptable?

p3.12   Record the reading shown on the following figure to the proper number of significant figures, and include the precision.

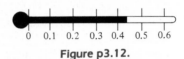

Figure p3.12.

p3.13   For the following meter, record the reading to the proper number of significant figures.

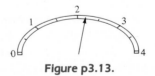

Figure p3.13.

p3.14   When using the following measuring device, what is the maximum amount that a measured value is likely to differ from the true value?

Figure p3.14.

p3.15   Pressure readings taken from the following gage are likely to be accurate to plus or minus what value?

Figure p3.15.

p3.16 A multimeter used for taking current readings was later found to be miscalibrated so that all readings obtained were 0.13 milliamps too low. What should be the corrected value for a reading of 23.69 milliamps?

p3.17 A steel tape thought to be 100 m long was actually found to be only 99.8 m. A distance measured as 5000 m with the tape would really be how many meters?

p3.18 A pressure gage was miscalibrated so that all readings were 2.0 percent too low. Determine the correct pressure for the following readings: (a) 106 psi, (b) 251 psi, (c) 27 psi, (d) 5 psi.

p3.19 A thermometer used for measuring body temperature was found to yield results that were consistently too high by 3.0 percent. A reading of 103.4°C should be corrected to what temperature?

p3.20 Round the following numbers to four significant figures:
(a) 64.321 98   (b) 8937.182   (c) 436.1800
(d) 549 998.21   (e) 0.003 4000   (f) 0.091 682

p3.21 Round the following numbers to two significant figures:
(a) 46.392   (b) 8986.23   (c) 0.004 29   (d) 0.1931

p3.22 Round the following numbers to one significant figure:
(a) 87.329   (b) 46 321.1   (c) 0.001 73   (d) 0.099 83

p3.23 Round the following numbers to three significant figures:
(a) 49.361 492   (b) 649.9326   (c) 60 009.34   (d) 0.004 923

p3.24 Add the following numbers and express the answer to the proper number of significant figures:

(a)   1.3625   (b) 0.0321   (c) 5736.13
     35.21   6.9320   000.2185
    163.194   15.0060   1.3710
                                        06.312

p3.25 Add the following numbers and express the answer to the proper number of significant figures:

(a) 2.311×10^2 (b) 1.5×10^2
    1.9×10^{-2} 6.3×10^3
                       4.821×10^1

(c) 9.200×10^1 (d) 4.832 E2
    3.7612×10^2 6.10 E-1
    7.001×10^{-1}

p3.26   Subtract and express the answer to the proper number of significant figures:

(a)   3219   (b)   45.2931   (c)   114.9630   (d)   193.2968
          -1701 -23.16 -12.3511 -00.1411

p3.27   Multiply and express the answer to the proper number of significant figures:

(a) 39.346   (b)   87.310   (c)   0.003 92
      23.14 -32.109 10.100 76

p3.28   Divide and express the answer to the proper number of significant figures:

(a) $\dfrac{45.32}{29.1}$ (b) $\dfrac{0.396\ 21}{0.046}$ (c) $\dfrac{8362.1}{459}$ (d) $\dfrac{0.0021}{0.015\ 639}$

p3.29   Divide and express the answer to the proper number of significant figures:

(a) $\dfrac{6.213 \times 10^{-2}}{1.59}$ (b) $\dfrac{8.3000 \times 10^{-1}}{0.002\ 91}$ (c) $\dfrac{6.8019 \times 10^{-3}}{4.631\ 07 \times 10^{2}}$

p3.30   Divide and express the answer to the proper number of significant figures:

(a) $\dfrac{6.3921 \times 10^{1}}{4.0100 \times 10^{-1}}$ (b) $\dfrac{2.1020 \times 10^{4}}{4.973\ E2}$ (c) $\dfrac{5.30 \times 10^{4}}{3.986\ 14\ E3}$

p3.31   Complete the following mathematical operations, and express the answer to the proper number of significant figures:

(a)   5.3910   (b) 9632.14
          46.239 16 -79.0371
          $+0.149\ 02$

(c) 642.396/2.91   (d) 43.20 × 6.13

p3.32   From the following readings, determine the highest value possible from addition of the numbers when the precision is taken into account (express answer to proper number of significant figures):

$$
\begin{array}{ll}
36.35 & \pm 0.04 \\
1063.1 & \pm 0.5 \\
163 & \pm 2 \\
\underline{0.0133} & \underline{\pm 0.0004}
\end{array}
$$

4

Hand-held Calculators

The hand-held calculator is an indispensable tool for both professionals and students who must make mathematical calculations daily. Although computers can perform some of the work, a hand-held calculator is used much of the time. Technical students should buy a calculator early in their academic career. Although many students will have mastered calculators before high school graduation, this chapter is an introduction to help technical students select and use the appropriate calculator for their studies.

Objective: The objective of this chapter is to enable you to identify the different types of calculators and to perform mathematical operations with them.

Criteria: After completing this chapter you should be able to do the following:

- **4.1** From a description of the mathematical operations that a calculator can perform and/or of the keys on the calculator, identify it as (a) a four-function calculator, (b) a multiple-function scientific calculator, or (c) a programmable calculator.
- **4.2** Given a set of mathematical operations to be performed, list in the correct order the keystrokes necessary to carry out the operations on an algebraic and/or a reverse Polish notation (RPN) calculator, and perform the necessary operations, recording the correct answer.

▲ 4.1 Types of Calculators

Since the advent of hand-held calculators in the early seventies, they have increased in utility and decreased in cost. At the present time most calculators are battery operated although many are powered by available light. Many have a light-emitting diode (LED) display and rechargeable or replaceable batteries, but most have a liquid crystal display (LCD) with replaceable batteries. The LCD display has become more popular because it requires a very small electric current, thus enabling the batteries to last a very long time, usually over a year.

Although there is an overlap among the types of calculators, for learning purposes we shall divide them into three categories: four-function calculators, multiple-function scientific calculators, and progammable calculators.

Four-Function Calculators   The least expensive and least versatile calculator is the four-function calculator, so called because it can perform only four functions: addition, subtraction, multiplication, and division. A typical

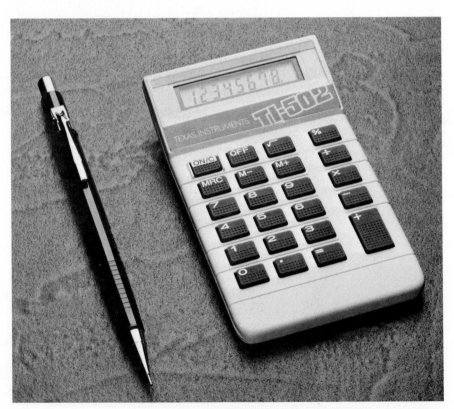

Illustration 4.1 Four-function calculator. (Courtesy Texas Instruments)

four-function calculator is shown in Illustration 4.1. Although labeled a four-function calculator, this type of calculator often has other function keys, such as percent $\boxed{\%}$, clear entry $\boxed{\text{CE}}$, all-clear $\boxed{\text{AC}}$, and store $\boxed{\text{STO}}$. This calculator can be used for simple algebra and arithmetic, but it has limited use for engineering and technology students.

Multiple-Function Scientific Calculators The multiple-function scientific calculator can perform more than four functions, which distinguishes it from the four-function type. Some multiple-function calculators are used mainly for business and statistical purposes and are not scientific, but we will be interested only in scientific calculators, which are the most useful for engineers and technologists.

Scientific calculators can perform various operations in addition to the basic four functions (see Illustration 4.2). Engineering students need a scientific calculator that has at least the following functions: $\boxed{y^x}$, numbers to a power; $\boxed{\text{LN}}$, natural logarithms; $\boxed{\text{LOG}}$, base 10 logarithms; $\boxed{\text{SIN}}$ $\boxed{\text{COS}}$

Illustration 4.2 Multiple-function scientific calculator

$\boxed{\text{TAN}}$, trigonometric functions and the inverses; $\boxed{\sqrt{x}}$, square root; $\boxed{+/-}$, change of sign; and π, the constant pi. The calculator should also have an optional floating point decimal operation system with overflow into scientific notation. In general, scientific calculators have at least one memory register and often more. Other useful functions and operations available on many scientific calculators are $\boxed{e^x}$, powers of the natural number e; $\boxed{x^2}$, square of a number; $\boxed{n!}$, factorial of a number; $\boxed{1/x}$, reciprocal of a number; $\boxed{\Sigma}$, summation; $\boxed{x \rightleftarrows y}$, register interchange; and hyperbolic trigonometric functions. In addition, some scientific calculators have a built-in program to calculate the mean and standard deviation of a set of numbers. Another feature that will be discussed further in a later section of this chapter is the calculator's logic system. The two available logic systems are the algebraic logic system and the reverse Polish notation (RPN) logic system.

Programmable Calculators Not long after the hand-held calculator became popular, programmable hand-held calculators were introduced. These calculators have progressed from those into which the program is keyed and stored electronically while the calculator is on, to those using magnetic cards to introduce external programs, to those that interface with

Illustration 4.3 Programmable calculator. (Courtesy Texas Instruments)

Illustration 4.4 Programmable calculator

computers and input/output devices. The distinction between the hand-held calculator and the personal computer thus has diminished.

Programmable scientific calculators can be used as multiple-function scientific calculators, and the programming is an additional feature. The programmable calculators permit more and more programming steps and are becoming easier and easier to use, so that now they can be used for much of the engineering computation that was previously done only on computers. However, small computers are so readily available and inexpensive that the advantage of a programmable calculator over a computer is not always obvious.

The procedures and languages for programmable calculators vary with the manufacturer and will not be discussed here. Nevertheless, the programmable calculator is powerful and versatile. Engineers or engineering students can do on a programmable calculator much computational work that cannot be done on a scientific calculator. Typical programmable calculators are shown in Illustrations 4.3 and 4.4. As can be seen, they have the same keys as do multiple-function scientific calculators but also have other programming keys such as $\boxed{\text{GTO}}$, go to; $\boxed{\text{P/R}}$ or $\boxed{\text{PRGM}}$, program; $\boxed{\text{COMP}}$, compute; and $\boxed{\text{R/S}}$, run/stop. The function keys for calculators are labeled in various ways. The labels used here are common, but may not be the same as the calculator that you are using. Many functions require two keys on some calculators, but that will not be indicated here. For example, for the inverse sine function, some calculators require the two keys, $\boxed{\text{INV}}$ and $\boxed{\text{SIN}}$, while others have just one key $\boxed{\text{SIN}^{-1}}$.

▲ 4.2 Calculator Logic

The main decision in choosing a scientific calculator is that of the logic system, either algebraic logic or reverse Polish notation (RPN). There are advantages and disadvantages to either, but once the choice is made, it is easy to operate either.

Algebraic Logic In the algebraic logic system, the keys are punched in the same order as the mathematical expression is read, that is, from left to right, with a few exceptions. The expression

$$6 - 2 + 3$$

is keyed into the calculator as

$$\boxed{6}\ \boxed{-}\ \boxed{2}\ \boxed{+}\ \boxed{3}\ \boxed{=}$$

The equal key $\boxed{=}$ instructs the calculator to perform the operations that have been keyed in. When the equal key $\boxed{=}$ is punched in this sequence, the answer, 7, is displayed. An additional $\boxed{=}$ could have been punched in:

$$\boxed{6}\ \boxed{-}\ \boxed{2}\ \boxed{=}\ \boxed{+}\ \boxed{3}\ \boxed{=}$$

The intermediate result, 4, would have been displayed after the first $\boxed{=}$.

An algebraic logic system may or may not have hierarchy. Having hierarchy means that without parentheses, the algebraic operations are performed according to a set order. A simple algebraic system without hierarchy performs the calculations in the order of their entry unless parentheses are used. Operations within the parentheses are performed first. But most algebraic logic systems do have a hierarchy of operations, as follows:

1. Evaluation of scientific functions such as log or sin.
2. Performance of exponentiation such as e^x and y^x.
3. Performance of multiplication and division in order of first entry to the last, or left to right, in a written expression.
4. Performance of addition and subtraction, in order of first entry to last, or left to right, in a written expression.

To demonstrate hierarchy, the expression

$$\frac{6}{2} + 7$$

is keyed in as

$$\boxed{6}\ \boxed{\div}\ \boxed{2}\ \boxed{+}\ \boxed{7}\ \boxed{=}$$

The correct answer, 10, is displayed. The operation $6 \div 2$ is carried out first because division has higher priority in the hierarchy of operations. The expression

$$\frac{6+7}{2}$$

is keyed in as

$$\boxed{(} \;\; \boxed{6} \;\; \boxed{+} \;\; \boxed{7} \;\; \boxed{)} \;\; \boxed{\div} \;\; \boxed{2} \;\; \boxed{=}$$

The correct answer, 6.5, is displayed. The parentheses must be used because the addition must be performed before the division. That is, if the order of key strokes were

$$\boxed{6} \;\; \boxed{+} \;\; \boxed{7} \;\; \boxed{\div} \;\; \boxed{2} \;\; \boxed{=} \quad \text{(INCORRECT)}$$

the answer displayed would be 9.5 because the division would have been performed before the addition. An alternative way of keying in this expression would be to insert an intermediate $\boxed{=}$:

$$\boxed{6} \;\; \boxed{+} \;\; \boxed{7} \;\; \boxed{=} \;\; \boxed{\div} \;\; \boxed{2} \;\; \boxed{=}$$

The exceptions to this order of keystroke are the scientific functions. To perform the operation

$$\sin(30°)$$

key in

$$\boxed{3} \;\; \boxed{0} \;\; \boxed{\text{SIN}}$$

and the answer, 0.5, will be displayed. An additional feature for trigonometric functions is the argument. Most scientific calculators allow the argument of the trigonometric function to be in either degrees or radians. The calculator must be set in the correct mode. Either mode can also be used for the inverse trigonometric functions.

To obtain

$$\ln(72.7)$$

key in

$$\boxed{7} \;\; \boxed{2} \;\; \boxed{.} \;\; \boxed{7} \;\; \boxed{\text{LN}}$$

The answer, 4.286341, is displayed.
To perform the operation

$$(6.8)^{1.3}$$

key in

$$\boxed{6} \;\; \boxed{.} \;\; \boxed{8} \;\; \boxed{y^x} \;\; \boxed{1} \;\; \boxed{.} \;\; \boxed{3} \;\; \boxed{=}$$

The correct answer, 12.085416, is displayed.

The following are examples of expressions with the correct order of keystrokes for an algebraic logic system with hierarchy:

Example 4.1: $\dfrac{349.2 - 284.7}{43.2}$

Solution: Keystrokes, in order

$\boxed{(}\ \boxed{3}\ \boxed{4}\ \boxed{9}\ \boxed{.}\ \boxed{2}\ \boxed{-}\ \boxed{2}\ \boxed{8}\ \boxed{4}\ \boxed{.}\ \boxed{7}\ \boxed{)}\ \boxed{\div}\ \boxed{4}\ \boxed{3}\ \boxed{.}\ \boxed{2}\ \boxed{=}$

Displayed answer: 1.493056.

Comment: Parentheses must be used in order for the subtraction to be carried out before the division.

Example 4.2: $\pi^2 + \sin(64.3°)$

Solution: Keystrokes, in order

$\boxed{\pi}\ \boxed{x^2}\ \boxed{+}\ \boxed{6}\ \boxed{4}\ \boxed{.}\ \boxed{3}\ \boxed{\text{SIN}}\ \boxed{=}$

Displayed answer: 10.770681.

Comment: The calculator must be set in the degree mode.

Example 4.3: $\dfrac{(4.2 + 7.3)(18.2)}{(2.7 + 8.4)}$

Solution: Keystrokes, in order

$\boxed{(}\ \boxed{4}\ \boxed{.}\ \boxed{2}\ \boxed{+}\ \boxed{7}\ \boxed{.}\ \boxed{3}\ \boxed{)}\ \boxed{X}\ \boxed{1}\ \boxed{8}\ \boxed{.}\ \boxed{2}\ \boxed{\div}\ \boxed{(}\ \boxed{2}\ \boxed{.}\ \boxed{7}\ \boxed{+}$
$\boxed{8}\ \boxed{.}\ \boxed{4}\ \boxed{)}\ \boxed{=}$

Displayed answer: 18.855856.

Example 4.4: $(2 + e^{3.2})[1 + \cos(27.4°)]$

Solution: Keystrokes, in order

$\boxed{(}\ \boxed{2}\ \boxed{+}\ \boxed{3}\ \boxed{.}\ \boxed{2}\ \boxed{e^x}\ \boxed{)}\ \boxed{X}\ \boxed{(}\ \boxed{1}\ \boxed{+}\ \boxed{2}\ \boxed{7}\ \boxed{.}\ \boxed{4}$
$\boxed{\text{COS}}\ \boxed{)}\ \boxed{=}$

Displayed answer: 50.088519.

Example 4.5: $\dfrac{3.2 \times 10^{-4}}{\tan(142.73°) + 0.923}$

Solution: Keystrokes, in order

$\boxed{3}\ \boxed{.}\ \boxed{2}\ \boxed{\text{EXP}}\ \boxed{4}\ \boxed{+/-}\ \boxed{\div}\ \boxed{(}\ \boxed{1}\ \boxed{4}\ \boxed{2}\ \boxed{.}\ \boxed{7}\ \boxed{3}\ \boxed{\text{TAN}}\ \boxed{+}$

$\boxed{.}\ \boxed{9}\ \boxed{2}\ \boxed{3}\ \boxed{)}\ \boxed{=}$

Displayed answer: 0.001975.

Comment: If the calculator is in the scientific notation mode with six decimal places, the displayed answer will be 1.974927-03.

Example 4.6: $\left[\dfrac{6.3 \times 10^3}{2.8 \times 10^8} + 7.3 \times 10^{-5}\right]^{2.7}$

Solution: Keystrokes, in order

$\boxed{(}\ \boxed{6}\ \boxed{.}\ \boxed{3}\ \boxed{\text{EXP}}\ \boxed{3}\ \boxed{\div}\ \boxed{2}\ \boxed{.}\ \boxed{8}\ \boxed{\text{EXP}}\ \boxed{8}\ \boxed{+}\ \boxed{7}\ \boxed{.}\ \boxed{3}$

$\boxed{\text{EXP}}\ \boxed{5}\ \boxed{+/-}\ \boxed{)}\ \boxed{y^x}\ \boxed{2}\ \boxed{.}\ \boxed{7}\ \boxed{=}$

Displayed answer: 1.399617 − 11.

Comment: The number 0.00000000001399617 cannot be displayed in fixed decimal form and thus is displayed in scientific notation, regardless of the mode for input.

Reverse Polish Notation In the reverse Polish notation (RPN) logic, first the operands are entered into the calculator and then the operator, rather than entering the operator between the operands, as in the algebraic logic notation. To separate the operands, an enter $\boxed{\text{ENTER}}$ key is used. The expression

$$6 - 2 + 3$$

is keyed in as

$\boxed{6}\ \boxed{\text{ENTER}}\ \boxed{2}\ \boxed{-}\ \boxed{3}\ \boxed{+}$

The answer is displayed as 7. As you can see, this is different from the algebraic logic system, as the RPN system requires no equal $\boxed{=}$ key and no parentheses.

Calculators using the RPN system employ a memory "stack" of usually four registers. A picture of this stack of registers clarifies the explanation of the RPN system. The registers are usually noted as X, Y, Z, and T. The X register is the display in the calculator. To calculate the expression

$$6 - 2 + 3$$

assume that all the registers are initially zero:

Key in:	The stack will contain:

6

T	0.0
Z	0.0
Y	0.0
X	6	←— display

ENTER

T	0.0
Z	0.0
Y	6.0
X	6.0	←— display

2

T	0.0
Z	0.0
Y	6.0
X	2	←— display

−

T	0.0
Z	0.0
Y	0.0
X	4.0	←— display

As you can see, the operands, that is, 6 and 2, were entered first and then the operator, −. When the operator key is pressed, the operation begins. To complete this expression,

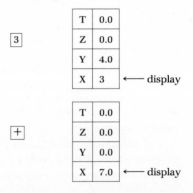

3

T	0.0
Z	0.0
Y	4.0
X	3	←— display

+

T	0.0
Z	0.0
Y	0.0
X	7.0	←— display

The correct answer, 7.0, is displayed.

Let us try another simple operation:

$$\frac{6}{2} + 7$$

For RPN, key in:	The stack will contain:

6

T	0.0
Z	0.0
Y	0.0
X	6	← display

ENTER

T	0.0
Z	0.0
Y	6.0
X	6.0	← display

2

T	0.0
Z	0.0
Y	6.0
X	2	← display

÷

T	0.0
Z	0.0
Y	0.0
X	3.0	← display

7

T	0.0
Z	0.0
Y	3.0
X	7	← display

+

T	0.0
Z	0.0
Y	0.0
X	10.0	← display

The correct answer, 10.0, is displayed.
For the expression

$$\frac{6 + 7}{2}$$

Key in:	The stack will contain:		
6	T	0.0	
	Z	0.0	
	Y	0.0	
	X	6	← display
ENTER	T	0.0	
	Z	0.0	
	Y	6.0	
	X	6.0	← display
7	T	0.0	
	Z	0.0	
	Y	6.0	
	X	7	← display
+	T	0.0	
	Z	0.0	
	Y	0.0	
	X	13.0	← display
2	T	0.0	
	Z	0.0	
	Y	13.0	
	X	2	← display
÷	T	0.0	
	Z	0.0	
	Y	0.0	
	X	6.5	← display

The correct answer, 6.5, is displayed.

The scientific functions are used in the same way for RPN calculators as for algebraic logic calculators except for carrying a number to a power, y^x. To perform the operation

$$(6.8)^{1.3}$$

key in

$$\boxed{6}\ \boxed{.}\ \boxed{8}\ \boxed{\text{ENTER}}\ \boxed{1}\ \boxed{.}\ \boxed{3}\ \boxed{y^x}$$

The correct answer, 12.085416, is displayed. As before, both of the operands are entered before the operator. To demonstrate the RPN logic use further, we offer the following examples:

Example 4.7: $\dfrac{349.2 - 284.7}{43.2}$

Solution: Keystrokes, in order

$$\boxed{3}\ \boxed{4}\ \boxed{9}\ \boxed{.}\ \boxed{2}\ \boxed{\text{ENTER}}\ \boxed{2}\ \boxed{8}\ \boxed{4}\ \boxed{.}\ \boxed{7}\ \boxed{-}\ \boxed{4}\ \boxed{3}\ \boxed{.}\ \boxed{2}\ \boxed{\div}$$

The correct answer, 1.493056, is displayed.

Example 4.8: $\pi^2 + \sin(64.3°)$

Solution: Keystrokes, in order

$$\boxed{\pi}\ \boxed{x^2}\ \boxed{6}\ \boxed{4}\ \boxed{.}\ \boxed{3}\ \boxed{\text{SIN}}\ \boxed{+}$$

The correct answer, 10.770681, is displayed.

Example 4.9: $\dfrac{(4.2 + 7.3)(18.2)}{(2.7 + 8.4)}$

Solution: Keystrokes, in order

$$\boxed{4}\ \boxed{.}\ \boxed{2}\ \boxed{\text{ENTER}}\ \boxed{7}\ \boxed{.}\ \boxed{3}\ \boxed{+}\ \boxed{1}\ \boxed{8}\ \boxed{.}\ \boxed{2}\ \boxed{X}\ \boxed{2}\ \boxed{.}\ \boxed{7}$$

$$\boxed{\text{ENTER}}\ \boxed{8}\ \boxed{.}\ \boxed{4}\ \boxed{+}\ \boxed{\div}$$

The correct answer, 18.855856, is displayed.

Example 4.10: $(2 + e^{3.2})[1 + \cos(27.4°)]$

Solution: Keystrokes, in order

| 2 | | ENTER | | 3 | | . | | 2 | | e^x | | + | | 1 | | ENTER | | 2 | | 7 | | . | | 4 | | COS | | + | | X |

The correct answer, 50.088519, is displayed.

Example 4.11: $\dfrac{3.2 \times 10^{-4}}{\tan(142.73°) + 0.923}$

Solution: Keystrokes, in order

| 3 | | . | | 2 | | EEX | | 4 | | +/− | | ENTER | | 1 | | 4 | | 2 | | . | | 7 | | 3 | | TAN |

| . | | 9 | | 2 | | 3 | | + | | ÷ |

The correct answer, 0.001975, is displayed.

Example 4.12: $\left[\dfrac{6.3 \times 10^3}{2.8 \times 10^8} + 7.3 \times 10^{-5} \right]^{2.7}$

Solution: Keystrokes, in order

| 6 | | . | | 3 | | EEX | | 3 | | ENTER | | 2 | | . | | 8 | | EEX | | 8 | | ÷ | | 7 | | . | | 3 | | EEX |

| 5 | | +/− | | + | | 2 | | . | | 7 | | y^x |

The correct answer, 1.399617 −11, is displayed.

● CHAPTER SUMMARY

This chapter emphasized the importance of a hand-held calculator for technical students. Four-function calculators, multiple-function scientific calculators, and programmable calculators were briefly described. We explained the algebraic logic system and the reverse Polish notation (RPN) logic system for calculators and, through examples, many of the functions for each system.

Supplementary Examples

Example 4.13: List the keystrokes, in order, to determine the value of the following expression for:
a. a calculator using algebraic logic with hierarchy.
b. a calculator using RPN logic.

$$\frac{(643.7)[\sin(0.428) + (1.7)\cos(0.672)]}{\ln(2.73)} =$$

Solution: The calculator must be set for the argument of the trigonometric functions to be in radians.

a. Keystrokes, in order

| 6 | 4 | 3 | . | 7 | X | (| (| . | 4 | 2 | 8 | SIN |

| + | 1 | . | 7 | X | . | 6 | 7 | 2 | COS |) | = |

| ÷ | 2 | . | 7 | 3 | LN | = |

Displayed answer: 1118.72410.

b. Keystrokes, in order

| 6 | 4 | 3 | . | 7 | ENTER | . | 4 | 2 | 8 | SIN |

| 1 | . | 7 | ENTER | . | 6 | 7 | 2 | COS | X | + |

| X | 2 | . | 7 | 3 | LN | ÷ |

Displayed answer: 1118.72410.

Example 4.14: List the keystrokes, in order, to determine the value of the following expression, for:
a. a calculator using algebraic logic with hierarchy.
b. a calculator using RPN logic.

$$\frac{8.43}{5.62} - (6.33 \times 10^{-4} + 2.77 \times 10^{-4})^{0.023} =$$

Solution:

a. Keystrokes, in order

| 8 | . | 4 | 3 | ÷ | 5 | . | 6 | 2 | = | − | (| (|

| 6 | . | 3 | 3 | EE | 4 | +/− | + | 2 | . | 7 | 7 | EE |

| 4 | +/− |) | y^x | . | 0 | 2 | 3 |) | = |

Displayed answer: 0.64875.

b. Keystrokes, in order

| 8 | . | 4 | 3 | ENTER | 5 | . | 6 | 2 | ÷ | 6 | . | 3 |

$$\boxed{3}\ \boxed{EEX}\ \boxed{4}\ \boxed{CHS}\ \boxed{ENTER}\ \boxed{2}\ \boxed{.}\ \boxed{7}\ \boxed{7}\ \boxed{EEX}\ \boxed{4}$$
$$\boxed{CHS}\ \boxed{+}\ \boxed{.}\ \boxed{0}\ \boxed{2}\ \boxed{3}\ \boxed{y^x}\ \boxed{-}$$

Displayed answer: 0.64875.

Comment:
a. The sequence of entries $\boxed{6}\ \boxed{.}\ \boxed{3}\ \boxed{3}\ \boxed{EE}\ \boxed{4}\ \boxed{+/-}$ establishes scientific notation; the $\boxed{+/-}$ is the sign change for making the power of 10 equal to negative 4.
b. The sequence of entries $\boxed{6}\ \boxed{.}\ \boxed{3}\ \boxed{3}\ \boxed{EEX}\ \boxed{4}\ \boxed{CHS}$ establishes scientific notation; the $\boxed{CHS}$ is the sign change for making the power of 10 equal to negative 4.

▲ Problems

p4.1–4.16   For the following mathematical expressions, list in the correct order the keystrokes necessary to perform the operations on:
(a) a calculator using algebraic logic with hierarchy.
(b) a calculator using reverse Polish notation.

p4.1 $\dfrac{256.8}{4} + 75.8 =$

p4.2 $\dfrac{391.4 + 218.5}{5.2} =$

p4.3 $\dfrac{(1.63)(2.78) - 2.47}{0.822} =$

p4.4 $(4.7)^3 + (2.3)^2 =$
p4.5 $2.783 - \ln(7.33) =$
p4.6 $0.134 - e^{-2.5} =$
p4.7 $1.66 - 2[\tan(18°)]$

p4.8 $\dfrac{184.75}{6.56} + (3.75)^{2.44} =$

p4.9 $\dfrac{\sin(62.4°) + \cos(48.5°)}{0.32} =$

p4.10 $(2.63)[1.36 + \sin(72.8°)] =$

p4.11 $\dfrac{(2500 + 8900 - 3300)(0.176)}{2.73 + \pi} =$

p4.12 $\dfrac{e^{3.4} + \tan(126°)}{e^{2.4} - \sin(294°)} =$

p4.13 $\dfrac{(19\ 275)^{2.556}}{1.66 \times 10^8} =$

p4.14 $\dfrac{0.356 + (2.2)(0.284) - (1.83)(0.54)}{1.33 + [\sin(.32)]^2} =$

p4.15 $\dfrac{3.25 \times 10^6}{0.32} - \dfrac{1.76 \times 10^6}{0.84} + \dfrac{6.94 \times 10^4}{0.04} =$

p4.16 $\{\ln[1.73 + \sin^2(0.72)] - (0.284)(5.622)\}(104) =$

p4.17–p4.35 For the following mathematical expressions, perform the operations and record the answer using a hand-held calculator:

p4.17 $\dfrac{3.641}{3} + 2.478 =$

p4.18 $\dfrac{5200 + 6170}{18} - (293)(1.6) =$

p4.19 $(1.3)^3 + (2.7)^{2.5} + (3.1)^{0.8} - (1.9)^{4.2} =$

p4.20 $(294 + 266 - 185 - 91)(3.26 - 1.75 + 2.67) =$

p4.21 $e^{6.52} + (2.6)(158.4) - \dfrac{2648}{\ln(0.25)} =$

p4.22 $\sin(12.3°) + \cos(65.3°) =$

p4.23 $\dfrac{\tan(118°)}{0.0138} + \dfrac{\tan(64.1°)}{0.0537} =$

p4.24 $\left[\dfrac{(7)(772)(590)}{654}\right]^2 \ln(50) =$

p4.25 $[1.629 - \cos^2(2.4\pi)]^{1/4.7} =$

p4.26 $[(6.3 \times 10^4)(0.112) + (5.2 \times 10^3)(2.793)]^{1/3} =$

p4.27 $\dfrac{2\pi(0.53)(75)(726 - 418)}{\log\left(\dfrac{392}{5.6}\right)} =$

p4.28 $(0.023)\left(\dfrac{0.056}{0.4}\right)\left[\dfrac{(6)(120)(5500)(1.521)}{0.203}\right]^{0.77} =$

p4.29 $\sqrt{3(60)^2 - (31 - 16)^2} + (56.3)\sin(1.7\pi) =$

p4.30 $\dfrac{2\pi(3000)(2.7)}{12}\left[\sin(54°) + \dfrac{3}{7}\sin(54°)\cos(54°)\right] =$

p4.31 $(2 - e^{-1.2}) + (3 - e^{-1.8})(e^{-1.1} + 4) =$

p4.32 $\dfrac{(6.3)^{0.32} + 4.3}{\left(2 - \dfrac{1}{e}\right)} + \dfrac{(2.7)^{1.2} + 3.6}{\left(3 - \dfrac{1}{e^2}\right)} =$

p4.33 $\dfrac{(5.3 \times 10^8 + 6.7 \times 10^8)}{(2.5 \times 10^4)^{1.7}} - \dfrac{(3.6 \times 10^7 - 2.7 \times 10^7)}{(8.2 \times 10^3)^{1.4}} =$

p4.34 $0.2387 + (1.2985)\tan^{-1}(1/3) - (0.6431)\cos^{-1}(7/8) =$

p4.35 $\left[\dfrac{(1 + 0.234)^{1.72}}{(2 + 1.373)^{0.82}}\right]^{2.22} - \left[\dfrac{(8.146 - 3)^{0.063}}{(5.279 - 2)}\right]^{3.28} =$

CHAPTER 5

Dimensions and Units

In order to characterize quantities in terms of their length, weight, temperature, or any other quantitative measure, recognized standards of reference must be used. Complete sets of reference standards (i.e., measurement standards for length, mass, force, and the like) are called *systems of units.* This chapter will examine the systems of units used by the scientific and engineering communities.

Objective: The objective of this chapter is to introduce the measuring systems in common use throughout the world and show how they are related.

Criteria: After completing this chapter, you should be able to do the following:

- **5.1** Define dimension, fundamental dimension, derived dimension, unit, length, mass, force, time, and temperature.
- **5.2** Determine the dimensions or units associated with a conversion factor k in a homogenous equation, given the equation and information about the dimensions or units of the variables involved.
- **5.3** State the difference between the absolute and gravitational systems of units, and identify the fundamental dimensions and units for mechanical systems in the English gravitational, SI, and American Engineering systems of units.
- **5.4** List the base units and supplementary units of the SI system, and apply the SI system's rules to symbols, names, numbers, and calculations.
- **5.5** Convert numbers from one system of units into another, and determine the value of a specified variable in an equation, given the equation and values for the other variables in various units.

▲ 5.1 Dimensions and Units

Information is communicated from one person to another primarily through spoken and written words. Such communication requires the use of previously defined, basic characters, the complete set of which is commonly known as an alphabet. Likewise, the scientific community has, in effect, established an alphabet of its own. The elements, or most basic parts of this communication system, are known as *dimensions.* A dimension is simply a shared attribute of all matter. The following are a few common dimensions and their definitions:

Length (L) is a dimension that is rather easy to define. A simple definition is the distance in space from one point to another. It is usually represented by the capital letter *L.*

Mass (M), on the other hand, is a dimension that is not as easy to comprehend. It refers to the substance of which something is composed. Every object has a mass that does not change as the object is moved from one place to another. Thus, the mass of a loaf of bread would be the same on Mars as it is on earth because the matter of which it is composed remains the same.

A *force (F)* is commonly understood to be a push or pull exerted on an object. A force can be applied through direct physical contact, as when we push or pull on a door to open it, or by gravitational, electric, or magnetic fields.

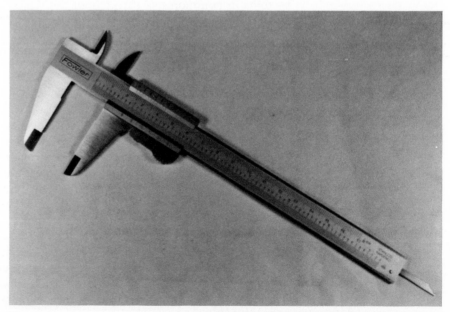

Illustration 5.1 A micrometer measures length with high precision.

　　Time (T) can be defined as a period or interval between two events. Although the concept of the reversibility of time is widely debated among physicists, in this text, we shall be concerned only with the one-way flow of time as poetically stated by Ogden Nash: "Time Marches On."

　　Temperature (Θ) is the degree of hotness or coldness of anything, as measured on one of several arbitrary scales. In a scientific sense, the temperature of a substance is a measure of the kinetic energy (i.e., energy caused by movement of its molecules). Kinetic energy is assumed to cease at zero degrees on an absolute temperature scale (absolute zero), but most people are familiar with the Celsius and Fahrenheit scales, neither of which is an absolute scale. The absolute scales that correspond to the Celsius and Fahrenheit scales are the Kelvin and Rankine scales, respectively. It is simple to convert from one to the other by means of one or more of the following equations:

$$°C = \frac{5}{9} \left(°F - 32\right)$$

$$K = °C + 273.16$$

$$°R = °F + 459.67$$

$$K = \frac{5}{9} °R$$

　　After a few dimensions are defined, it should be obvious that other dimensions can be obtained by combining one or more of them. This observation leads to the need to differentiate between the "original" dimensions and the "combined" dimensions, and thus the terms *fundamental* and *derived* dimensions were born. The most elementary dimensions, like length, mass, and time, are known as *fundamental dimensions.* The others, obtained from combinations of the "originals," are called *derived dimensions.*

　　Area (L^2) and volume (L^3) are examples of derived dimensions obtained by combining the same dimension (i.e., L). Velocity (L/T), acceleration (L/T^2), and pressure (F/L^2), on the other hand, are examples of derived dimensions obtained by combining different fundamental dimensions (i.e., F, L, and T).

　　Although dimensions are necessary to describe an object or an event, they are not sufficient. That is, it could be correctly stated that both a football field and a match stick possess the fundamental dimension of length, but if one were interested in knowing their relative sizes, additional information would obviously have to be provided about the dimension of length. This additional information is provided in the form of the *units* associated with each dimension. A unit is the standard of measurement applicable to a given dimension. For example, inches, feet, meters, furlongs, and fathoms all are units associated with the dimension of length. Similarly, cubic inches, liters, cubic meters, and gallons are units associated with the dimension of vol-

Illustration 5.2 This transducer measures pressure by converting displacement to voltage.

ume. Throughout history, different units have been adopted for quantifying the various dimensions, as illustrated for length and volume. Therefore, we may often need to convert numbers from one set of units into another (e.g., feet to meters, yards to centimeters). In Section 5.5, we discuss various systems of units, including the procedures for converting from one to the other.

Problems p5.1–p5.4

▲ 5.2 Dimensionally Homogeneous Equations

The development and use of equations are commonplace in the scientific community. These equations are generated either by developing and manipulating the theoretical considerations relevant to the situation or by collecting data from experimental studies and generalizing the results. The latter method is usually used when the theories involved are not well understood or when the phenomena under investigation are so complex that purely mathematical solutions are not possible. Equations developed in this manner are called *empirical equations*. Frequently, empirical equations require the introduction of a conversion factor, *k*, so that the dimensions or units on both sides of the equal sign are the same. The procedure for determining the dimensions or units on *k* can best be illustrated through an example. Suppose that a track coach believed that the time required for a male college student to run a hundred-yard dash was strictly a function of his height and weight. In order to prove his point, let us assume that he collected data on the times recorded by five different runners and from these data, he developed the following equation:

$$DT = (5) \left(\frac{WT}{HT} \right)$$

where

DT = dash time, in seconds

WT = weight, in pounds

HT = height, in inches

5 = constant

When we write the dimensions on both sides of the equation, we find that they are not the same, because the left side has dimensions of time and the right side has dimensions of force (i.e., weight) and length (i.e., height). Because all equations must be dimensionally homogeneous, the constant (i.e., 5) must have dimensions that will cause the right-hand side of the equation also to have dimensions of time. The dimensions required on the conversion factor, then, can be determined by writing the equation in its dimensional form and solving for *k*. Thus,

$$T = k \frac{F}{L}$$

$$k = \frac{LT}{F}$$

This result can be checked by inserting *k* into the original equation and then verifying that both sides contain the same dimensions. Thus,

$$T = \left(\frac{LT}{F} \right) \left(\frac{F}{L} \right)$$

$$T = T \quad \text{(The solution for } k \text{ is verified)}$$

In addition to dimensions, the units associated with *k* can be determined in a similar manner (see Section 5.5 for an example). In the example about runners, determining the dimensions required on *k* to achieve dimensional homogeneity is normally only an intermediate step in a process designed to explain the variables in physical systems. This process, therefore, is an effective tool for experimental design and data interpretation.

Example 5.1: Determine the dimensions on k in the following dimensionally homogeneous equation:

$$\frac{L}{T^2} = \frac{kML^2\theta^{0.5}}{T^2}$$

Solution: Solving for k,

$$k = \frac{LT^2}{T^2ML^2\theta^{0.5}} = \frac{1}{ML\theta^{0.5}}$$

Check:

$$\frac{L}{T^2} = \left(\frac{1}{ML\theta^{0.5}}\right)\left(\frac{ML^2\theta^{0.5}}{T^2}\right)$$

$$\frac{L}{T^2} = \frac{L}{T^2} \quad \text{O.K.}$$

Supplementary Examples 5.5, 5.6
Problems p5.5–p5.12

▲ 5.3 Systems of Units

In Section 5.1, units were defined as a standard of measurement applicable to a given dimension. In years past, different groups of people defined various sets of units for each of the fundamental and derived dimensions that were important to them. Complete sets of such units are called *systems of units*. In many cases, a particular unit may have served the limited needs of a limited constituency very well for a certain period of time, but as technology improved our ability to measure and to communicate with one another, some sets of units were displaced by others that were perhaps more exact or otherwise more appropriate. As a result, one can find in recorded history literally hundreds of standards of measurement for the most common fundamental dimensions. The dimension of length, for example, has been expressed in such unfamiliar units as ells, hands, links, nails, and paces. Even today, however, the height of a horse is expressed in terms of *hands* (which, in olden times, was defined as the width of a person's open hand).

Today, there are essentially three systems of units in common use throughout the world. These unit systems are the English gravitational (also called the U.S. Customary), SI (Système International d'Unités), and the American Engineering System.

In order to understand the differences among these systems of units, it is important to remember that in the seventeenth century, Isaac Newton formulated his well-known second law of motion which stated that an object subjected to a force, F, will have an acceleration proportional to that force. In equation form, Newton's second law is

$$F = ma \qquad (5.1)$$

where F is a force acting on a rigid body of mass m and a is its resulting acceleration.

A manifestation of Newton's equation that we all understand is that it takes twice as much push to remove a two-ton stalled automobile from the road as it does to remove one that weighs only one ton. As discussed in Section 5.2, equations must have the same dimensions on both sides of the equal sign in order to be dimensionally homogeneous. If length and time are among the fundamental dimensions in a given system of units, then Equation 5.1 can be written dimensionally as

$$F = M\,(L/T^2) \qquad (5.2)$$

where L/T^2 represents the dimensions for acceleration.

Equation 5.2 shows that when length and time are used as two of the fundamental dimensions in a system of units, then only one of the other components of the equation (i.e., F or M) can be included as a fundamental dimension without requiring the introduction of a conversion factor, k. The one that is not included becomes a derived dimension from Equation 5.2. The alternative is to define all four terms (i.e., F, M, L, and T) and include a conversion factor for dimensional homogeneity in Equation 5.1, as follows:

$$F = kma \qquad (5.3)$$

The dimensions and units for homogeneity in Equation 5.3 are discussed below for various systems of units.

The U.S. Customary, SI, and American Engineering systems of units all differ with respect to which of the components of Newton's equation they define. All three systems define length and time as fundamental dimensions, but their treatment of force and mass is not the same. The U.S. Customary system of units defines force as a fundamental dimension, and mass, therefore, as a derived dimension. Systems that define force as one of the fundamental dimensions are known as *gravitational systems,* because the definitions must take into account the effects of gravity. In the U.S. Customary system, then, mass has derived dimensions of

$$m = \frac{F}{a} = \frac{F}{L/T^2} = \frac{FT^2}{L}$$

The units defined for the fundamental dimensions of force, length, and time in the U.S. Customary system are the pound (lb), foot (ft), and second (s). The units of mass, therefore, are lb · s²/ft, as follows:

$$m = \frac{FT^2}{L} = \frac{\text{lb} \cdot \text{s}^2}{\text{ft}}$$

In order to avoid having to say the rather cumbersome "pound second squared per foot" every time one speaks about a certain mass, this combination of units was given the much simpler name of *slugs*. Thus, a mass of 20 lb · sec²/ft is also a mass of 20 slugs.

The SI system of units is an outgrowth of the metric system, which defines mass as a fundamental dimension and force as a dimension derived from Newton's law. The dimensions for force, therefore, are ML/T^2, as follows:

$$F = ma = \frac{ML}{T^2}$$

The units defined for mass, length, and time in the SI system are the kilogram (kg), meter (m), and second (s). The derived units for force therefore are kg · m/s², and again, in the interest of simplicity in writing or speaking about this unit, a kg · m/s² is called a *newton* (N). Thus, a force of 200 kg · m/s² is also a force of 200 N.

The American Engineering system of units is a gravitational system because it defines force as a fundamental dimension. However, it also defines mass as a fundamental dimension, which creates a problem with respect to dimensional homogeneity in Newton's law. A conversion factor must be introduced, as shown in Equation 5.3, which has dimensions of FT^2/ML:

$$k = \frac{F}{ma} = \frac{F}{ML/T^2} = \frac{FT^2}{ML}$$

The American engineering system of units (also called the English engineering system) complicates matters even more because of a rather inappropriate selection of units for the fundamental dimensions. That is, the units for length, time, force, and mass are feet, seconds, pounds, and pounds, respectively. Because the term *pound* is used for both a unit of force and a unit of mass and because a force and a mass are obviously not the same, it is necessary to differentiate between the two quantities by identifying the units of force as *pounds force* (abbreviated lb_f) and the units of mass as *pounds mass* (abbreviated lb_m). When the subscript is omitted from the abbreviation lb, it usually refers to pound force. When pound mass is intended, the subscript m is added. This convention will be followed hereafter in this book.

It clearly would have been better if units of mass had been called anything else besides pound, but since this was not the case, practitioners will have to use extra caution when dealing with the term pound in the

TABLE 5.1 Systems of Units

Fundamental Dimensions	SI (Absolute)	U.S. Customary (Gravitational)	American (Gravitational)
Force (F)	—	lb_f	lb_f
Mass (M)	kg	—	lb_m
Length (L)	m	ft	ft
Time (T)	s	s	s
Derived Dimensions			
Force (F)	$kg \cdot m/s^2$ (called a newton, N)	—	—
Mass (M)	—	$lb_f \cdot s^2/ft$ (called a slug)	—
Area (L^2)	m^2	ft^2	ft^2
Volume (L^3)	m^3	ft^3	ft^3
Velocity (L/T)	m/s	ft/s	ft/s
Acceleration (L/T^2)	m/s^2	ft/s^2	ft/s^2
Density (M/L^3)	kg/m^3	$lb_f \cdot s^2/ft^4$	lb_m/ft^3
Specific weight (F/L^3)	N/m^3	lb_f/ft^3	lb_f/ft^3
Pressure (F/L^2)	N/m^2	lb_f/ft^2	lb_f/ft^2
Energy (FL)	$N \cdot m$	$ft \cdot lb_f$	$ft \cdot lb_f$
Power (FL/T)	$N \cdot m/s$	$ft \cdot lb_f/s$	$ft \cdot lb_f/s$

American engineering system of units. Table 5.1 shows some of the fundamental dimensions and units for each of the three systems.

There is an advantage to using the American Engineering system of units for calculations for physical systems located where the acceleration due to gravity (g) is 32.174 ft/s². This advantage results from the American system's definition of force and mass: a one-pound force will accelerate a one-pound mass at a rate of 32.174 ft/s². Thus,

$$F = kma$$

$$1 \ lb_f = k(1 \ lb_m)(32.174 \ ft/s^2)$$

$$1 \ lb_f = (k)(32.174) \ lb_m \cdot ft/s^2$$

Thus,

$$k = \frac{1}{32.174} \frac{lb_f \cdot s^2}{lb_m \cdot ft}$$

When this value of k is put back into Newton's equation (as required for dimensional homogeneity),

$$F = \frac{1}{32.174} ma$$

At a place where the acceleration due to gravity is 32.174 ft/s², the force is

Illustration 5.3 A pyranometer measures solar radiation

numerically equal to the mass:

$$F = \frac{1}{32.174}\, m \;(32.174)$$
$$F = m$$

Since the variation in g is relatively small anywhere on earth, no calculations are required to obtain the force when mass is expressed in terms of lb_m rather than slugs. The relationship between pounds mass (lb_m) and slugs can be obtained from Newton's law. Thus, using the American Engineering system of units,

$$1\ lb_f = (1\ lb_m)(32.174\ ft/s^2) = 32.174\ lb_m \cdot ft/s^2$$

For the English system of units, a one-pound force will accelerate a one-slug mass at 1 ft/s². Thus,

$$1\ lb_f = (1\ slug)(1\ ft/s^2) = 1\ slug \cdot ft/s^2$$

If the previous two equations are set equal to each other,

$$32.174\ \frac{lb_m \cdot ft}{s^2} = 1\ \frac{slug \cdot ft}{s^2}$$

$$\therefore 1\ slug = 32.174\ lb_m$$

Even though legislation was enacted by the United States Congress in 1974 for the adoption of SI units, it is quite clear that portions of all three of these systems (and a few others as well) will be used to some extent for many years. Since engineers practicing in this generation must be able to transfer

TABLE 5.2 SI Base Units

Quantity	Name	Symbol
length	meter	m
mass	kilogram	kg
time	second	s
electric current	ampere	A
thermodynamic temperature	kelvin	K
amount of substance	mole	mol
luminous intensity	candela	cd

from one system of units to another, the units used in the problems and discussion in this text will be randomly varied among these three systems. Section 5.5 discusses the procedure for converting from one system of units into another.

Problems p5.13 – p5.17

▲ 5.4 The SI System of Units

As stated in Section 5.3, the SI system of units was created in 1960 as an outgrowth of the metric system of units. The Metric Conversion Act of 1975 was signed on December 23, 1975, declaring "a national policy of coordinating the increasing use of the metric system in the United States."

Considerable progress has been achieved toward this end, but the mountains of books, tools, machines, gauges, and the like that were produced using American units before 1974 (and after) cause one to wonder whether the changeover in the United States will be complete even fifty years from now. In any case, since the SI system is used in most of the other nations of the world and since an increasing number of household, commercial, and industrial products in common use in the United States are manufactured abroad, the pressure to change to the "unified" system can only become stronger. This section examines some of the details associated with correct usage of the SI system.

Table 5.1 presented some of the fundamental and derived units associated with the English, SI, and American systems of units. SI units are more correctly divided into three classes: base units, derived units, and supplementary units. The seven base units of the SI system are listed in Table 5.2 with their names and symbols. The definition of each base unit follows the table. (The unit of measurement for each base unit is also provided.)

1. Length: The meter is the length equal to the distance traveled by light in a vacuum during $1/299\ 792\ 458$ s.
2. Mass: The kilogram is the unit of mass and is equal to the mass of a

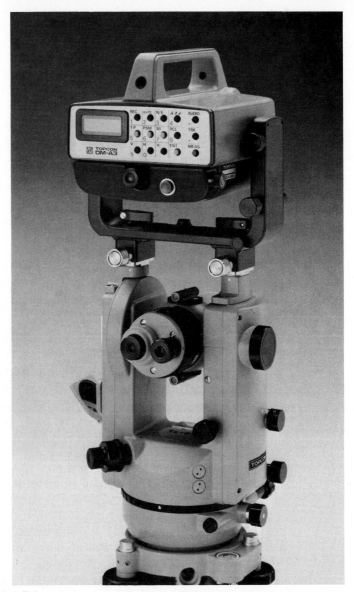

Illustration 5.4 The electronic theodolite measures angle and distance accurately and precisely. (Courtesy Topcon Instrument Corporation of America)

platinum-iridium alloy cylinder that is kept at the International Bureau of Weights and Measures in France.

3. Time: The second is the duration of 9 192 631 770 periods of the radiation corresponding to the transition between the two hyperfine levels of the ground state of the cesium-133 atom.

TABLE 5.3 Examples of SI-derived Units*

Quantity	Name	Symbol	Expression in Terms of Other Units	Expression in Terms of SI Base Units
area	square meter	m²	—	—
volume	cubic meter	m³	—	—
velocity	meter per second	m/s	—	—
acceleration	meter per second squared	m/s²	—	—
density	kilogram per cubic meter	kg/m³	—	—
specific weight	newton per cubic meter	N/m³	—	—
current density	ampere per square meter	A/m²	—	—
specific volume	cubic meter per kilogram	m³/kg	—	—
luminance	candela per square meter	cd/m²	—	—
frequency	hertz	Hz	—	s^{-1}
force	newton	N	—	$m \cdot kg \cdot s^{-2}$
pressure	pascal	Pa	N/m²	$m^{-1} \cdot kg \cdot s^{-2}$
energy, work	joule	J	N · m	$m^2 \cdot kg \cdot s^{-2}$
power	watt	W	J/s	$m^2 \cdot kg \cdot s^{-3}$
electric potential	volt	V	W/A	$m^2 \cdot kg \cdot s^{-3} \cdot A^{-1}$

* NBS Special Publication 330 (Washington, D.C.: U.S. Dept. of Commerce, National Bureau of Standards, 1977).

4. Electric Current: The ampere is the constant current that, if maintained in two straight parallel conductors of infinite length and of negligible circular cross section and placed 1 meter apart in a vacuum, would produce between these conductors a force equal to 2×10^{-7} newton per meter of length.

5. Temperature: The kelvin, a unit of thermodynamic temperature, is the fraction 1/273.16 of the thermodynamic temperature of the triple point of water.

6. Amount of Substance: The mole is the amount of substance of a system that contains as many elementary entities as there are atoms in 0.012 kilogram of carbon 12.

7. Luminous intensity: The candela is the luminous intensity in a given direction of a source that emits monochromatic radiation of frequency 540×10^{12} hertz and that has a radiant intensity in that direction of 1/683 watts per steradian.

Table 5.3 lists some of the derived units expressed in terms of the base units. The lower half of the table shows derived units with special names. Table 5.4 lists the supplementary units, and as shown, there are only two: the plane angle and the solid angle.

When dealing with quantities too large or too small to be conveniently handled with the standard SI units, multiples or submultiples may be formed by adding the appropriate prefix. The prefixes and their symbols are shown in Table 5.5. Note that the prefix symbol for milli (m) is the same as the base unit symbol for meter.

TABLE 5.4 SI Supplementary Units

Quantity	Name	Symbol
plane angle	radian	rad
solid angle	steradian	sr

In order to eliminate any confusion in the use of SI units, certain guidelines and recommendations have been established governing their use. The most important of these are the following:

1. Unit symbols are printed in lowercase Roman (upright) type, except when the symbols are derived from proper names, in which case capital Roman type is used. Periods are never used after the symbol unless the symbol is at the end of a sentence.

   For example: m, N, kg, or A—*not* KG, N., or m.

2. Prefix symbols are printed in Roman type without a space between the prefix symbol and unit symbol. Double prefixes should not be used.

   For example: pm, GN, and mW—*not* p m, G N, or μmN

3. The product of two or more units is indicated by a dot or space between the units. This differentiates between symbols used as prefixes and those forming a product.

   For example: N m, N · m, or kg · s^{-3}—*not* Nm or kgs^{-3}

4. A solidus (/), horizontal line, or negative power may be used to express a unit formed from another by division. The solidus or horizontal line

Illustration 5.5 This special instrumentation is for precisely measuring steering wheel angles. (Courtesy General Motors)

TABLE 5.5 SI Unit Prefixes

Factor by Which Unit is Multiplied	Prefix	Symbol
10^{-18}	atto	a
10^{-15}	femto	f
10^{-12}	pico	p
10^{-9}	nano	n
10^{-6}	micro	μ
10^{-3}	milli	m
10^{-2}	centi	c
10^{-1}	deci	d
10^{1}	deka	da
10^{2}	hecto	h
10^{3}	kilo	k
10^{6}	mega	M
10^{9}	giga	G
10^{12}	tera	T
10^{15}	peta	P
10^{18}	exa	E

should not be repeated on the same line. Parentheses may be used to avoid ambiguity.

$$\text{For example: } m/s, \frac{N}{m}, \frac{m \cdot kg}{s^2} \text{ or } m \cdot s^{-2} - not\ m/s/s, \frac{m}{\frac{s}{s}}, \text{ or } \frac{m}{s/s}$$

5. Unit names should not be capitalized (even if derived from a proper name) unless they are in a title or at the beginning of a sentence.

6. In general, unit names and symbols should not be mixed, with the use of symbols preferred. When symbols are used, there should be a space between the number and the unit symbol.

    For example: 5 m, 2 N or one meter — *not* 2N or 1 meter

7. When unit names are written out, plurals should be used as necessary. For the symbols, however, the singular and plural are the same.

    For example: 5 m, 2 N, two newtons — *not* 5 m's, two newton

8. When writing numbers, commas should not be used to separate groups of digits (In some countries, a comma is used as a period). Rather, a space should be left after every third digit. If there are only four digits to the left or right of the decimal point, the space is optional.

    For example: 1 000 or 25 396 219 — *not* 3,000 or 73,629,432

9. Numbers less than 1 should be preceded by a zero.

    For example: 0.63 or 0.932 158 — *not* .63 or .932 158

10. A space should be left on each side of the signs for addition, subtraction, multiplication, and division.

    For example: 5 m + 2 m — *not* 5 m+2 m

Problems p5.18 – p5.20

▲ 5.5 Conversion of Units

Because different unit systems are still used throughout the world, the ability to convert from one system of units into another will be required for many years. This procedure generally requires using a conversion table, an example of which is shown in Table 5.6. (Appendix C is a more comprehensive listing of conversion factors.)

The units to be converted are in column 1, the conversion factors in column 2, and the desired units in column 3. Thus, one can find the number of liters in three cubic feet by multiplying 3 by 2.832×10^1:

$$\text{liters} = 3.0 \times 2.832 \times 10^1 = 84.96 \text{ L}$$
$$= 85 \text{ L}$$

It is good practice to write the units beside each component of a mathematical equation. This procedure helps eliminate errors caused by the careless manipulation of units. Thus, a better way to write the preceding equation is as follows:

$$\text{liters} = 3.0 \text{ ft}^3 \times 2.832 \times 10^1 \text{ L/ft}^3 = 84.96 \text{ L}$$
$$= 85 \text{ L}$$

Obviously, the units for the numbers in column 2 are equal to those in column 3, divided by those in column 1.

Units converted from one system into another should maintain the implied precision of the original units. Precision is implied through significant digits. In general, implied precision will be maintained if the number of significant digits remains the same after the conversion. We shall illustrate the meaning of maintaining implied precision by converting a force of 1.5 pounds into newtons:

$$F = (1.5 \text{ lb}) \left(4.448 \, \frac{\text{N}}{\text{lb}} \right)$$
$$= 6.672 \text{ N}$$

It is not logical to leave the converted value as shown because the original implied precision was not as great. More logically, the converted force should be

$$F = 6.7 \text{ N}$$

where the original implied precision is maintained.

TABLE 5.6 Conversion Factors

To Convert	Multiply by	To Obtain
feet	1.2×10^1	inches
acres	4.047×10^3	square meters
centimeters	3.281×10^{-2}	feet
cubic feet	2.832×10^1	liters
pounds	4.448	newtons

Example 5.2: The Not-2-Slick oil company (N-2-S) owns an oil well that is producing two barrels of oil per hour. How many cubic meters per hour is this?

Solution:

$$m^3/h = (2.0 \text{ bbl/h})(4.2 \times 10^1 \text{ gal/bbl})(3.785 \times 10^{-3} \text{ m}^3/\text{gal})$$
$$= 0.32 \text{ m}^3/h$$

Section 5.2 discussed the requirement for dimensional homogeneity in equations, and although that discussion focused on the homogeneity of dimensions, the same requirement applies to units. Often the data given to engineers for analysis or design purposes are not in consistent units. Since these data are generally used in mathematical equations involving several variables, it is frequently necessary to convert the units of one or more of the variables into units that will render the equation homogeneous. The next two examples illustrate this concept.

Example 5.3: The owner of a 600-acre farm was approached by a state highway official and told that some of his land was needed for a right-of-way. Specifically, the highway department wanted a strip 80.0 ft wide by 10 000 ft long. If the farmer sold the land to the state, how many acres would he have left?

Solution: The first step is find out how many acres the state wants. Thus,

$$A = 10\ 000 \text{ ft} \times 80.0 \text{ ft} = 800\ 000 \text{ ft}^2$$

$$A = 800\ 000 \text{ ft}^2 \times 2.296 \times 10^{-5} \text{ acres/ft}^2$$
$$= 18.4 \text{ acres}$$

The amount of land the farmer would have left, therefore, would be

$$\text{land left} = 600 - 18.4 = 582 \text{ acres}$$

Example 5.4: The flow rate of a liquid through a conduit can be calculated from the equation Q = AV, where Q is the flow rate, A is the area of the conduit, and V is the velocity. If a rectangular channel is 15 in wide by 10 in high, what will be the flow rate, in ft³/s when the velocity is 3.0 ft/s?

Solution: Since units of ft³/s are desired on the left side of the equation, the units on the right side must also be ft³/s. If the area is expressed in square feet, then this will be accomplished. Thus,

$$A = (15 \times 11) \text{ in}^2 \times 6.944 \times 10^{-3} \text{ ft}^2/\text{in}^2$$
$$= 1.15 \text{ ft}^2$$

Thus,

$$Q = 1.15 \text{ ft}^2 \times 3.0 \text{ ft/s} = 3.5 \text{ ft}^3/\text{s}$$

Supplementary Example 5.7
Problems p5.21–p5.31

● CHAPTER SUMMARY

This chapter considered the measuring systems most widely used today. Section 5.1 examined the dimension and unit as the basis for measuring systems. Next, we looked at dimensionally homogeneous equations in terms of dimensional and unit conversion factors. Sections 5.3 and 5.4 discussed the bases for unit systems (i.e., absolute or gravitational) and three systems of units. The last section explained the procedures for converting from one system of units into another.

Supplementary Examples

Example 5.5: Determine the dimensions for the conversion factor k in the following equation:

$$\frac{FLM}{\theta T} = \frac{k M^3 L^{2/3}}{T F^2 \theta}$$

Solution:

$$k = \frac{(FLM)(T F^2 \theta)}{(\theta T)(M^3 L^{2/3})}$$
$$k = \frac{F^3 L^{1/3}}{M^2}$$

Comment: The solution can be checked by substituting the value of k back into the original equation.

Example 5.6: For the equation $y = 0.5\,DRT^{0.5}$, the units for y are m³/s. If the units for D are m/s and for T are m², what units will be required for R in order to render the equation homogeneous?

Solution:

$$\text{m}^3/\text{s} = \text{m/s} \cdot \text{R} \cdot (\text{m}^2)^{0.5}$$

$$\text{m}^3/\text{s} = \text{m}^2/\text{s} \cdot \text{R}$$

$$R = \frac{(\text{m}^3/\text{s})}{(\text{m}^2/\text{s})} = \text{m}$$

$\therefore R$ must have units of meters

Example 5.7: The equation $Q = CiA$ is widely used for calculating the rainfall runoff from a given area (A) after a rainfall of a certain intensity (i). The runoff Q is expressed in units of ft³/s; C is a dimensionless coefficient of runoff; i is the rainfall intensity in in/h; and A is the drainage area in acres. In order to make the equation homogeneous in terms of units, a factor, k, must be included. Determine the value and units for k.

Solution: The general equation is

$$Q = kCiA$$

Plugging the units into the equation,

$$\frac{\text{ft}^3}{\text{s}} = (k)\left(\frac{\text{in}}{\text{h}}\right)(\text{acres})$$

$$k = \left(\frac{\text{ft}^3 \cdot \text{h}}{\text{s} \cdot \text{in} \cdot \text{acres}}\right)\left(\frac{12\ \text{in}}{\text{ft}}\right)\left(2.296 \times 10^{-5}\ \frac{\text{acres}}{\text{ft}^2}\right)\left(3600\ \frac{\text{s}}{\text{h}}\right)$$

$$k = 0.992 \approx 1$$

Therefore, k has a value of 1 with no units.

Comment: The result obtained here (i.e., $k = 1$) is very unusual. Most of the time, the numerical value for k for such conversions is a value other than 1.

▲ Problems

p5.1   Identify the following as either dimensions or units:
(a) length   (b) second   (c) pound   (d) time
(e) mass   (f) velocity   (g) area   (h) m³

p5.2   Convert 75°C to (a) °F, (b) °R, and (c) K.

p5.3   Convert 20°F to (a) °C, (b) °R, and (c) K.

p5.4   Convert the temperatures below as indicated:

(a) 212 °F = _____ °C   (b) −120°C = _____ K

(c) 600 °F = _____ °R   (d) 1000 K = _____ °R

p5.5   Determine the dimensions for the conversion factor k so that the following equation will be dimensionally homogeneous:

$$\frac{FTL^2}{\Theta^2 M^3} = k \frac{ML^2 F}{T^2 \Theta^2}$$

p5.6   Solve for the conversion factor, k, in the following dimensionally homogeneous equation:

$$k(F^2 T^{-2} \sqrt{L^2 \Theta^{-6}}) = \Theta^{-3} T^{-2} LM$$

p5.7   Determine the fundamental dimensions on the conversion factor, k, in the following dimensionally homogeneous equation:

$$\frac{kLM}{\Theta^2} = \frac{TM^3}{L^2}$$

p5.8   Determine the fundamental dimensions on k in the following equation:

$$k\,ML^{1/2}\sqrt{T^2 \Theta^2} = T\Theta\sqrt{M^2 L}$$

p5.9   In the equation $Q = AV$, if the units on A are m² and on V are m/s, what will be the units on Q?

p5.10 In the equation $E = mc^2$, if the units on m are (lb · s²/ft) and c has units of ft/s, what will be the units on E?

p5.11 For the equation $H = f(L/D)(V^2/2g)$, what will be the units on H if f is dimensionless, L is in ft, D is in ft, V is in ft/s, and g is in ft/s²?

p5.12 For the equation $KE = (1/2)\,mV^2$, what will be the units on m if KE is in ft · lb and V is in ft/s?

p5.13 Identify the fundamental or derived dimensions associated with the following quantities in the SI system of units: (a) mass, (b) force, (c) area, (d) volume, (e) velocity, and (f) π.

p5.14 Work p5.13 in the American Engineering system of units.

p5.15 For Newton's equation $F = ma$, identify the fundamental dimensions that apply to (a) the SI system of units, (b) the English system of units, and (c) the American Engineering system of units.

p5.16 Identify the units associated with the dimensions of length, time, force, and mass in (a) the SI system of units and (b) the American Engineering system of units.

p5.17 In the SI system of units, identify the following as either fundamental or derived dimensions:

(a) force   (b) mass   (c) acceleration

(d) volume   (e) temperature   (f) time

(g) pressure

p5.18 Affix the appropriate prefix symbol so that each of the following numbers will be expressed as a number between 1 and 10 (for example, 1200 m would be 1.2 km):
- (a) 0.0011 m
- (b) 0.01 m
- (c) 5 165 000 N
- (d) 0.000 0025 kg
- (e) 7.32 N
- (f) 21 cm
- (g) 0.0074 mm

p5.19 In the following list, one or more SI system rules have been violated. Make the appropriate corrections.
- (a) 67.3 Newt
- (b) 7.3 hr
- (c) 72 Pa's
- (d) .73 m
- (e) 14 m/s/sec
- (f) 6 m per second

p5.20 Correct the following unit symbols in accordance with SI system rules:
- (a) 18 sec
- (b) 75 met.
- (c) 4 m/hr
- (d) 6 amps
- (e) 9 milli-meters
- (f) 7 N meters

p5.21 Perform the following conversions, maintaining the implied precision:
- (a) $265 \text{ N} = $ _____ lb
- (b) $4.31 \text{ slugs} = $ _____ lb_m
- (c) $6.4 \text{ m}^2 = $ _____ ft^2
- (d) $3001 \text{ lb} = $ _____ tons (short)

p5.22 Perform the following conversions, maintaining the implied precision:
- (a) $7.4 \text{ rods} = $ _____ in
- (b) $8326 \text{ yd}^3 = $ _____ m^3
- (c) $3000 \text{ L} = $ _____ m^3
- (d) $120 \text{ kw} = $ _____ hp

p5.23 Perform the following conversions, maintaining the implied precision:
- (a) $10 \text{ million gal/day} = $ _____ m^3/min
- (b) $60 \text{ km/h} = $ _____ ft/s
- (c) $13 \text{ lb/in}^2 = $ _____ ft of water
- (d) $23.00 \text{ ft/s} = $ _____ m/h
- (e) $60.00 \text{ quarts/s} = $ _____ ft^3/h

p5.24 In the equation $Q = AV$, Q is a flow rate, A is an area, and V is a velocity. If Q is 320 ft^3/min and A is 0.13 m^2, find V in m/s.

p5.25 In Newton's equation $F = ma$, if F is 65 N and m is 3 kg, find a in m/min^2.

p5.26 In the equation $P_1 V_1 = P_2 V_2$, P_1 and P_2 are pressures, and V_1 and V_2 are volumes. If $P_1 = 70$ lb/in^2, $V_1 = 50$ L, and $P_2 = 260$ lb/ft^2, solve for V_2 and express the answer in m^3.

p5.27 The equation $H = f(L/D)(V^2/2g)$ is used to find the pressure loss in closed conduits. If f is 0.03 (dimensionless), L is 400 m, D is 0.25 m, V is 90 m/min, and g is 32 ft/s^2, find H in m.

p5.28 The speed limit in a certain school zone is 620 m/min. If a speeding motorist traveling at a rate of 30 miles/h is caught by a police officer and fined at a rate of $1.00 per m/min above 620 m/min, how much will the fine be?

p5.29 If the cost of electricity is 10 cents per kilowatt-hour (kWh) up to 1500 kWh and 13 cents per kWh thereafter, how much will the bill be for a power demand of 30 kW for 10 days?

p5.30 If the Fly-by-Nite smelter discharges sulfur dioxide (SO_2) through its smokestack at a rate of 300 lb/h from 9:00 P.M. until 5:00 A.M., how many tons of SO_2 will be released in 30 days?

p5.31 If 10 000 people flush their toilets within a 1-min time interval (e.g., during a time-out of the Super Bowl), what will the wastewater flow rate be in this minute in million gallons per day (MGD). Assume that one flush releases 5 gal.

CHAPTER 6

Equation Solution Techniques

One of the most important skills that an engineer can possess is the ability to solve accurately and quickly various kinds of mathematical equations. Complex equations, or systems of equations, are often solved using digital computers. For simpler equations, however, solutions may be readily obtained with a pocket calculator and a sheet of graph paper. This chapter will present various ways of categorizing and then solving the different classes of equations.

Objective: The objective of this chapter is to teach you how to recognize various classes of equations and solve them using the appropriate techniques.

Criteria: After completing this chapter you should be able to do the following:

■ **6.1** Identify a given equation as one of the following types:

    a. linear algebraic
    b. nonlinear algebraic
    c. logarithmic
    d. trigonometric

■ **6.2** Solve a linear algebraic equation by direct algebraic rearrangement.

■ **6.3** Solve a linear algebraic equation by either substitution or elimination.

■ **6.4** Identify and solve a quadratic equation using the quadratic formula and determine the number of roots for a given nonlinear algebraic equation.

■ **6.5** Find the real root(s) of a nonlinear equation using graphical methods.

■ **6.6** Find a real root of an equation within a specified interval using the method of bisection.

Linear Equations

Form	Solution Technique
$Ax + B = 0$ or $y = mx + b$	Algebraic manipulation to solve for x. Graph as a straight line with slope m and y-intercept b.

Nonlinear Equations

Category	Solution Technique
Polynomial: $Ax^n + Bx^{n-1} +$ $\quad \ldots + Cx + D = 0$	Factor by inspection, graph or use numerical technique
Quadratic: $Ax^2 + Bx + C = 0$	Use quadratic formula $$x = \frac{-B \pm \sqrt{B^2 - 4AC}}{2A}$$
Logarithmic or Trigonometric:	Graphical method Method of bisection Other numerical methods

Figure 6.1 Various categories of equations and solution techniques.

▲ 6.1 Identifying Equation Types

The first step in solving an equation is to recognize the particular type of equation to be solved so that the appropriate solution techniques can be applied. The various classes of equations and appropriate solution techniques are shown in Figure 6.1.

Supplementary Example 6.12
Problem p6.1

▲ 6.2 Linear Equations

The simplest equations contain only one unknown, which is raised to the first power. Examples of such equations are

a. $3x - 6 = 21$

b. $2x - 7 = 5x + 4$

c. $3x + 2x + 6 = 31 + x$

Such equations are said to be *linear equations*. Note that the unknown, x, may appear more than once, but its exponent in all terms must be one. Such equations are also said to be of the first degree in x. They may be solved for x by simple algebraic rearrangement. The solutions to the above equations are

a. $\qquad\qquad\qquad\qquad x = 9 \qquad$ Answer

b. $\qquad\qquad\qquad\qquad x = \dfrac{-11}{3} \qquad$ Answer

c. $\qquad\qquad\qquad\qquad x = \dfrac{25}{4} \qquad$ Answer

Many processes encountered in engineering can be controlled and measured producing tabulated values and graphs that show how one quantity varies with another. The plotting of such tabulated values gives a good graphic indication of the relationships among the various quantities and helps explain the system in question. Such relationships can be formalized by defining the concept of a function as follows: If x and y represent real numbers, then y is said to be a function of x if y is uniquely determined by the value of x. Since y is determined by x, y is said to be the *dependent* variable, and x is said to be the *independent* variable. When performing an experiment to determine how y and x are related, various values of x are chosen, and the corresponding values of y are measured and tabulated.

Fortunately, many frequently used relationships in engineering produce curves that are nearly straight lines (or may be treated as straight lines over limited ranges of the variables). Recall that straight lines may be represented by an equation of the form

$$y = mx + b \tag{6.1}$$

where x and y are the independent and dependent variables, respectively; m is the slope of the resulting line; and b is the y-intercept. Such an equation defines a linear function. An alternative general form for a linear equation is

$$Ax + By + C = 0 \tag{6.2}$$

where A, B, and C are nonzero constants. This equation is a first-degree equation in x and y and defines y as a function of x if $B \neq 0$. Equations having the form of Equation 6.2 are generally rearranged into the form of Equation 6.1 for analysis.

Example 6.1: Solve the following linear equation for y and determine the straight line that it represents:

$$3x + 4y + 2 = 0$$

Solution: The equation is solved for y as follows:

$$4y = -3x - 2$$

$$y = \frac{-3}{4}x - \frac{1}{2}$$

The straight line represented by this relationship is shown in Figure 6.2.

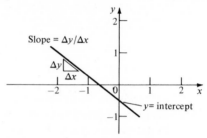

Figure 6.2 Graph of $y = -3/4x - 1/2$

Comment: In this case, the line intersects the y-axis at $-1/2$ and has a slope of $-3/4$.

Example 6.2: Suppose the graph of Figure 6.3 is obtained for two variables, x and y. What does this situation imply?

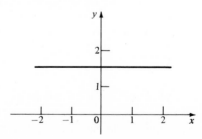

Figure 6.3 Graph of horizontal straight line ($y = 1.5$).

Solution: The horizontal line of the graph implies that the value of the quantity represented by y does not change as the quantity represented by x is varied. The slope of the straight line is zero, and y is said to be independent of x.

Supplementary Examples 6.13–6.14
Problems p6.2–p6.7

▲ 6.3 Solution of Linear Algebraic Equations

Technical people involved in research or analytical work frequently encounter situations involving more than one variable. In order to determine the values of these variables, it is necessary to work with more than one equation. (In fact, the number of equations that must be handled is equal to the number of unknowns.) The consideration of more than one equation at the same time is referred to by mathematicians as *simultaneous* equations or systems of equations. A number of methods can be employed to solve simultaneous equations, but the method selected is usually a function of the complexity of the equations involved. Two of the most common methods used for solving relatively simple systems of equations are *substitution* and *elimination*.

As the name implies, the *substitution method* involves replacing a variable contained in one equation by the value of that variable obtained from another equation. When only two simultaneous equations are to be solved, only one substitution must be made, but as the number of equations under consideration increases, so does the number of substitutions that must be made. Obviously, there is a point beyond which the substitution method becomes too unwieldy, so that other techniques would be preferred. The following example illustrates the steps to be followed in solving two simple linear equations by the method of substitution.

Example 6.3: Solve for x and y in the following system of equations:

$$6x + 13y = -8$$
$$2x - 3y = 12$$

Solution: As a first step, solve for either x or y in either one of the equations. Solving the first equation for x yields

$$x = \frac{-8 - 13y}{6}$$

The next step involves substituting the value of x into the second equation and solving for y as follows:

$$2\left(\frac{-8 - 13y}{6}\right) - 3y = 12$$

$$\frac{-16 - 26y}{6} - 3y = 12$$

$$-16 - 26y - 18y = 72$$
$$-44y = 88$$
$$y = -2$$

Finally, substitute this value of y into either of the original equations and solve for x. Thus, using the first equation,

---

$$6x + 13(-2) = -8$$
$$6x = -8 + 26$$
$$6x = 18$$
$$x = 3$$

The solution to the given set of equations, therefore, is:

$$x = 3$$
$$y = -2$$

Comment: The accuracy of the answers can be checked by substituting them into either of the original equations and checking for equality. For example:

$$6(3) + 13(-2) = -8$$
$$18 - 26 = -8$$
$$-8 = -8 \qquad \text{O.K}$$

or

$$2(3) - 3(-2) = 12$$
$$6 + 6 = 12$$
$$12 = 12 \qquad \text{O.K.}$$

Supplementary Example 6.13 shows how three equations can be solved by the substitution method.

In the *elimination method* of solving equations, one or more of the mathematical operations of multiplication, division, addition, or subtraction is used to eliminate variables until an equation is obtained which contains only one of the variables. The process can then be repeated to find the remaining variable. It is usually easier, however, to use the method of substitution after one variable has been determined. The procedure is illustrated in the next example.

Example 6.4: Solve the following equations by the method of elimination.

$$4x + y = 28$$
$$2x + 3y = 24$$

Solution: There are many ways to eliminate one of the variables from the two equations. Two ways will be shown here.

Method 1: Multiply the first equation by 3 and then substract the second equation:

$$12x + 3y = 84$$
$$\underline{-(2x + 3y = 24)}$$
$$10x = 60$$
$$x = 6$$

Substituting this value into the first equation yields:

$$4(6) + y = 28$$
$$y = 4$$

Method 2: Multiply the second equation by 2 and then subtract:

$$
\begin{array}{r}
4x + y = 28 \\
-(4x + 6y = 48) \\
\hline
-5y = -20 \\
y = 4
\end{array}
$$

The methods of substitution and elimination can be used for nonlinear equations as well. However, as equations increase in number and complexity, other methods are usually more suitable. Some of the more advanced methods are presented in subsequent sections of this chapter while others (such as matrix methods) are beyond the scope of this book.

Supplementary Example 6.15
Problems p6.8 – p6.13

▲ 6.4 Nonlinear Algebraic Equations

Whenever possible, engineers like to represent relationships among various quantities using linear equations because the resulting mathematical descriptions are relatively easy to manipulate. Unfortunately, this may cause significant errors in certain types of problems. To produce sufficiently accu-

than one (nonlinear algebraic equations), or the equations may contain trigonometric or logarithmic functions. All such equations are *nonlinear equations*. The implication is that the relationships among the variables are not "straight line" relationships.

Traditional approaches to solving nonlinear equations depend on the specific category of nonlinear terms appearing in a given equation. Most modern techniques use digital computers and numerical techniques to produce a solution to a specific equation. The solution itself is not a continuous function; rather, it is a set of tabulated values that indicate the relationships among the various quantities of interest. The following sections summarize several techniques that may be used to solve different types of nonlinear equations.

Quadratic Equations

The easiest nonlinear equations to solve are polynomial equations of the second degree. The general form of this category is

$$Ax^2 + Bx + C = 0 \tag{6.3}$$

Such equations are called *general quadratic equations* and will usually have two roots or solutions. A special case results when B in Equation 6.3 is zero. Such an equation is called a *pure quadratic equation* and is

$$Ax^2 + C = 0 \tag{6.4}$$

This equation may be solved by rearranging the terms so that the square of the unknown appears only on the left side of the equal sign. The square root of both sides of the equation is then determined, producing the desired answers. The required steps are illustrated in Examples 6.5 and 6.6.

Example 6.5:   Solve $3x^2 = 48$

Solution: Rearrange the equation so that x^2 appears on the left side of the equal sign.

$$x^2 = \frac{48}{3} = 16$$

Now take the square root of both sides:

$$x = \pm 4$$

Comment: Both $+4$ and -4 may be substituted into $3x^2 = 48$ to produce the identity $48 = 48$, and hence, both are correct answers in a mathematical sense. But in many situations, one of the solutions may be rejected because it represents an impossible physical situation.

Example 6.6:   Solve $5x^2 + 45 = 0$

Solution: The equation is again arranged so that x^2 appears on the left:

$$x^2 = \frac{-45}{5}$$

$$= -9$$

and the square root of both sides is taken:

$$x = \sqrt{-9}$$

$$x = \pm i3$$

Comment: Taking the square root of a negative number produces an imaginary number, indicated by the i in the answer. Since the symbol i is defined as $\sqrt{-1}$, i^2 is -1.

The first step in solving general quadratic equations is to manipulate them into the standard algebraic form of

$$Ax^2 + Bx + C = 0 \qquad (6.3)$$

Once the equation is in this form, it may be possible to factor the equation by inspection, but a more general approach, which ensures an immediate solution, is to use the following quadratic formula:

$$x = \frac{-B \pm \sqrt{(B^2 - 4AC)}}{2A} \qquad (6.5)$$

Evaluation of this expression yields the two roots of the quadratic equation. The resulting roots will be real if the quantity $B^2 - 4AC$ is positive. Should this quantity be negative, the result will be roots having imaginary parts that are complex conjugates.

Example 6.7: Find the solutions for $3x^2 + 2x + 1 = 0$.

Solution: The equation is already in standard form, and so $A = 3$, $B = 2$, and $C = 1$. The roots are evaluated using the quadratic formula as follows:

$$x = \frac{-B \pm \sqrt{(B^2 - 4AC)}}{2A}$$

$$= \frac{-2 \pm \sqrt{(2^2 - 4(3)(1))}}{2(3)}$$

$$= \frac{-2 \pm \sqrt{(4 - 12)}}{6}$$

$$= -\frac{1}{3} \pm \frac{i\sqrt{2}}{3}$$

$$x = -0.33 \pm i0.47$$

Comment: For this example, the roots are $x_1 = -0.33 + i0.47$ and $x_2 = -0.33 - i0.47$, which form a complex conjugate pair.

Example 6.8: Find the solution to $2x^2 + 2x - 12 = 0$.

Solution: Some computational effort would be saved by dividing all terms by 2. This, of course, does not affect the answer to the problem. The resulting equation produces the following values: $A = 1$, $B = 1$, $C = -6$. The quadratic formula is again used to produce the final result:

$$x = \frac{-B \pm \sqrt{(B^2 - 4AC)}}{2A}$$

$$= \frac{-1 \pm \sqrt{(1^2 - 4(1)(-6))}}{2}$$

$$= \frac{-1 \pm \sqrt{(1 + 24)}}{2}$$

$$= -\frac{1}{2} \pm \frac{5}{2}$$

so

$$x_1 = -\frac{1}{2} + \frac{5}{2} = 2$$

$$x_2 = -\frac{1}{2} - \frac{5}{2} = -3$$

Comment: In this example, both roots were real, but one was positive and the other was negative. Often, in this situation, one or the other of the solutions is rejected because the problem's physical constraints do not allow that particular root.

Polynomial Equations of Degree Greater Than Two

Polynomial equations having an order greater than two can always be manipulated into the following standard form:

$$Ax^n + Bx^{n-1} + Cx^{n-2} + \ldots + Dx^1 + E = 0 \tag{6.6}$$

Determination of the highest power, n, of the unknown quantity provides specific information about the roots of the equation. This information is the following:

1. The total number of roots of the equation is equal to the highest power of the unknown (n).
2. If the highest power of the unknown is odd, the equation will have an odd number of real roots. (Every such equation must have at least one real root.)
3. Complex roots will always occur in pairs.

Example 6.9: Which of the following polynomial equations must have at least one real root?

a. $2x = 10$

b. $2x = -10$

c. $x^2 - 4x + 3 = 0$

d. $x^3 - 2x^2 + 4x + 1 = 0$

e. $x^5 - 3x = 0$

f. $x^4 + 3x^3 + 5x + 7 = 0$

Solution: Equations a, b, d, and e all have at least one real root, as the highest power of the unknown is odd. The number of real roots in Equations c and f is not obvious because each has an even number of roots, which may be real or complex conjugate pairs. The quadratic formula may be used to find the roots of Equation c, which are $+1$ and $+3$. Thus this equation has two real roots. Equation f will have a total of four roots, as the highest power of the unknown is 4. The number of real roots can be determined only by solving the equation as discussed in the following sections.

Supplementary Example 6.16
Problems p6.8–p6.12

When an equation does not have additional information, it is usually not apparent in which numeric range the roots are located. In the following sections, we shall describe the analytical techniques that allow the determination of the roots of nonlinear equations by beginning with reasonable guesses. After engineers have studied various systems for some period of time, they are able to estimate closely the values of roots that may be expected, as the roots of the pertinent equations determine how the system under investigation will react. What might appear as a complex searching process in the following discussion is in reality conducted over a very narrow and known range.

▲ 6.5 Graphical Solutions of Nonlinear Equations

One way to solve nonlinear equations is to rearrange the equation into the form $f(x) = 0$ and then plot $f(x)$ against x. Any point where $f(x)$ intersects the abscissa will be a value of x that causes $f(x)$ to equal zero. This value of x represents a real root of the equation. This approach requires a degree of judgment in its application. Typically, a number of values for x will be chosen, after which $f(x)$ is computed and then plotted for each corresponding value. The selection of appropriate values for x involves some guesswork and an element of luck. The idea is to select two values of x that produce one positive and one negative value for $f(x)$. When this has been accomplished, it will be known that at least one root of the equation lies between the two adjacent values of x. Once two values of x are found that cause a sign change in $f(x)$, the region being searched can be plotted, allowing a reasonably accurate estimate of the root location. Graphical solutions will typically yield results accurate to two or three significant digits, which is sufficient for many applications.

Example 6.10: Find a positive root of the equation

$$x^3 = 5 \sin x + 1$$

Solution: First rearrange the equation so that $f(x) = 0$.

$$f(x) = x^3 - 5 \sin x - 1 = 0$$

Now construct a table of values choosing x in such a way that $f(x)$ takes on both positive and negative values. In this case, the numbers 1 and 2 are tried, producing the results shown in Table 6.1.

TABLE 6.1 Initial Guesses Used to Find Positive and Negative $f(x)$

x	0	1	2
$f(x)$	-1	-4.207	2.454

Because $f(x)$ changes sign as x goes from 1 to 2, at least one root appears between these two values. Table 6.2 is now constructed with x ranging between 1 and 2. In this case, five values will be chosen, having equal increments of 0.2. The particular range chosen and the number of values plotted are matters of judgment, which generally determine the effort required to produce the solution and the relative accuracy of the final result.

TABLE 6.2 $f(x) = x^3 - 5 \sin x - 1$

x	1.0	1.2	1.4	1.6	1.8	2.0
$f(x)$	-4.207	-3.932	-3.183	-1.902	-0.037	2.454

The values of Table 6.2 are plotted in Figure 6.4. The point where $f(x)$ crosses the x-axis is a root of the equation. In this case, the root is at about 1.80.

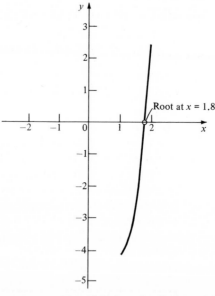

Figure 6.4 Plot of $f(x) = x^3 - 5 \sin x - 1$.

Supplementary Example 6.17
Problems p6.13–p6.16

▲ 6.6 Method of Bisection

The graphical approach just demonstrated gives a reasonably good estimate of a root's value, which is sufficient for many purposes. If additional accuracy is required, other methods are available. One of the easier techniques to understand and apply is the *method of bisection*. The method's geometric interpretation is shown in Figure 6.5.

The method is like the graphical method in that two values of x are found that produce one positive and one negative value for $f(x)$. The values producing this condition are called a_0 and b_0. As before, it is assumed that a single real root of the function exists within the interval $a_0 \leq x \leq b_0$. A necessary condition is that the function $f(x)$ will cross the x-axis once, and only once, on this interval. When this crossing point is found, the root of $f(x)$ is determined.

The method of bisection is a repetitive process in which the region under consideration is successively split into two parts by choosing a value of x_{mi} midway between the two end points currently being considered (a_i

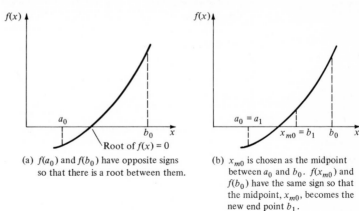

(a) $f(a_0)$ and $f(b_0)$ have opposite signs so that there is a root between them.

(b) x_{m0} is chosen as the midpoint between a_0 and b_0. $f(x_{m0})$ and $f(b_0)$ have the same sign so that the midpoint, x_{m0}, becomes the new end point b_1.

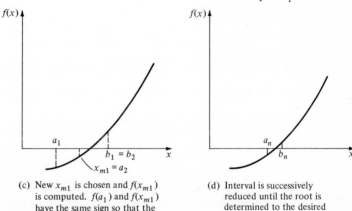

(c) New x_{m1} is chosen and $f(x_{m1})$ is computed. $f(a_1)$ and $f(x_{m1})$ have the same sign so that the new interval is a_2 to b_2.

(d) Interval is successively reduced until the root is determined to the desired accuracy.

Figure 6.5 Method of bisection.

Example 6.11: Find a positive root of the equation $x^3 = 5 \sin x + 1$ using the method of bisection.

Solution: The equation is put into the form $f(x) = 0$, as follows:

$$f(x) = x^3 - 5 \sin x - 1 = 0$$

As in the graphical approach, two values of x are found that produce a sign change in $f(x)$ without regard to order. From Example 6.10, it is known that $f(1) = -4.207$ and $f(2) = 2.454$. Because of the sign change, at least one root of $f(x)$ lies between $x = 1$ and $x = 2$. New values of x are now chosen that successively narrow the possible range of values. The region containing the root is cut in half by choosing $x_{mi} = 1.5$, which represents half the distance between 1 and 2. The function is evaluated at this point, producing $f(1.5) = -2.612$. The negative sign associated with this answer indicates that the desired root is on the interval between 1.5 and 2.0, as a sign change in $f(x)$ occurs within this region. The process is now repeated, with 1.5 and 2.0 serving as the end points. The new intermediate value of $x_{mi} = 1.75$ is again chosen to be halfway between these two values. Successive application of this method results in determining the root to an accuracy dependent on the number of significant digits available in the calculator or computer, rather than on the method itself. Table 6.3 shows the progression of the process. After nine steps, the root is estimated to be 1.804.

TABLE 6.3 Result of Method in Bisection Applied to
$f(x) = x^3 - 5 \sin x - 1$

Interval Considered		f(x) at Beginning of Interval	f(x) at End of Interval	Midpoint to Be Used in Next Iterative Step	Value of f(x) at Midpoint
1.0	→ 2.0	−4.207	2.454	1.5	−2.612
1.5	→ 2.0	−2.612	2.454	1.75	−0.561
1.75	→ 2.0	−0.561	2.454	1.875	0.822
1.75	→ 1.875	−0.561	0.822	1.8125	0.0993
1.75	→ 1.8125	−0.561	0.0993	1.78125	−0.2376
1.78125	→ 1.8125	−0.2376	0.0993	1.797	−0.070
1.797	→ 1.8125	−0.070	0.0993	1.805	0.018
1.797	→ 1.805	−0.070	0.018	1.801	−0.026
1.801	→ 1.805	−0.026	0.018	1.803	−0.0048
1.803	→ 1.805	estimate the root to be half way between at 1.804			

Supplementary Example 6.18
Problems p6.17 – p6.20

and b_i). The function $f(x)$ is then evaluated at this midpoint. The sign of $f(x_{mi})$ will be the same as either $f(a_i)$ or $f(b_i)$. The end point (a_i or b_i) having the same sign as $f(x_{mi})$ is then replaced with x_{mi}, and the process is repeated. The interval from a_i to b_i is halved at each iterative step, and by making the interval sufficiently small, the root is determined to the desired accuracy. Note that half of the interval under consideration is eliminated at each step. The root that is to be determined cannot lie in the rejected subinterval, as there is no change in sign of $f(x)$ on that subinterval. This implies that $f(x)$ does not cross the x-axis on this subinterval, and therefore, the root cannot lie in this region.

● CHAPTER SUMMARY

Success in virtually any technical profession requires some facility in solving mathematical equations. The first step in the equation solution process is recognizing the type of equation to be solved, and the first section of this chapter dealt with that problem. In subsequent sections, we described some of the methods which can be used for solving linear and nonlinear equations including algebraic methods, graphical techniques, and the numerical method of bisection.

Supplementary Examples

Example 6.12: Indicate the category (i.e., a–d) of each of the following equations:

Categories

a. linear algebraic
b. nonlinear algebraic
c. logarithmic
d. trigonometric

Equations

1. $f(x) = x^3 - 1$
2. $f(x) = 2x^5 - 3x^2 + 3$
3. $f(x) = 2^x$
4. $f(x) = x \sin x$
5. $f(X) = 2 + \sec x$
6. $f(x) = 2x - 4$
7. $f(x) = k/(x - a)$
8. $f(x) = 2x + 4x - 5$
9. $f(x) = 2e^{-x} + 4$
10. $f(x) = 4 \ln (3x + 1) + 5$
11. $f(x) = (\sin 2x)/x$
12. $f(x) = 4 - x$

Solution: The equations are categorized by inspecting their terms as follows:
(a) linear algebraic (Equations 6, 8, 12)
(b) nonlinear algebraic (Equations 1, 2, 7)
(c) logarithmic (Equations 3, 9, 10)
(d) trigonometric (Equations 4, 5, 11)

Example 6.13: Solve $f(x) = 2|x|$ and determine the linear approximations for this function.

Solution: Technically, this is not a linear equation, but over certain ranges it may be treated as one. The regions to be considered are selected as follows:

(a) $\qquad\qquad\qquad\qquad\qquad f(x) = 2x + 0 \quad x > 0$

(b) $\qquad\qquad\qquad\qquad\qquad f(x) = 0 \qquad\quad x = 0$

(c) $\qquad\qquad\qquad\qquad\qquad f(x) = -2x \qquad x < 0$

The equations may be rewritten as follows:

(a) $\qquad\qquad\qquad\qquad\qquad y = 2x + 0 \qquad x > 0$

(b) $\qquad\qquad\qquad\qquad\qquad y = 0 \qquad\qquad x = 0$

(c) $\qquad\qquad\qquad\qquad\qquad y = -2x + 0 \quad x < 0$

The solutions are as follows:

(a) $\qquad\qquad\qquad\qquad\qquad x = \dfrac{y}{2} \qquad x > 0$

(b) $\qquad\qquad\qquad\qquad\qquad x = 0 \qquad\quad x = 0$

(c) $\qquad\qquad\qquad\qquad\qquad x = \dfrac{-y}{2} \quad x < 0$

Comment: When plotted, the first equation is a straight line with a positive slope of $+2$ and a y-axis intercept of zero. The second equation ($y = 0$ when $x = 0$) is just a single point at the origin. The third equation is a straight line in the second quadrant having a negative slope of -2 and a y-axis intercept that is also zero.

Example 6.14: Consider the equation $y = \sqrt{x - 1}$. Determine a linear approximation to the positive portion of this equation for $2 \leq x \leq 5$.

Solution: The function (positive values only) is plotted in Figure 5.6. This equation describes a parabola opening to the right. Between $2 \leq x \leq 5$,

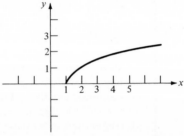

Figure 6.6 Graph of $y = +\sqrt{x - 1}$.

the side of the parabola has only a small amount of curvature. For many applications, in this range, the equation can be linearized (replaced with a straight-line approximation). One way of accomplishing this is to draw a straight line through the point (2,1) and (5,2). The general form for such an equation is

$$\frac{y - y_1}{y_2 - y_1} = \frac{x - x_1}{x_2 - x_1}$$

When the specific points are substituted, the result is as follows:

$$(x_1, y_1) = (2,1)$$

$$(x_2, y_2) = (5,2)$$

$$\frac{y - 1}{2 - 1} = \frac{x - 2}{5 - 2}$$

$$3y - 3 = x - 2$$

$$x = 3y - 1$$

The equation of the straight-line approximation may also be found:

$$y = \frac{x}{3} + \frac{1}{3}$$

Example 6.15: Solve the equations below by the methods of (a) substitution and (b) elimination

$$2x + 2y - 4z = 2$$
$$5x - y - 2z = -3$$
$$6x + 4y + 3z = 28$$

Solution: (a) First solve one of the equations for one of the variables and substitute the value into the other two equations. Solving the first equation for x:

$$2x + 2y - 4z = 2$$
$$2x = 2 - 2y + 4z$$
$$x = \frac{2 - 2y + 4z}{2}$$

Substituting this value into the other two equations:

$$5\left(\frac{2 - 2y + 4z}{2}\right) - y - 2z = -3$$

$$6\left(\frac{2 - 2y + 4z}{2}\right) + 4y + 3z = 28$$

Simplifying these equations yields:

$$-12y + 16z = -16$$
$$-4y + 30z = 44$$

Next, solve one of these equations for y or z and substitute into the other equation. Solving the first equation for y:

$$-12y + 16z = -16$$
$$-12y = -16 - 16z$$
$$y = \frac{16 + 16z}{12}$$

Substituting this value of y into the other equation and simplifying:

$$-4\left(\frac{16 + 16z}{12}\right) + 30z = 44$$
$$296z = 592$$
$$z = 2$$

Substituting this value of z into one of the two previous equations will yield the value of y. Thus,

$$-12y + 16(2) = -16$$
$$y = 4$$

Finally, substituting the values of y and z into one of the original equations will provide the value of x as follows:

$$2x + 2(4) - 4(2) = 2$$
$$x = 1$$

Therefore, the solution to the equations is

$$x = 1, y = 4, \text{ and } z = 2$$

(b) In the elimination method, one of the variables must be eliminated from two of the equations to yield two new equations in two unknowns. The first of the new equations can be obtained by dividing the first equation by 2 and adding it to the middle equation to eliminate y as follows:

$$\begin{array}{rr} x + y - 2z = & 1 \\ \underline{5x - y - 2z =} & \underline{-3} \\ 6x \quad\quad - 4z = & -2 \end{array}$$

The second new equation can be obtained by multiplying the middle equation by 4 and adding it to the bottom one as follows

$$\begin{array}{rr} 20x - 4y - 8z = & -12 \\ \underline{6x + 4y + 3z =} & \underline{28} \\ 26x \quad\quad - 5z = & 16 \end{array}$$

Now, the process can be repeated to eliminate either x or z from the two new equations, as shown in Example 6.4. The completion of this problem is left as an exercise to the reader.

Example 6.16: A projectile is fired straight up at an initial velocity of 160 m/s. The distance above the ground is given by

$$d = -4t^2 + 160t \text{ m}$$

where t is in seconds. When will the projectile be 100 m above the ground? When will it hit the ground?

Solution: The projectile will be 100 m above the ground twice—once on its way up and once when it is falling. For either situation, $d = 100$ m, and t is unknown.

$$100 = -4t^2 + 160t$$

$$4t^2 - 160t + 100 = 0$$

$$t_1, t_2 = \frac{-B \pm \sqrt{B^2 - 4AC}}{2A}$$

$$= \frac{-(-160) \pm \sqrt{(-160)^2 - 4(4)(100)}}{2(4)}$$

$$= \frac{160 \pm \sqrt{25600 - 1600}}{8}$$

$$= \frac{160 \pm \sqrt{24000}}{8}$$

$$= \frac{160 \pm 154.92}{8}$$

$$t_1 = 0.635 \text{ s}$$

$$t_2 = 39.36 \text{ s}$$

The projectile will also be at ground level twice, but one solution is trivial, since at $t = 0$, d will also equal 0. The time required for the projectile to go up and back down is found from

$$d = 0$$

$$4t^2 - 160\,t = 0$$

$$= -4t^2 + 160t$$

$$4t = 160$$

$$t = 40 \text{ s}$$

Example 6.17: Determine the approximate roots of

$$y = 2^{-x} \sin x$$

using graphical analysis. Consider only roots near the origin.

Solution: Table 6.4 shows the function evaluated at various points. The function is plotted in Figure 6.7. Inspection of this graph shows the x-axis crossing points at about -3.1, 0.0, 3.1, and 6.3. Since this function is a product of sin x, roots should be found at multiples of π, and they are.

TABLE 6.4 Evaluation of $f(x) = 2^{-x} \sin x$

x	f(x)
-4.0	12.109
-3.5	3.969
-3.0	-1.129
-2.5	-3.385
-2.0	-3.637
-1.5	-2.821
-1.0	-1.683
-0.5	-0.678
0.0	0.000
0.5	0.339
1.0	0.421
1.5	0.353
2.0	0.227
2.5	0.106
3.0	0.018
3.5	-0.031
4.0	-0.047
4.5	-0.043
5.0	-0.030
5.5	-0.016
6.0	$-4.366\ \mathrm{E}-03$
6.5	$2.377\ \mathrm{E}-03$

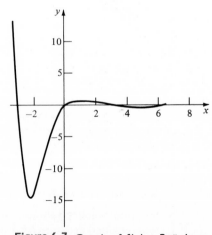

Figure 6.7 Graph of $f(x) = 2^{-x} \sin x$

Example 6.18: Determine, using the method of bisection, the location of the roots near the origin of the equation

$$y = 2^{-x} \sin x$$

Solution: The date in Table 6.4 are examined for changes in sign, indicating that a root is present in the intervening region. The results of this investigation are shown in Table 6.5.

TABLE 6.5 Regions Where Roots Exist

Region	Range of x	Sign Change
1	−3.5 to −3.0	+ to −
2	−0.5 to 0.5	− to +
3	3.0 to 3.5	+ to −
4	6.0 to 6.5	− to +

▲ Problems

p6.1   Indicate the category (i.e., a–d) of each of the following equations:
(a) linear   (b) nonlinear algebraic
(c) logarithmic   (d) trigonometric

(1) $x^5 + 4x^2 - 2x + 1 = 0$ (2) $5 \sin x = \sin 2x$
(3) $x^3 = 3 \cos x$ (4) $v = 2\,e^{-0.2t}$
(5) $\ln x = 1 - 1/x^2$ (6) $3x + 4y + 2 = 0$
(7) $a \log b = c$

p6.2   Find the slope and y-intercept of $3x + 2y + 4 = 0$

p6.3   Solve the following equation for x: $3x - 35 = 41 - x$

p6.4   Solve the following equation for x: $2x^2 + 5x - 15 = 10x - 20 + 2x^2$

p6.5   Find a linear approximation to $f(x) = 2^x$ for $2 < x < 3$.
p6.6   Repeat p6.5 for $-3 < x < -1$.
p6.7   Find a linear representation for $f(x) = x^3/2$ for $0 < x < 1$.
p6.8   Solve the following equations for x and y using the methods of (a) substitution, and (b) elimination.

$$2x + 7y = 31$$
$$4x + 10y = 50$$

p6.9   Solve the following equations for i and j using the methods of (a) substitution, and (b) elimination.

$$4i + 3j = -7$$
$$-6i - 4j = 8$$

p6.10   Solve the following equations for k and t using the methods of (a) substitution, and (b) elimination.

$$5k + 2t = -6$$
$$-6k - 4t = -4$$

p6.11   Solve the following equations for p and q using the methods of (a) substitution, and (b) elimination

$$\tfrac{1}{2}p + \tfrac{2}{3}q = 6$$
$$\tfrac{3}{8}p - 2q = -3$$

p6.12   Solve the following equations for x, y, and z using the methods of (a) substitution, and (b) elimination.

$$x - 3y + 2z = 27$$
$$4x + 2y - 3z = -11$$
$$5x - 3y + 7z = 78$$

p6.13   Solve the following equations for b, m, and w, using the methods of (a) substitution and (b) elimination.

$$4b + 3m + 5w = 27$$
$$2b - m + 2w = 6$$
$$3b + 4m - w = 0$$

p6.14   Solve $x^2 + 50 = 0$.

p6.15   Solve $x^2 + 2x - 8 = 0$.

p6.16   Solve $x^2 - 2x + 6 = 0$.

p6.17   Solve $x^2 + 3x + 12 = 0$.

p6.18   Solve $5x^2 + 8x + 16 = 0$.

p6.19   Find all roots of the following equation using the graphical method:

$$x^3 - 7x^2 + 14x - 8 = 0$$

p6.20   Find the roots of the following equation using the graphical method:

$$x^2 - 4x - 5 = 0$$

p6.21   Find the roots of the following equation using the graphical method:

$$x^2 + 4x + 8 = 0$$

p6.22   Find the roots of the following equation using the graphical method:

$$f(x) = x^4 - 4x^3 + 3x^2 = 0$$

p6.23   Using the method of bisection, find the smallest positive root of

$$3x = \tan 2x$$

p6.24   Find a root of the following equation using the method of bisection:

$$x^2 = 5 \cos x + 2$$

p6.25   Find a solution for the following equation using the method of bisection:

$$x + \sin x = \cos x - 1$$

p6.26   Find a solution for the following equation using the method of bisection:

$$10\, e^{-2x} + x = 5$$

7

Graphs

Much of the information communicated by technical professionals is not through words alone. Frequently, some type of graphical communication is needed. To present data, professionals often use graphs that visually display relationships, trends, or relative magnitudes. This chapter discusses the use of graphs.

Objective: The objective of this chapter is to introduce the various methods that are used to present data in graphic form.

Criteria: After completing this chapter, you should be able to do the following:

- **7.1** Construct a circle chart, complete with labels, from data presenting the division of a particular quantity.
- **7.2** Construct a bar graph, complete with labels, from appropriate data.
- **7.3** Construct a line graph, complete with labels, from data relating two variables, on rectangular coordinate graph paper with linear scales.
- **7.4** For data that approximate a straight line on rectangular coordinate graph paper with linear scales, draw a straight line through the data points, "by eye," and determine the equation of the straight line by selecting two points on the line and solving the resulting two simultaneous equations.
- **7.5** Construct a line graph, complete with labels, on semilog graph paper from data relating two variables.
- **7.6** Given data that approximate a straight line on semilog graph paper, draw the straight line "by eye," and determine the equation relating the two variables by solving two simultaneous equations.
- **7.7** Construct a line graph, complete with labels, on log-log graph paper from data relating two variables.
- **7.8** Given data that approximate a straight line on log-log graph paper,

draw the straight line, "by eye," and determine the equation relating the two variables by solving two simultaneous equations.

Before discussing the particular types of graphs, there are a few ideas that apply to all graphs. The purpose of graphs is to help the reader grasp the significance of data quickly and easily. Therefore, graphs should be simple, with few lines and words. However, the words or titles and labels on a graph are important. They should clearly describe the graph so that all variables are apparent. If possible, the reader should be able to grasp the significance of the data presented by the graph without having to read the text.

▲ 7.1 Circle Charts

Circle charts, or *pie charts,* as they are often called, effectively depict the division of a quantity. A circle chart shows the relative size of the fractions or percentages of a quantity that make up the whole and can be understood quickly by nearly any reader.

An example of a circle chart is shown in Figure 7.1, depicting the various fractions or percentages of the total college expenses for an average student at a private college.

The steps to follow in constructing a circle chart are:

Steps to Construct a Circle Chart

1. Determine the fraction or percentage of the whole for each part comprising the quantity.
2. Determine the number of degrees or angle of each part. This is the fraction of each part times 360 degrees.

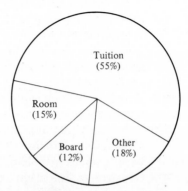

Figure 7.1 Circle chart. Distribution of Expenses for the Average Student at a Private College.

3. Construct the circle and divide it into the angles required.
4. Label the circle and title the chart.

The following example shows how to construct a circle chart:

Example 7.1: Construct a circle chart of the distribution of students enrolled in an engineering college according to discipline. Use the following data:

Engineering Discipline	Number of Students
Civil	463
Electrical	807
Industrial	245
Mechanical	512
Metallurgical	168
Total	2195

Solution: Since the graph is to depict the relative size of the parts of the whole, the fraction of each discipline must be determined.

$$\text{Civil fraction} \qquad \frac{463}{2195} = 0.21$$

$$\text{Electrical fraction} \qquad \frac{807}{2195} = 0.37$$

$$\text{Industrial fraction} \qquad \frac{245}{2195} = 0.11$$

$$\text{Mechanical fraction} \qquad \frac{512}{2195} = 0.23$$

$$\text{Metallurgical fraction} \qquad \frac{168}{2195} = \underline{0.08}$$

$$\text{Total} \qquad\qquad\qquad 1.00$$

Of course, the fractions must add up to the whole, 1.00. But because the fractions are rounded, an adjustment may need to be made to one or two of the fractions to ensure that the total is exactly 1.00.

The number of degrees, or the angle of each part of the whole, must be determined for each discipline.

$$\text{Civil angle} \qquad (0.21)(360°) = \quad 75°$$

$$\text{Electrical angle} \qquad (0.37)(360°) = 133°$$

$$\text{Industrial angle} \qquad (0.11)(360°) = \quad 40°$$

$$\text{Mechanical angle} \qquad (0.23)(360°) = \quad 83°$$

$$\text{Metallurgical angle} \qquad (0.08)(360°) = \underline{\quad 29°}$$

$$\text{Total} \qquad\qquad\qquad\qquad 360°$$

As it is a circle, the total of the angles must be 360°, and again, because the numbers are rounded, adjustments may be needed. The graph can be constructed and labeled as shown in Figure 7.2.

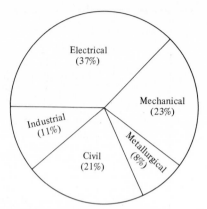

Figure 7.2 Circle chart for Example 7.1. Distribution of Students in an Engineering College According to Discipline.

Problems p7.1–p7.6

▲ 7.2 Bar Graphs

The *bar graph* is a chart made of bars and is a good way of expressing comparisons of increases or decreases over a period of time. The concept depicted by a bar graph is usually simple and easily grasped by any reader. An example of a bar graph is shown in Figure 7.3, which presents the average temperature for each month of the year at a particular location.

The steps in constructing a bar graph are as follows:

Steps to Construct a Bar Graph

1. Determine whether the bars will be vertical or horizontal, a matter of choice.
2. Determine the length of the maximum bar, and construct a linear scale that will allow the length of the longest bar to span most of the available scale. The scale for the bars will normally be linear, and the bars will be constructed from zero to give a true comparison of the bars' lengths.
3. Determine the necessary number of bars, and locate them on the linear axis to cover the space available.
4. Construct the bars, and label and title the graph.

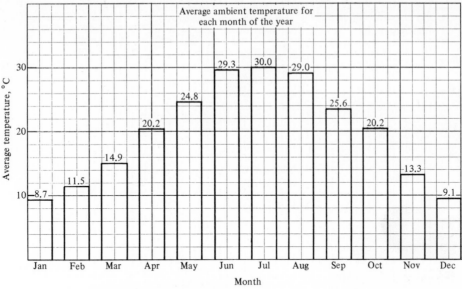

Figure 7.3 Vertical bar chart.

An example illustrates these steps.

Example 7.2: The following data are the electrical energy use in a typical three-bedroom home in a particular locale. Use a bar graph to show the trends.

Electrical Energy Use in a Typical Three-Bedroom Home During a Calendar Year

Month	Electrical Energy Used (kWh)
January	700
February	680
March	640
April	650
May	690
June	810
July	980
August	960
September	840
October	690
November	650
December	710

Applying the steps in order, it is first arbitrarily decided that these bars will be vertical. The longest bar will be the month of July and will represent 980 kWh. The ordinate scale is constructed from 1 to 1000 to cover the range necessary. There will be twelve bars, evenly spaced along the abscissa to cover the area available. The bars are constructed, the graph is titled and labeled, and the result is shown in Figure 7.4.

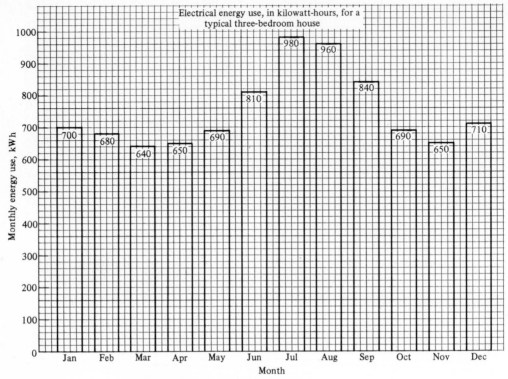

Figure 7.4 Bar graph for Example 7.2.

Problems p7.7 – p7.13

▲ 7.3 Line Graphs

Line graphs on rectangular coordinate graph paper are the most widely used method of presenting engineering data. In this section we shall discuss the construction and use of these graphs with linear scales. Most of the rules applying to linear-scale graphs also apply to graphs with log scales, which are discussed in the next sections.

Graphs are made to enable the viewer to understand quickly the variation of one quantity with respect to another. Even though the data presented in a table may be exactly the same as those presented in a graph, the variation usually cannot be as easily grasped by looking at the tabulated numbers. Figures 7.5 through 7.7 show some typical line graphs. The following are steps for constructing a line graph, as well as some rules:

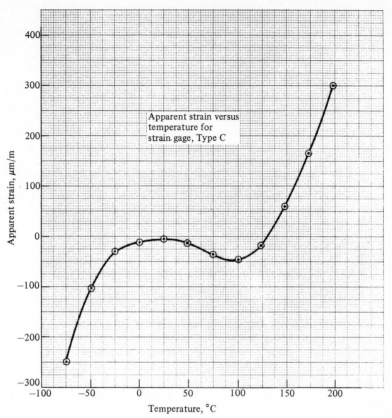

Figure 7.5 A line graph on linear-scale graph paper. The experimental data points are plotted with circle symbols.

Steps and Rules for Constructing a Line Graph

1. Decide whether the graph paper is to have linear or log scales. (Log scales will be discussed in the next section.) This choice will not always be obvious, and in fact, a graph may first be plotted on one type of graph paper and then on another.
2. Determine which variable, or set of data, will be on the ordinate and which will be on the abscissa. Normally, the ordinate is the dependent variable, and the abscissa is the independent variable.
3. Determine the approximate locations of the axes and their zero positions. These will depend on the signs and the range of the values of the data or variables. Some scales may have both positive and negative values. The zero position is normally shown for each scale, but this is not necessary if the data values are not near zero. Under this circumstance a break in the

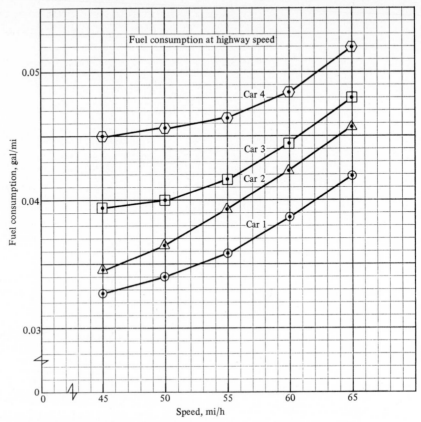

Figure 7.6 A line graph with four curves, each plotted with a different symbol.

scale can be used, but a scale not containing zero, or containing a break, should not mislead the viewer. See Figures 7.5 through 7.7 for examples of zero position, axis placement, and breaks in the scale.

4. Choose a linear scale for each axis. Many choices are available in commercial graph paper, and several samples are shown in Figure 7.8. The plotted data on the graph should cover the area available. To select a scale for each variable, or a particular linear scale, a preliminary scale value can be determined for each axis:

$$\text{scale value} = \frac{\text{range of variable or data}}{\text{available length of graph paper}}$$

The scale value will have units of

$$\frac{\text{units of variable or data}}{\text{length of graph paper}}$$

This preliminary scale value can be helpful in choosing a linear ruling for the graph or in determining the calibration of the scale if a particular ruling has already been chosen.

5. When selecting scales, the minimum division on a scale should be 1, 2, or 5 times 10 to an integer power. For example, on one scale the minimum division might be 0.02, or 2×10^{-2}. Or the minimum division might be 500, 5×10^2. It is customary in graphing to obey the "1, 2, 5 rule," although sometimes it is more appropriate to use a scale not following this rule. For instance, if data were given in 1/4 in increments, the minimum division might logically be 1/4 in, even though this does not obey the 1, 2, 5 rule.

6. The axes should be calibrated; that is, the axes should be marked with numerical values, thus making it easy to read the scale. The minimum division should be easily identified when viewing the calibrated scale, and the numbers on the axes should not be crowded. Some sample scales and calibrations are shown in Figure 7.9.

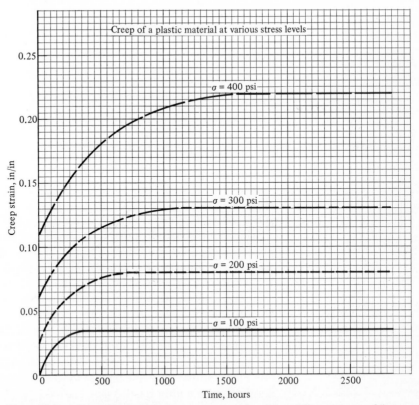

Figure 7.7 A line graph with four curves, each with a different type of line.

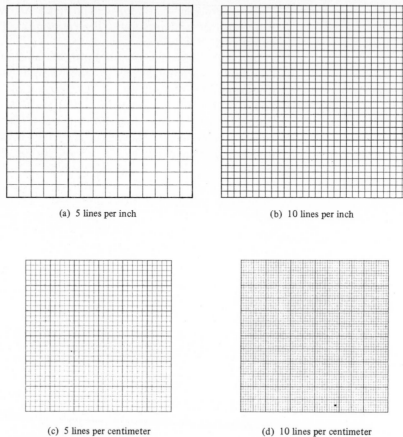

(a) 5 lines per inch

(b) 10 lines per inch

(c) 5 lines per centimeter

(d) 10 lines per centimeter

Figure 7.8 Samples of commercially available linear-scale graph paper.

7. If the data are determined experimentally, the plotted points should be marked by a circle. If more than one set of data is plotted on the same graph, each set of points can be marked by different symbols, such as triangles or squares (see Figure 7.6). For experimentally determined data, the points can be connected by straight lines, as shown in Figure 7.6, or if an empirical relationship is desired, the data can be approximated by a smooth curve, as shown in Figure 7.5. Lines drawn to connect points or to form a smooth curve should touch the circles or other symbols but should not be drawn through the symbol. If several lines are drawn on the same graph, they can most easily be distinguished if they are differ- ent. For example, one line can be solid, another can be short dashes, and another can be long dashes (see Figure 7.7).

8. Both axes should be labeled with a description of the variable and the units. For example, the label might be "Force, newtons," "Velocity, ft/s," or "Time, seconds." Sometimes it is appropriate to include also the symbol for the variable. For example, the label might be "Force, F, newtons," "Velocity, V, ft/s," or "Time, t, seconds." The axis label should be outside the axis and parallel to it.

9. A graph should be labeled and titled clearly and completely; that is, the reader should to be able to understand the graph quickly and completely without having to read any text. Although the labeling should be complete, the page should not be crowded and confusing.

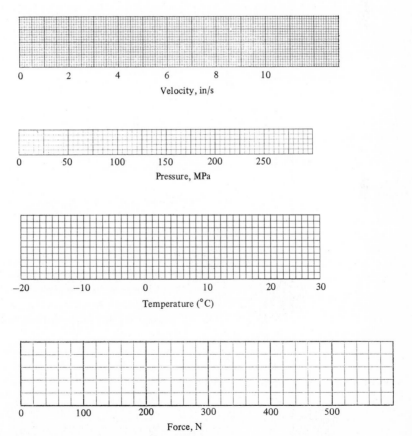

Figure 7.9 Sample scales and calibrations.

Example 7.3: The following data were obtained experimentally during the loading of a particular structure. Graph them on rectangular coordinate graph paper, with force as the independent variable and deflection as the dependent variable.

Deflection (mm)	Force (kN)
0	0
1.2	200
2.3	400
3.4	600
4.8	800
5.9	1000
7.0	1200
7.9	1400

Solution: Assume that graph paper with 5 divisions per inch will be used, with approximately 5 in for the abscissa and 8 in for the ordinate. The preliminary scale values would be

abscissa (force):

$$\text{scale value} = \frac{1400 \text{ kN}}{5 \text{ in}}$$

$$= 280 \frac{\text{kN}}{\text{inch of graph paper}}$$

ordinate (deflection):

$$\text{scale value} = \frac{8 \text{ mm}}{8 \text{ in}}$$

$$= 1 \frac{\text{mm}}{\text{inch of graph paper}}$$

In this case the preliminary scale value for the ordinate can be used as the scale value. The scale value of 280 kN/in of graph paper cannot be used for the abscissa because it does not obey the 1, 2, 5 rule. If we tried to use a smaller scale value, like 250, more than 5 in of graph paper would be needed for the abscissa. For 5 in of scale, the range of the variable would be

$$\text{range} = \left(250 \frac{\text{kN}}{\text{in}}\right)(5 \text{ in}) = 1250 \text{ kN}$$

This range is not enough. Assuming that only 5 in are available, the smallest scale value that can be used is 500. The minimum division using this paper with 5 divisions per inch would be

$$\frac{500 \text{ kN/in}}{5 \text{ divisions/in}} = 100 \frac{\text{kN}}{\text{division}}$$

This scale would obey the 1, 2, 5 rule, but only approximately 3 in of the 5 in of graph paper available would be used, which is unavoidable if this graph paper must be used.

The graph is shown in Figure 7.10, completely labeled. The relationship is approximated by a straight line drawn "by eye."

Problems p7.14 – p7.24

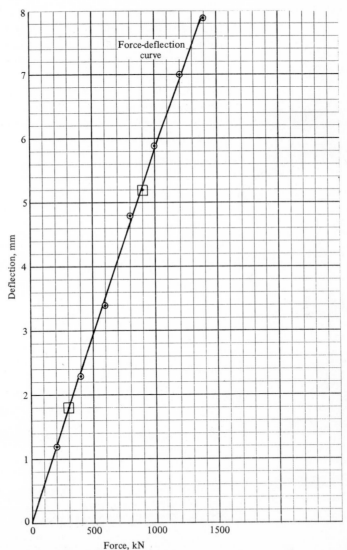

Figure 7.10 Line graph for Example 7.3

▲ 7.4 Equation of a Straight Line

The equation for a straight line, presented in Chapter 6, is

$$y = mx + b \tag{7.1}$$

Recall that in this form, x is the independent variable, y is the dependent variable, m is the slope, and b is the y-intercept. To obtain the equation of a straight line from data that approximate a straight line, the procedure is as follows:

1. Draw a straight line "by eye" through the data points. (A more sophisticated procedure for drawing straight lines through data points is presented in Section 8.7 of the next chapter.)
2. Choose two points on the straight line, preferably one near each end of the line.
3. Determine the coordinates of these two points.
4. Use the coordinates of the two points in Equation 7.1 to solve two simultaneous equations for m and b.

An example illustrates this.

Example 7.4: Determine the equation of the straight line approximated by the data in Example 7.3.

Solution: The equation of the line will have the form

$$d = mf + b.$$

where

$$d = \text{deflection, mm}$$

$$f = \text{force, kN}$$

Two points on the line are selected, which are marked on Figure 7.10 by squares:

$$f = 300 \text{ kN}, \quad d = 1.8 \text{ mm}$$

$$f = 900 \text{ kN}, \quad d = 5.2 \text{ mm}$$

Substituting those values into the equation of the line, the following two equations are obtained:

$$1.8 = 300m + b$$

$$5.2 = 900m + b$$

Solving these simultaneously using the techniques from Chapter 5 results in

$$m = 5.67 \times 10^{-3}$$

$$b = 0.1$$

Therefore the equation describing the data is

$$d = (5.67 \times 10^{-3})f + 0.1$$

Comment: Once the equation for the data has been obtained, it is prudent to choose another point to check the equation. For example, choose the point, $f = 700$ kN. Substituting this into the equation,

$$d = (5.67 \times 10^{-3})(700) + 0.1$$

$$d = 4.07 \text{ mm}$$

This is correct according to Figure 7.10.

Problems p7.25 – p7.27

▲ 7.5 Semilog Graph Paper

In addition to the linear graph scales there are a number of other scales that are widely used for graphing data. One of the most common of these other scales is the log scale. There are several reasons for using log scales rather than linear scales to graph data. Graphing on a log scale essentially compresses the larger values of the data on the scale, which is frequently desirable when the data cover a large range. Also, log scales often cause nonlinear data to approximate a straight line.

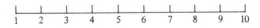

(a) The integers $N = 1$ to 10 on a linear scale.

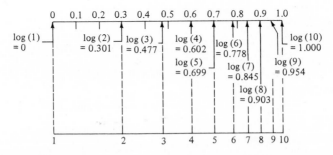

(b) Log to the base 10 of the integers $N = 1$ to 10 on a linear scale.

(c) Same scale as in (b) except the integer N is at the position where the $\log_{10}(N)$ is on the linear scale in (b). This is the log scale that is on log graph paper.

Figure 7.11 Log scales.

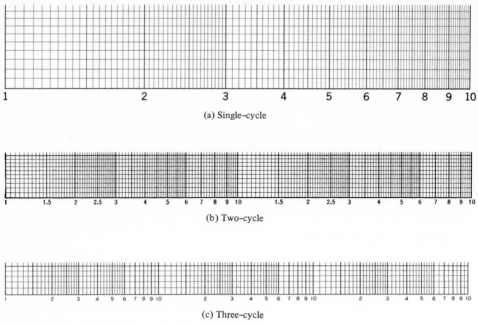

(a) Single–cycle

(b) Two–cycle

(c) Three–cycle

Figure 7.12 Samples of log scales.

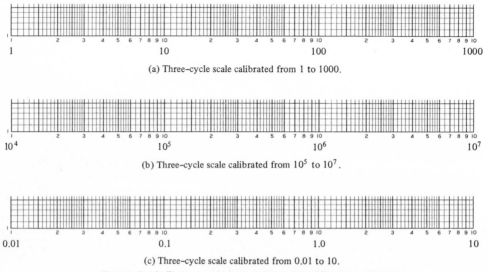

(a) Three–cycle scale calibrated from 1 to 1000.

(b) Three–cycle scale calibrated from 10^5 to 10^7.

(c) Three–cycle scale calibrated from 0.01 to 10.

Figure 7.13 Three-cycle log scales with different calibrations.

The log scale is a scale of the log to the base 10 of the numbers rather than a scale of the numbers themselves. An explanation of these scales is shown in Figure 7.11. Log scales are available in several cycles, as shown in Figure 7.12. This is necessary because one cycle of the log scale can cover only one multiple of 10. The log scales chosen can be calibrated to cover the range necessary if the correct number of cycles is chosen. For instance, a three-cycle log scale can be calibrated as shown in Figure 7.13(a) to cover the range from 1 to 1000 or, as shown in Figure 7.13(b), to cover the range from 1×10^4 to 1×10^7 or, as shown in Figure 7.13(c), to cover the range from 0.01 to 10.

Semilog graph paper has one scale as a log scale and the other as a linear scale. This type of graph paper is available with from one to five cycles of the log scale on the paper. When using semilog paper it is desirable to use graph paper with the smallest number of cycles necessary, as then most of the available area of the graph paper will be used.

Problems p7.28 – p7.37

▲ 7.6 Straight Lines on Semilog Graph Paper

Equations of the general form

$$y = ke^{ax} \tag{7.2}$$

graph as a straight line on semilog graph paper. In Equation 7.2, k and a are real values, y is the dependent variable, and x is the independent variable. To see why this graphs as a straight line, take the log of both sides of Equation 7.2 as follows:

$$\log y = \log(ke^{ax})$$
$$= \log k + \log(e^{ax})$$

$$\log y = a(\log e)x + \log k \tag{7.3}$$

If the constant, a ($\log e$), is replaced by m and $\log k$ by b, the equation will be

$$\log y = mx + b$$

This will be a linear equation if x is considered to be one variable and $\log y$ the other variable. Therefore if the ordinate is a log scale and the abscissa is a linear scale, Equation 7.2 will graph as a straight line on semilog graph paper, with the ordinate as the log scale. As an example of this, Figure 7.14 shows the graph of the equation

$$y = 0.7e^{0.5x} \tag{7.4}$$

on linear graph paper. It is certainly not a straight line, but when plotted on

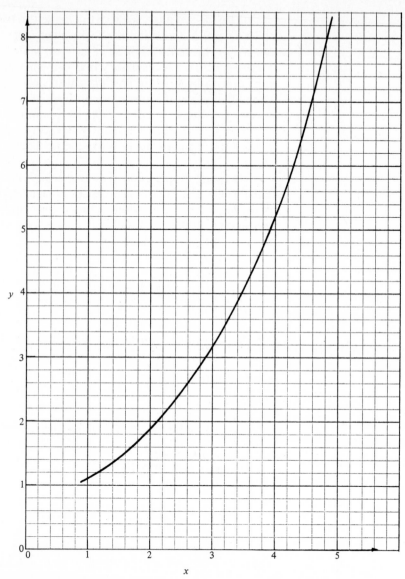

Figure 7.14 Graph of the equation $y = 0.7e^{0.5x}$ on linear-scale graph paper.

semilog graph paper with the ordinate or y-axis as the log scale, it is a straight line, as shown in Figure 7.15.

Sometimes when data are graphed on semilog graph paper and they approximate a straight line, it is desirable to determine the equation of the data. From what was previously discussed, if the data graphs as a straight line on semilog graph paper, the equation for the data will be in the form of

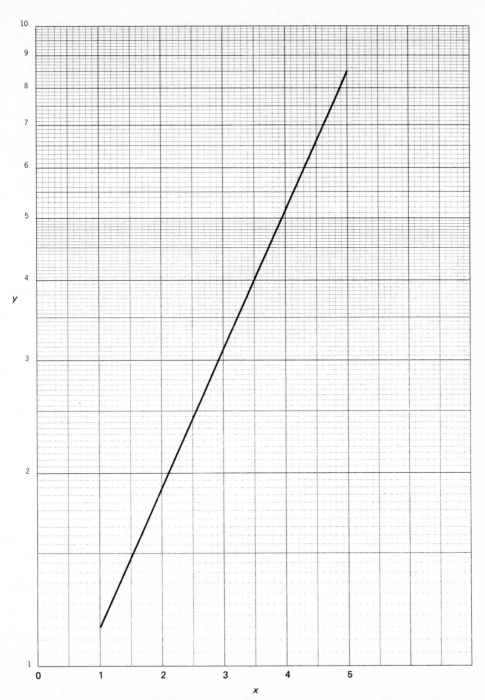

Figure 7.15 Graph of the equation $y = 0.7e^{0.5x}$ on semilog graph paper.

Equation 7.2. It is only necessary to determine the values for *k* and *a*. Since two points on a straight line define that line uniquely, and since the equation for the data that graph as a straight line on semilog graph paper is Equation 7.3, the values of *a* and *k* can be determined by substituting the coordinate values for the two points into Equation 7.3 and solving the two equations simultaneously. The following example illustrates this:

Example 7.5: A series of machine parts was tested to determine the number of cycles required to produce fatigue failure for different values of load. The results are shown below. Choose a semilog paper and graph the results, with the load as the linear ordinate and the number of cycles to failure as the log scale abscissa.

Load, L (lb)	Cycles to Failure, N
61	1.35×10^5
50	2.50×10^5
42	4.00×10^5
36	6.10×10^5
27	1.13×10^6
21	1.97×10^6
14	2.75×10^6
10	4.09×10^6

Solution: The number of cycles to failure scale must be represented in two log cycles in order to cover the range 1×10^5 to 1×10^6 and 1×10^6 to 1×10^7. The data are graphed in Figure 7.16, and a straight line is drawn through the points. Two points on the line are chosen to determine the equation of the data, as follows:

$$N = 1.5 \times 10^5, L = 58$$

$$N = 5.0 \times 10^6, L = 6$$

Since the number of cycles, *N*, is the log scale, the data will have an equation in the form

$$N = ke^{aL}$$

and Equation 7.3 is, with *N* and *L* as the variables,

$$\log N = \log k + \log(e^{aL})$$

Rearranging,

$$\log N = a(\log e)L + \log k$$

Substituting the above values into this equation,

$$\log(5 \times 10^6) = a(\log e)(6) + \log k$$

$$\log(1.5 \times 10^5) = a(\log e)(58) + \log k$$

$$6.69897 = 2.60577a + \log k$$

$$5.17609 = 25.18908a + \log k$$

Subtracting the second equation from the first,

$$1.52288 = -22.58331a$$

$$a = -0.06743$$

Solving the first equation for k,

$$\log k = 6.69897 - (2.60577)(-0.06743)$$
$$= 6.87468$$

$$k = 7.4934 \times 10^6$$

Rounding a and k, the equation of the data is

$$N = (7.49 \times 10^6)e^{-0.067L}$$

Comment: To check this equation, choose another point on the straight line, such as $L = 40$. Substituting this value into the equation gives $N = 5.1 \times 10^5$, which Figure 7.16 shows to be correct.

Problems p7.38–p7.40

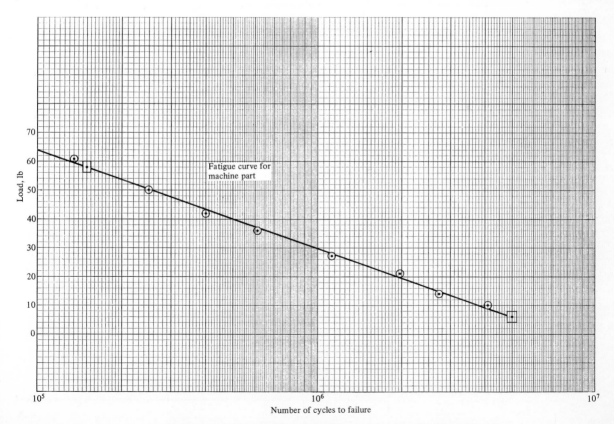

Figure 7.16 Line graph on semilog graph paper for Example 7.5.

▲ 7.7 Log-Log Graph Paper

Log-log graph paper is commercially available with several combinations of cycles on the scales. If possible, choose scales that the data will fill as much as possible. Sometimes, if one or two points are omitted, one cycle can be omitted from the graph paper. Of course, these data should not be omitted if they will affect the graph's results.

Problems p7.41 – p7.43

▲ 7.8 Straight Lines on Log-Log Graph Paper

Equations of the general form

$$y = kx^a \qquad (7.5)$$

with k and a as real values, y as the independent variable, and x as the dependent variable, graph as a straight line on log-log graph paper. This is graph paper with both axes as log scales. To show that this equation graphs

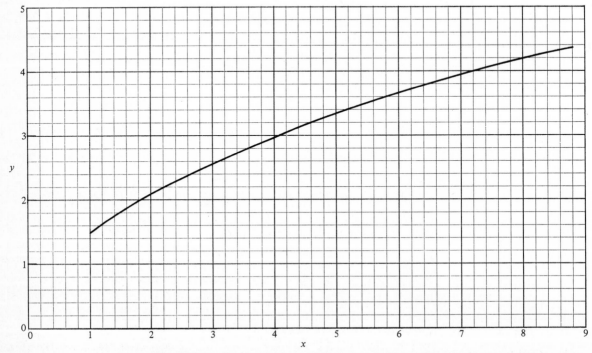

Figure 7.17 Graph of the equation $y = 1.5x^{0.5}$ on linear-scale graph paper.

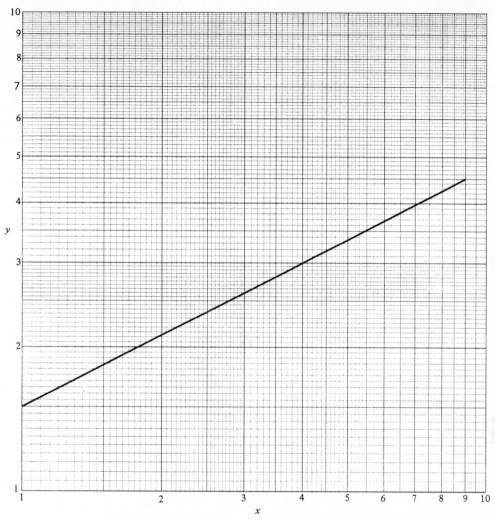

Figure 7.18 Graph of the equation $y = 1.5x^{0.5}$ on log-log graph paper.

as a straight line, the log of both sides of Equation 7.5 is taken:

$$\log y = \log(kx^a)$$
$$= \log k + \log(x^a)$$

$$\log y = a \log x + \log k \qquad (7.6)$$

If the constant, $\log k$, is replaced by b, the following equation will result:

$$\log y = a \log x + b$$

This equation will be a linear equation if one variable is considered as $\log x$ and the other variable as $\log y$. Therefore if the axes are log scales, Equation 7.6 will graph as a straight line. As an example, Figure 7.17 shows a graph of the equation

$$y = 1.5x^{0.5}$$

This is not a straight line, but when graphed on log-log paper, a straight line is produced, as shown in Figure 7.18.

When data are graphed that approximate a straight line on log-log graph paper, the equation for these data is in the form of Equation 7.5. To determine the equation for the data, the values for a and k must be determined. As discussed in Section 7.6, this can be accomplished by choosing two points on the straight line, substituting the values for y and x at those points into Equation 7.6, and solving the two equations for a and k. The following example illustrates this:

Example 7.6:
a. Choose the appropriate log-log graph paper for the data shown below, graph the data and approximate them by a straight line.
b. Determine the equation of the data.

x	y
1.14	3.20
1.66	4.33
2.01	5.45
3.32	8.40
5.10	12.90
7.28	18.40

Solution:
a. The log-log graph paper necessary is one cycle for the x-axis (1 to 10) and two cycles for the y-axis (1 to 10 and 10 to 100). The data are graphed in Figure 7.19, and a straight line is drawn to approximate them.
b. The two points on the straight line chosen to determine the equation for the data are enclosed in squares and are

$$x = 1.10, y = 3.0$$

$$x = 9.00, y = 22.0$$

These values are substituted into Equation 7.6:

$$\log(22) = a \log(9.0) + \log k$$

$$\log(3) = a \log(1.1) + \log k$$

$$1.34242 = a(0.95424) + \log k$$

$$0.47712 = a(0.04139) + \log k$$

Subtracting the second equation from the first eliminates $\log k$ and results in

$$0.86530 = a(0.91285)$$

$$a = 0.94791$$

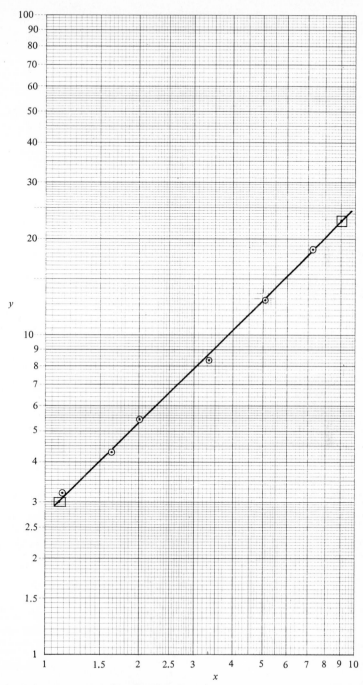

Figure 7.19 Log-log graph for Example 7.6.

Substituting a into the first equation and solving for k,

$$\log k = 1.34242 - (0.94791)(0.95424)$$
$$= 0.43789$$

$$k = 2.74088$$

Rounding a and k, the equation for the data is

$$y = 2.74x^{0.95}$$

Comment: To check this equation, choose another value of x, for example, 4.0. Substituting this value into the equation yields a correct result, as shown by Figure 7.19.

$$y = 2.74(4)^{0.95}$$

$$y = 10.23$$

Problems p7.44 – p7.47

● CHAPTER SUMMARY

This chapter introduced the most commonly used graphs for engineers and technologists: the circle chart, the bar graph, and the line graph. We then presented, step by step, the rules for constructing the graphs. We discussed line graphs, not only for rectangular coordinate graph paper, but also for semilog and log-log graph paper. Finally, we described, for data that graph as a straight line on any of these three types of graph paper, a method for determining the equation that relates the variables.

▲ Problems

p7.1   The labor distribution, by time, for the assembly of a product is shown in Table p7.1. Construct a circle chart showing this distribution.

TABLE p7.1 Labor Distribution

Description	Time (seconds)
Subassembly	12
Clip	18
Leak test	31
Dry	8
Label	7
O-ring and screw	14
Box	28

p7.2   Construct a circle chart depicting the distribution of grades for a class according to the following data:

Grade	A	B	C	D	F
No. of students	4	10	23	12	8

p7.3   Construct a circle chart depicting the distribution of sales for a department store by department according to the data in Table p7.3.

TABLE p7.3 Sales for Year 1985

Department	Sales ($)
Men's clothing	213 000
Women's clothing	549 000
Children's clothing	362 000
Housewares	146 000
Furniture	473 000

p7.4   The distribution, by age, of employees working for a particular company is shown below. Construct a pie chart to show this distribution.

Age group	<20	20 – 29	30 – 39	40 – 49	50 – 59	>59
No. of employees	32	67	85	73	47	18

p7.5   With the outside air temperature at 25°F, the heat transfer from a particular building is shown in Table p7.5. Construct a circle chart depicting the distribution of heat transfer from the building.

TABLE p7.5 Heat Transfer from Building

Section of Building	Heat Transfer (Btu/h)
Walls	34 370
Windows	16 690
Doors	1 170
Slab	17 970
Ceiling	65 530

p7.6   An energy audit for an office building results in a savings of electrical energy usage for a year, as shown in Table p7.6. Construct a circle chart to depict the distribution of savings in the various categories.

TABLE p7.6 Electrical Energy Savings

Category	Savings (kWh)
Lighting	622
Heating	327
A/C and ventilation	178
Refrigeration	23
Water heating	75
Other	57

p7.7 Construct a bar chart showing the distribution of grades in a class, as shown in p7.2.

p7.8 Construct a bar chart showing the distribution, by age, of employees working for a particular company, as shown in p7.4.

p7.9 The earnings history for Acme Engineering, Inc. is as shown below. Construct a bar graph to depict this history.

Year	1980	1981	1982	1983	1984	1985
Earnings ($1,000's)	18.2	16.9	16.7	14.5	21.5	24.3

p7.10 The rainfall at the Greenville weather station has been recorded by month, as shown below. Construct a bar chart to depict these data.

Month	J	F	M	A	M	J	J	A	S	O	N	D
Rainfall (in)	2.3	1.8	3.2	2.8	3.5	2.9	4.5	5.3	4.2	2.9	2.8	3.2

p7.11 The sound pressure levels near fans used in a factory were recorded before and after silencers for the fans were installed. The data are shown in Table p7.11. Construct one bar graph to present the results from before and after the installation.

TABLE p7.11 Fan Noise

Octave Band	Fan Noise	Fan Noise
Center Frequency (Hz)	Sound Pressure Level (dB)	Sound Pressure Level with Silencers (dB)
125	91	83
250	90	84
500	94	83
1000	94	82
2000	91	79
4000	86	72
8000	81	68

p7.12   The average monthly home energy use for home cooling in a particular locale is shown below. Construct a bar chart to show this energy use.

Month	May	June	July	Aug.	Sept.	Oct.
Energy use (kWh)	402	490	560	565	537	420

p7.13   The weekly production rate forecast for two different electric motors is shown in Table p7.13. Construct one bar chart to depict this forecast.

TABLE p7.13 Forecast of Weekly Production Rate

Year	Electric Motor A2	Electric Motor B7
1987	625	750
1988	700	890
1989	750	920
1990	600	1050
1991	400	1570
1992	0	2100

p7.14   The data for force in newtons vary from 4 N to 360 N. Construct a linear scale, to fit in a space 8 in long, for these data. Be sure that the scale conforms to the 1, 2, 5 rule. Calibrate and label the scale.

p7.15   The data for voltage in volts vary from 0.6 V to 86 V. Construct a linear scale for the data to fit in a space 5 in long. Be sure that the scale conforms to the 1, 2, 5 rule. Calibrate and label the scale.

p7.16   Temperature, in degrees Fahrenheit, is to be plotted on a linear scale that is to fit in a space 5 in long. The temperature varies from $-65°F$ to $120°F$. Construct, calibrate, and label a scale conforming to the 1, 2, 5 rule.

p7.17   Power, in horsepower, is to be plotted on a linear scale to fit in a space 6 in long. The power varies from 45 hp to 90 hp. Construct, calibrate, and label a scale conforming to the 1, 2, 5 rule.

p7.18   Drill speed, in revolutions per minute, is to be plotted in a space 5 in long. The speed varies from 2200 rpm to 5100 rpm. Construct, calibrate, and label a linear scale conforming to the 1, 2, 5 rule.

p7.19   To determine the friction between two surfaces, sliding force in pounds versus normal force in pounds is measured and recorded in Table p7.19. Construct, calibrate, and label a line graph on rectangular coordinate graph paper with linear scales for these data. Normal force should be the independent variable.

TABLE p7.19 Determination of Friction

Normal Force (lb)	Sliding Force (lb)
0.2	0.052
0.4	0.100
0.6	0.144
0.8	0.217
1.0	0.252

p7.20 For two kinds of epoxy, the value of modulus of elasticity, in pounds per square inch, varies with cure temperature, as measured and recorded in Table p7.20. Construct, calibrate, and label a line graph on rectangular coordinate graph paper with linear scales for these data. Plot the data for both epoxies on the same graph, with cure temperature as the independent variable.

TABLE p7.20 Modulus of Elasticity Variation

Cure Temperature (°F)	Modulus of Elasticity (1000 psi)	
	Epoxy A	Epoxy B
150	470	560
175	410	530
200	390	485
225	370	470
250	365	460
275	360	455
300	355	450

p7.21 A heat transfer experiment results in the temperature-time data in Table p7.21. Construct, calibrate, and label a line graph on rectangular coordinate graph paper with linear scales for these data.

TABLE p7.21 Time Versus Temperature

Time (seconds)	Temperature (°Celsius)
0	−20
5	−17
10	−12
15	− 7
20	− 3
25	+ 2
30	8
35	15
40	18
45	21
50	25

p7.22 In a machine with a paper-feeding mechanism, the pressure plate exerts force against the paper. The measurement of the pressure plate force versus the pressure plate displacement results in the data in Table p17.22. Construct, calibrate, and label a line graph on rectangular coordinate graph paper with linear scales for these data.

TABLE p7.22 Pressure Plate Force Variation

Pressure Plate Force (N)	Displacement of Pressure Plate (mm)
2.4	0
2.6	5
2.7	10
2.8	15
2.8	20
3.1	25
3.4	30
3.5	35
3.7	40
3.8	45
4.0	50

p7.23 For a demand-response short-trip bus, the data relating cost per trip versus trip per hour are given in Table p7.23. Construct, calibrate, and label a line graph on rectangular coordinate graph paper with linear scales for these data.

TABLE p7.23 Trip Cost of Bus

Trips per Hour	Cost per Trip ($)
2	3.25
4	2.10
6	1.50
8	1.05
10	0.90
12	0.80

p7.24 A capacitor, charged with an initial voltage, is discharged into a circuit, and the voltage across the capacitor is measured and recorded at regular time intervals, as shown in Table p7.24. Construct, calibrate, and label a line graph on rectangular coordinate graph paper with linear scales for these data.

TABLE p7.24 Discharge of a Capacitor

Time (seconds)	Voltage (volts)
1	335
2	226
3	148
4	102
5	65
6	47
7	31
8	19
9	14

p7.25 For the graph in p7.19 draw a straight line "by eye" through the data, and determine the equation for the straight line, relating sliding force to normal force. Let normal force be the independent variable.

p7.26 For the graph in p7.21 draw a straight line "by eye" through the data, and determine the equation for the straight line, relating time and temperature, with time as the independent variable.

p7.27 For the graph in p7.22 draw a straight line "by eye" through the data, and determine the equation for the straight line, relating force and displacement, with displacement as the independent variable.

p7.28 The data for a force in newtons vary from 1.2 to 8.6 N. Choose and calibrate an appropriate log scale for these data.

p7.29 The data for electric current in amperes vary from zero to 640 amps. Choose and calibrate an appropriate log scale for these data.

p7.30 The data for stress in pounds per square inch vary from 3500 psi to 47 000 psi. Choose and calibrate an appropriate log scale for these data.

p7.31 The data for displacement in meters vary from 0.000 23 to 0.675 00. Choose and calibrate an appropriate log scale for these data.

p7.32 The data for velocity in miles per hour vary from 120 to 260 mph. Choose and calibrate an appropriate log scale for these data.

p7.33 Plot the data from p7.22 on appropriate semilog graph paper, with displacement as the dependent variable on a log scale. Calibrate and label the graph.

p7.34 Plot the data from p7.24 on appropriate semilog graph paper, with voltage as the dependent variable on a log scale. Calibrate and label the graph.

p7.35 Plot the data from p7.21 on appropriate semilog graph paper, with time as the independent variable on a log scale. Calibrate and label the graph.

p7.36 Plot the data from p7.23 on appropriate semilog graph paper, with cost as the dependent variable on a log scale. Calibrate and label the graph.

p7.37 The production in a new manufacturing facility is as shown in Table p7.37. Choose appropriate semilog graph paper to plot the production data, with pieces as the dependent variable on a log scale. Calibrate and label the graph.

TABLE p7.37 Production Increase in New Plant

Production (Number of Pieces)	Time (Week)
1 700	1
2 900	2
5 100	3
8 000	4
16 500	5
28 500	6

p7.38 For the graph in p7.34, draw a straight line "by eye" through the data, and determine the equation relating voltage and time, with voltage as the dependent variable.

p7.39 For the graph in p7.37, draw a straight line "by eye" through the data, and determine the equation relating number of pieces produced to week number, using number of pieces produced as the dependent variable.

p7.40 A machine part is decelerated during its operating cycle, and the velocity is measured and recorded in Table p7.40. Plot the data on semilog graph paper, with velocity as the dependent variable on a log scale. Draw a straight line "by eye" through the data, and determine the equation, relating velocity and time.

TABLE p7.40 Machine-Part Velocity

Velocity (mm/s)	Time (s)
760	0.01
535	0.02
400	0.03
270	0.04
180	0.05

p7.41 Plot the data from p7.22 on appropriate log-log graph paper, with force as the dependent variable.

p7.42 Plot the data from p7.23 on appropriate log-log graph paper, with trips per hour as the independent variable.

p7.43 Plot the data from p7.24 on appropriate log-log graph paper, with voltage as the dependent variable.

p7.44 For the graph in p7.42, draw a straight line "by eye" through the data, and determine the equation relating cost per trip and trips per hour, with trips per hour as the independent variable.

p7.45 The variation of the period of a vibrating system with weight is measured and recorded, as shown in Table p7.45. Construct, calibrate, and label a graph for these data on appropriate log-log graph paper, with period as the dependent variable. Draw a straight line "by eye" through the data, and determine the equation relating period and weight.

TABLE p7.45 Period of a Vibration System

Weight (lb)	Period (s)
150	0.062
200	0.071
300	0.088
500	0.112
700	0.134
1000	0.160

p7.46 Plot the data in Table p7.46 on appropriate log-log graph paper with correct calibration and labels. Sketch a best-fit straight line "by eye" through the data, and determine the equation relating deflection and force, with deflection as the dependent variable.

TABLE p7.46 Behavior of a Nonlinear Spring

Deflection of Spring (mm)	Force Applied to Spring (N)
2.0	11
3.0	31
4.0	64
5.0	112
6.0	176
7.0	259
8.0	362

p7.47 The velocity of an airplane is measured as a function of time, and the data are recorded in Table p7.47. Choose an appropriate log-log graph paper, and plot the data, with velocity as the dependent variable. Sketch a straight line "by eye" through the data, and determine the equation, relating velocity and time.

TABLE p7.47 Velocity of an Airplane

Time (s)	Velocity (ft/s)
0	0
5	10
10	24
15	46
20	71
30	118
40	184
50	253
60	317

Statistics

Statistics is defined as the collection, organization, and interpretation of numerical data. Whether or not we are aware of it, we are bombarded with statistics on topics ranging from increases or decreases in monthly inflation to who is most likely to win a political election. In the engineering profession, the need to understand statistics is obvious because engineers are continually handling numerical data. This chapter discusses the statistical manipulation of data.

Objective: The objective of this chapter is to introduce some of the basic concepts of statistical analysis of data.

Criteria: After completing this chapter, you should be able to do the following:

- **8.1** State what is meant by a frequency distribution and determine the cell width, cell boundaries, and cell midpoints for constructing a histogram, given the observed values and the number of cells desired.
- **8.2** Tabulate and graph a cumulative frequency distribution and determine the frequency of occurrence of specified values, given the cell boundaries and the observed values.
- **8.3** State what is meant by a normal distribution and determine the mean, mode, and median of a given set of numbers.
- **8.4** Define what is meant by range and standard deviation and determine their values, given the data and the equation for calculating the standard deviation.
- **8.5** Define what is meant by a normal distribution and determine the value of a data point located a specified number of standard deviations from the mean, given the mean and standard deviation of the data.

- **8.6** Compute the correlation coefficient (r) between two variables, given the data and the formula for calculating r.
- **8.7** Determine the best-fitting linear regression line between two variables, given the data, the regression line formula, and the equation for calculating the slope of the line.

▲ 8.1 Frequency Distribution

Engineers and scientists are constantly collecting and analyzing data in order to make recommendations or draw conclusions about a related project. When analyzing data, it is always advantageous to be able to categorize or classify the information in ways that make it easier to interpret. One method of grouping or summarizing relatively large amounts of data is through a frequency distribution.

A *frequency distribution* is a tabulation or, more commonly, a graph showing the number of times a particular event has occurred. This "event" can relate to a variable that is either discrete or continuous. A *discrete variable* is one that can have only a limited number of values in a certain range. For example, if one were to count the number of cars passing through a certain intersection in different 5-min time periods, the results obtained would be a series of integer numbers, like 20, 51, 33, 8. It would not be possible to obtain a result such as 31.3 or 18.73. On the other hand, a *continuous variable* can assume virtually any value within a given data range. Thus, if one were to record the speed of automobiles traveling along a certain highway, the values obtained could span a continuous range from the lowest to the highest speed recorded, with the number of significant digits limited only by the accuracy of the measuring device.

After the data are obtained, it is frequently necessary to group some values together into what are called *cells*, so that an appropriate distribution pattern will be formed. This is especially necessary for continuous data when the frequency of occurrence of the individual data items is very low. For example, if one were to obtain the weights of 100 people selected at random, there would not be many values, if any, that would be the same. However, if the data were grouped into cells of, say, 20-lb increments, some cells would contain many values, so that the predominant weight ranges would be readily discernable.

After it has been determined that the data must be grouped, adherence to the following guidelines will generally yield a satisfactory frequency distribution:

1. For fewer than 50 data points, there should be between 5 and 10 cells. For more than 50 points, as many as 20 cells may be used.
2. The approximate size of each cell can be determined from the following equation:

$$\text{cell size, } c = \frac{\text{max. value} - \text{min. value}}{\text{no. of cells, } k} \tag{8.1}$$

If the maximum and minimum values are far above or below the next highest or lowest values, they should not be used in Equation 8.1, but they would be included in open-ended beginning and final cells designated "greater than—" or "less than—".

3. The cell boundaries can be determined by starting with a data value one-half measurement unit smaller than the lowest value and adding the cell size, c. This will ensure that each value is included in only one cell. The procedure should be continued until the upper cell boundary is greater than the last data point.
4. The number of data values in each cell should be determined and tabulated. These results (i.e., the frequency distribution) can then be plotted to form a *histogram*.

The procedure for preparing a frequency distribution for grouped data is illustrated in Example 8.1.

Example 8.1: The hours of running time per week for a generator in a manufacturing plant are as follows: 20, 75, 43, 62, 51, 52, 78, 33, 28, 39, 61, 56, 43, 49, 48, 49, 71, 53, 57, 46, 42, 41, 63, 36, 51, 59, 40, 32, 37, 29, 26. Construct a frequency distribution and draw the histogram.

Solution: Since there are fewer than 50 data points, try 5 cells. The cell size, then, would be

$$C = \frac{78 - 20}{5} \simeq 12$$

The first cell boundary would be at 19.5 (one-half unit below the first data point). The cell boundaries and frequencies for each cell are shown in Table 8.1.

TABLE 8.1 Cell Boundaries and Frequencies

Cell Boundaries	Frequencies
19.5–31.5	4
31.5–43.5	10
43.5–55.5	8
55.5–67.5	6
67.5–79.5	3

The histogram is shown in Figure 8.1.

Comment: When the cell end points are close together, it is permissible to show only the cell midpoint on the x-axis, to avoid crowding of numbers. Also, note that histograms of different shapes may be obtained for different k values. When this occurs, the preparer must decide which histogram displays the information in the most desirable or beneficial way.

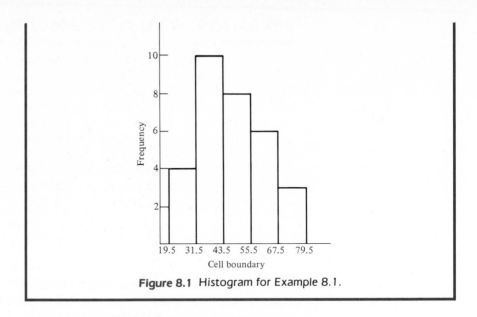

Figure 8.1 Histogram for Example 8.1.

By using cell boundaries that are more accurate than the data, it is never possible to have a data point fall on a boundary. Some practitioners, however, use cell boundaries that are of the same accuracy as the data, and in this case, some of the data values may fall on a boundary. When this occurs, the standard practice is to include the data point in *the cell to the right of this boundary.* In other words, the upper cell boundary is *not* included in the cell. For example, if the cell boundaries in Example 8.1 were 20–32, 32–44, 44–56, 56–68, and 68–80, the value 32 would be included in the 32–44 cell. Similarly, the value 56 would be included in the 56–68 cell. This procedure will be used hereafter in this text.

Problems p8.1–p8.5

▲ 8.2 Cumulative Frequency Distributions

As discussed in Section 8.1, a frequency distribution provides information regarding the number of times that an event of a given magnitude has occurred. Sometimes, however, an investigator needs to have frequency information not only about one particular magnitude, but also about the frequency of occurrences less than, greater than, or in between specific magnitudes. This type of information is readily obtained from a cumulative frequency distribution. A *cumulative frequency distribution* is the summation of all data values less than or greater than a particular specified value. Thus, if an engineer wanted to know the number of times that fewer than five cars were involved in the same accident on a certain section of freeway,

TABLE 8.2 Cumulative Frequency Distribution

Rainfall Intensity, in/h	Frequency	Cumulative Frequency
(1)	(2)	(3)
<0.2	43	43
0.2–0.4	12	55
0.4–0.6	9	64
0.6–0.8	5	69
0.8–1.0	1	70
1.0–1.2	2	72
1.2–1.4	1	73
>1.4	1	74

the answer would be the summation of the number of 1, 2, 3, and 4 car accidents. Cumulative frequency distributions constructed so that the frequency values represent less than the respective upper cell boundaries are called *less-than* cumulative frequency distributions. Those whose cumulative frequency values are equal to or greater than the lower boundary are known as *or-more* cumulative distributions. The less-than type is usually implied unless otherwise specified.

As is the case for frequency distributions, cumulative frequency distributions are usually first tabulated and then graphed. Column 3 in Table 8.2 shows the cumulative frequency distribution for rainfalls of a given intensity in a one-year period of time at a precipitation recording station. This is obviously a less-than cumulative frequency distribution.

In preparing a graph of a cumulative frequency distribution, the data values are placed along the abscissa, with the cumulative frequency along

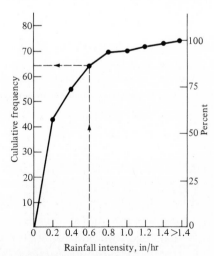

Figure 8.2 Cumulative frequency distribution.

the ordinate. The cumulative frequency values (i.e., column 3) for *grouped* data are always plotted at the upper cell boundary. Therefore, the frequencies associated with a particular data value are "less than," not "less than or equal to" the stated amount, because the upper cell boundary is never included in the cell. For ungrouped data values, the cumulative frequency distributions would be read "less than or equal to." Figure 8.2 is a plot of the cumulative frequency distribution of Table 8.2.

Note in Figure 8.2 that a percentage scale was added as the right vertical axis. The percentages are obtained by dividing the cumulative frequency at any point by the largest cumulative value (74 in this case). Cumulative frequency distributions are often prepared to obtain percentage values. Example 8.2 illustrates this.

Example 8.2: From Figure 8.2, determine the following:

a. The number of times the intensity (i) was less than 0.6 in/hr.
b. The lowest intensity for which 50 rainfalls occurred.
c. The number of times the intensity was greater than or equal to 0.8 in/hr.
d. The number of times the intensity was at least 0.2 and less than 0.6 in/hr.
e. The percentage of rainfalls less than 1.0 in/hr.

Solution:

a. From Figure 8.2, the number of times the intensity was less than 0.6 in/hr can be read directly from the graph as 64.
b. Entering the y-axis at 50, the intensity that occurred 50 times was less than 0.3 in/hr.
c. The number of times i was ≥ 0.8 is equal to the cumulative total minus the number of times the intensity was less than 0.8. Thus,

$$\text{no. times} \geq 0.8 = 74 - 69 = 5$$

d. The number of times $0.2 \leq i < 0.6$ is

$$\text{no. times} = 64 - 43 = 21$$

e. Entering the x-axis at 1.0 in/hr, the percentage can be read from the right vertical axis as approximately 95 percent.

Supplementary Examples 8.7, 8.8
Problems p8.6 – p8.11

▲ 8.3 Measures of Central Tendency

Much of the information that technical people must deal with is numerical in nature, and quite often, it is necessary or desirable to be able to summarize it. Just as the abstract of an article is supposed to provide a clear, concise, and accurate representation of the text, a summary of numerical information is supposed to accomplish the same thing for numbers. Single numbers that are said to represent large groups of numbers are called *measures of central tendency.* There are three common measures of central tendency in widespread use: the arithmetic mean, the median, and the mode.

The *arithmetic mean* is undoubtedly the most common measure of central tendency and is thus well understood. When someone mentions the word *average,* he or she is usually referring to the arithmetic mean. The equation for calculating the arithmetic mean of *n* numbers is

$$\bar{x} = \frac{\sum_{i=1}^{n} x_i}{n} = \frac{x_1 + x_2 + x_3 + \cdots + x_n}{n} \qquad (8.2)$$

where

$\bar{x}$ = arithmetic mean
Σ = greek letter sigma meaning "summation of"
x_i = individual data values, with i varying from 1 to n
n = number of data values

For example, the arithmetic mean of the numbers 3, 6, 7, 2, 1, 3, and 6 would be

$$\bar{x} = \frac{3 + 6 + 7 + 2 + 1 + 3 + 6}{7} = \frac{28}{7} = 4$$

It should be pointed out that $\bar{x}$ is only an *estimate* of the true population from which it was drawn. The true mean is represented by the Greek letter μ and can be determined only when all of the values that constitute the population are included in the calculation of the mean. Most of the time, only a part of the population is observed and included in the calculation, in which case the mean is properly represented as $\bar{x}$.

When the numbers to be summarized contain a few values that are much larger or smaller than most of the other numbers, the arithmetic mean may yield a value that does not really represent the data. For example, an entrepreneurial civil engineer may decide to begin a home-building business in which he plans to build houses in the price range representative of the greatest number of sales. Let us assume he obtained the following information about home sale prices from the local board of realtors:

$72 000, $81 000, $69 000, $385 000, $79 000, and $70 000.

The arithmetic mean of these prices is $126 000, yet not one of the houses sold was even close to this value. Clearly, the engineer should build houses in the $70 000 to $80 000 price range if he wants to build an "average" house. In this case, the arithmetic mean is misleading, and so some other measure of central tendency should be used.

The *median* is defined as the middle value of an array of numbers that are arranged in order of magnitude, from the smallest to the largest. Half of the values are less than or equal to the median, and half are greater than or equal to it. Thus, for the numbers 1, 8, 5, 1, 4, the median is 4, because it is the middle value of the ranked observations (i.e., 1, 1, 4, 5, 8). For an even number of observations, the median is the arithmetic mean of the two middle values. Hence, for the home sale prices given above, the median would be $75 500, that is, (72 000 + 79 000)/2. A disadvantage of the median is that it tends to vary from one sample to another more than does the mean.

A third method of describing the central tendency of a set of data values is by determining the mode. The *mode* is the value that occurs the greatest number of times. The mode is sometimes a much better representation of the data than is either the mean or the median. For example, if our entrepreneur were the owner of a wholesale automobile tire distributorship, he would have to know which sizes of tires should be stocked in the largest quantities. Assuming that the numbers 2, 2, 7, 2, 7, 2, 6, 9, 8 represented meaningful tire sizes recently sold in the city, he obviously should have the largest stock in tires of size 2, but the mean would suggest size 5 and the median size 6. The mode would clearly have been more representative of the data in this case.

A disadvantage of the mode compared with either the mean or the

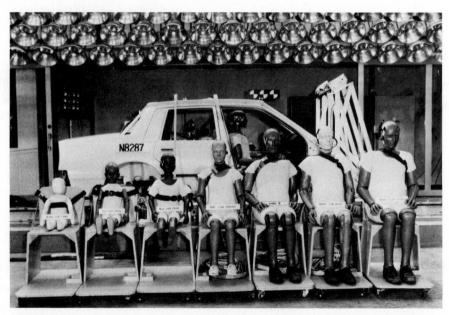

Illustration 8.1 Statistics are used to determine the physical characteristics of anthropomorphic dummies. The second and third from the right represent 50th percentile males, meaning that their weight and height places them in the middle of the male population. The far right dummy is a 95th percentile male. (Courtesy General Motors)

median is that a true mode may not always exist and that if it does, it may not be unique. The numbers below illustrate these problems:

$$1, 2, 5, 3, 9, 4 \quad \text{no mode}$$

$$5, 5, 6, 3, 1, 1 \quad \text{two modes}$$

When groups of numbers are represented by a single number, a choice obviously has to be made regarding the measure adopted. Common sense should always dictate which method is finally chosen, but if there is a chance of confusion, it is reasonable to use more than just one of the measures of central tendency.

Problems p8.12 – p8.16

▲ 8.4 Standard Deviation

In Section 8.3, we described the mean, median, and mode as measures of central tendency. Each of these methods has limitations peculiar to that particular method, but a deficiency that all three have with respect to adequately describing and summarizing data values is that none provides information about the data's dispersion or scatter. Without such information, gross errors can be made when generalizations are based solely on "average" values. For example, the mean and median of the numbers 3, 40, and 77 both are 40, but the value 40 can hardly be said to be representative of the observations involved.

There are several measures commonly used to describe the dispersion of data, but we shall discuss only two, range and standard deviation. The *range* is the simplest and crudest measure of deviation and is simply the difference between the highest and lowest values in a data set. Its usefulness is limited, however, because only two items in the data set are used, and therefore, it provides no information about how far the other values are from the "average." This deficiency is illustrated in Table 8.3, which presents four data sets.

In case 1, even though the arithmetic means are the same for data sets *a* and *b*, the large difference in the range for each one should warn the observer that these two data sets are not alike. In case 2, however, both the

TABLE 8.3 Range as a Measure of Dispersion

	Data Set	Data Values	Mean	Range	Discrimination
Case 1	a	10, 20, 40, 60, 70	40	60	good
	b	39, 40, 40, 40, 41	40	2	
Case 2	c	10, 11, 12, 68, 69, 70	40	60	poor
	d	10, 40, 40, 40, 40, 70	40	60	

mean and the range are the same for data sets c and d, but the observations within them are hardly the same. In this case, a person who did not see the data values themselves might be misled into thinking that the data sets are the same.

A better expression of dispersion among the items in a data set may be obtained by first calculating the differences between the mean and each of the individual observations and then summing these differences. When this is done, however, the sum will always come out to zero, because in essence, the definition of arithmetic mean is the value that will cause this to happen. One way to overcome this problem is to disregard the sign of the difference values (i.e., take their absolute values) and then find the mean of these differences. The resulting value is known as the *average deviation*. A second way to overcome this problem (and, as it turns out, a better way) is to square the differences and then find their mean. The square root of this mean is called the *standard deviation, s,* and is represented mathematically as follows:

$$s = \sqrt{\frac{\Sigma(x_i - \bar{x})^2}{n-1}} \qquad\qquad (8.3)$$

where

$$s = \text{standard deviation}$$

$$(x_i - \bar{x})^2 = \text{summation of the squares of the differences between the observations and the arithmetic mean}$$

Note that the denominator of Equation 8.3 contains $n-1$ instead of n. This is because statisticians have observed that better estimates of the true standard deviation (σ) are obtained when $n-1$ is used instead of n. Example 8.3 shows the steps in calculating a standard deviation.

Example 8.3: An engineer was asked to determine whether the average air quality in a certain assembly plant was within the OSHA guidelines. The following air-quality readings were collected: 81, 86, 80, 91, 83, 83, 96, 85, 89. Calculate (a) the arithmetic mean, (b) the range, and (c) the standard deviation of these readings.

Solution: (a) The arithmetic mean is calculated from Equation 8.2:

$$\bar{x} = \frac{\Sigma x_i}{n} = \frac{774}{9} = 86$$

(b) The range is obtained by subtracting the smallest from the largest reading; thus,

$$\text{Range} = 96 - 80 = 16$$

(c) The standard deviation is calculated using Equation 8.3 and the values from Table 8.4.

TABLE 8.4 Standard Deviation Computations

Reading, X_i	Mean, $\bar{x}$	$X_i - \bar{x}$	$(X_i - \bar{x})^2$
81	86	−5	25
86	86	0	0
80	86	−6	36
91	86	5	25
83	86	−3	9
83	86	−3	9
96	86	10	100
85	86	−1	1
89	86	3	9
$\Sigma X_i = 774$	$\bar{x} = \dfrac{\Sigma X_i}{n} = 86$	$\Sigma(X_i - \bar{x}) = 0$	$\Sigma(X_i - \bar{x})^2 = 214$

$$s = \sqrt{\frac{214}{9-1}} = 5.17$$

Problems p8.17–p8.21

▲ 8.5 The Normal Distribution

It was recognized long ago that after repeating an experiment many times, it is possible to characterize the results obtained in a given trial as being either more common or more uncommon. For example, if someone who had previously never seen a pair of dice wanted to know the likelihood of rolling a 2, 5, 12, or any other possible number, that person would roll the dice hundreds of times and observe the results. In this case, the person would find that 7 occurs much more frequently than either 2 or 12 does. Comparatively speaking, then, 7 would be common and 2 or 12 rare. If the frequency of occurrence of each number (as obtained from many repeated experiments) is plotted, a graph showing the pattern of occurrence will be obtained. Such a graph is called a *distribution* (as discussed in Section 8.1), and from it, the likelihood of occurrence of a given number can be obtained. This information can then be used, for example, to determine whether a process is in or out of control or if a treatment applied to a test group has been effective.

It should be pointed out that commonly occurring distributions come in many different shapes. The only one that will be described here is the most important one and is known as the normal distribution. A *normal distribution* is a bell-shaped curve that is symmetrical around its highest point. The highest point on the curve corresponds to the arithmetic mean, the median (because it is symmetrical) and the mode (because it represents the value that occurs the greatest number of times). Figure 8.3 is a graph of a

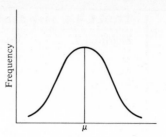

Figure 8.3 Normal curve.

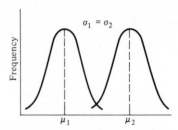

Figure 8.4 Different means, same standard deviation.

normal curve, which shows that the frequency associated with any observation decreases as its distance from the mean increases.

   Although all normal curves have the same general shape, their exact
shape is a function of two things, the mean and the standard deviation.
Figures 8.4 and 8.5 illustrate the effects of different means and standard
deviations.

   An important characteristic of all normal distributions is that for any
specified number of standard deviations away from the mean, the proportion of the total area under the curve *will always be the same*. Thus, in Figure
8.6, the distributions have different means and different standard deviations, but the proportional areas (and hence the proportion of observations)

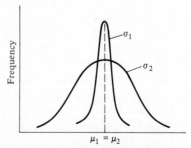

Figure 8.5 Different standard deviations, same means.

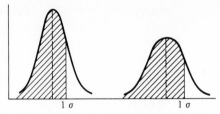

Figure 8.6 Equal proportions under normal curves.

to the left of $\mu + 1\sigma$ are exactly the same. This information can be used to make inferences regarding the likelihood that the means of two sets of data are the same, but such a determination is beyond the scope of this book.

The area under a given portion of the distribution can be determined by referring to tables that show the relationship between z scores and areas under the curve. A z score is simply the number of standard deviations away from the mean that a given point is located. For example, a z score of $+2$ refers to the point two standard deviations *above* the mean. A z score of -0.75 refers to a point 0.75 standard deviations *below* the mean. The z score for any point x along the x-axis can be determined from Equation 8.4:

$$z = \frac{x - \bar{x}}{s} \tag{8.4}$$

Table 8.5 shows the area under the normal curve *to the left of* the respective z values. Thus, for z = 0 (i.e., at an x value equal to the mean), the area to the left of that point is 0.50, meaning that 50 percent of the observations fall below that point. Similarly, for a z score of -1.96, only 2.5 percent of the

TABLE 8.5 Area Under Curve to Left of z

z Score	Proportion of area to left of z
-3.0	0.001
-2.58	0.005
-2.33	0.01
-2.0	0.023
-1.96	0.025
-1.65	0.05
-1.0	0.16
0	0.50
$+1.0$	0.84
$+1.65$	0.95
$+1.96$	0.975
$+2.0$	0.977
$+2.33$	0.99
$+2.58$	0.995
$+3.0$	0.999

observations are below that point. Obviously, if the mean and standard deviation are known, the z score can be converted into an *x*-value, as illustrated in Example 8.4.

Example 8.4: A data set consisting of 120 numbers is known to have a mean of 32 and a standard deviation of 6.10. Determine (a) the number of points to the left of a z score of $+1.0$, (b) the data value associated with a z score of -1.0, and (c) the number of observations between the z scores of $+1.96$ and -1.96.

Solution: (a) From Table 8.5, the proportion of the area to the left of $+1.0$ is 0.84, or 84 percent. Therefore, the number of data points is

$$\text{no. pts.} = (0.84)(120) = 101$$

(b) Use Equation 8.4 to convert a z score (z) to a raw score (x):

$$-1.0 = \frac{x - 32}{6.10}$$

$$x = 25.9$$

(c) The number of observations between $z = +1.96$ and $z = -1.96$ is proportional to the area under the curve between the two values. The area between $z = +1.96$ and -1.96 is equal to the area to the left of $+1.96$ minus the area to the left of -1.96 (see Figure 8.7). Thus,

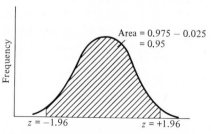

Figure 8.7 Area between $z = -1.96$ and $z = +1.96$.

$$\text{area} = 0.975 - 0.025 = 0.95 = 95\%$$

The number of observations within this area, then, is

$$\text{no. pts.} = (0.95)(120) = 114$$

Comment: From part (c), the number of data points within ± 1.96 standard deviations of the mean was shown to be 95 percent. As an exercise, show that 68 percent of the points fall between ± 1 standard deviation.

Supplementary Example 8.9
Problems p8.22 – p8.28

▲ 8.6 Coefficient of Correlation

Scientists and engineers continually make investigations, and many times, these investigations are for determining the relationship, or correlation, between two variables. When the relationship between the variables can best be described by a straight line, the variables are said to be *linearly correlated*. Figure 8.8 shows a perfect linear correlation between two variables, identified as P and Q.

This correlation is described as "perfect" because every point falls exactly on the straight line that connects them. Most of the time, even when two variables are linearly related, not all of the data points fall on the line. In Figure 8.9, for example, the linear relationship between U and R is not perfect.

When two variables are linearly correlated, but the correlation is not perfect, it is certainly desirable to be able to determine the extent to which the variables are related. Such a measure has been developed, and it is called the *Pearson coefficient of correlation*, represented by the letter r.

The correlation coefficient measures the extent to which the variation in one variable is explained by the variation in the other. In a perfect *direct* correlation, each unit of change in the variable plotted on the x-axis causes a unit of change in the same direction for the variable plotted on the y-axis. In such a case (Figure 8.8), the correlation coefficient would be $+1$. A perfect *negative* correlation exists when an increase in one variable causes a decrease in the other. Figure 8.10 shows a perfect negative correlation between V and W, for which r would be -1.

For either direct or negative correlations that are not perfect, r values between -1 and $+1$ are obtained, with an r value of zero meaning that the two variables are not linearly correlated. The correlation coefficient, r, between two variables can be determined from the following equation:

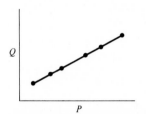
Figure 8.8 Perfect linear correlation.

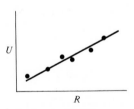
Figure 8.9 Imperfect linear correlation.

$$r = \frac{n\Sigma xy - (\Sigma x)(\Sigma y)}{\sqrt{[n\Sigma x^2 - (\Sigma x)^2][n\Sigma y^2 - (\Sigma y)^2]}} \qquad (8.5)$$

where

$$x, y = \text{variables}$$

$$n = \text{no. of pairs of variables}$$

If the value obtained from Equation 8.5 is squared (i.e., r^2), a better measure of the association between the variables involved will be obtained. This measure is called the *coefficient of determination*, and it represents the *fraction* of the variation in y that is accounted for by the variation in x. Example 8.5 illustrates the calculation of r and r^2.

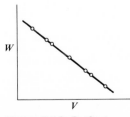
Figure 8.10 Perfect negative correlation.

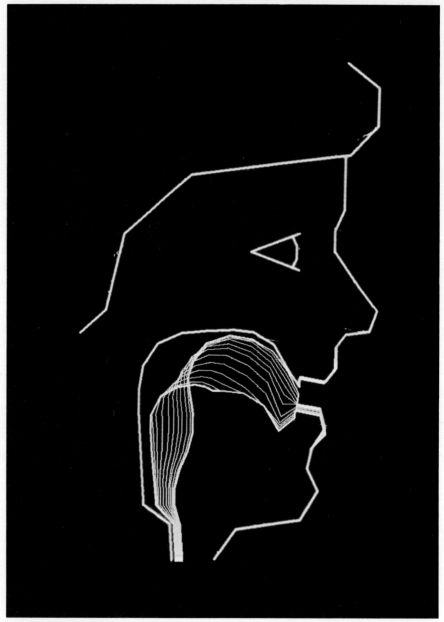

Illustration 8.2 Statistical techniques are widely used in voice recognition systems. (Courtesy AT&T, Bell Laboratories)

Example 8.5: Students in a strength-of-materials class were told that the elongation of an axially loaded bar is a function of several variables, including the bar's cross-sectional area. The students decided to set up an experiment to collect data on elongation (δ) versus area (A) for a plastic material and calculate the correlation coefficient and coefficient of determination. Their data are as follows:

A, cm²	0.6	1	2	5	8	11
δ, cm	2.5	1.5	0.8	0.3	0.2	0.1

Solution: The values needed in Equation 8.5 are most easily obtained from a table such as that shown below, in which x was arbitrarily chosen to represent variable A and y variable δ.

TABLE 8.6 Calculation of Coefficient of Correlation

x	y	x^2	y^2	xy
0.6	2.5	0.36	6.25	1.5
1	1.5	1	2.25	1.5
2	0.8	4	0.64	1.6
5	0.3	25	0.09	1.5
8	0.2	64	0.04	1.6
11	0.1	121	0.01	1.1
27.6	5.4	215.36	9.28	8.8

$$r = \frac{6(8.8) - (27.6)(5.4)}{\sqrt{[6(215.36) - (27.6)^2][6(9.28) - (5.4)^2]}}$$
$$= -0.81$$

$$r^2 = 0.66$$

The negative r value indicates that the variables studied are negatively related. The r^2 value of 0.66 means that approximately 66 percent of the variation observed in elongation (y) can be explained by the variation in the cross-sectional area (x) of the material.

Comment: Even though relatively high values were obtained for r and r^2, the plotted data in Figure 8.11 show that a curvilinear relationship would be more appropriate than the linear one assumed here. A graph showing the relationship between the variables under consideration is called a *scattergram* and obviously is an important part of determining correlation.

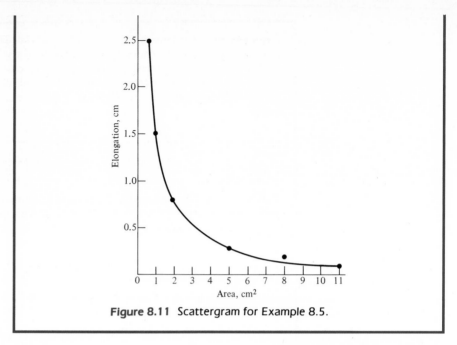

Figure 8.11 Scattergram for Example 8.5.

Supplementary Example 8.10
Problems p8.29–p8.35

▲ 8.7 Least Squares Regression

One reason to collect information about the relationship between two variables is for prediction. That is, in scientific investigation or engineering design, it is desirable to be able to predict the value of one variable from knowledge about the other. This process of finding the relationship between variables and using it to make predictions is called *regression analysis*. In order to do this, the mathematical equation that expresses the relationship between the two variables must be determined. The variable that can be arbitrarily manipulated is called the *independent variable* and is usually represented by x. The other is the *dependent variable* and is represented by y.

When two variables are linearly related, the relational mathematical expression is in the form $y = a + bx$. (This equation is the same as that introduced in Chapter 6 as $y = mx + b$, but the form used here is that most commonly found in textbooks on statistics). The problem, then, is to find the values of a and b that will provide the best-fitting line (i.e., the regression line) through the points. There are several methods for accomplishing this from experimental data, but only the most commonly used one, the least squares method, will be discussed here.

The *least squares method* is based on the premise that the best-fitting

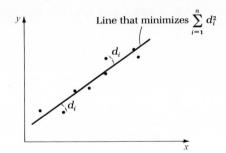

Figure 8.12 Least squares regression line.

line is the one that will minimize the sum of the squares of the differences between the data points and the line. In Figure 8.12, the best line is the one that minimizes the sum of d_i^2.

For the least squares method, the straight-line equation is usually expressed in the following form:

$$y = \bar{y} + b(x - \bar{x}) \tag{8.6}$$

where

$$\bar{y} = \text{mean of } y\text{-values (dependent variable)}$$

$$\bar{x} = \text{mean of } x\text{-values (independent variable)}$$

$$b = \text{slope of line}$$

The value of b can be determined from Equation 8.7:

$$b = \frac{n\Sigma xy - (\Sigma x)(\Sigma y)}{n\Sigma x^2 - (\Sigma x)^2} \tag{8.7}$$

The determination of a regression line using the least squares method is illustrated in Example 8.6.

Example 8.6: In certain colored solutions, the absorption of monochromatic light is proportional to the concentration of the substance causing the color. The straight line produced from such solutions is called a *standard curve*. From five concentrations of an unknown solution, students in a chemistry lab collected the following data:

concentration, x	0.50	1.0	1.5	2.0	3.0
absorbance, y	0.15	0.30	0.41	0.56	0.80

Determine the equation of the line of best fit through the five points.

Solution: The values required for Equations 8.6 and 8.7 can be obtained from Table 8.7.

TABLE 8.7 Values for Calculating b

x	y	x^2	xy
0.50	0.15	0.25	0.08
1.0	0.30	1.00	0.30
1.5	0.41	2.25	0.62
2.0	0.56	4.00	1.12
3.0	0.80	9.00	2.40
$\Sigma x = 8.0$	$\Sigma y = 2.22$	$\Sigma x^2 = 16.50$	$\Sigma xy = 4.52$

Solving for b (from Equation 8.7), $\bar{x}$, and $\bar{y}$:

$$b = \frac{5(4.52) - (8.0)(2.22)}{5(16.50) - (8)^2} = 0.26$$

$$\bar{x} = \frac{\Sigma x}{5} = \frac{8.0}{5} = 1.6$$

$$\bar{y} = \frac{\Sigma y}{5} = \frac{2.22}{5} = 0.44$$

The equation for the line, therefore, is

$$y = 0.44 + 0.26(x - 1.6)$$

Supplementary Example 8.10
Problems p8.36 – p8.39

● CHAPTER SUMMARY

This chapter described the most common techniques of data manipulation: frequency distributions, cumulative frequency distributions, the normal distribution, and three measures of central tendency. For determining the dispersion of data about the mean, we explained the concept of standard deviation and the relationship between standard deviation and z scores. Finally, we discussed the meaning of the Pearson correlation coefficient and the least squares method of linear regression.

Supplementary Examples

Example 8.7: From the following frequency distribution, determine (a) the cell that contains the value 10, (b) the total number of data points, and (c) the percentage of values with magnitudes of less than 40.

Cell Boundaries	Frequency
0 – 10	5
10 – 20	21
20 – 30	9

30–40	7
40–50	5
>50	4

Solution: (a) The upper cell boundary is not included in the cell. Therefore, the value 10 is in the 10–20 cell.

(b) The total number of data points is equal to the sum of the frequencies:

$$\text{no. points} = 5 + 21 + 9 + 7 + 5 + 4 = 51$$

(c) The percentage of values <40 is

$$\% < 40 = \frac{5 + 21 + 9 + 7}{51} \times 100 = 82\%$$

Example 8.8: From the data in Example 8.7, construct an "or more" cumulative frequency table.

Solution: In this type of frequency distribution, the frequencies represent the number of times the lower cell boundary has been equaled or exceeded. The tabulation for this condition is as follows:

Data Value	*Cumulative Frequency*
0 or more	51
10 or more	46
20 or more	25
30 or more	16
40 or more	9
50 or more	4

Example 8.9: (a) Calculate the z score for an x value of 9.3 if the data are from a normal distribution having a mean of 7.1 and a standard deviation of 1.3. (b) What x value would be equal to or greater than 99 percent of the x values?

Solution: (a) From equation 8.4, the z score is

$$z = \frac{9.3 - 7.1}{1.3} = 1.69$$

(b) From Table 8.4, a z score of 2.58 would include 99 percent of the values. The x value associated with a z score of 2.58 is

$$2.58 = \frac{x - 7.1}{1.3}$$

$$x = 10.5$$

Example 8.10: An engineering student who was studying the effect of a toxic pollutant on a certain type of fish conducted a bioassay test and collected the following data:

Pollutant Concentration, mg/L	Percent of Fish Surviving After Two Days
20	2
15	10
10	40
5	70
1	99

(a) Calculate the correlation coefficient between the variables and (b) determine the equation of the straight line of best fit.

Solution: (a) Table 8.8 contains the values needed for calculating the correlation coefficient. The pollutant concentration is represented by x and the percent of fish surviving is represented by y.

TABLE 8.8 Values for calculating *r*

x	y	x^2	y^2	xy
20	2	400	4	40
15	10	225	100	150
10	40	100	1600	400
5	70	25	4900	350
1	99	1	9801	99
$\Sigma x = 51$	$\Sigma y = 221$	$\Sigma x^2 = 751$	$\Sigma y^2 = 16\ 405$	$\Sigma xy = 1039$

The correlation coefficient is calculated from Equation 8.5 as follows:

$$r = \frac{(5)(1039) - (51)(221)}{\sqrt{[5(751) - (51)^2][5(16\ 405) - (221)^2]}}$$

$$r = -0.98$$

Thus, there is a very strong negative correlation between pollutant concentration and fish survivability.

(b) The least squares regression line is obtained from Equation 8.6. The calculation of $\bar{x}$ and $\bar{y}$ is as follows:

$$\bar{x} = \frac{51}{5} = 10.2 \quad \bar{y} = \frac{221}{5} = 44.2$$

The value of b is determined from Equation 8.7 using the totals from Table 8.8 in part (a)

$$b = \frac{5(1039) - (51)(221)}{(5)(751) - (51)^2}$$

$$b = -5.3$$

The equation for the regression line, therefore, is

$$y = 44.2 - 5.3(x - 10.2)$$

Comment: You can check the reasonableness of the equation by inserting various values of x and then comparing the resulting y-values to those of the original data.

▲ Problems

p8.1   From the following data, determine the frequency for each of the cells shown below:

1, 9, 10, 8, 5, 3, 2, 3, 2, 3, 7, 9, 10, 14, 3, 15, 2,
9, 1, 7, 8, 3, 3, 2, 9, 7, 6, 15, 3, 2, 1, 4, 4, 12

Cell Boundaries
1–4
4–8
8–12
12–16

p8.2   The heights of buildings in a certain downtown section of a small city were recorded as follows (in meters):

6, 10, 8, 7, 5, 4, 6, 7, 4, 9, 5, 4, 6, 11, 5, 6, 9.

If a histogram with four cells were desired, (a) what would be the cell width, (b) what would be the lowest cell boundary if no data points are to fall on the boundaries, (c) what would be the lower and upper boundaries for the first cell, and (d) how many points would be in each cell?

p8.3   The speeds of automobiles at a radar checkpoint on a freeway were measured as follows (in mph):

56, 50, 62, 68, 57, 55, 53, 59, 62, 71, 70, 54,
58, 61, 62, 56, 56, 73, 69, 49, 54, 59, 61

For a histogram with 5 cells, (a) what cell width would you recommend, (b) what would be the lowest cell boundary if the boundaries are to be more accurate than the data are, and (c) how many data points would be in each cell?

p8.4   In preparing a histogram from collected data, an engineer decided to use the following grouping of values: 0–3, 3–6, 6–9, 9–12, and 12–15. (a) What is the cell width, and (b) what cell would contain the value of 9?

p8.5   For the frequency distribution shown below, determine (a) the cell width, (b) the cell that contains the value 15, and (c) the frequency of occurrence of values that are greater than or equal to 5 but less than 10.

Cell Boundaries	Frequency
0–5	3
5–10	9
10–15	11
15–20	2

p8.6 Prepare a cumulative frequency distribution for the data from p8.5.

p8.7 For the frequency distribution shown below, determine (a) the cell width, (b) the number of values whose magnitude is less than 125, and (c) the percentage of values with a magnitude less than 150.

Cell Boundaries	Frequency
50–75	35
75–100	50
100–125	60
125–150	63
150–175	47

p8.8 The following running times were recorded for a lift station pump (in h/day):

12.3, 15.1, 6.3, 9.1, 20.7, 15.4, 11.9, 9.3, 17.9, 8.2,
7.9, 7.6, 14.3, 14.2, 10.8, 8.6, 13.4, 10.2, 9.8

Group the data in the cells shown below, and determine (a) the frequency of running times equal to or greater than 9.0, (b) the number of running times that were less than 18.0 h/day, and (c) the number of values greater than or equal to 9.0 but less than 18.0 h/day.

Cell Boundaries
6.0–9.0
9.0–12.0
12.0–15.0
15.0–18.0
18.0–21.0

p8.9 For the data set that includes the numbers from 1 to 100, an initial cell boundary of 0.5, and a cell width of 5, determine (a) the number of values included in the first cell, (b) the number of values that are less than 35.5, (c) the number of values between 20.5 and 75.5, and (d) the percentage of values that are less than 40.5.

p8.10 For the data set that includes all odd numbers between 20 and 70, start with an initial lower cell boundary of 20 and use a cell width of 6 to determine (a) the number of values less than 52 (b) the number of values between 40 and 60, and (c) the percentage of values between 32 and 64.

p8.11   From the grouped, discrete data shown below, determine (a) the cell width, (b) the number of cells, (c) the number of data points, (c) the percentage of readings that have a value less than or equal to 12, (e) the percentage of readings that have a value less than 13, and (f) the percentage of readings having a value less than or equal to 24 but greater than 8.

Cell Boundaries	Frequency
1–4	8
5–8	6
9–12	14
13–16	9
17–20	5
21–24	4

p8.12   For the following numbers, determine (a) the mean, (b) the median, and (c) the mode:

3, 6, 9, 3, 4, 2, 8, 7, 6, 5, 5, 3, 9, 1, 4, 3, 8, 10, 11

p8.13   From the following data, determine (a) the mean, (b) the median, and (c) the mode:

4, 7, 2, 6, 9, 3, 5, 6, 2, 9, 4, 6, 3, 5, 4, 8, 6

p8.14   The wastewater flow rate into a small wastewater treatment plant varies with the time of day. The following flow rates were measured on an "average" day, beginning at 12:00 midnight (all values in m^3/h):

300, 290, 250, 210, 205, 285, 380, 505, 490, 420, 400,
450, 500, 420, 390, 380, 425, 500, 540, 500, 440, 400, 350, 330

Determine (a) the mean, (b) the median, and (c) the mode.

p8.15   Traffic counts along a certain four-lane highway were summarized as follows:

Time of Day	Cars/h
12:00 midnight–6:00 A.M.	110
6:00 A.M.–10:00 A.M.	900
10:00 A.M.–1:00 P.M.	600
1:00 P.M.–4:00 P.M.	500
4:00 P.M.–8:00 P.M.	1000
8:00 P.M.–12:00 midnight	300

Determine (a) the mean, (b) the median, and (c) the mode in units of cars/h.

p8.16   For the van pool data shown below, determine (a) the mean, (b) the median, and (c) the mode of the number of persons per van.

Persons/Van	Frequency
2	10
3	14
4	13
5	24
6	15
7	5
8	3
9	1

p8.17   If the $\Sigma(x_i - \bar{x})^2$ for 40 numbers is equal to 926, what is the standard deviation?

p8.18   Calculate the standard deviation using the information in the following table:

x	$(x_i - \bar{x})$	$(x_i - \bar{x})^2$
8	3	9
5	0	0
3	−2	4
7	2	4
2	−3	9

p8.19   For the following numbers, determine (a) the range and (b) the standard deviation:

$$5, \quad 4, \quad 3, \quad 4, \quad 4, \quad 4$$

p8.20   Find the standard deviation for the following numbers:

$$7, \quad 8, \quad 4, \quad 9, \quad 7, \quad 2, \quad 3$$

p8.21   The monthly kWh readings in a small manufacturing plant are 185, 230, 160, 310, 196, 375, and 280. Determine (a) the mean and (b) the standard deviation of the readings.

p8.22   If two sets of numbers (i.e., set 1 and set 2) both have a mean of 50 but set 1 has a standard deviation of 2.0 and set 2 has a standard deviation of 8.0, show clearly, through a sketch, the difference between the two sets.

p8.23   Determine the proportion of the area under a normal curve (a) to the left of a z value of −1.96, (b) between the z values of +1.65 and −1.96, (c) between the z values of +2.33 and +1.0, and (d) between the z values of +1.65 and −2.58.

p8.24   For data that have a mean of 15 and a standard deviation of 5, determine the z score for (a) $x = 20$, (b) $x = 15$, and (c) $x = 5$.

p8.25   For data that have a mean of 220 and a standard deviation of 25, determine (a) the z score at $x = 280$ and (b) the area to the left of $x = 280$.

p8.26   For data that have a mean of 66 and a standard deviation of 12, find the value of x that corresponds to a z score of (a) +1.96, (b) +1.0, (c) zero, and (d) −1.25.

p8.27 In order to determine the number of black jelly beans in a 1-lb bag, 300 bags were counted. The mean number of blacks was 18, with a standard deviation of 5. How many of the bags contained (a) 18 or fewer black ones, (b) more than 23 black ones, (c) between 18 and 23 blacks, and (d) less than 8 blacks?

p8.28 If 2500 concrete samples had a mean compressive strength of 3000 psi, with a standard deviation of 200, how many of the samples had compressive strengths (a) less than 2500 psi, (b) greater than 2700 psi, and (c) between 2700 and 3100 psi?

p8.29 If two variables were known to be correlated, the correlation coefficient would lie between what values if the correlation were (a) positive and (b) negative?

p8.30 Determine the correlation coefficient from the following information: $n = 30$, $\Sigma xy = 350$, $\Sigma x = 63$, $\Sigma y = 91$, $\Sigma x^2 = 420$, $\Sigma y^2 = 506$.

p8.31 Calculate the correlation coefficient from the following information: $n = 17$, $\Sigma xy = 1037$, $\Sigma x = 175$, $\Sigma y = 75$, $\Sigma x^2 = 463$, $\Sigma y^2 = 254$.

p8.32 From the data below, calculate Σx^2, Σxy, $(\Sigma y)^2$, and $n\Sigma y^2$.

x	2, 5, 6, 8, 9
y	1, 3, 3, 5, 7

p8.33 Find the correlation coefficient for the data in p8.32.

p8.34 In order to determine the relationship, if any, between the total liters of gasoline pumped and the average traffic count at a location, an engineer collected the following data:

Liters Pumped/h	Traffic Count, Hundreds of Cars/h
10	3
11	4
15	7
21	10
6	2
8	3
7	2

What is (a) the dependent variable, (b) the value of Σxy, and (c) the correlation coefficient?

p8.35 In an electrical engineering laboratory experiment, the relationship between voltage and current flow in a particular circuit was found to be as follows:

v, volts	10	15	25	40	49	64
I, amps	1	1.6	2.8	4.3	5.0	6.2

If voltage is represented as x and current flow as y, solve for the following: (a) $(\Sigma x)^2$, (b) Σy^2, (c) $(\Sigma x)(\Sigma y)$, and (d) the correlation coefficient, r.

p8.36 For the data of p8.35, determine the equation of the line of best fit using the least squares method.

p8.37 From the data shown below, determine the equation of the line of best fit using the least squares method.

x	8	6	3	5	9
y	3	2	1	2	4

p8.38 From the data shown below, determine the equation of the line of best fit using the least squares method.

x	26	42	12	75	3	10	30
y	60	100	20	200	5	25	70

p8.39 In a biology experiment studying bacterial inhibitors in tooth paste, the following data were collected:

inhibitor concentration, %	0.1	0.50	1.0	1.5	2.0	2.5	3.0
viable cells after 10 min	4000	3600	3000	2500	2200	1800	1000

Determine the equation of the line of best fit using the least squares method.

9

Computers

The development of the transistor, followed by a series of discoveries concerning the miniaturization of electronic circuits, has made possible the construction of computers in their present forms. Each new series of computers is smaller, cheaper, and more powerful than the preceding one. Computers represent one of a very few product areas whose price-to-performance ratio has steadily improved with time.

There are at least two ways to study computers. The computer may be viewed as a tool to be used in solving a particular problem or as an engineering system that itself is to be studied and further improved. Virtually without exception, all engineers and technicians now use computers to perform a wide range of engineering and management tasks. It is helpful to such users to understand generally how computers work, their capabilities, and their limitations.

In the first part of this chapter we will discuss some of the fundamental concepts concerning how computers are built and operate. In a later section some current applications of computers will be presented including computer workstations and computer-aided engineering.

Objective: The objective of this chapter is to introduce some of the basic principles concerning how computers operate and are used.

Criteria: After completing this chapter, you should be able to do the following:

- **9.1** Count in a given number system and state why nearly all digital computers use the binary number system.
- **9.2** Convert the contents of an 8-bit binary word into one of the following forms, depending on the desired interpretation: decimal, hexadecimal, or ASCII.

179

Illustration 9.1 The first transistors were primitive by today's standards, yet they revolutionized the electronics industry. Transistors provided the reliability required to make computers practical devices. (Courtesy AT&T, Bell Laboratories)

Illustration 9.2 One of the world's first commercial electronic computers was used to predict the outcome of the 1952 Presidential election. (Courtesy Sperry Corporation)

■ **9.3** Draw the logic symbol and list the truth table for any given logic gate, and develop the corresponding truth table for a logic circuit containing no more than six logic gates.

■ **9.4** List the elements necessary to construct a microcomputer and explain their function.

■ **9.5** Briefly describe each of the following uses of computers.

    a. Electronic Communications
    b. Word Processing
    c. Spreadsheet Programs
    d. Data Base Management Systems
    e. Computer-Aided Design
    f. Computer-Aided Manufacturing

▲ 9.1 Number Systems

Before describing the binary, or base 2, number system used in modern digital computers, we shall review the decimal or base 10 number system. Consider the meaning implied by the number 1432.56. The digits in the number have a place value associated with their position relative to the decimal point. For example, the 2 has a place value of 1, or more properly, 10^0, associated with it. Similarly, the place value of the 4 is 100, or 10^2, and the place value of the 6 is 0.01, or 10^{-2}. The number 1432.56 can be written in an expanded form showing the place value of its digits, as follows:

$$1 \times 10^3 + 4 \times 10^2 + 3 \times 10^1 + 2 \times 10^0 + 5 \times 10^{-1} + 6 \times 10^{-2}$$

Although this expression is correct mathematically, it would be exceedingly clumsy to write all numbers in this expanded form. Hence only the coefficients that multiply the various powers of the number system base are written. The place value or, equivalently, the appropriate power of the base is implied by the position of the digit relative to, in this case, the decimal point.

Also note that in a base 10 system, exactly ten symbols are needed for the coefficients that are multiplied by the various powers of the number system base. Consider the process of counting in base 10. The sequence of numbers generated is as follows:

$$0 \times 10^0$$
$$1 \times 10^0$$
$$\cdot$$
$$\cdot$$
$$\cdot$$
$$9 \times 10^0$$
$$1 \times 10^1 + 0 \times 10^0$$

$$1 \times 10^1 + 1 \times 10^0$$
$$\cdot$$
$$\cdot$$
$$\cdot$$

The next-to-last expression in this sequence is of particular interest. Note that an eleventh unique symbol is not needed for the number 11 (or any higher number) and that its inclusion would, in fact, destroy the systematic process of writing coefficients and assigning to them understood place values. In the base 10 system, only ten unique symbols are required for coefficients.

The counting process is implemented in exactly the same manner in number systems having other bases. For example, counting upward in a base 5 system would produce the following sequence:

0, 1, 2, 3, 4, 10, 11, 12, 13, 14, 20, 21, 22, 23, 24, 30 . . .

Observe that only five coefficients (0, 1, 2, 3, 4) are needed. The place value of the right most digit is 5^0, and the place value of the next digit is 5^1. As larger base 5 numbers are written, the additional coefficients may be added as needed, with their place values assuming correspondingly higher powers of 5.

In order to discuss numbers written using various bases, a small subscript (also sometimes called a *radix*) is often used. Thus, 241_{10} is a base 10 number, and $A2F_{16}$ is a hexadecimal number. Using this notational scheme, is it true that $4_{10} = 4_7$? To answer this question, the meaning of the coefficient 4 must be understood. In both number systems, the 4 means that four things are being counted or referenced. Appearing between the following parentheses are four X's (XXXX). In any number system with a base of 5 or more, the number of X's is said to be four. The following always holds:

$$4_5 = 4_6 = 4_7 = \cdot \cdot \cdot = 4_{10} = 4_{16} = \cdot \cdot \cdot$$

Another concept related to number system theory that causes a great deal of confusion is illustrated by the following question: Does $10_8 = 8_{10}$? This question may be answered by writing the numbers in an expanded form consisting of coefficients multiplied by the corresponding place values.

$$10_8 = ?\ 8_{10}$$
$$1_8 \times 8_{10}^1 + 0_8 \times 8_{10}^0 = ?\ 8_{10}$$
$$1_{10} \times 8_{10}^1 + 0_{10} \times 8_{10}^0 = ?\ 8_{10}$$
$$8_{10} + 0_{10} = 8_{10}$$

The two expressions are seen to be equivalent. Table 9.1 provides a convenient way of comparing equivalent numbers expressed in various number systems.

TABLE 9.1 Equivalent Decimal, Binary, Octal, and Hexadecimal Numbers

Decimal	Binary	Octal	Hexadecimal
0	0	0	0
1	1	1	1
2	10	2	2
3	11	3	3
4	100	4	4
5	101	5	5
6	110	6	6
7	111	7	7
8	1000	10	8
9	1001	11	9
10	1010	12	A
11	1011	13	B
12	1100	14	C
13	1101	15	D
14	1110	16	E
15	1111	17	F
16	10000	20	10
17	10001	21	11
18	10010	22	12
19	10011	23	13
20	10100	24	14

Binary Number System and Computers

To understand why the binary number system is so widely used in digital computers, consider the following example. Suppose it is desired to represent numbers by cutting matchsticks into various lengths that are proportional to the number being represented. The available matchsticks have a length of 4 cm, and the number 7_{10} is to be represented. Since the base 10 system is being used and a given match stick is to represent a coefficient, each match stick must be cut into one of ten unique lengths. For the example being considered, the match stick could be cut to $7/10 \times 4$ cm $= 2.8$ cm. Similarly, a 6_{10} would be represented by a match stick 2.4 cm long, and an 8_{10} would require a match stick 3.2 cm long. A number like 14_{10} would be represented by two appropriately arranged match sticks.

A system based on the above ideas, although primitive, would certainly work, but consider the accuracy required both to cut and later to interpret the lengths of the various matchsticks. Suppose the 2.8-cm matchstick of the above example were mixed with other matchsticks representing other coefficients. A ruler and a rather tedious search would probably be required to find the 2.8-cm matchstick. In an analogous way, it is certainly possible to build digital computers based on electronic circuits having ten unique voltage or current levels, each representing a base 10 coefficient, but this is not particularly easy or cheap when compared with other alterna-

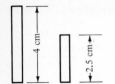

Figure 9.1 Matchsticks representing the number 7_{10}.

tives. In the previous example, suppose it were agreed to use matchsticks having lengths of 1, 2.5, or 4 cm only. It would be very easy to distinguish among the various lengths, but now a single matchstick could represent only a coefficient of 0, 1, or 2. Numbers of arbitrary size or, equivalently, containing arbitrary numbers of coefficients could still be represented, but a large number of matchsticks might have to be used in combination to represent them. The number 7_{10} from the previous discussion could be represented by two matchsticks, as shown in Figure 9.1. The first would be 4 cm long and represent a 2, and the second would be 2.5 cm long and represent a 1. This version of the representation of the number 7 is based on a base 3 system in which

$$7_{10} = 2_3 \times 3_{10}^1 + 1_3 \times 3_{10}^0$$
$$= 21_3$$

The simplest and cheapest possible electrical circuits are those that have only two possible states (on and off). Modern integrated-circuit technology allows hundreds of thousands of such circuits to be packaged in a very small volume at a very low cost. Because of this technology, virtually all modern digital computers are based on a binary number system. The choice is arbitrary, but often an ON state is represented as a 1 and an OFF state becomes a binary 0. Information stored in a computer becomes strings of ones and zeroes that are the coefficients of the binary numbers used to represent the information.

When dealing with computers, hexadecimal numbers are also widely used. To see the reason for this, consider the following binary number: 1011010111011111_2. Look away from this page and try to recite this number. Most people have difficulty remembering long strings of binary digits like this. But when this binary number is converted into a hexadecimal number, it becomes $B5DF_{16}$. Most people find this number easier to remember because they find it easier to deal with smaller groups of a large variety of symbols than large groups of similar symbols. Since conversion from binary into hexadecimal and back is relatively easy, much of the information pertinent to computers supplies numbers in hexadecimal form, even though the computers actually are binary devices.

Supplementary Examples 9.9 – 9.10
Problems p9.1 – p9.4

▲ 9.2 Binary Representations of Information

A binary number system is based on powers of 2, and only two different digits or coefficients are permitted. The coefficients of a binary number are called *bits*, and a group of bits when considered together is called a *word*. The exact number of bits that comprise a word varies depending on the

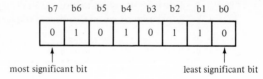

b7	b6	b5	b4	b3	b2	b1	b0
0	1	0	1	0	1	1	0

most significant bit   least significant bit

Figure 9.2 An eight-bit word.

computer design. Many current designs of small computers are based on words containing eight bits, and this length will be assumed in the following discussion.

A word within a computer may be visualized as a box containing eight compartments, each of which holds one bit. This idea is shown in Figure 9.2. The bits within a word are often identified by number (b7–b0), as shown in the figure. The terms *most significant bit* and *least significant bit* are also used to refer to the left-most and right-most bits, respectively.

The specific meaning attached to the contents of one or more words is determined by the program using the words rather than by the physical or electrical characteristics of the word itself. The same 8-bit word could, for example, store a binary number, a binary number with an associated sign, a binary code representing a letter of the alphabet, two 4-bit codes representing two decimal coefficients or hexadecimal coefficients, or even a binary code that directly instructs the computer to perform a specific task.

Decimal Interpretation of a Binary Word

Binary numbers may be converted into their base 10 equivalents by explicitly writing the binary coefficients times their respective place values and performing the indicated mathematical operations. The following example illustrates this process:

Example 9.1: Convert 01010110_2 into its base 10 equivalent.

Solution: The number is first rewritten as follows:

$$0_2 \times 2_{10}^7 + 1_2 \times 2_{10}^6 + 0_2 \times 2_{10}^5 + 1_2 \times 2_{10}^4 + 0_2 \times 2_{10}^3$$
$$+ 1_2 \times 2_{10}^2 + 1_2 \times 2_{10}^1 + 0_2 \times 2_{10}^0$$

The coefficients can immediately be converted into their base 10 equivalents, and the various powers of 2 can be substituted, producing the following result:

$$0_{10} \times 128_{10} + 1_{10} \times 64_{10} + 0_{10} \times 32_{10} + 1_{10} \times 16_{10} + 0_{10} \times 8_{10}$$
$$+ 1_{10} \times 4_{10} + 1_{10} \times 2_{10} + 0_{10} \times 1_{10}$$

which becomes

$$64_{10} + 16_{10} + 4_{10} + 2_{10} = 86_{10}$$

Comment: The various powers of 2 produce a relatively easily remembered sequence of numbers that is extremely useful and is as follows:

$$1, 2, 4, 8, 16, 32, 64, 128, 256, 512, 1024, 2048, 4096, 8192 \ldots$$

The binary-to-decimal conversion process then considers the binary number one bit at a time, starting with the least significant one. If the bit is a 1, then the corresponding term from the above sequence will be included in the sum that produces the answer. If the bit is a zero, the corresponding term will be omitted in the summing process. Figure 9.3 shows the place values of the bits in an 8-bit word.

128   64   32   16   8   4   2   1

Figure 9.3 Place values of bits in an eight-bit word.

Example 9.2: Convert 10110101_2 into decimal.

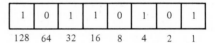

128   64   32   16   8   4   2   1

Figure 9.4 Eight-bit binary number and corresponding place values.

Solution: The number and the corresponding place values are shown in Figure 9.4. The answer is obtained by summing the place values for which the corresponding binary digit is a 1. The result is

$$128_{10} + 32_{10} + 16_{10} + 4_{10} + 1_{10} = 181_{10}$$

Hexadecimal Numbers

The term *hexadecimal* means sixteen, implying that sixteen coefficients are required and that the values of the place holders are powers of 16. The symbols 0 – 9 are used for the first ten symbols, but $10_{10} - 15_{10}$ are not acceptable, since they involve two symbols and would destroy the concept of place value. Additional single symbols thus are needed, and for convenience the first six letters of the alphabet are universally used. The following are equivalent:

$$10_{10} = A_{16}$$

$$11_{10} = B_{16}$$

$$12_{10} = C_{16}$$

$$13_{10} = D_{16}$$

$$14_{10} = E_{16}$$

$$15_{10} = F_{16}$$

Hexadecimal numbers are formed by using the same concepts as numbers in any other base system. The hexadecimal number $A2E4_{16}$ can be thought of as representing a compact way of writing the following mathematical expression:

$$A_{16} \times 16_{10}^3 + 2_{16} \times 16_{10}^2 + E_{16} \times 16_{10}^1 + 4_{16} \times 16_{10}^0$$

Hexadecimal Interpretation of a Binary Word

As previously pointed out, a hexadecimal number is composed of various combinations of exactly sixteen coefficients (0_{16} to F_{16}). To investigate the relationship between binary numbers and hexadecimal numbers, consider how the hexadecimal coefficients could be equivalently represented in binary forms. Since 16_{10} possible digits must be represented, exactly 4_{10} binary digits must be used. (It takes 4_{10} binary digits to count from 0_{10} to 15_{10}.) As a result, an 8-bit binary word can store exactly two hexadecimal digits. The left four binary digits store the most significant hexadecimal digit, and the right four binary digits store the least significant hexadecimal digit. Figure 9.5 shows how this is done.

Example 9.3: Convert 10110111_2 into its hexadecimal equivalent.

Solution: The binary number is split into two parts of four digits each.

$$1011_2 \quad 0111_2$$
$$\text{MSD} \quad \text{LSD}$$

The left pattern is examined first:

$$1011_2 = 8_{10} + 2_{10} + 1_{10}$$
$$= 11_{10}$$
$$= B_{16}$$

The right pattern is then examined:

$$0111_2 = 4_{10} + 2_{10} + 1_{10}$$
$$= 7_{10}$$
$$= 7_{16}$$

so

$$10110111_2 = B7_{16}$$

Comment: Eight-bit binary words are often called *bytes*, and 4-bit parts, such as those considered here, are referred to as *nibbles*.

Binary numbers with more than eight bits may also be converted into hexadecimal numbers, using essentially the same process. This is illustrated in Example 9.4.

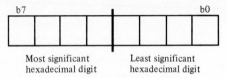

Figure 9.5 Hexadecimal interpretation of binary word.

Example 9.4: Convert 101101101_2 into hexadecimal.

Solution: Starting at the least significant bit, the binary number is divided into groups of four bits. Zeros may be added as most significant digits to ensure that each group has exactly four bits. The result is

$$0001 \quad 0110 \quad 1101_2$$

Each group of four bits is replaced by its hexadecimal equivalent, producing the desired result.

$$16D_{16}$$

Comment: Consider the middle group of four bits and the resulting 6_{16} in the final answer. Because of the place value associated with the middle group of bits, they can be rewritten as follows:

$$0_{10} \times 2_{10}^7 + 1_{10} \times 2_{10}^6 + 1_{10} \times 2_{10}^5 + 0_{10} \times 2_{10}^4$$

A 2_{10}^4 can be factored from each term, producing the following expression:

$$(0_{10} \times 2_{10}^3 + 1_{10} \times 2_{10}^2 + 1_{10} \times 2_{10}^1 + 0_{10} \times 2_{10}^0) \times 2_{10}^4$$

The expression within the parentheses may be evaluated, producing

$$6_{10} \times 2_{10}^4$$

but 2_{10}^4 is just 16_{10}, and so the following results:

$$6_{10} \times 16_{10}^1$$

which may be rewritten as

$$6_{16} \times 16_{10}^1$$

For comparison, the initial answer may be written out, showing the place value of the coefficients, as follows:

$$1_{16} \times 16_{10}^2 + 6_{16} \times 16_{10}^1 + D_{16} \times 16_{10}^0$$

The two expressions are the same. The above process does produce the correct result with regard to both the coefficients produced and their corresponding place values.

TABLE 9.2 ASCII Codes

Most Significant Digit		0	1	2	3	4	5	6	7
	0	NUL	DLE	SP	0	@	P		p
	1	SOH	DC1	!	1	A	Q	a	q
	2	STX	DC2	"	2	B	R	b	r
	3	ETX	DC3	#	3	C	S	c	s
	4	EOT	DC4	$	4	D	T	d	t
	5	ENQ	NAK	%	5	E	U	e	u
	6	ACK	SYN	&	6	F	V	f	v
Least Significant	7	BEL	ETB	'	7	G	W	g	w
Digit	8	BS	CAN	(	8	H	X	h	x
	9	HT	EM	)	9	I	Y	i	y
	A	LF	SUB	*	:	J	Z	j	z
	B	VT	ESC	+	;	K	[	k	{
	C	FF	FS	,	<	L	/	l	/
	D	CR	GS	−	=	M	]	m	}
	E	SO	RS	.	>	N	↑	n	≈
	F	SI	US	/	?	O	→	o	DEL

ASCII Interpretation of a Binary Word

In addition to storing numeric information, most computers must also be capable of storing symbols like letters of the alphabet and punctuation marks. Such storage is useful for keeping copies of the source listings of programs and for storing text, such as in word-processing functions. ASCII (American Standard Code for Information Interchange and pronounced "askey") is the system used by most computer manufacturers. Each letter or other symbol is represented by a unique binary code. Table 9.2 defines for each included symbol the corresponding binary code.

The table is used by first locating the desired symbol and then moving up to the corresponding column heading. This heading provides the most significant four bits of the required code. Moving to the left horizontally from the desired symbol provides the least significant four bits. The ASCII code for A is $41_{16} = 01000001_2$, and for B the code is $42_{16} = 01000010_2$.

Adoption of standards like the ASCII code offers many benefits, both to the companies producing computer equipment and to those using it. Today most serial printers use ASCII code, permitting a printer built by one company to be driven by a computer produced by another. To some extent computer peripherals are interchangeable as a result of this code standardization.

A binary word is a perfectly general storage concept. Storage locations are exactly the same whether they are used to store decimal numbers, hexadecimal numbers, or symbols. The way that the contents of a particular storage location are interpreted depends on the program being run, and not on some sort of electrical characteristic. In addition to those concepts presented here, binary words can store many other types of information.

Supplementary Examples 9.11, 9.12
Problems p9.5 – p9.13

▲ 9.3 Logic Gates

Modern digital computers contain complicated electronic circuits that operate at extremely high speeds and can be used to solve an amazingly wide variety of problems. Although the circuitry is complex, the various elements of a digital computer are constructed from simpler devices which may be viewed as building blocks or components of the more complex electronic structures. These building blocks are called *logic gates*. In digital computers, logic gates are constructed with transistors and other electrical devices connected to accomplish a specific task. It is possible to build relatively simple computers that use a flow of fluid, typically air or oil, instead of a flow of electricity to accomplish limited computations. Such computers also contain logic gates and use the same mathematical concepts to be described here.

The concept of a logic gate is really a mathematical definition of the relationship of certain inputs and certain outputs. Figure 9.6 illustrates a logic gate. The inputs and outputs of logic gates are normally binary numbers, which may be viewed as logic "1's" or logic "0's." In electrical circuits, voltage levels can be used to represent logic levels. A commonly used system assigns a logic level of 1 to voltages at or near 5 volts and a logic level of 0 to voltages approaching zero volts.

The term *input* implies a logic signal (voltage level) that is produced elsewhere and contains the information needed to make some type of decision. The simplest logic gates typically have two inputs and one output, although gates with more than two inputs and/or outputs are also quite common. The logic gate combines the information (binary signals) to be acted upon according to a predefined set of rules (truth table), so as to produce a response or "answer" as the output. This response also consists of one or more binary digits that may be directly utilized or may be routed to still other logic gates where they become inputs for additional processing stages. The interconnection of logic gates allows extremely complex processes to be carried out rapidly and accurately.

Most of the integrated circuits used in digital computers may be

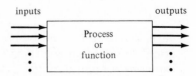

Figure 9.6 Logic gate.

TABLE 9.3 Commonly Used Logic Gates

Name	Symbol	Truth Table		Boolean Expression
Invertor	A $\overline{\text{A}}$ Pen 1	Input Output 0 1 1 0		$A = \overline{A}$
AND	A B Y	Inputs Output 0 0 0 0 1 0 1 0 0 1 1 1		$A \cdot B = Y$ $A B = Y$ $A \times B = Y$
OR	A B Y	Inputs Output 0 0 0 0 1 1 1 0 1 1 1 1		$A + B = Y$ $A \vee B = Y$
Exclusive OR	A B Y	Inputs Output 0 0 0 0 1 1 1 0 1 1 1 0		$A \oplus B = Y$ $A \veebar B = Y$

viewed as convenient packages that may contain tens or even hundreds of thousands of logic gates interconnected in such a way as to accomplish a specific task or set of tasks. Table 9.3 defines the most commonly used, two-input, one-output logic gates and a special logic gate called an *invertor*. The logic gate symbols are used by interconnecting them in larger diagrams to represent circuits that are used to construct specific computer components. The truth tables define, for each possible set of inputs, what the resulting output will be and how the logic gates will act on any possible set of inputs. The Boolean expressions form the basis of a mathematical notational scheme that allows a convenient and concise analysis of more complex systems constructed from logic gates.

Computers are widely used to control various types of processes, but for simple tasks, a few appropriately connected logic gates may provide a more cost-effective controlling device, as Example 9.5 illustrates.

Example 9.5: A device is needed to control the watering of a lawn. An electrically operated valve is to be placed in the pipe supplying water to the sprinkler heads. This valve allows water to flow only when it receives a logic 1 signal. The grass is to be watered only between the hours of 5 A.M. and 8 A.M., only when water is actually needed, and only when it is not raining. Build a controller using logic gates to accomplish this task.

Solution: Careful analysis of the statement of the problem reveals that three simultaneous conditions must be satisfied before the water control valve will be turned on. These conditions are:

a. correct time interval
b. need of water
c. presence (or absence) of rainfall

Note that each of these conditions either are conducive to watering or preclude watering at a given time. Each of the three conditions is binary in nature. The system does not need to know how dry the lawn is or how much water to supply. It shall be assumed that appropriate devices are available to produce logic signals indicating the current state of each required condition. Figure 9.7 shows these devices.

The first device is a clock that supplies a logic 1 signal only between 5 A.M. and 8 A.M. The second device is capable of sensing whether or not it is raining and is designed to put out a logic 1 only when it detects that rain is falling. The last device senses the moisture content of the lawn and provides a logic 1 when additional moisture is needed. These three signals are the inputs to the system that is to be designed, as they collectively contain all the information needed to decide whether or not water is needed. The particular logic element needed is a three-input, one-output gate.

Some experience is often helpful in selecting the particular logic gate required for a specific task. Fortunately, the meanings of the words AND and OR are similar to those used in the technical definition of the logic gates. One way to determine the type of logic gate needed is to state, in an abbreviated form using English, what the problem solution requires. For the current example, this might be as follows:

The water is to be turned on when

1. the time interval is correct

AND

2. it is *not* raining

AND

3. the grass is too dry

Otherwise the water is to be kept off.

The appearance of the word AND in the statement suggests that an AND gate may form the basis of the controller design. Inspection of the truth table for an AND gate in Table 9.3 shows that an output of a logic 1 occurs only when both inputs are logic 1's. This is the right idea, but a three-input gate that functions in the same way is needed. The truth table for the controller is shown in Table 9.4.

TABLE 9.4 Truth Table for Watering System

Correct Time	Not Raining	Grass Dry	Water Valve On
0	0	0	0
0	0	1	0
0	1	0	0
0	1	1	0
1	0	0	0
1	0	1	0
1	1	0	0
1	1	1	1

Inspection of the truth table shows that water is supplied to the lawn only when all inputs are in their logic 1 states. This is exactly what the problem statement requires.

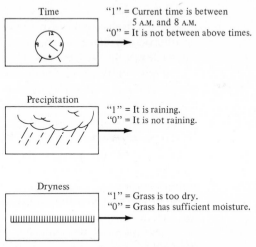

Figure 9.7 Sensors for lawn watering system.

The sensor that indicates whether or not it is raining needs additional attention. As shown in Figure 9.7, the sensor provides a logic 1 signal when it is raining, but the logic of Table 9.4 requires a logic 1 signal when it is *not* raining. The "sense" of this signal must be reversed. This is accomplished by using a special logic gate shown in Table 9.3 and called an *invertor*. The final design for the lawn watering system is shown in Figure 9.8.

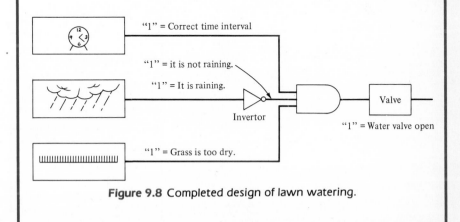

Figure 9.8 Completed design of lawn watering.

Supplementary Examples 9.13 – 9.14
Problems p9.14 – p9.15

▲ 9.4 Microcomputers

The logic gates discussed in the previous section may be used as building blocks to construct devices of arbitrary function and complexity. The ways that large classes of engineering problems are solved have dramatically changed as a result of the availability of cheap and reliable microcomputers or microcontrollers. In this section, we shall explain the components of microcomputer systems and how they function.

Figure 9.9 depicts the elements necessary to construct a simple computer. The heart of a microcomputer is a microprocessor that is normally contained within a single integrated circuit. This device controls the computer's overall operation and may be thought of as its brain. The computer has some type of memory in which the programs are to be executed and the results of these programs can be stored. Finally, the computer system must receive information from the external world and supply information, which may include controlling signals, to the external world. Devices that permit these functions are called *input* and *output devices*, often abbreviated as *I/O devices* or *ports*.

The memory of a microcomputer provides a good starting point for discussion. In many ways, a microcomputer memory bank is like a long

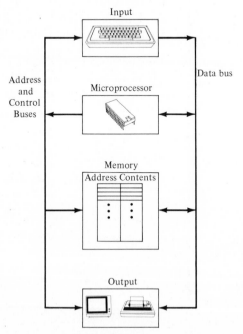

Figure 9.9 Key components of a microcomputer.

string of mailboxes. When a letter is sent to someone, two items are essential. The first is the contents of the letter, which might be viewed as information or data. The second is where the letter is to be sent, or the address. In an analogous way, microprocessor communication with memory has two elements. First, the microcomputer must signal the appropriate memory location with which it wishes to communicate, by supplying an appropriate address and auxiliary control signals, and second, the microcomputer must transmit or receive the required information or data. The information a microcomputer handles at this level is much simpler than someone's street address or the body of a letter. The microprocessor actually deals with just two binary numbers, as shown in Figure 9.10. The actual information for many microcomputers consists of an 8-bit binary number and its associated 16-bit address, which indicates where in memory the binary number is to be stored. The memory of a microcomputer is a collection of electronic circuits, each capable of storing an 8-bit binary number (data) and responding to a unique 16-bit code (address). A microcomputer's memory is usually packaged in one or more integrated circuits.

Computer memory may be divided into two categories. The first is called *read only memory* (ROM). The concepts of address and contents are still valid, but in normal operation, this type of memory permits only the extraction of information. No provision is made to insert new or modified information into the memory. ROM is most commonly used to store programs and/or data tables that the computer needs frequently enough to justify permanent storage. The ROM is programmed once as a part of the manufacturing process, and thereafter its contents cannot be changed without destroying the device.

Random access memory (RAM) is the second type of computer memory. This type permits the bidirectional flow of data, in that new information may be inserted into memory or extracted from it as required by the computer program. The programs entered by a computer operator and the results of programmed computations are examples of items typically stored in RAM memory.

ROM and RAM memories for microcomputers are relatively cheap and allow extremely rapid storage and retrieval of information, but for certain applications, RAM and ROM memories alone do not provide sufficient storage capability or permanence. Many of the microcomputers in current use provide only sixteen bits for memory addresses, which limits to 65536_{10} the number of storage locations with which the microcomputer can communicate. Such a computer is said to be able to access directly 64k (64 kilobytes) of

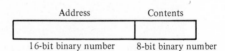

Address   Contents

16-bit binary number   8-bit binary number

Figure 9.10 Microcomputer memory.

memory, where k $= 1024_{10}$. Should additional storage be required, an auxiliary device, such as a hard or floppy disk, is included in the system. Such devices store information on magnetic media instead of in electronic circuits, and although they provide slower access to the information, the volume of information available is tens or hundreds of millions of bytes. Such devices are called *mass storage devices*.

Microcomputers send and receive information to and from the external world through special electronic circuits called *ports* or *interfaces*. In many systems, these ports look very much like memory locations except for how the contents of the port are treated. If the port is designed for input, then some external device will put an 8-bit binary number into the port by setting high and/or low voltage levels on certain wires. Subsequently, the microcomputer can read or "pick up" this number and use it. For an output port, the microcomputer puts a number into the port which is converted by the circuitry to high or low voltages (depending on the digits within the binary number) which are available to some external device that the microcomputer is controlling.

Many I/O devices are available for microcomputers. Some of the most common input devices are keyboards, various types of readers (an example of which is the bar-code reader widely used in retail sales), and sensing devices that allow computers to measure physical quantities like voltage, current, temperature, pressure, velocity, and acceleration. Probably the most common output devices consist of CRT (cathode ray tube) displays and

Illustration 9.3 A microprocessor chip in an electronic engine control system. The needle and thread show its extremely small size. (Courtesy Delco Electronics)

various types of printers, although an almost endless list of other output devices utilizing motors, valves, solenoids, and other actuators driven by computer signals also can be compiled.

Problems p9.16 – p9.18

▲ 9.5 Uses of Computers

Computers have been available for many years and have been extensively used for certain categories of problem solving. But because the early computers were large and expensive, it was necessary to share them. Because of the high cost of the computers and their limited accessibility owing to many users, the kinds of problems solved on these computers usually were those requiring intense computation or manipulation of large amounts of data. Such problems were expensive to solve using large digital computers, but often this was the only practical way to produce answers in reasonable periods of time. Although these early computers could perform many other functions, they often were not implemented because cheaper alternative methods were available.

But as new technologies evolved, the cost of computing fell dramatically, and consequently, many more tasks could be economically performed on a computer. The large central computer is still found in many companies, but most engineers and technicians now have a smaller personal computer or workstation sitting on their desk.

Often these computers are linked through various types of networking schemes to a larger computer system. People with such systems have at their disposal a very powerful computing and data-processing facility. The ability to access information within the large companywide computers allows users to obtain the most recently available information both locally and from other company locations, which might be thousands of miles away. Such systems permit everyone within the company to use the same information at the same time. This capability dramatically reduces problems related to the communication of information among various individuals or groups. When a particular problem becomes too large for a personal computer — from a computational or data storage standpoint — the personal computer can be used to submit the problem to the main-frame computer and, after the problem is solved, to retrieve the solution for subsequent review.

The performance of personal computers has greatly improved, and a great deal has been learned about designing programs that can be easily used on them. At one point, most people who used computers were also programmers or at least supervised the work of programmers. The need for developing specialized programs still exists, but many programs are currently available that are capable of doing most types of routine engineering work. Many of these programs are simple to use and require no programming skills and only minimal training. We shall discuss some of the more widely used programs in this section.

Illustration 9.4 Engineers and technicians now commonly use personal computers for computation, word processing, spreadsheet analysis, and data base management. (Courtesy AT&T)

Electronic Communications

Many engineers and technicians find it necessary to communicate periodically the results of their efforts. Much of this communication must be written and may consist of memos, letters, reports, manuals, proposals, or articles. Not so long ago, the initial copies of such materials were handwritten. Then they were typed by a secretary and reviewed, revised, and retyped until the finished version was produced. The materials were finally reproduced and mailed to those needing copies.

Illustration 9.5 This satellite communications dish is one method of sending and receiving electronic communications. (Courtesy Electronic Data Systems)

This process often required much time to complete, and there was ample opportunity for the introduction of errors, since a number of different people were involved in the process, and some had little or no understanding of the materials' technical content.

Word processing and telecommunications are rapidly growing uses of personal computers, for both engineers and others. Instead of preparing written materials in longhand, many people compose documents directly on a personal computer by typing them in on the keyboard. Once the material is entered, it may be stored, retrieved, and modified as necessary, by either the engineer or others who are professionally trained as technical writers or editors. Expecting professionals to do their own typing might initially be viewed as a waste of time, but after some practice, many find that they can type the initial draft of their material faster than they can write it in longhand. Once the information is typed in, the text can be corrected without introducing new errors, which frequently occur when longhand manuscripts are typed by secretaries. The time-consuming process of proofreading is thereby considerably reduced.

The real time savings in the process is realized after the final version of the material is available. Data communication networks that are now widely available allow the material to be electronically stored in computer memory banks and accessed by others at remote locations. Should hard copies of the material be desired at another location, the material is electronically transferred from the initial computer to a remote computer where it can then be printed out. But for many purposes, it is not necessary to print the material. Personnel needing to read the documents have the option of simply transferring them to their personal computers and then reading them from the screen. Using this technology, it is entirely possible to arrive at work at 8:00 A.M., write a short report, edit and correct it, transmit it to one or more remote locations, have others read it, and receive their comments before a midmorning coffee break.

From the author's standpoint, three things are necessary to be able to use such a system efficiently. The first is the ability to type and compose at the same time at a personal computer keyboard. The second is a familiarity with the system-specific commands necessary to create, store, transmit, and receive data files using the information system to which the personal computer is connected. The third is a working knowledge of the word-processing program that is run on the personal computer, because this facilitates the creation of the initial data file containing the manuscript.

Word Processing

Almost all popular personal computers have one or more word-processing programs available that vary considerably in cost, capability, and complexity. We shall describe the commonly available capabilities of some of the better programs. The commands necessary to implement a specific feature differ from program to program and, for this reason, will not be presented here. Most word-processing programs come with extensive manuals of these commands.

Most of the better word-processing programs are designed so that they can easily be used. Many commands are required to carry out various word-processing functions, and at least initially, it is difficult to remember the command for a specific purpose. Because of this, most programs provide a series of menus that display on the screen a list of tasks that can be selected at any given time. Along with each task is the specific command that must be issued. Usually, the commands consist of pressing one key or several keys in combination. Once the keys are pressed, the computer executes the command. The menu may remain on all or part of the screen, or it may be replaced by text or another menu, depending on the program and the system itself. There is almost always a provision to transfer from menu to menu and back so that most tasks can be accomplished without regard to their specific order.

One of the most basic commands permits the insertion of text into the computer. One or more commands are issued, after which the computer acts very much as a typewriter. As various keys are pressed, the corresponding symbols appear on the screen and are stored in computer memory. A cursor, which is usually a flashing underline symbol, indicates where the next letter will be placed on the screen. Most word-processing programs incorporate what is called *full-screen text editing.* This is the ability to move the cursor to any position on the screen by pressing controlling keys on the keyboard. Once the cursor is positioned, symbols at the cursor position may be deleted or changed, or new symbols may be added.

The cursor is really a pointer that allows the computer to identify a specific location that the operator wishes to reference. As such, it can be used to mark certain sections of text. Suppose that a paragraph is out of order and needs to be moved to a new position. The cursor is positioned at both the beginning and end of the paragraph to be moved, and special characters are inserted marking each of these locations. The cursor is then moved to the position where the paragraph that is to be moved is to begin. A single command copies the paragraph to the new position. Other commands are usually available to delete the old version of the marked paragraph from the text.

Most word processors can search for a specified string of characters. The cursor may stop at each occurrence of the given string, or it may find all occurrences of a given string and replace them with a new string. Such a capability is helpful when it is discovered that a certain word has been consistently misspelled or something like a chapter number or name must be changed throughout the text.

Most word processors also have spelling checkers that look up each word contained in the text in a data file called a *dictionary.* The program indicates to the operator all words that do not appear in this file and may therefore indicate possible errors. It usually enables newly encountered words to be inserted that are correctly spelled but not contained in the dictionary file. Over a period of time, with continued usage, a supplementary dictionary is created that contains most of the technical words associated with a particular discipline or job function.

One or more of the word-processing menus are concerned with the storage and retrieval of the text that was typed into the system. The textual data will usually be stored locally on floppy or hard disks and may also be sent to another computer through a communication link. At a later time, this same menu provides the command(s) necessary to retrieve the information, so that additions or changes can readily be made. There is also provision to combine files so that two or more different documents can be merged into one.

Another group of word processor commands facilitate the printing of the file on a printer if this is desired. Typical commands in this group specify parameters like margins, characters per line, line spacing, right justification, and page numbering. Additional commands establish the details of the data communication channel so that the information supplied by the personal computer is consistent in form with that expected by the printer. One of the most important of these is the *baud rate*, which determines the speed of data transmission.

A final group of commands are *embedded commands.* These occur as needed in the text and issue special instructions to the printer. An example is to center a title on the page. When this command is encountered, the computer determines how many spaces need to precede the first printed character so that the line appears centered. Other commands allow the printer carriage to advance or back up, enabling the printing of superscripts or subscripts, and allow backspacing, enabling underlining.

The convenience and cost savings permitted by the use of computerized word-processing systems have made them widely accepted in both the scientific and engineering communities and the business world. Almost all professionally written materials are now produced on such systems (this book included).

Spreadsheet Programs

Although initially designed for accounting, forecasting, and other financial purposes, spreadsheet programs are also widely used by engineers and technicians. Depending on the program and its complexity, a great many capabilities may be provided, but basically, spreadsheet programs permit the efficient and orderly manipulation of tabular information. These programs permit the entry of rows and/or columns of data and appropriate headings. Once this information is entered, equations can also be provided that allow additional columns, rows, or elements, called *cells*, to be computed from previously entered or computed information.

A spreadsheet consists of initial information and defining mathematical relationships that relate various rows and/or columns as needed to compute automatically additional rows and columns of new information. The real utility of the program is that once the initial information and equations are entered, a subsequent change in any number will result in the recomputing and updating of all numbers whose values depend on this modified data value. Various types of "what if" questions can be readily answered using such programs. How this is accomplished, conceptually, is shown in a series of examples, starting with Example 9.6.

Example 9.6: Suppose you are the president of a local parent–teacher organization and you must decide on the price of tickets for a local high school's football games. From previous years' experience, you know that if adult ticket prices are $3.00, approximately 1000 adults will attend each game and that for each $0.10 increase in ticket prices, 20 fewer adults will come. Similarly, for each $0.10 decrease in the ticket prices, 20 more adults will show up. On the average, it can be assumed that each adult will be accompanied by one student. The admission price for a student has been fixed by the school board at $1.00. Your job is to price the adult tickets in such a way that the maximum possible profit will be made on each game.

Solution: This problem can be solved using hand computations, by preparing a table of required values based on a number of guesses for ticket prices. Such a tabulation is presented in Table 9.5. Initially, a range of ticket prices is chosen that is believed to include the desired one. These ticket prices are listed in column A. Note that it was arbitrarily decided to use a sequence of values having increments of $0.10 each for convenience in making change when tickets are sold. The adult attendance corresponding to each ticket price is computed and shown in column B. The total revenue from adult ticket sales is found by multiplying the adult ticket price by the corresponding number of tickets sold. This information is also computed and shown in column C. Since the student ticket prices will not change, all entries in column D are the same. The number of student tickets sold is the same as the number of adult tickets sold, and so column E is a copy of column B. Revenue from student ticket sales is the product of the corresponding numbers in columns D and E, as shown in column F. Finally, the total revenue generated by all ticket sales is found by summing the corresponding numbers in columns C and F and placing the result in column G. The answer to this problem is found by inspecting column G to determine the largest value, which is found to be $4050, and indicates that an adult ticket price of $3.50 would produce the largest revenue.

Comment: Some care must be exercised in choosing the range of ticket prices to be investigated. In more complex problems, it is possible that two or more relative maximum values may be found. Furthermore, another possibility is that the range of values investigated may not contain the absolute maximum.

TABLE 9.5 Determination of Optimal Prices for Football Tickets

	A	B	C	D	E	F	G
1	ADULT	ADULT	ADULT	STUDENT	STUDENT	STUDENT	TOTAL
2	TICKET	ATTEND	SALES	TICKET	ATTEND	SALES	SALES
3	PRICE			PRICE			
4	3.00	1000	3000	1.00	1000	1000	4000
5	3.10	980	3038	1.00	980	980	4018
6	3.20	960	3072	1.00	960	960	4032
7	3.30	940	3102	1.00	940	940	4042
8	3.40	920	3128	1.00	920	920	4048
9	3.50	900	3150	1.00	900	900	4050
10	3.60	880	3168	1.00	880	880	4048
11	3.70	860	3182	1.00	860	860	4042
12	3.80	840	3192	1.00	840	840	4032
13	3.90	820	3198	1.00	820	820	4018
14	4.00	800	3200	1.00	800	800	4000

The above problem could also have been solved by writing a short computer program in a high-level language like FORTRAN or BASIC. Such a program would consist of a loop, several arithmetic statements, and a print statement to produce the table of values. The production of such a program, however, requires at least some programming skill which many people do not possess. Spreadsheet programs solve this problem by providing a structure for the initial data entry and defining how any supplementary data should be computed. Once this information, which is called a *template,* is available, the user can change one or more numbers or relationships and have the resulting changes in all other numbers automatically computed and displayed.

Example 9.7 shows how the data and defining relationships developed for Example 9.6 can be used in another problem that, in effect, defines a template for this type of problem.

Example 9.7: Consider the problem explained in Example 9.6 and develop a similar table, but instead of entering numerical values, enter wherever possible the mathematical expressions that allow the computation of the corresponding value. The numerical values for the first row of the table are assumed to be known.

Solution: Columns are assigned a letter, and rows are assigned a number so that a value stored in a particular cell can be referenced by its row and column position. Thus A4 means the contents of the cell in column A and row 4. For this example, the value of A4 is $3.00. The required mathematical relationships are shown in Table 9.6. Thus, the value needed for cell A5 is the value in cell A4 plus 0.10, and so on.

TABLE 9.6 Mathematical Relationships of a Spreadsheet Program

	A	B	C	D	E	F	G
1	ADULT	ADULT	ADULT	STUDENT	STUDENT	STUDENT	TOTAL
2	TICKET	ATTEND	SALES	TICKET	ATTEND	SALES	SALES
3	PRICE			PRICE			
4	3.00	1000	A4*B4	1.00	B4	D4*E4	C4 + F4
5	A4 + 0.10	B4 − 20	A5*B5	D4	B5	D5*E5	C5 + F5
6	A5 + 0.10	B5 − 20	A6*B6	D4	B6	D6*E6	C6 + F6
7	A6 + 0.10	B6 − 20	A7*B7	D4	B7	D7*E7	C7 + F7
8	A7 + 0.10	B7 − 20	A8*B8	D4	B8	D8*E8	C8 + F8
9	A8 + 0.10	B8 − 20	A9*B9	D4	B9	D9*E9	C9 + F9
10	A9 + 0.10	B9 − 20	A10*B10	D4	B10	D10*E10	C10 + F10
11	A10 + 0.10	B10 − 20	A11*B11	D4	B11	D11*E11	C11 + F11
12	A11 + 0.10	B11 − 20	A12*B12	D4	B12	D12*E12	C12 + F12
13	A12 + 0.10	B12 − 20	A13*B13	D4	B13	D13*E13	C13 + F13

Comment: The real value of a spreadsheet program lies in two areas. First, no programming skills are needed. Numbers and equations are simply typed into the computer as required. The second and main advantage occurs when a series of "what if" questions need to be answered. The following example presents one such "what if" computation.

Example 9.8: "What if" all information of Example 9.6 remained the same except that 1000 adults would attend at a price of $3.20 each? At this new rate, what adult ticket price would produce the most profit?

Solution: If a spreadsheet program were used to solve the problem, entry A4 would be changed to $3.20, and the computer would be commanded to update all entries according to the rules of Table 9.6. The results are shown in Table 9.7. For the cases investigated, the maximum profit is now realized for an adult ticket price of $3.60, and the total revenue generated has increased to $4232, from the previous amount of $4050.

TABLE 9.7 Determination of Best Ticket Price Using New Data

	A	B	C	D	E	F	G
1	ADULT	ADULT	ADULT	STUDENT	STUDENT	STUDENT	TOTAL
2	TICKET	ATTEND	SALES	TICKET	ATTEND	SALES	SALES
3	PRICE			PRICE			
4	3.20	1000	3200	1.00	1000	1000	4200
5	3.30	980	3234	1.00	980	980	4214
6	3.40	960	3264	1.00	960	960	4224
7	3.50	940	3290	1.00	940	940	4230
8	3.60	920	3312	1.00	920	920	4232

9	3.70	900	3330	1.00	900	900	4230
10	3.80	880	3344	1.00	880	880	4224
11	3.90	860	3354	1.00	860	860	4214
12	4.00	840	3360	1.00	840	840	4200

The financial uses of spreadsheets include rather obvious applications. Many additional applications are possible, however. A number of companies are currently selling what are called templates for a multitude of applications. These templates can be stored on a floppy or hard disk and are loaded into a compatible spreadsheet program by one or more appropriate commands. These templates consist of the information necessary to set up the spreadsheet program for a specific task. Such information might include column headings, titles, various types of graphic information, and perhaps even various known constants or parameters, in addition to the mathematical relationships among the contents of the various cells. The user simply supplies an initial set of data for the specific problem and commands the spreadsheet program to do the required computations. The template supplies the additional information needed for the desired solution. If changes in data or new constraints are to be introduced that would produce variations of the initial problem, this can also be easily accomplished.

Data Base Management Systems

Data base management programs are also widely used on personal computers. Such programs allow the user to create, update, sort, and print files of information. But before discussing data base managers, we shall describe several simpler concepts.

A data base is a collection of facts organized for a specific purpose, and a computerized data base is a collection of facts encoded and stored in such a way that a computer can access and manipulate them. According to this definition, such things as card catalogs, telephone directories, and dictionaries are simple data bases. A telephone directory is a good example of a file and its component parts. The entire residential directory is a file. A telephone directory consists of many listings having the same form or format. Any individual listing is known as a *record*. Such a listing consists of a name, address, and telephone number. Each of these elements is termed a *field*, and together they make up the record. All records within the file use this same structure. Thus, a field is a piece of information within a record, and a group of records comprises a file.

Programs capable of creating, inserting, deleting, changing, sorting, and displaying only single files are file management programs, file management systems, or filing programs. Such programs can deal with only a single subject or one type of information. They are useful because they are fairly simple to operate, even by people with little or no computer experience, but they are limited in what they can do.

Data base management systems (DBMS) are much more flexible in creating and using the data base and are also considerably more complex. Such systems allow users to store data in more than one file and to rearrange fields within records, create new files from existing ones, and extract information from a number of files for subsequent processing.

There are three types of data base management systems: relational, hierarchical, and networking. A relational data base is made up of many tables or files capable of storing one or more types of information. The entries in these files are structured in such a way that there is a known relationship or logical connection among corresponding entries in the various files. Suppose that information concerning a part used in the manufacture of several machines is stored in a data base. Such information might include the name of the piece, its part number, its cost, the material from which it is manufactured, the number currently available in inventory for delivery, and a list of specific machines that use this particular part.

A system using a relational data base would, if appropriate commands were issued, indicate all machines utilizing this part if the user simply specified the part number. If the data base contained similar information about many parts, the current value of all parts in inventory for a specific machine could be determined by accessing the files specifying the different machines, the number of each part fitting that particular machine, and finally, the cost of each part. Such data bases are extremely useful because of their ability to retrieve and cross-reference data.

A hierarchical data base system may be compared to a company's organization. At the highest level is the company president, followed by the vice-presidents, division managers, project directors, engineers, and technicians. In a hierarchical data base system, different pieces of data are organized in a similar structure. Obtaining a piece of information from one of the lower levels requires accessing it from the top of the pyramid down to the appropriate level. If one of the higher-level blocks linking the system happened to be changed or deleted, the only way to find the desired information would be through an exhaustive search.

A networking data base has records in a hierarchical arrangement, but a given record can participate in more than one relationship. This is analogous to having an engineer report to more than one project manager. In a hierarchical data base, there is only one superior for a particular data set, but in a network data base system, there may be several superiors for a given data set, allowing access by more than one path.

The capabilities of spreadsheet programs, data base managers, and graphics programs have been integrated into single software systems permitting the storage, analysis, and display of relatively complex problems. Such packages do not require a knowledge of programming, and yet they permit utilization of a computer's computational and storage abilities. Depending on the features available to the user, the skill and knowledge required by the operator can vary significantly.

Computer-Aided Design (CAD)

The abbreviation CAD/CAM, which stands for computer-aided design and computer-aided manufacturing, is a widely used acronym that identifies a broad spectrum of activities related to the engineering and manufacturing processes, the efficiency of which can be improved through the use of computers. We shall now discuss some aspects of CAD/CAM and its implications.

A typical CAD/CAM work station consists of a moderately powerful computer, a variety of peripheral devices, a communication link to a mainframe computer with extensive data and program storage, and various programs.

The main display device is usually a cathode ray tube (CRT) which looks very much like a television set but produces much better quality picture displays. The CRT display is usually about 19 inches across (diagonally) and is commonly divided into an array of 4096×4096 or more small elements called *pixels*. Each pixel can be individually controlled by the work station processor and can be set to one of sixteen or more colors at various intensity levels. The CRT allows not only text to be displayed but also almost any type of high-quality graphical image. In fact, the engineer can sit in front of the CRT and "see" the object that has been designed before one is actually built.

In response to instructions from the engineer, the work station computer (and the associated program) develops a set of numbers called a *data set* which completely describe the object being designed. Work stations with a variety of performance levels are currently available. All levels are based on the computer's and the CRT's ability to display "primitives," the graphics building blocks from which complete images are formed. The simplest primitives are points, lines, and text strings. A system that can display only these can produce several line drawings and can be quite useful to design engineers and draftspersons.

The next higher level of primitive is the representation of a surface using polygons made from connected line segments that form a closed figure. The polygons can be assigned various color values, and the result starts to appear as a solid object.

Illustration 9.6 Engineering computer-aided design work station.
(Courtesy T&W Systems)

Curved surfaces represented by conic section curves consisting of circles, arcs, ellipses, parabolas, and hyperbolas result in additional sophistication and better graphic rendition. The highest level of such primitives is called a *free-form curve* and is generated by an algorithm within the graphics program or a series of points supplied by the user.

Most systems allow the primitives to be assigned additional properties, called *attributes*. Attributes include line style, line width, display intensity, color, visibility or invisibility, highlighting, and detectability.

Wire-Frame Models Through the use of primitives and attributes, it is possible to display various representations of an object that look more or less like the object itself. The wire-frame display is the simplest display of a

Illustration 9.7 While this appears to be a photograph of a Chevrolet Camaro, in reality it is merely a synthetic image of this vehicle drawn on a graphics terminal. (Courtesy General Motors)

three-dimensional object. Each edge of the object is displayed as a straight or curved line. The object appears to be transparent, as single edges, normally hidden from the viewer, are also displayed. A hidden line algorithm is often used to remove these lines, resulting in a more visually pleasing model. Wire-frame models are relatively easy to create and are widely used for engineering drafting, 2- and 2.5-axis numerical control machine programming, and computations involving areas of the object. The wire-frame models have several limitations, including the inability to produce blended and rounded surfaces instead of sharp edges, lack of information about the surface mathematics, and the inability to differentiate between the inside and outside of objects.

Surface Modeling Surface modeling represents an intermediate stage between wire-frame models and solid, three-dimensional models. This technique is particularly useful for products made from sheet metal and thinly molded plastic parts. Surface models can be useful in producing color-shaded, three-dimensional views of the product.

Surface modeling is accomplished by initially creating a wire-frame model of the figure's edges. Flat surfaces are modeled by placing planes between the wire-frame edges. Surfaces of revolution are used to represent surface portions with axial symmetry. More complicated surfaces are created in a variety of ways, including sweep surfaces constructed by having one curve translate through another curve to trace out an area. Finally, the edges and corners are rounded, and fillets are added where necessary to produce the final model.

Solid Modeling Solid modeling represents the highest levels of graphics displays. The representation developed in the computer is sufficient to allow the computation of any well-defined geometric property and a multicolor (almost photographic quality) picture to be displayed for the designer. Various parts can be color keyed, and the appropriate fit of components, including tolerances, can be checked. Additionally, a normally hidden internal structure can be shown by producing various types of section cuts in the part under examination.

Uses of Computer Graphics Virtually all advanced work stations provide commands to manipulate the object being displayed. These manipulations are called *geometric transformations* and permit at least the following three functions:

1. Translation, which is the movement of an object along a straight line.
2. Scaling, which allows the designer to increase or decrease the object's size.
3. Rotation, which allows the object to be viewed from any desired vantage point.

These commands allow the designer to see the object as it is being designed and, if necessary, to modify the design before actually producing the object. Because the object is completely described within the computer's data base, such things as the object's center of gravity and its weight when constructed of a given material all are readily available.

Many work stations offer programs permitting what is called *finite element analysis.* In this mathematical analysis technique, a three-dimensional object is broken down into a network of simple elements for which stress and deflection characteristics can be easily computed. Many equations are then generated and solved. The design engineer can request the stresses and deflections occurring in various parts of the object for a variety of loading conditions. Thus the engineer can decide whether the design under consideration is sufficiently strong or too strong and heavy, or whether another type of material might produce a better part.

In general, the hardware capabilities of currently used engineering work stations have exceeded those of the various programs used in the actual design process. The number of good software programs is rapidly expanding, however. Three areas that are often cited for their early use of effective CAD programs are architectural engineering, integrated circuit design, and various uses of animation.

Much of the work in architectural engineering is repetitive, and so the designs for one particular project may well be used again in the same project or in closely related ones. Programs are currently available to do electrical, plumbing, water-supply-system, and air-conditioning duct layouts. These programs can coordinate the design process so that plans do not call for two different utilities to be placed in the same position, resulting in a costly mistake that must be corrected. Piping programs are also available that lay out pipe arrangements for refineries and chemical-processing plants. From large libraries of standard parts descriptions, these programs extract and locate fittings like tees and elbows and even more complex devices like pumps, generators, and heat exchangers. Some of the more elaborate programs even do finite element analysis of the resulting configurations to ensure that the design is structurally adequate.

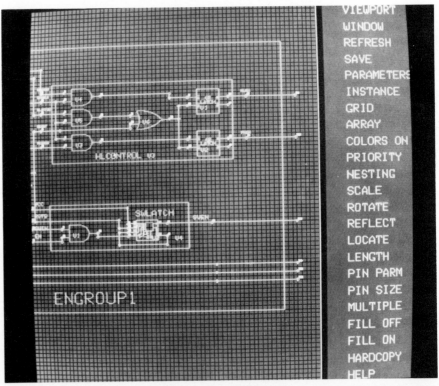

Illustration 9.8 Computer-assisted design of integrated circuits reduces design and test times by a factor of 10. (Courtesy General Motors)

Most large integrated circuit (IC) designs are created using workstations. The photomasks necessary to produce the IC chips themselves and to verify the correct interconnection of the circuit components can be cheaply produced using these design tools.

Computer animation is now widely used in television commercials and has for some time been used in the automotive industry to model the activities of people in and around a car. This technology is also particularly valuable in the study of robotics, for which appropriate animation programs can be written that show how manufacturing cells consisting of robots, machine tools, and transport systems will interact with one another.

Computer-Aided Manufacturing (CAM)

The engineering work station forms only one component of a production system that promises to revolutionize the way that the products consumed by our society are produced. Many people predict that by the year 2000, the assembly lines used to mass-produce many items like cars, appliances, and electronic devices will have few if any humans working on them. Most of these products will be produced by industrial robots and associated computer-controlled equipment. In this section, we shall consider some of the other technologies necessary for computer-aided design and manufacturing.

At the conclusion of the design phase of a new part's production, the processor in the workstation or a mainframe computer has stored within it a mathematical description of the desired object. Numerically controlled machines have for some time been available that, once started, will accomplish a variety of machine operations according to a predefined program, without operator intervention. Computer programs are now becoming available that translate the mathematical description of the part into the required series of operations for such a machine. Ideally, this translation process should be carried out by computer programs with little or no human intervention.

In certain situations, an engineer may wish to examine how the machine tool moves relative to the part being produced. Graphics simulation packages using animation are available that provide this capability for certain classes of problems. The result is a sequence of instructions that allows a numerically or computer-controlled machine to perform the desired operations with little or no human intervention.

Until recently, humans were used to bring raw materials from storage to the numerically controlled machine and to return the machined part to a storage area or to the area where the next step in the manufacturing process took place. There is currently a great deal of money and effort being expended to automate these and other tasks using industrial robots. In a completely automated system, raw materials are received and stored, machined or otherwise processed as required, tested, assembled, retested, packaged, and shipped with little or no direct human intervention. The movement of the parts, assembly, and testing functions all are done using computer-controlled machines and robots.

Industrial robots look very different from these created by science fiction writers. Figure 9.11 shows the main types of fixed industrial robots. In general, industrial robots perform a series of material-moving, manipulating, or assembly functions within a limited work space volume. They consist of a gripping or holding mechanism attached to a mechanical arm that performs the required motion. In addition, the robot contains a controlling computer and some type of power supply. The mechanics in a robot typically require electrical, hydraulic, or pneumatic power for operation, in addition to the electrical power required for the computer.

A robot is capable of a variety of actions and can be reprogrammed as the manufacturing tasks change. In the future, the programs that control robot motions may be generated by workstation simulations, but at present, robots are usually programmed by a human using what is called a *teaching pendant* (i.e., a control panel that controls the robot's motion). The required sequence of events is determined as the human operator takes the robot through the required routine one step at a time in response to switches or buttons pressed on the teaching pendant. As various motions are com-

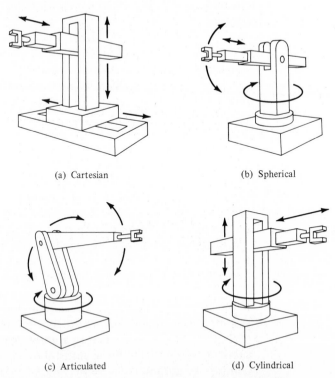

(a) Cartesian   (b) Spherical

(c) Articulated   (d) Cylindrical

Figure 9.11 Four common arm geometrics for industrial robots.

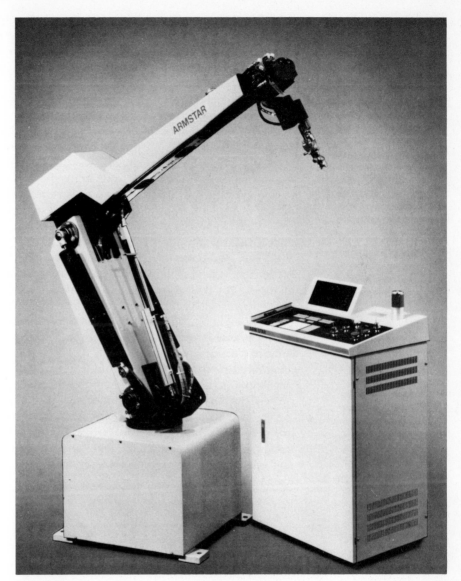

Illustration 9.9 "Armstar" painting robot with robot controller. (Courtesy Tokico America, Inc.)

pleted, the robot's computer keeps track of them. At the conclusion of the training phase, the computer contains a complete program of the various motions required to complete the routine, and thereafter, the robot can execute this sequence without further intervention. After it is given a start signal, the robot goes through exactly the same sequence of motions for which it was programmed.

Considerable effort is currently being directed toward giving robots the ability to sense and interpret visual and tactile data. With such information, the robot control computer could adjust the preprogrammed sequence of motions. An example of this is a robot picking a part from a bin in which a variety of parts are stored in random orientations. Attempts are also being made to incorporate into robots various aspects of artificial intelligence. Such robots will eventually be able to interpret and execute commands like "Get a 1/4 inch nut from bin C and screw it on bolt 26 in the assembly." The control computer will decide and execute the motions necessary for these tasks and will be able to verify and modify, as required, their performance. A manufacturing facility based on computer-aided design, computer-controlled machines, and industrial robots represents a huge investment, but once it is available, considerable benefits usually result.

Traditional manufacturing techniques have emphasized the cost benefits of mass production, but these techniques have tended to standardize products. When an assembly line was switched from one product to another, the process often involved weeks of time and expensive tooling changes. But it is predicted now that the computerized manufacturing concept will lead to what has been termed *flexible manufacturing*. In principle, at least, one product would switch to another by simply loading different programs into the various machines and robots. Such loading could be done in seconds instead of days or weeks. It is even possible to envision an assembly line that could intermix the manufacture of various parts. As a particular part moved through the various work cells, the programs required for that part would be loaded and executed. The next part arriving at a particular workstation might require a different sequence of operations, and so another program would be loaded and executed. Standardization for the purpose of manufacturing economy would no longer be necessary. In fact, each individual part or assembly could be customized to fit exactly a user's needs.

Problems p9.19 – p9.33

● CHAPTER SUMMARY

The study of computers as an engineering system is based on concepts related to number systems theory. Modern digital computers use a binary system, as the resulting electronic circuits are simple and cheap. The building blocks from which computers are constructed are logic gates, whose operation is defined by truth tables. Microcomputers are widely used in a range of scientific and consumer products because they provide cheaper and more reliable operation than do other possible design options.

The way our society produces many of the goods it needs will be drastically changed by the end of this century. Extensive assembly lines used for the mass production of standardized parts and requiring hundreds of people for their operation will be replaced by computer-controlled auto-mated production facilities employing relatively small numbers of people. Substantial adjustments to our social and economical systems will be re-quired as the nature of the work force changes. The driving force behind automation is largely economic. Advances in computer and robotic technol-ogies will ultimately make it cheaper to produce goods by automated means than by traditional assembly line techniques. Furthermore, additional auto-mation does not necessarily imply increased standardization. As the capa-bilities of industrial robots and computer-controlled machines increase, it may be possible to custom-manufacture individual parts to meet exactly an individual customer's needs.

The integration of computers into engineering promises to be exciting for at least two reasons: additional gains are possible in the economics of the manufacturing process, and changes in the manufacturing process may greatly change society.

Supplementary Examples

Example 9.9: Count to 25_{10} in a number system using 18_{10} as its base.

Solution: Eighteen coefficients are now required. Following the pattern used for hexadecimal numbers, add $G = 16_{10}$ and $H = 17_{10}$. The resulting sequence is as follows:

0, 1, 2, 3, 4, 5, 6, 7, 8, 9, A, B, C, D, E, F, G, H, 10, 11, 12, 13, 14, 15, 16, 17

Example 9.10: Suppose a computer were to be built using a base 4 system. How many discrete voltage levels would the input and output lines of logic gates be required to have?

Solution: Four unique voltage levels for the inputs would appear to be re-quired, since the coefficient of a number must be uniquely represented by a voltage level.

Each of the two input signals may assume four distinct levels. Therefore, the number of possibilities for the two lines is $4^2 = 16$. Not all of the corre-sponding output states would necessarily be unique, but the circuit design and logic design would be much more complex than for binary computers and considerably more expensive.

Example 9.11: Store 29_{10} in BCD form.

Solution: The initials BCD stand for binary-coded decimal notation. Exactly four binary digits are used to store each decimal digit. Thus the binary pattern $1001_2 = 9_{10}$ is the largest that would appear. The decimal digits themselves are stored as binary equivalents. Thus

$$29_{10} = \underbrace{0010_2}_{2} \quad \underbrace{1001_2}_{9}$$

$$= \quad 00101001_2$$

Comment: BCD routines are particularly useful in programs that cannot tolerate rounding or truncation, such as those used for financial computations.

Example 9.12: Determine the message contained in the following data, which is expressed in hexadecimal forms:

$$48 \quad 45 \quad 4C \quad 4C \quad 4F$$

Solution: These numbers are hexademical representations of ASCII codes. The patterns are looked up in a table of ASCII codes, producing

HELLO

Example 9.13: Find the truth table for the circuit of Figure 9.12.

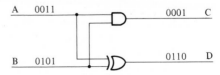

Figure 9.12 Circuit used in Example 9.13.

Solution: Inputs A and B may assume two values. Thus, four inputs are possible. The possibilities and corresponding outputs are shown in Table 9.8.

TABLE 9.8 Truth Table for Example 9.13

Inputs		Outputs	
A	B	C	D
0	0	0	0
0	1	0	1
1	0	0	1
1	1	1	0

Comment: This circuit is called a *binary half adder*. It adds two single-digit binary numbers, producing a sum output (D) and a carry output (C).

Example 9.14: Find the truth table for the circuit shown in Figure 9.13.

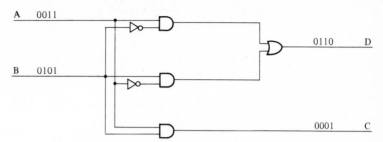

Figure 9.13 Circuit used in Example 9.14.

Solution: As in the previous example, there are two inputs (so that the truth table will have four rows) and two outputs. All possibilities are again investigated.

TABLE 9.9 Truth Table for Example 9.14

Inputs		Outputs	
A	B	C	D
0	0	0	0
0	1	0	1
1	0	0	1
1	1	1	0

Comment: This circuit produces exactly the same truth table as the previous one did, and it is also a binary half adder. Note that the circuit of the previous example used two logic gates and that this one required six, making it a much more expensive and less desirable design. Determining the best design for the more complex circuits is often not a simple task.

▲ Problems

p9.1   Show the results of counting by 1 from 0_3 to 1000_3.

p9.2   Count from 0_{10} to 20_{10} in a base 9 system.

p9.3   Count from 15_{10} to 30_{10} in a base 20 system.

p9.4   What is the place value of each coefficient in the following binary number?

$$101.0111_2$$

p9.5   Which of the following equalities are true?
  (a) $10_{16} = 16_{10}$ (b) $16_8 = 8_{16}$ (c) $5_4 = 4_5$
  (d) $10_2 = 2_{10}$ (e) $5_6 = 5_{12}$

p9.6 Convert each of the following numbers into its base 10 equivalent:

(a) 0101101_2 (b) 647_8 (c) 2132_4

(d) $B4D_{16}$ (e) 543_7

p9.7 Perform the indicated conversions:

(a) $01011011010_2 = \underline{\hspace{0.5cm}}_{16}$ (b) $0110101101_2 = \underline{\hspace{0.5cm}}_8$ (c) $4735_8 = \underline{\hspace{0.5cm}}_{16}$

(d) $A3D_{16} = \underline{\hspace{0.5cm}}_2$ (e) $631_8 = \underline{\hspace{0.5cm}}_2$

p9.8 Can the binary equivalent of three octal digits be stored in an 8-bit binary word? Explain.

p9.9 Find two ways of storing 76_{10} in an 8-bit binary word.

p9.10 Determine the binary contents of the memory locations used to store the following word in ASCII:

BYTE

p9.11 A certain memory location contains 10110101_2. Is this a valid BCD number? Explain.

p9.12 A certain memory location contains 10000101_2. Convert this binary number into BCD.

p9.13 If only numbers without a sign are considered, what is the largest base 10 number that can be stored in an 8-bit binary word?

p9.14 Using the appropriate logic gates, design a device that will convert base 10 numbers into their corresponding binary equivalent. The device is to have ten input lines representing the digits 0 to 9_{10}. A logic 1 placed on any one of these lines should cause the corresponding binary number to appear on the output lines. Figure p9.14 shows the input and corresponding output resulting when a logic 1 is placed on the 5_{10} line.

p9.15 A control circuit for a solar heating system is to be designed using logic gates. The controller must receive a signal from a thermostat indicating a need for heat. Whenever heat is required, a circulating fan is to be turned on. The source of the required heat is to be from a solar heat storage device if the

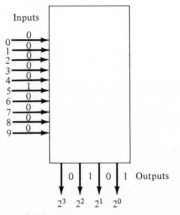

Figure p9.14 Decimal to binary convertor.

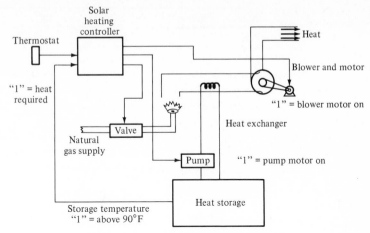

Figure p9.15 Controller for solar heating.

temperature of the storage medium is 90°F or greater. If the temperature of the storage medium is lower than 90°F, a natural gas valve is to be opened, and the resulting combustion is to be used to supply the needed heat. Figure p9.15 shows the details of the system.

p9.16 Explain the difference between the contents of a memory location and the address of a memory location.

p9.17 A certain peripheral device is connected to a microcomputer through an 8-bit port. The peripheral is constructed in such a way that all 8-bits must be available simultaneously. How many different commands can be issued to the peripheral?

p9.18 Suppose that a certain ROM has ten address lines. How many memory locations does the device contain?

p9.19 If one is available, access or log onto a mainframe computer from a personal computer and transmit a file both to and from the small computer.

p9.20 Use a personal computer to access one of the commercial data base systems, and retrieve some specific item like a weather report or a current news item.

p9.21 Use the computer system in your local library, if available, to perform a bibliographic search concerning a subject of interest to you.

p9.22 If one is available, and you do not regularly do so, use a word processor to prepare a written assignment, lecture outline, or laboratory report.

p9.23 If you are not familiar with word processors, ask someone who knows how to use one to demonstrate how it works.

p9.24 If an appropriate computer system with a spreadsheet program is available, use it to compute the total price of the following order. If the total price of any item exceeds $100, a discount of 10 percent will be allowed on that item. A tax of 5 percent is to be charged on all items, and the total price of each item is to be listed in addition to the total cost of the order.

Number of items	20	10	50	5	10
Cost	$10.00	$5.00	$5.00	$3.00	$2.00

p9.25 Suppose that all the conditions of Example 9.6 are the same except that it is known that 1000 adults will come when the ticket price is $2.80. Determine, to the nearest $0.10, what the selling price should be to produce the maximum profit.

p9.26 Explain how the various pieces of information found in a card catalog can be equated to the concepts of file, record, and field.

p9.27 Cite one example from everyday experiences of each of the following:

relational data base

hierarchical data base

networking data base

p9.28 Draw a wire-frame model of a matchbox. Redraw the matchbox, removing all hidden lines. The matchbox measures 1.5 in × 3 in × 5 in. Draw your wire-frame model to scale.

p9.29 Using a coordinate system, store the image created in p9.28 in a data file. Each record should consist of three fields, each containing a single coordinate. How many records will be in the file? What assumptions need to be made about the structure of the data storage and the image being stored?

p9.30 An entire matchbox is to be rotated counterclockwise about the vertical axis by 30° and the result is to be stored in a second data file. What mathematical processes are needed to generate the new representation? Does the size of the data file remain the same?

p9.31 Four basic arm geometries of robot arm designs are shown in Figure 9.11. For each case, what is the characteristic shape of the geometric volume in which the robot can reach and grasp?

p9.32 If you were writing computer programs to control the robotic arms shown in Figure 9.11, on what coordinate system would you base each program?

p9.33 If each robot in Figure 9.11 is equipped with a gripper that can both grip and twist, how many totally different motions (articulations) do each of the designs allow?

CHAPTER 10

Chemistry

If any single discipline could be said to form the foundation for engineering and technology, science would have to be at the top of the list. Within the sciences, chemistry and physics surely play the most prominent roles. This chapter examines the concepts of chemistry that are most relevant to engineering and technology.

Objective: The objective of this chapter is to review some of the fundamentals of chemistry that are important to engineers, technologists, and technicians.

Criteria: After completing this chapter, you should be able to do the following:

■ **10.1** Define the terms atomic number, mass number, and isotope, and determine the number of protons, neutrons, and electrons in an atom, given its nuclear symbol.

■ **10.2** Determine the empirical and molecular formulas of a compound, given the percent composition of each element and the compound's molecular weight.

■ **10.3** Given a chemical equation, balance the equation and calculate the amount of products (or reactants) expected for a given concentration of one of the reactants (or products).

■ **10.4** Make calculations pertaining to stoichiometry of solutions, given information for determining the molarity and/or the normality of the solutions involved.

■ **10.5** Make calculations based on the ideal gas law, given the ideal gas law equation and the respective pressures, volumes, and temperatures of the gases.

■ **10.6** Define alpha, beta, and gamma decay, and make calculations based on radionuclei half-lives.

▲ 10.1 Atomic Number, Mass Number, and Atomic Weight

Although the exact date for the beginning of chemistry can be debated ad infinitum, there is no question about our desire to understand our universe. Such an understanding necessarily requires investigations of the nature of matter itself, and as early as 400 B.C., there were theories about the composition of matter. It was not until the early nineteenth century, however, that John Dalton formulated the atomic theory that created the foundation for several of the basic laws of chemistry.

One of the main postulates of the Dalton theory states that all elements are composed of extremely small particles, called *atoms*. Although Dalton believed that atoms were solid, indivisible objects, subsequent experiments revealed that atoms are made up of even smaller particles called *protons*, *neutrons*, and *electrons*, with all elements except hydrogen containing at least one of each particle. (Hydrogen is composed of one proton and one electron only.) Protons and neutrons were found to have the same mass $(1.67 \times 10^{-24}g)$, but protons possess a positive charge, and neutrons are neutral. Electrons are negatively charged particles, but their mass is only about 1/1835 as great as that of a neutron or proton.

These particles are arranged in an atom in a very dense nucleus of protons and neutrons surrounded by electrons traveling in various shells around the nucleus and held in orbit by the force of attraction to the positively charged protons. Since the electrons are located at the periphery of the atom, many chemical reactions can be explained by the interaction of the orbiting electrons in the outermost shell of the elements involved.

Inasmuch as all elements are composed of various combinations of protons, neutrons, and electrons, one way to differentiate among the elements is on the basis of the number of these particles they contain. It was discovered long ago that each element contains a unique number of protons. Therefore, if the number of protons in the nucleus of one atom of the element were known, the element itself could be identified. The number of protons in an atom is its *atomic number* and is written as a subscript beside

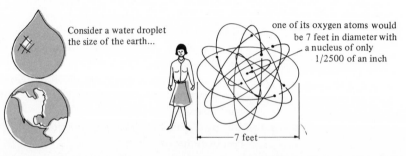

Consider a water droplet the size of the earth... one of its oxygen atoms would be 7 feet in diameter with a nucleus of only 1/2500 of an inch

Illustration 10.1 This illustrates graphically the incredibly small size of the atom.

the element symbol. Thus, $_7N$ refers to the element nitrogen, which has seven protons in its nucleus. The number of electrons in the atom must be equal to its number of protons (seven in this case), because all elements are electrically neutral. The number of neutrons present in an atom, however, is not as obvious.

In general, as the number of protons in the nucleus of an atom increases, the ratio of the number of neutrons to the number of protons also increases. Since the mass of a proton or neutron is much greater than that of an electron, the mass of an atom is essentially equal to the sum of the masses of the protons and neutrons. This sum is known as the *mass number* of an element and is represented as a superscript beside the element symbol. Thus, $_7^{14}N$ refers to the element nitrogen, which has seven protons and a total of fourteen protons and neutrons. Since the atomic number for a given element is always the same, the subscript is frequently omitted from the symbol of the element. Therefore, nitrogen with a mass number of 14 would be represented as ^{14}N.

Because a neutron is a particle that has no charge, many elements can have nuclei that have different numbers of neutrons. For example, the carbon atom, which has six protons, can have six, seven, or eight neutrons (i.e., a mass number of 12, 13, or 14, respectively). Atoms of a given element that have different mass numbers are called *isotopes* of that element.

In equation form, the mass number of an element is determined as follows:

$$\text{Mass number} = \text{number of protons} + \text{number of neutrons}$$

Example 10.1:

(a) Write the nuclear symbols for the three isotopes of oxygen (atomic number = 8) for which the mass numbers are 16, 17, and 18, respectively.
(b) How many neutrons are in the nucleus of the isotope of oxygen having a mass number of 18?

Solution:

(a) The nuclear symbols are ^{16}O, ^{17}O, and ^{18}O, respectively.
(b) Mass no. = no. protons + no. neutrons.

$$18 = 8 + \text{no. neutrons}$$

$$\text{no. neutrons} = 18 - 8 = 10$$

Comment: The number of electrons in each of the three isotopes of oxygen is 8, because the number of electrons is equal to the atomic number.

Although the early scientists investigating atomic structure did not know how to measure the extremely small masses of the atoms themselves, they were able to measure the mass of one atom relative to that of another.

TABLE 10.1 Atomic Weight of Selected Elements

Element	Symbol	Atomic Number	Atomic Weight
Carbon	C	6	12.01115
Gold	Au	79	196.967
Hydrogen	H	1	1.00797
Oxygen	O	8	15.9994
Sulfur	S	16	32.064
Uranium	U	92	238.03

This determination of the relative masses of the atoms established what is commonly called their *atomic weights,* even though, strictly speaking, it is a relative atomic mass and not a weight. Throughout history, various elements have been used as the reference element, but in 1961, it was decided to use the most common isotope of carbon as the reference and to assign it the value of exactly twelve *atomic mass units* (AMU). The atomic weight of carbon, like that of most other elements, is not a whole number because its atomic weight is a weighted average of its isotopes. That is, because carbon has two stable isotopes, ^{12}C and ^{13}C, which occur in relative proportions of 98.89 and 1.11 percent, respectively, its atomic weight is $0.9889 \times 12 + 0.0111 \times 13 = 12.0111$ AMU. Table 10.1 lists several common elements with their symbols, atomic numbers, and atomic weights. A complete table of the elements is in Appendix D.

Problems p10.1–p10.7

▲ 10.2 Empirical and Molecular Formulas

In the previous section, we discussed the basic building blocks of matter (i.e., atoms). Except in rare circumstances, matter is not composed of isolated atoms but, rather, of combinations of atoms called *molecules.* Just as the number of protons, neutrons, and electrons differentiate one type of atom from another, the particular combinations of atoms that comprise a molecule can be used to differentiate among molecules. The simplest combination of atoms in whole-number ratios that make up a molecule is called its *empirical formula.* The *actual* number of atoms in the molecule is its *molecular formula,* from which its molecular weight (i.e., the sum of the atomic weights of the atoms in the molecular formula) can be determined.

Thus, the empirical formula for glucose is CH_2O; its molecular formula is $C_6H_{12}O_6$; and its molecular weight is 180 (i.e., $6 \times 12 + 12 \times 1 + 6 \times 16$). The empirical formula can be determined from an elemental analysis of the compound. The molecular formula is a whole-number multiple of the empirical formula and can be found from its molecular weight. The procedure for determining the empirical and molecular formulas for a given compound is relatively straightforward and can be summarized as follows:

1. Obtain an analysis of the elements present in the compound. The analysis can be the percentages of each element present (for example, 20 percent hydrogen, 30 percent carbon, and the like) or the actual amounts available (38 g of oxygen, 40 g of carbon, and so on).
2. If the analysis is in percentages, convert them to masses by assuming that the amount of the compound analyzed was a certain amount, like 100 g.
3. Divide the mass of each element by its atomic weight.
4. Divide the resulting numbers by the smallest number obtained in Step 3.
5. If the result of Step 4 contains fractions, multiply all numbers by the smallest whole number that will yield all integer values. At this point, some rounding may be necessary to account for small inaccuracies in data acquisition. For example, 1.95 should be rounded to 2.
6. Write the empirical formula as $X_A Y_B Z_C$, where X, Y, and Z are the elements involved, and A, B, and C are the whole numbers obtained in Step 5. The empirical formula provides the formula weight.
7. If the molecular formula is desired, divide the molecular weight by the formula weight and multiply the A's, B's, C's, and so forth of Step 6 by the number obtained.
8. Write the molecular formula as the $X_D Y_E Z_F$, where X, Y, and Z are as defined previously, and D, E, and F are the integers obtained in Step 7.

Example 10.2 illustrates the determination of empirical and molecular formulas.

Example 10.2: Analysis of a carefully purified sample of an alcohol revealed that the weight percentages of carbon, hydrogen, and oxygen were 52.22 percent, 13.17 percent, and 34.78 percent, respectively. If the molecular weight of the alcohol is 46.08 AMU, determine its molecular formula.

Solution: The first step is to convert the element percentages into masses. Assuming an initial alcohol mass of 100 g, the element masses would be 52.22 g, 13.17 g, and 34.78 g. Next, these masses must be divided by their atomic weights:

$$\text{no. gram atomic weights of C} = \frac{52.22}{12.01} = 4.348$$

$$\text{no. gram atomic weights of H} = \frac{13.17}{1.01} = 13.04$$

$$\text{no. gram atomic weights of O} = \frac{34.78}{16.00} = 2.174$$

Now, divide each gram atomic weight by the smallest ratio obtained, 2.174:

$$C = \frac{4.348}{2.174} = 2.00$$

$$H = \frac{13.04}{2.174} = 6.00$$

$$O = \frac{2.174}{2.174} = 1.00$$

The empirical formula is C_2H_6O. Therefore, the formula weight is

$$\text{Formula Weight} = 12.01 \times 2 + 1.01 \times 6 + 16.00 \times 1$$
$$= 46.08$$

Dividing the molecular weight by the formula weight:

$$\text{multiplier} = \frac{46.08}{46.08} = 1$$

Therefore, the empirical formula and molecular formula are the same:

$$C_2H_6O$$

Comment: If the multiplier obtained above had been 2 instead of 1, the molecular formula would be $C_4H_{12}O_2$.

Empirical formula determinations are conducted when identifying unknown compounds in gaseous, liquid, or solid substances. For example, the first step in identifying the major constituents in a recycled wastewater sample might be determining the empirical formulas of the compounds present. This determination usually provides important information about the classes or types of compounds that should be checked.

Problems p10.8–p10.13

▲ 10.3 Balancing Equations

Engineers and scientists often use diagrams or symbols to simplify complex phenomena. Chemists do this by means of chemical equations that symbolically represent chemical reactions. The equation is written with certain substances on the left-hand side of an arrow (the reactants) and other substances on the right-hand side (the products), with the arrow showing the direction of the chemical reaction. For example, Equation 10.1 shows the reaction of carbon and oxygen to form carbon dioxide:

$$C + O_2 \longrightarrow CO_2 \tag{10.1}$$

Because of the law of conservation of mass, the number of atoms on both sides of the equation must be equal, in which case the equation is said to be balanced. Equation 10.1 is balanced because both sides contain one carbon and two oxygen atoms.

The procedure for balancing chemical equations requires the trial-and-error method. In certain complex equations, other techniques can profitably be used, but they will not be necessary for the level of material presented in this text. It is common practice to balance equations in a manner that will yield whole numbers as coefficients for the reactants and products. Thus, although Equation 10.2 is balanced, the equation is normally written as Equation 10.3, in which all coefficients have been multiplied by 2 so as to eliminate the fractional coefficient ahead of the oxygen molecule.

$$C_2H_6 + 3.5\ O_2 \longrightarrow 2\ CO_2 + 3\ H_2O \tag{10.2}$$

$$2\ C_2H_6 + 7\ O_2 \longrightarrow 4\ CO_2 + 6\ H_2O \tag{10.3}$$

Once an equation has been balanced, it provides quantitative information regarding the amounts of reactants necessary to complete the reaction and the amount of products that will result. That is, the coefficients ahead of the substances in a chemical equation represent the number of molecular weights of the substance in the reaction. From Equation 10.3, for example, it is known that 224 AMU of oxygen (i.e., 7×32) will be required for the complete combustion of 60 AMU of ethane (i.e., 2×30). The products will be 176 AMU of carbon dioxide and 108 AMU of water.

At this point, an obvious question might be, "What is the relationship between AMU and grams, pounds, or any other unit of measure?" To answer that question, one must understand the definition of a mole. A *mole* of any element is the amount of the element that contains the same number of atoms as exactly 12 g of ^{12}C. It has been experimentally determined that the number of atoms in 12 g of ^{12}C is 6.022×10^{23}, a very large number known as Avogadro's number. Thus, a mole of anything contains Avogadro's number of those things. For example, a mole of bananas is 6.022×10^{23} bananas. Since 12 g of ^{12}C is 1 mole, and since the atomic weight of ^{12}C is 12 AMU, and since atomic mass units are *relative* measures of mass, it follows that 14 g of ^{14}N contains 6.022×10^{23} atoms. Obviously then, 1 mole of anything is equal to its atomic or molecular weight expressed in grams instead of AMU.

Example 10.3: How many moles of glucose, $C_6H_{12}O_6$, are contained in 234 g of glucose?

Solution: One molecular weight of glucose is 180 AMU. Therefore, 1 mole of glucose is equal to 180 g. The number of moles in 234 g, therefore, is

$$\text{no. moles } C_6H_{12}O_6 = \frac{234}{180} = 1.3 \text{ moles}$$

Example 10.4: How many atoms are contained in 3.21 moles of oxygen (O_2)? In 3.21 moles of gold (Au)?

Solution: Since 1 mole of an element contains 6.022×10^{23} atoms, the number of atoms in 3.21 moles of oxygen, gold, or any other element is

$$\text{no. atoms} = 3.21 \times 6.022 \times 10^{23}$$
$$= 1.933 \times 10^{24} \text{ atoms}$$

Example 10.5: Calculate the amount of oxygen (O_2) required to burn completely 100 g of methane (CH_4). The chemical equation for combustion is

$$CH_4 + O_2 \longrightarrow CO_2 + H_2O$$

Solution: As a first step, the equation must be balanced. Thus,

$$CH_4 + 2\,O_2 \longrightarrow CO_2 + 2\,H_2O$$

The balanced equation reveals that 1 mole of methane requires 2 moles of oxygen, or 1×16 g of methane requires 2×32 g of oxygen. The amount of oxygen required for 100 g of methane, then, is

$$\text{amount } O_2 \text{ required} = 100 \times \frac{64}{16} = 400 \text{ g}$$

Comment: Once an equation has been balanced, any units of mass or weight can be used. Thus, from the relationship just determined between methane and oxygen in the above equation, 100 lbs of methane will require 400 lbs of oxygen, or 50 tons of methane will require 200 tons of oxygen, and so on.

Problems p10.14–p10.21

▲ 10.4 Solution Stoichiometry

When someone mentions the word *solution,* we frequently think of a liquid (usually water) that has something dissolved in it (usually a solid). However, because a solution is defined as a homogeneous mixture of two or more substances, there can be other types of solutions besides solids dissolved in liquids. For example, air is a solution of several different gases (i.e., oxygen, nitrogen, carbon dioxide, and so on), and brass is a solution of solids (i.e., copper and zinc). In this section, we shall look at concepts describing liquid solutions and their reactants.

In order to describe the amount of one substance contained in another, the term *concentration* is used. In liquid solutions, concentration is most conveniently expressed as either molarity M or normality N. The *molarity* of a solution is the number of moles of a substance in 1 liter of the solution.

TABLE 10.2 Valence and Equivalent Weight

Name	Symbol or Formula	Atomic or Molecular Weight	Valence	Equivalent Weight
Hydrogen	H	1.0079	1	1.0079
Oxygen	O	15.9994	2	7.9997
Sulfur	S	32.06	2, 3, or 4	—
Sodium Hydroxide	NaOH	40	1	40
Hydrochloric Acid	HCl	36	1	36
Sulfuric Acid	H_2SO_4	98	2	49
Ferric Chloride	$FeCL_3$	162	3	54
Ferric Sulfate	$Fe_2(SO_4)_3$	400	6	66.7

Thus, a 1-molar solution of sodium chloride (i.e., NaCl) contains 58 g of NaCl per liter, since 1 molecular weight of sodium chloride is 58 g. Similarly, a 5.3-molar solution of glucose ($C_6H_{12}O_6$) contains 954 g of glucose (i.e., 5.3 × 180).

Normality is the number of equivalent weights (EW) of a substance in 1 liter of solution, where the equivalent weight of a substance is equal to its molecular weight divided by its valence. The *valence* of an element refers to the combining power of that element relative to that of hydrogen and is related to the number of electrons in the atom's outermost shell. An atom's or molecule's valence can be determined from a balanced chemical equation involving that substance. Since some substances are capable of exhibiting more than one valence state, in this text the valence will be provided when needed. Table 10.2 lists several common elements and compounds with their molecular weights, valences, and equivalent weights.

Example 10.6: Calculate the molarity and normality of a solution of lime (CaO) that has a concentration of 135 g/L. The valence of lime is 2.

Solution: The molecular weight of CaO is 56 (i.e., 40 + 16). Therefore, the number of moles of CaO per liter, that is, the molarity of the solution, is

$$\text{molarity} = \frac{135}{56} = 2.41 \ M$$

The equivalent weight of lime is 56/2 = 28 g. The normality of the solution is the number of equivalents per liter. Thus,

$$\text{normality} = \frac{135}{28} = 4.82$$

Comment: The normality of a solution can be calculated directly from the molarity by multiplying by the valence. Thus, in this example, $N = 2.41 \times 2 = 4.82 \ N$.

Example 10.7: How many grams of $CaCl_2$ are required to make 1.5 L of a 1.2 M solution?

Solution: The molecular weight of $CaCl_2$ is 110. A 1 molar solution, therefore, requires 110 g $CaCl_2$ per liter. The amount of $CaCl_2$ required for a 1.2 M solution is

$$\text{amount} = 110 \times 1.2 = 132 \text{ g}$$

The 132 g are adequate for 1 L. For 1.5 L,

$$\text{total amount required} = 132 \times 1.5$$
$$= 198 \text{ g}$$

A common method for determining the concentration of a substance in a given solution is by using a procedure called *titration*. This method adds one solution containing a known amount of a reactant to a measured volume of another solution containing the substance to be measured. The known solution is added incrementally to the unknown solution until the chemical reaction is complete, as indicated by a solution color change or other end-point determination technique. The normality of the unknown substance (and, therefore, its concentration) can then be determined from the following familiar equation:

$$N_1 V_1 = N_2 V_2 \tag{10.4}$$

where

$$N_1 = \text{normality of solution 1}$$

$$V_1 = \text{volume of solution 1}$$

$$N_2 = \text{normality of solution 2}$$

$$V_2 = \text{volume of solution 2}$$

The following example illustrates the use of Equation 10.4:

Example 10.8: Determine the hardness of a solution as measured by the concentration of calcium carbonate, $CaCO_3$, if 100 mL of the solution required 20 mL of a titrant that has a normality of 0.25 N. The valence of $CaCO_3$ is 2.

Solution: The normality of the $CaCO_3$ solution can be determined from Equation 10.4, as follows:

$$N_1 V_1 = N_2 V_2$$
$$(0.25)(20) = (N_2)(100)$$
$$N_2 = 0.05$$

The concentration can be converted into units of g/L by multiplying the normality by the equivalent weight of $CaCO_3$. Thus,

$$\begin{aligned}
\text{concentration in g/L} &= (0.05)(\text{EW CaCO}_3) \\
&= 0.05(100/2) \\
&= 2.5 \text{ g/L}
\end{aligned}$$

Supplementary Examples 10.12 – 10.15
Problems p10.22 – p10.26

▲ 10.5 Ideal Gases

In the previous section, we pointed out that a solution can exist in a solid, liquid, or gaseous state. Most pure substances also can exist in any one of these three states. In this section, we shall consider the properties of substances in the gaseous state.

Gases differ from liquids in many respects, but the most obvious differences are in their expandability and compressibility. If a gaseous substance is placed in either an empty vessel or one containing another gas, it will expand uniformly until the space is occupied completely. Compared with liquids and solids, there will be large empty spaces between the molecules of a gaseous substance, and because of this, the gas can be compressed. If one recognizes pressure as the force exerted by the molecules of a gas on a unit area of a container, it should be obvious that as the size of the container is decreased, the pressure must increase, as long as the number of molecules and temperature of the gas remains the same (see Figure 10.1). Robert Boyle was the first to discover this property of gases, which can be quantitatively formulated as follows:

$$P_1V_1 = P_2V_2 \tag{10.5}$$

where P_1 and P_2 are pressures in any units and V_1 and V_2 are volumes in any units.

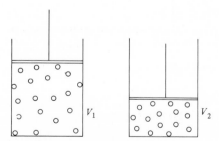

Pressure in V_2 is twice as great as that in V_1 because in a given period of time, there would be twice as many collisions with the walls of the container.

Figure 10.1 Pressure exerted by a gas.

Temperature is a manifestation of the average kinetic energy of a substance's molecules. As the average speed of a substance's molecules increases, so does its temperature. The number of collisions with the sides of a fixed container, occurring in a given period of time, also increases. To maintain a given pressure, therefore, the volume of the container must increase. That volume is directly related to temperature was first discovered by Jacques Charles. In equation form, Charles' law can be written as

$$\frac{V_1}{T_1} = \frac{V_2}{T_2} \qquad (10.6)$$

where V_1 and V_2 are volumes in any units and T_1 and T_2 are temperatures in absolute units.

If Boyle's law and Charles' law are combined, the general formula for the combined gas laws (commonly called the ideal gas law) is produced:

$$\frac{P_1 V_1}{T_1} = \frac{P_2 V_2}{T_2} \qquad (10.7)$$

where the units of P, V, and T are as previously stated.

Example 10.9: An ideal gas at a pressure of 5.0 kPa is compressed from a volume of 3.0 m³ to 2.0 m³. If the initial temperature were 120°C and the final temperature 210°C, what would be the pressure?

Solution: The temperature used in the ideal gas law must be an absolute temperature. Therefore,

$$T_1 = 120 + 273.15 = 393.15 \text{ K}$$

$$T_2 = 210 + 273.15 = 483.15 \text{ K}$$

Now,

$$\frac{(5)(3)}{393.15} = \frac{(P_2)(2)}{483.15}$$

$$P_2 = 9.2 \text{ kPa}$$

Supplementary Example 10.16
Problems p10.27 – p10.32

▲ 10.6 Nuclear Chemistry

Most of the chemical reactions between elements and compounds involve changes in the electrons that are farthest from the atom's nucleus. For some elements, however, these reactions are caused by changes in the atom's nucleus rather than in its outermost electrons. These elements are said to be *radioactive,* and this phenomenon is known as *radioactivity* or *radioactive decay.*

Radioactive decay is the spontaneous ejection of particles or electromagnetic radiation from an atom's nucleus. The three most common types of radiation are alpha (α), beta (β), and gamma (γ) rays.

Alpha radiation is the emission of nuclei of the helium atom, that is, two protons and two neutrons. This obviously changes both the atomic number and the mass number of the nucleus, thereby altering the identity of the original element. Equation 10.8 shows that the radioactive decay of uranium 238 results in the production of thorium 234:

$$^{238}_{92}U \longrightarrow {}^{234}_{90}Th + {}^{4}_{2}He \tag{10.8}$$

Beta decay is the emission of particles that have all the properties of electrons. Since the nucleus of an atom does not contain any electrons, the negatively charged particles must have been formed from the transformation of a neutron into a proton. This transformation results in an atom that has the same mass number as the original atom but a higher atomic number by one. As in alpha decay, therefore, the element formed through beta decay is different from the original one. This is shown in Equation 10.9, in which the radioactive decay of zirconium 97 results in the formation of niobium 97:

$$Zr^{97}_{40} \longrightarrow {}^{97}_{41}Nb + {}^{0}_{-1}e \tag{10.9}$$

Gamma rays consist of high-energy photons that have neither mass nor charge. Since there is no change in the atomic number of the element involved in this kind of radiation, there is no new element formed, as with alpha or beta radiation.

As our understanding of nuclear transformations has increased, our ability to exploit the effects of these processes has similarly expanded. The tremendous amounts of energy released from the rearrangement of atomic nuclei have been used to make bombs and to generate electricity. The gamma rays emitted from cobalt 60 have been used beneficially in activities as diverse as treating cancer, disinfecting meat, and conditioning wastewater. The uniformity and predictability of the decay process itself have been used by scientists and engineers as a rather sophisticated time clock. This technique is based on knowing the time required for an element to decay and is described next.

Radioactive decomposition is a unimolecular reaction that occurs at a constant rate. For such reactions, it is possible to define, for the element involved, its *half-life* as the time required for half of a given number of atoms to disintegrate. In equation form, the half-life is

$$t_{1/2} = \frac{0.693\,t}{\ln \dfrac{C_o}{C_t}} \tag{10.10}$$

where

$$t_{1/2} = \text{half-life}$$

$$t = \text{time associated with certain amount of decay}$$

$$C_o = \text{initial amount of radioactive nuclei}$$

$$C_t = \text{amount of radioactive nuclei remaining after time } t$$

Equation 10.10 can be solved for any of the terms by rearranging the equation. Example 10.10 illustrates this procedure.

Example 10.10:

(a) Calculate the half-life of ^{24}Na if an initial mass of 2.00 g is reduced to 1.80 g in 2.28 h.

(b) How much will remain after 10 h?

Solution: (a) From Equation 10.10,

$$t_{1/2} = \frac{(0.693)(2.28)}{\ln \dfrac{2.0}{1.8}} = 15 \text{ h}$$

(b) Equation 10.10 can be solved for C_o/C_t as follows:

$$\ln \frac{C_o}{C_t} = \frac{(0.693)(10)}{t_{1/2}} = \frac{6.93}{15}$$

$$\ln \frac{C_o}{C_t} = 0.462$$

$$\frac{C_o}{C_t} = 1.587$$

But

$$C_o = 2.0 \text{ g}$$

$$\therefore C_t = \frac{2.0}{1.587} = 1.26 \text{ g}$$

Information about the half-lives of radioactive materials can be used to determine the age of artifacts or other important archaeological materials. Rock deposits can be dated by measuring the amount of ^{238}U and ^{206}Pb they contain because it is known that the overall decay equation ends with the production of lead. By knowing the half-life of the process, the elapsed time from the solidification of the rock can be determined.

For materials that were once living, ^{14}C can be used to date them. This is based on the fact that the carbon dioxide in the atmosphere is made up of atoms of ^{12}C, ^{13}C, and ^{14}C. The ratio of radioactive ^{14}C to nonradioactive ^{12}C has remained relatively constant throughout the ages. When a living plant

Illustration 10.2 Artist's conception of a space-based nuclear power source. (Courtesy Department of Defense)

converts atmospheric CO_2 into cell mass by means of photosynthesis, the ratio of ^{14}C to ^{12}C in the plant is the same as that of the atmosphere. The higher forms of life that consume the plants have the ^{14}C incorporated into their cell mass as well. When the organism dies, however, the amount of radioactive ^{14}C decreases in accordance with its 5570-year half-life, altering the ratio between ^{14}C and ^{12}C. The extent of change in this ratio can be used to determine when the carbon-containing material stopped living. Example 10.11 illustrates the calculations involved.

Example 10.11: In a cave believed to have been occupied by prehistoric people, archaeologists found a piece of wood that was only 25 percent as radioactive as present-day wood is. How long had the tree been dead?

Solution: The ratio of $\dfrac{C_t}{C_o} = 0.25$. Therefore,

$$\frac{C_o}{C_t} = \frac{1}{0.25} = 4.0$$

From Equation 10.10 using $t_{1/2}$ of 5570:

$$5570 = \frac{0.693\,t}{\ln 4.0}$$

$$t = 11\ 142 \text{ yrs}$$

Problems p10.33 – p10.40

● CHAPTER SUMMARY
_____

Because the field of chemistry is so broad, any review of the subject that is limited to one chapter will necessarily omit some areas that are important to some engineers. In this chapter, we attempted to select those topics having the widest applications: the structure of atoms, the combination of these atoms to form molecules, and the determination of molecular formulas. The relationship between products and reactants was shown by way of the balanced chemical equation. Application of the balanced equation to liquid solutions led to solution stoichiometry and the concepts of molarity and normality. And we briefly examined the relationship among the pressure, volume, and temperature of ideal gases and the concepts of radioactive decay and radionuclei half-lives for artifact dating.

Supplementary Examples

Example 10.12: Calcium hypochlorite, $Ca(OCl)_2 \cdot 2H_2O$, is commonly used to chlorinate residential swimming pools. If the commercially available calcium hypochlorite is 65 percent pure, (a) how many grams must be added to a 20 000-gal pool in order to provide a chlorine concentration of 2 mg/L; and (b) if the calcium hypochlorite costs $1.35 per lb, what will be the monthly chlorination cost if the dosage rate specified in part (a) is required daily?

Solution: (a) The amount of chlorine in 20 000 gal of water containing 2 mg/L is

$$\text{amount Cl} = 20\ 000 \text{ gal} \times 3.785 \text{ L/gal} \times 2 \text{ mg/L}$$
$$= 151\ 400 \text{ mg or } 151.4 \text{ g}$$

The percentage of Cl in pure calcium hypochlorite is

$$\% \text{ Cl} = \frac{2(35)}{178} \times 100 = 39.3\%$$

Thus, each gram of pure calcium hypochlorite contains 0.393 g of chlorine, but since the commercially available calcium hypochlorite is only 65 percent pure, each gram contains

$$Cl/g = 0.393 \times 0.65 = 0.255 \text{ g Cl}$$

In order to provide 151.4 g, the amount of calcium hypochlorite to be added is

$$\text{amt Ca(OCl)}_2 \cdot 2H_2O \text{ req'd} = \frac{151.4}{0.255}$$
$$= 594 \text{ g}$$

(b) The daily dosage rate in lb/day is

$$\text{dosage/day} = 594 \text{ g} \times 2.205 \times 10^{-3} \text{ lb/g}$$
$$= 1.3 \text{ lb/day}$$

Assuming 30 days per month,

$$\text{cost/mo} = 1.3 \text{ lb/day} \times 1.35 \text{ \$/lb} \times 30 \text{ days/mo}$$
$$= \$52.65/\text{mo}$$

Example 10.13: If 360 g of $CaCO_3$ is dissolved in water and diluted to 3 L, calculate (a) the molarity and (b) the normality of the solution.

Solution: (a) The concentration of $CaCO_3$ in solution is

$$\text{conc} = \frac{360 \text{ g}}{3 \text{ L}} = 120 \text{ g/L}$$

The molecular weight of $CaCO_3$ is 100 g. Therefore, the molarity is

$$\text{molarity} = \frac{120}{100} = 1.2 \text{ M}$$

(b) The equivalent weight of $CaCO_3$ is 50 g (i.e., 100/2). The number of equivalents/liter, therefore, is

$$\text{normality} = \frac{120}{50} = 2.4 \text{ N}$$

Example 10.14: If a liter of grain alcohol is 95 percent ethanol (C_2H_5OH) by weight, what will be its molarity if the bottle contains 800 g of liquid?

Solution: The amount of ethanol in the solution is

$$\text{amount ethanol} = 800 \times 0.95 = 760 \text{ g}$$

The molecular weight of ethanol is 46 g. Therefore, the molarity is

$$\text{molarity} = \frac{760}{46} = 16.5 \text{ M}$$

Example 10.15: How many grams of lime (CaO) would be required to neutralize 4 L of a 1.5 N solution of HCl according to the following equation?

$$HCl + CaO \longrightarrow CaCl_2 + H_2O$$

Solution: The first step is to balance the equation as follows:

$$2HCl + CaO \longrightarrow CaCl_2 + H_2O$$

Next, the amount of HCl in the solution must be determined:

$$EW = \frac{\text{molecular wt.}}{\text{valence}} = \frac{36}{1} = 36$$

A 1.5 N solution contains $1.5 \times 36 = 54$ g of HCl per liter. Four liters, then, contain

$$\text{amt HCl} = 54 \times 4 = 216 \text{ g}$$

Finally, from the balanced equation, 72 g of HCl require 56 g of CaO. The amount of CaO required for 216 g of HCl is

$$\text{CaO req'd} = \left(\frac{56}{72}\right)(216) = 168 \text{ g}$$

Example 10.16: Three cubic meters of a gas at 10 psi pressure were compressed into a volume of 5 L. If the temperature were held constant throughout the compression process, what would be the final pressure?

Solution: Since the temperature was constant, it does not have to be included in the calculation. Using Equation 10.5 and converting m³ into liters,

$$P_1V_1 = P_2V_2$$

$$(10 \text{ psi})(3 \text{ m}^3)(10^3 \text{ L/m}^3) = (P_2)(5 \text{ L})$$

$$P_2 = 6000 \text{ psi}$$

▲ Problems

p10.1   Determine the number of protons, neutrons, and electrons in each of the following atoms:
(a) $^{63}_{29}\text{Cu}$ (b) $^{127}_{53}\text{I}$ (c) $^{200}_{80}\text{Hg}$

p10.2   Identify the elements that have the following atomic numbers:
(a) 16   (b) 74   (c) 98

p10.3   The identification of element X is unknown, but it is known that the mass of calcium is ten times greater than that of the unknown element. What is the unknown element?

p10.4   Chlorine has two isotopes, with masses of 34.969 and 36.966 AMU. If the percentage of occurrence of the former is 75.53 percent and the latter is 24.47 percent, what will be the average atomic weight of chlorine?

p10.5 The two isotopes of boron were found to have masses of 10.02 and 11.01 AMU. If the abundance of the first is 18.83 percent and of the latter is 81.17 percent, what will be the average atomic weight of boron?

p10.6 An analysis of the element neon indicated that it was made up of three isotopes with masses of 19.99, 20.99, and 21.99 AMU. If their percentages of occurrence were found to be 90.92, 0.25, and 8.83 percent, respectively, what would be the average atomic weight of neon?

p10.7 A sample of copper was found to contain two isotopes ^{63}Cu and ^{65}Cu with masses of 62.930 and 64.928 AMU. If the atomic weight of copper is 63.54 AMU, what will be the relative percentage of each isotope in the sample?

p10.8 Elemental analysis of an unknown compound revealed that it was composed of 2.0 percent hydrogen, 32.7 percent sulfur, and 65.3 percent oxygen. What is its (a) empirical formula and (b) formula weight?

p10.9 Analysis of a compound showed that it contained 83.72 percent carbon and 16.28 percent hydrogen. What are (a) its empirical formula and (b) its molecular formula if its molecular weight is 86?

p10.10 The analysis of 160 g of an unknown substance showed that it contains 64 g of copper, 32 g of sulfur, and 64 g of oxygen. What is its empirical formula?

p10.11 An unknown compound contains 3 g of hydrogen, 42 g of nitrogen, and 144 g of oxygen. What are its (a) empirical formula and (b) molecular formula if its molecular weight is 63?

p10.12 What is the molecular formula of a compound that has a molecular weight of 74 and contains 48.7 percent carbon, 8.1 percent hydrogen, and 43.2 percent oxygen?

p10.13 The molecular weight of glucose $(C_6H_{12}O_6)$ is 180. How many grams of carbon are contained in 600 g of glucose?

p10.14 The molecular formula for potassium dichromate is $K_2Cr_2O_7$. How many grams of chromium are in 3 moles?

p10.15 How many grams of $CoCl_2$ constitute 4.1 moles?

p10.16 How many NH_3 atoms are there in 1.3 moles?

p10.17 How many grams of NaOH are required to obtain 12.044×10^{23} atoms?

p10.18 How many moles of Na_2SO_4 are in 15.32×10^{24} atoms?

p10.19 Balance the following equation:

$$Al_2(SO_4)_3 + Ca(HCO_3)_2 \longrightarrow Al(OH)_3 + CaSO_4 + CO_2$$

p10.20 Balance the following equation and determine the amount of NaCl that is formed from 108 g of HCl:

$$HCl + Na_2CO_3 \longrightarrow NaCl + H_2CO_3$$

p10.21 Balance the following equation and determine the amount of $CaSO_4$ that is formed from 255 g of $Fe_2(SO_4)_3$:

$$Fe_2(SO_4)_3 + Ca(OH)_2 \longrightarrow Fe(OH)_3 + CaSO_4$$

p10.22 How may grams of calcium chloride, $CaCl_2$, are required to prepare (a) a 1 M solution, (b) a 3.3 M solution, and (c) a 3.3 N solution? The valence of $CaCl_2$ is 2.

p10.23   How many grams of sodium bicarbonate, $NaHCO_3$, are required to prepare (a) a 1 M solution, (b) a 7 M solution, and (c) a 7 N solution? The valence of $NaHCO_3$ is 1.

p10.24   If 200 mL of a 0.50 N solution are titrated with a 10.0 N solution, how many milliliters of titrant will be required?

p10.25   If 25 mL of a 0.02 N solution are titrated with a 0.05 N solution, how many milliliters of titrant will be required?

p10.26   If 40 mL of a 0.05 N solution of sodium hydroxide, $NaOH$, are required to neutralize 10 mL of a sulfuric acid solution (H_2SO_4), (a) what is the normality of the H_2SO_4 solution, (b) what is the molarity of the H_2SO_4, and (c) how many grams of H_2SO_4 are in the 10-mL solution (the valence of H_2SO_4 is 2)?

p10.27   A gas at a pressure of 3 kPa occupies a volume of 2 m³. If the gas is allowed to expand at a constant temperature into a volume of 6 m³, what will be its final pressure?

p10.28   An ideal gas has a volume of 4 L at 350 K and 8 lb/in² pressure. What will be its volume at 250 K and 16 lb/in²?

p10.29   A gas at 20°C and 14.7 lb/in² is heated to 70°C. If the volume remains constant, what will be its final pressure?

p10.30   If $P_1 = 10$ lb/in², $V_1 = 5$ ft³, and $T_1 = 60$°F, what will be T_2 in °F if $P_2 = 18$ lb/in² and $V_2 = 3$ ft³?

p10.31   A gas at 50°F occupies a volume of 10 m³. If the gas is heated to 200°F, what will be its final volume if the pressure during heating remains constant?

p10.32   The initial pressure, temperature, and volume of a gas are 5 kPa, 75°C, and 4 m³, respectively. If the final pressure and volume are 8 kPa and 10 m³, what will be its final temperature in °C?

p10.33   Tritium is a radioisotope of hydrogen that has the symbol ^3_1H. During the beta decay of tritium, (a) what element will be formed, (b) what will be the atomic number of the product, and (c) what will be the mass number of the product?

p10.34   During the beta decay of $^{35}_{32}S$, (a) what element will be formed, (b) what will be the atomic number of the product, and (c) what will be the mass number for the product?

p10.35   When radium, $^{226}_{88}Ra$, decays through the emission of an alpha particle, (a) what element will be formed, (b) what will be the atomic number of the product, and (c) what will be the mass number?

p10.36   Polonium, $^{218}_{84}Po$, decays by the emission of either an alpha or a beta particle. If an alpha particle is emitted, (a) what element will be formed, (b) what will be the atomic number of the product, and (c) what will be the mass number?

p10.37   Strontium 90, $^{90}_{38}Sr$, is a radioactive nuclide that has a half-life of 29 yrs. How long will it take for 300 g of strontium to be reduced to 100 g?

p10.38   Polonium, $^{218}_{84}Po$, has a half-life of 3.05 min. How long will it take for 300 g to be reduced to (a) 200 g, (b) 50 g, and (c) 3 g?

p10.39   How long will it be before the radiation from an element that has a half-life of 22 yrs is reduced by (a) 50 percent, (b) 90 percent, and (c) 99.9 percent?

p10.40   Determine the half-life of an element if an initial amount of 500 g is reduced to 7 g in 20 yrs.

CHAPTER 11

Electrical Engineering

Perhaps no other form of energy is as convenient or useful as electricity, for without it our complex technological society could not exist. This chapter discusses the utilization of electrical energy.

Objective: The objective of this chapter is to clarify basic electrical engineering terminology and simple electrical circuits.

Criteria: After you have completed this chapter you should be able to do the following:

- **11.1** Define the electrical quantities charge, current, voltage, and power, and state the units used to identify each one.
- **11.2** State Ohm's law and compute the unknown quantity for a resistor, assuming that two of the following three quantities are given: voltage, current, resistance.
- **11.3** Identify resistors connected in series and calculate their combined resistance, the current flow through them, and the voltage drop across each one.
- **11.4** Identify resistors connected in parallel and calculate their combined resistance, the current flow through each, and the voltage drop across the combination.
- **11.5** Calculate current flow through and voltage drop across any resistor in a series-parallel circuit containing a single voltage source.

▲ 11.1 Definitions

The following definitions related to electricity should be reviewed before studying additional concepts:

ampere (I) The basic unit of electrical charge movement or charge flow.
conductor A material that readily allows the flow of current.
conventional current flow The direction in which positive charge carriers would move if current flow were to result from positive charge motion instead of electron motion (which is the actual cause of current flow).
coulomb (Q) The basic unit of electrical charge.
current The movement of electrical charge.
joule (J) The unit of measurement of electrical work.
load The portion of an electrical circuit that converts electrical energy into some other form.
ohm (Ω) The unit of measurement of electrical resistance.
resistance (R) The opposition to the flow of electrical current.
source The part of an electrical circuit that supplies energy to other parts of a circuit.
volt (V) The unit of measurement of electrical potential.
voltage The electrical force or "electrical pressure" that forces current to flow in a circuit.
watt (W) The unit of measurement of electrical power.

▲ 11.2 Ohm's Law

Figure 11.1 shows a simple electrical circuit, consisting of a battery and a resistor connected by wires assumed to have zero resistance. The battery is the source of electrical energy within the circuit, and the resistor is the electrical load that utilizes the supplied energy.

Before discussing how the circuit operates, we shall describe how a battery functions. As a result of a chemical reaction, electrons are torn away

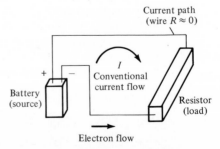

Figure 11.1 Electrical circuit with a battery and resistor.

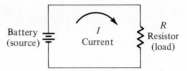

Figure 11.2 Schematic diagram of the electrical circuit with a battery and resistor.

from a material connected to the positive (+) terminal of the battery and forced to accumulate on a second material connected to the negative (−) side of the battery. This separation of charge creates an electrical potential difference, or electrical "pressure," because the electrons would "like" to recombine with the molecules from which they were removed. As a result of the pending chemical reaction, which could force additional electrons to move, the battery is said to have potential energy.

In order to utilize the potential energy, the electrons must be allowed to move from the battery's negative terminal back to the positive terminal. This movement is permitted by interconnecting wires and a load that, in this case, is a resistor. As the electrons move through the resistor, they collide, producing additional vibrations of the molecules within the resistor. Thus the resistor is heated, and the stored chemical energy in the battery is gradually converted to kinetic or thermal energy in the resistor. Actually, the connecting wires are also heated by the current flow, but because good electrical conductors are usually chosen, the heating effect in the wires is small and is usually neglected in computations.

Electrical circuits may involve many sources, loads, and interconnecting wires that, if represented in the form of a pictorial diagram as in Figure 11.1, could result in very complex and possibly confusing drawings. Thus a symbolic representation for each element in electrical circuits has been developed, and Figure 11.2 shows the circuit when redrawn using this notational scheme.

Note in Figure 11.2 that the arrow associated with current flow is pointing in a clockwise direction. Actually, the electrons are moving counterclockwise in the circuit, but in conformance with standard practice, we shall view current as the flow of positive charge (which moves opposite in direction to the electrons' movement). Thus, we say that current is flowing in a clockwise direction around the circuit. To avoid confusion, the term *current flow* is often replaced by the term *conventional current flow,* which implies the movement of positive charge in the direction of the arrow in Figure 11.2

Suppose we conduct the experiment implied by the schematic diagram in Figure 11.3. The arrow drawn across the battery symbol indicates that the resulting voltage may be adjusted to various desired values. If we measure and plot the current flow through the resistor for various values of voltage, the graph shown in Figure 11.4 will result.

Illustration 11.1 Size comparison of the conventional lead acid batteries in the foreground and the nickel-zinc oxide batteries in the rear. The battery packs have equal energy, but the nickel-zinc oxide is only half as large and weighs less than half as much. (Courtesy General Motors)

Observe that no current flows when the applied voltage is zero and that as the voltage is increased, the current also increases by a proportional amount. The relationship between I and V is given by the equation of a straight line:

$$y = mx + b$$

For this case specifically, the equation becomes

$$I = mV + 0 \tag{11.1}$$

where b, the y-intercept, is zero, since the V-versus-I characteristic goes

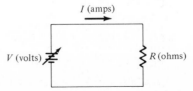

Figure 11.3 Variable voltage source connected to a resistor.

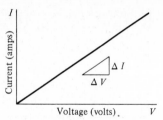

Figure 11.4 Current as a function of voltage for a fixed resistance.

through the origin. Further note that I and V are related by a constant of proportionality, m, which is the slope of the line. Recalling that resistance is defined as the opposition to the flow of electrical current in a circuit, one might suspect that this quantity should also appear in the equations. This suspicion is valid, for resistance is just the reciprocal of the slope of the line shown in Figure 11.4. Thus,

$$m = 1/R$$

and by rearranging Equation 11.1,

$$V = I\,R \tag{11.2}$$

This equation can be further manipulated into other forms, as follows:

$$I = V/R \tag{11.3}$$

$$R = V/I$$

The interrelationship of voltage, current, and resistance expressed by these equations is known as Ohm's law and is the most basic and often-used electrical theory. In words, Ohm's law is as follows:

> Current through a resistor is directly proportional to the voltage across the resistor and inversely proportional to the resistance of the resistor.

Example 11.1: A 2-ohm resistor is connected to a 10-volt battery. Compute the resulting current flow.

Solution: Using Ohm's law (Equation 11.3),

$$I = V/R$$

$$I = 10 \text{ volts}/2 \text{ ohms}$$
$$= 5 \text{ amps}$$

Example 11.2: The current flowing out of a 9-volt battery is to be no larger than 100 ma (0.1 amp). What is the smallest permitted value of load resistance?

Solution: Again using Ohm's law,

$$R_{min} = V/I$$
$$= 9 \text{ volts}/0.1 \text{ amps}$$
$$= 90 \text{ ohms}$$

Comment: Because of the inverse relationship between resistance and current, a resistance of 90 ohms or more limits the current to 100 ma or less.

Example 11.3: Compute the voltage across a 1000-ohm resistor if 0.2 amp is known to be flowing through it.

Solution: Using another form of Ohm's law,

$$V = I R$$

$$V = (0.2 \text{ amps})(1000 \text{ ohms})$$
$$= 200 \text{ volts}$$

Example 11.4: The voltage-versus-current characteristics of two different resistors are shown in Figure 11.5. Which of the two resistors is larger?

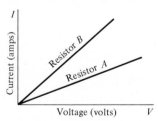

Figure 11.5 Voltage vs current characteristic for two resistors.

Solution: From Ohm's law and the equation of a straight line, it is known that slope and resistance are inversely related. The line associated with resistor A has a smaller slope than that associated with resistor B. Therefore, because of this inverse relationship, resistor A is larger than resistor B.

Problems p11.1–p11.6

▲ 11.3 Resistors in Series

Suppose a second resistor is added to the circuit shown in Figure 11.2. This may be done in one of the two ways, as shown in Figure 11.6.

Illustration 11.2 Development of a prototype electrical circuit using computer-aided design. (Courtesy AT&T, Bell Laboratories)

In this section, consider only the series connection of resistors shown in Figure 11.6(a). Resistors are said to be connected in series if the same current flows through both of them.

Note in Figure 11.6(a) that there is still only one path for current to follow as it flows out of the battery through the resistors and back into the battery. The same current must flow through each resistor, since only one current flows through the circuit. Also, only one end of each resistor is connected to the other, again implying that the same current must flow through both. Because resistors R_1 and R_2 have the same current flowing through them, they are said to be *in series.* As will be seen later, it is possible for two resistors to be connected in series without the resistors being located immediately adjacent to each other.

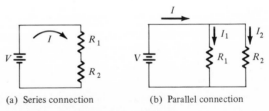

(a) Series connection   (b) Parallel connection

Figure 11.6 Two resistors connected to a battery.

In order to compute the current flow through these resistors, their combined effect must be determined. Recalling that resistance is defined as the opposition to current flow, as additional resistance is added to the circuit, this opposition would be expected to increase. That is, one would expect the two resistors to act just like a single resistor whose value was the sum of the two. This is, in fact, the situation, and this concept may be stated in the form of a rule:

> The combined resistance of resistors connected in series is equal to the sum of the individual resistances.

The corresponding equation for this rule is

$$R_{TOTAL} = R_1 + R_2 + R_3 + \ldots + R_n \tag{11.4}$$

Example 11.5: Compute the total resistance in the circuit of Figure 11.7.

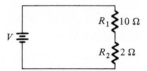

Figure 11.7 Circuit of Example 11.5

Solution: Since only one current can flow in the circuit, the resistors are in series, and the total resistance is found by means of addition as per equation 11.4

$$R_{TOTAL} = R_1 + R_2$$
$$= 10 \text{ ohms} + 2 \text{ ohms}$$
$$= 12 \text{ ohms}$$

Example 11.6: Compute the total resistance in the circuit shown in Figure 11.8.

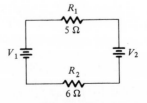

Figure 11.8 Circuit of Example 11.6.

Solution: There is only a single path for current flow. Therefore, R_1 and R_2 have the same current flowing through them, and the total resistance in the circuit is found by summing the values of R_1 and R_2.

$$R_{TOTAL} = R_1 + R_2$$
$$= 5 \text{ ohms} + 6 \text{ ohms}$$
$$= 11 \text{ ohms}$$

Comment: Note that even though R_1 and R_2 are not "next to" each other, they are in series, since the same current flows through both.

Example 11.7: Compute the total resistance in the circuit shown in Figure 11.9.

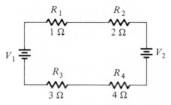

Figure 11.9 Circuit of Example 11.7.

Solution: Because there is only a single path for current flow, all four resistors are connected in series. Therefore,

$$R_{TOTAL} = R_1 + R_2 + R_3 + R_4$$
$$= 1 \text{ ohm} + 2 \text{ ohms} + 3 \text{ ohms} + 4 \text{ ohms}$$
$$= 10 \text{ ohms}$$

Problems p11.7 – p11.10

▲ 11.4 Resistors in Parallel

Figure 11.6(b) shows the other possible way of connecting resistors. This configuration is called a *parallel connection,* with the significant feature that both resistors have the same voltage across them. If the resistances are different but the voltage is the same, then two different currents will flow. The rule for combining resistors in parallel is as follows:

The reciprocal of the combined resistance of resistors connected in parallel is equal to the sum of the reciprocals of the individual resistors.

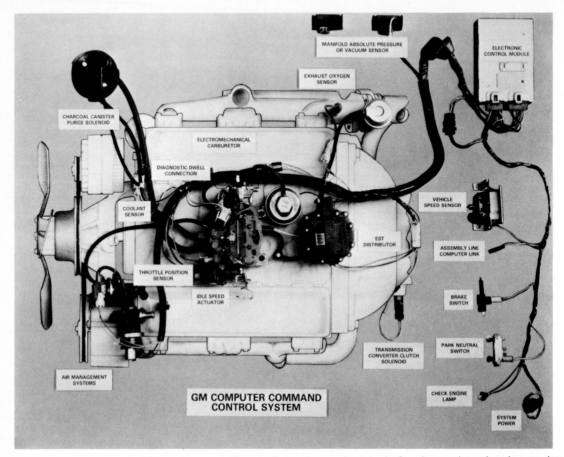

Illustration 11.3 Electronic sensing and control of an internal combustion engine. (Courtesy General Motors)

In equation form,

$$1/R_{\text{TOTAL}} = 1/R_1 + 1/R_2 + \ldots 1/R_n \tag{11.5}$$

Whenever resistors are connected in parallel, the resulting value will be less than that of any of the individual resistances.

Example 11.8: Find a convenient expression for computing the combined value of two resistors connected in parallel.

Solution: The rule for combining two resistors connected in parallel becomes

$$1/R_{\text{TOTAL}} = 1/R_1 + 1/R_2$$

First, find the lowest common denominator:

$$1/R_{\text{TOTAL}} = (R_2 + R_1)/R_1 R_2$$

Now, take the reciprocal of both sides of the equation to obtain:

$$R_{TOTAL} = R_1 R_2 / (R_1 + R_2)$$

Comment: For two resistors in parallel, the combined result is found by taking the "product over the sum." This can be done, however, for only *two* resistors. Thus,

$$R_{TOTAL} = R_1 R_2 R_3 / (R_1 + R_2 + R_3)$$

Is not correct.

Example 11.9: Find the combined resistance of the resistors in the circuit shown in Figure 11.10.

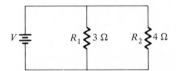

Figure 11.10 Circuit of Example 11.9.

Solution: Using the "product over the sum,"

$$R_{TOTAL} = R_1 R_2 / (R_1 + R_2)$$
$$= (3 \text{ ohms})(4 \text{ ohms}) / (3 \text{ ohms} + 4 \text{ ohms})$$
$$= 12/7 \text{ ohms}$$

Example 11.10: Find the combined resistance of the resistors in the circuit shown in Figure 11.11.

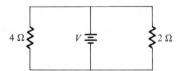

Figure 11.11 Circuit of Example 11.10.

Solution: The 4-ohm and the 2-ohm resistors are in parallel, since they still have the same voltage (V) across them.

$$R_{TOTAL} = (4 \text{ ohms})(2 \text{ ohms}) / (4 \text{ ohms} + 2 \text{ ohms})$$
$$= 8/6 \text{ ohms}$$
$$= 1\,1/3 \text{ ohms}$$

Comment: Note that the result of combining two or more resistors in parallel must always be less than the smallest of the individual resistors. Here 1 1/3 ohms is less than 2 ohms.

Example 11.11: Find the combined resistance of the resistors in the circuit of Figure 11.12.

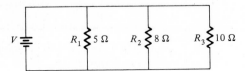

Figure 11.12 Circuit of Example 11.11.

Solution: Since there are now three resistors in parallel, revert to the basic rule for combining resistors in parallel:

$$1/R_{TOTAL} = 1/R_1 + 1/R_2 + 1/R_3$$
$$= 1/5 \text{ ohm} + 1/8 \text{ ohm} + 1/10 \text{ ohm}$$
$$= 0.2 + 0.125 + 0.1$$
$$= 0.425$$

Taking reciprocals on both sides of the equation,

$$R_{TOTAL} = 1/0.425$$
$$= 2.35 \text{ ohms}$$

Problems p11.11–p11.14

▲ 11.5 Computation of Current and Voltage in Series-Parallel Resistive Circuits

The circuits discussed previously may be viewed as components of more complex circuits that may be solved by sequentially applying the various techniques already described. Consider the circuit shown in Figure 11.13.

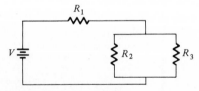

Figure 11.13 A series-parallel resistive circuit.

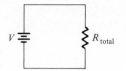

Figure 11.14 The circuit of Figure 11.13 redrawn in simplest form.

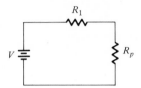

Figure 11.15 Simplified equivalent circuit of Figure 11.13.

This circuit may be simplified until it becomes the one shown in Figure 11.14. To do this, note that R_2 and R_3 are connected in parallel (i.e., have the same voltage). Combining these two resistances produces the circuit of Figure 11.15. Since R_1 and R_p are themselves connected in series (i.e., have the same current), they may be combined to produce the final circuit suggested by Figure 11.14.

Example 11.12: Simplify the circuit of Figure 11.16 as much as possible.

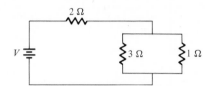

Figure 11.16 Circuit of Example 11.12.

Solution: The 1-ohm and 3-ohm resistors are in parallel and therefore can be combined:

$$R_p = (1 \text{ ohm})(3 \text{ ohms})/(1 \text{ ohm} + 3 \text{ ohms})$$
$$= 0.75 \text{ ohm}$$

Since the 2-ohm resistor and R_p are connected in series, the total circuit resistance is

$$R_{\text{TOTAL}} = R_p + 2 \text{ ohms}$$
$$= 0.75 + 2$$
$$= 2.75 \text{ ohms}$$

Once the circuit has been simplified by utilizing the series and parallel combination rules, the task of finding the voltages and currents associated with various components of a given circuit is obviously much easier. The next example illustrates this process.

Example 11.13: Find the current through and voltage across each resistor in the circuit shown in Figure 11.17.

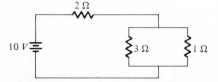

Figure 11.17 Circuit of Example 11.13 with voltage specified.

Solution: This is the same circuit as that in Example 11.12 except that the battery voltage is now specified. When the three resistors are properly combined, the following simplified circuit results:

Figure 11.18 Simplified equivalent circuit for Example 11.13.

Using Ohm's law, the current can readily be computed, as follows:

$$I_{BAT} = 10 \text{ volts}/2.75 \text{ ohms}$$
$$= 3.64 \text{ amps}$$

Certainly the current through the battery will not change as the various equivalent combinations of resistors are connected to it. After the current has been determined, it is possible to "move back one step" and consider the following circuit:

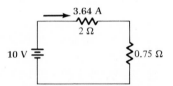

Figure 11.19 Intermediate equivalent circuit for Example 11.13.

Note that the 10-volt battery, the 2-ohm resistor, and the 0.75-ohm resistor all are connected in series (same current flows through them). Using Ohm's law, the voltage drop across the 2-ohm and 0.75-ohm resistors can now be found:

$$V_{2\Omega} = I_{2\Omega} \, (R_{2\Omega})$$
$$= I_{BAT} \, (R_{2\Omega})$$
$$= (3.64 \text{ amps})(2 \text{ ohms})$$
$$= 7.28 \text{ volts}$$

$$V_{0.75\Omega} = I_{0.75\Omega} \, (R_{0.75\Omega})$$
$$= I_{BAT}(R_{0.75\Omega})$$
$$= (3.64 \text{ amps})(0.75 \text{ ohms})$$
$$= 2.73 \text{ volts}$$

It is now possible to "back up" by one additional step. If the 0.75-ohm resistor "acts exactly like" the 3-ohm and 1-ohm resistors connected in parallel, then the voltage that was just computed ($V_{0.75\Omega} = 2.73$ volts) should not change when the 0.75-ohm resistor is replaced with the parallel combination of the 2-ohm and 3-ohm resistors. This is, in fact, the situation, and the initial circuit containing all known or previously computed values can be redrawn:

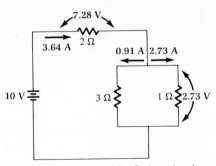

Figure 11.20 Initial circuit of Example 11.13 showing known and computed values.

The currents flowing through the 3-ohm and 1-ohm resistors can now be computed as follows:

$$I_{3\Omega} = V_{3\Omega}/R_{3\Omega}$$
$$= 2.73 \text{ volts/3 ohms}$$
$$= 0.91 \text{ amps}$$

$$I_{1\Omega} = V_{1\Omega}/R_{1\Omega}$$
$$= 2.73 \text{ volts/1 ohm}$$
$$= 2.73 \text{ amps}$$

At this point, the voltage across and current through each component in the circuit is known, and so the solution process is complete.

Comment: Note that if the two currents through the 3-ohm and 1-ohm resistors are added, the sum will be just the current through the battery or, equivalently, through the 2-ohm resistor.

$$I_{3\Omega} + I_{1\Omega} = 2.73 \text{ amps} + 0.91 \text{ amps}$$
$$= 3.64 \text{ amps}$$
$$= I_{BAT}$$

This, of course, is no accident. Current must flow in continuous closed paths, and if at some point the path divides, the sum of the currents in the two paths will always equal the initial current. This concept is known as *Kirchhoff's current law* and forms the basis for another way of analyzing electrical circuits but will not be discussed in this text.

By inspecting the voltages across the various elements in Example 11.13, it can be noted that the voltage across the 2-ohm resistor plus the voltage across the parallel combination (i.e., the 3-ohm and 1-ohm resistors) add up to 10 volts.

$$V_{2\Omega} + V_{3\Omega\|1\Omega} = 7.28 \text{ volts} + 2.73 \text{ volts}$$
$$= 10.01 \text{ volts}$$

Problems p11.15 – p11.19

● CHAPTER SUMMARY

Ohm's law forms the basis for virtually all circuit analysis techniques used in electrical engineering. When two or more resistors are connected in series, the result is larger than any of the individual resistors. The resistance that results when resistors are connected in parallel must be smaller than any of the individual resistances. Many circuits may be solved by combining series and parallel groups of resistors to simplify the resulting circuit. Resistive circuits with only one battery may be solved with extensions of this method.

Supplementary Examples

Example 11.14: Find the current flowing through all resistors in the following network.

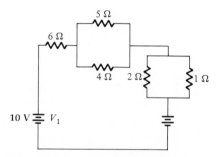

Figure 11.21 Circuit of Example 11.14.

Solution: The 1-ohm and 2-ohm resistors are in parallel and they can be combined, resulting in a single equivalent resistance. Similarly, the 4-ohm and 5-ohm resistors can also be combined.

$$R_{1\Omega\|2\Omega} = \frac{R_{1\Omega}R_{2\Omega}}{R_{1\Omega} + R_{2\Omega}}$$

$$= \frac{(1)(2)}{(1)+(2)} = \frac{2}{3} = 0.667 \text{ ohms}$$

$$R_{4\Omega\|5\Omega} = \frac{R_{4\Omega}R_{5\Omega}}{R_{4\Omega} + R_{5\Omega}}$$

$$= \frac{(4)(5)}{(4)+(5)} = \frac{20}{9} = 2.222 \text{ ohms}$$

The 6-ohm resistor is in series with each of the equivalent resistances computed above. The total circuit resistance is found by summing.

$$R_{\text{TOTAL}} = R_{6\Omega} + R_{1\Omega\|2\Omega} + R_{4\Omega\|5\Omega}$$
$$= 6.0 + 0.667 + 2.222 = 8.889 \text{ ohms}$$

The total current flow is now computed using Ohm's Law.

$$I_{\text{TOTAL}} = \frac{V_{\text{BAT}}}{R_{\text{TOTAL}}}$$

$$= \frac{10}{8.889} = 1.125 \text{ amps}$$

The total current flows through the 6-ohm resistor, so:

$$I_{6\Omega} = I_{\text{TOTAL}} = 1.125 \text{ amps}$$

One way to find the current through each resistor in a parallel combination is to first find the voltage across the parallel resistors and then compute individual currents using Ohm's Law.

$$V_{1\Omega\|2\Omega} = I_{\text{TOTAL}} R_{1\Omega\|2\Omega}$$
$$= (1.125 \text{ A})(0.667 \ \Omega) = 0.750 \text{ volts}$$

$$I_{1\Omega} = \frac{V_{1\Omega\|2\Omega}}{R_{1\Omega}} = \frac{0.750}{1.0} = 0.750 \text{ amps}$$

$$I_{2\Omega} = \frac{V_{1\Omega\|2\Omega}}{R_{2\Omega}} = \frac{0.750}{2.0} = 0.375 \text{ amps}$$

And

$$V_{4\Omega\|5\Omega} = I_{\text{TOTAL}} R_{4\Omega\|5\Omega}$$
$$= (1.125 \text{ A})(2.22 \ \Omega) = 2.5 \text{ volts}$$

$$I_{4\Omega} = \frac{V_{4\Omega\|5\Omega}}{R_{4\Omega}} = \frac{2.5}{4} = 0.625 \text{ amps}$$

$$I_{5\Omega} = \frac{V_{4\Omega\|5\Omega}}{R_{5\Omega}} = \frac{2.5}{5} = 0.5 \text{ amps}$$

COMMENT: The solution can be checked in a number of ways. One way is to sum the currents flowing through each resistor in a parallel combination. This sum should equal the total current flowing into that combination. Specifically for this problem:

$$I_{\text{TOTAL}} \overset{?}{=} I_{1\Omega} + I_{2\Omega}$$
$$\overset{?}{=} 0.075 + 0.375 = 1.125 = I_{\text{TOTAL}}$$
$$I_{\text{TOTAL}} \overset{?}{=} I_{4\Omega} + I_{5\Omega}$$
$$\overset{?}{=} 0.625 + 0.5 \quad = 1.125 = I_{\text{TOTAL}}$$

The currents found flowing in the individual resistors do sum to the correct total current.

▲ Problems

p11.1   A 25-ohm resistor is connected to a 12-volt battery. Compute the resulting current flow.

p11.2   A certain flashlight bulb filament has a resistance of 30 ohms when 200 milliamps are flowing through it. Compute the voltage of the battery used in the flashlight.

p11.3   The voltage-versus-current characteristic for a certain electrical device is shown in Figure 11.3. What is the device's resistance?

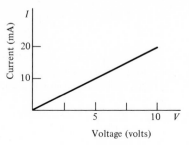

Figure p11.3 Voltage-current characteristic used for Problem p11.3.

p11.4   A 1.5-volt battery can, at most, deliver 50 milliamps. What is the smallest resistor that can be connected to the battery?

p11.5   Find the current in each of the resistors in the circuit shown in Figure p11.5.

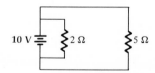

Figure p11.5 Circuit for Problem p11.5.

p11.6   Can the circuit shown in Figure p11.6 be solved using only Ohm's Law?

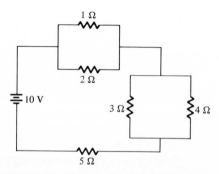

Figure p11.6 Circuit used in Problem p11.6

p11.7   A 2-ohm and a 5-ohm resistor are connected in series. Compute the resulting resistance.

p11.8   Find the total resistance in the circuit shown in Figure p11.8.

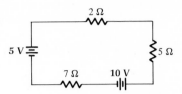

Figure p11.8 Circuit used for Problem p11.8.

p11.9   Which resistors are in series in the circuit shown in Figure p11.9?

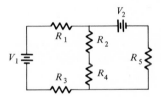

Figure p11.9 Circuit used for Problem p11.9.

p11.10   Current and voltage are measured in a circuit consisting of a variable power supply and a single resistor. The result is shown in Figure p11.10. A second resistor is added to the circuit in series with the first. If a new graph is made, will the resulting straight line fall above or below the initial line? Show the calculations that justify your answer.

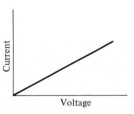

Figure p11.10 Graph used in Problem p11.10.

p11.11   A 2-ohm resistor is connected in parallel with a 12-ohm resistor. What is the resulting resistance?

p11.12   Three resistors (5 ohm, 7 ohm, and 3 ohm) are connected in parallel. Compute the resulting resistance.

p11.13   Five resistors all are connected in parallel. Their values are 2 ohms, 4 ohms, 8 ohms, 3.25 ohms, and 5.5 ohms. What statement can you make about the size of the resulting equivalent resistor?

p11.14   Shown in Figure p11.14 is a graph of voltage and current flow in a certain electrical circuit consisting of a variable voltage source and a resistor. If a second resistor is connected in parallel with the first, how will the graph be changed?

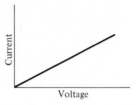

Figure p11.14 Graph used in Problem p11.14.

p11.15   Find the equivalent resistance of the circuit shown in Figure p11.15.

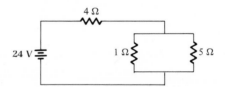

Figure p11.15 Circuit used in Problem p11.15.

p11.16   Find the total resistance of the circuit shown in Figure p11.16.

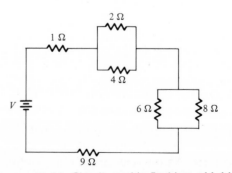

Figure p11.16 Circuit used in Problem p11.16.

p11.17   If the battery in the circuit of p11.15 is known to be 24 volts, compute the resulting current flow through it.

p11.18   Compute the voltage across the 4-ohm resistor of p11.15.

p11.19   How would the voltage across the 4-ohm resistor be changed if the battery voltage were decreased to 12 volts in the circuit of p11.15?

12

Statics

Statics is the area of rigid-body mechanics that pertains to the equilibrium of bodies. A body in equilibrium is either at rest or moving in a straight line with constant velocity, but in this chapter we shall discuss only bodies that are at rest. The concern in statics is defining the external loads or forces acting on a body and, from these, determining the internal forces. Engineers need to know the internal forces in a body or structure in order to be able to choose materials for it and determine the geometry of its design.

There are many different types of bodies or structures, with varying degrees of complexity. In this chapter we shall analyze only some simple structures in a plane.

Objective: The objective of this chapter is to enable you to determine the forces in a plane for a body in static equilibrium.

Criteria: After you have completed this chapter, you should be able to do the following:

- **12.1** Express a force vector in the x-y plane in terms of its Cartesian components in the x- and y-directions, and in polar vector form.
- **12.2** Determine the resultant of concurrent forces in a plane.
- **12.3** Determine the moment about a given point caused by concentrated forces and/or uniformly distributed forces in a plane.
- **12.4** From a diagram of a body in a plane with concentrated forces, concentrated moments, uniformly distributed forces, and supports and connections, draw a correct free-body diagram.

■ **12.5** For a body in a plane with concentrated forces, concentrated moments, uniformly distributed forces, and supports and connections, use the equations of equilibrium in a plane to determine the specified unknown.

▲ 12.1 Forces As Vectors

In mechanics, it is important to differentiate between quantities that possess only magnitude and quantities that possess both magnitude and direction. Quantities that possess only magnitude are called *scalars*. Examples of scalar quantities are length, area, and mass. Algebra is used to perform mathematical operations with scalars.

Quantities that possess both magnitude and direction are called *vectors*. Vector algebra is used to perform mathematical operations with vectors. A vector is represented graphically by an arrow, whose length represents the vector's magnitude and whose head represents the vector's direction. Several examples of vector representations and uses are shown in Figure 12.1.

A vector may be acting at a fixed point, as represented in Figure 12.1(a), or it may be acting along some line of action but not at a specific point, as shown in Figure 12.1(b). *Concurrent* vectors act at a point, or their lines of

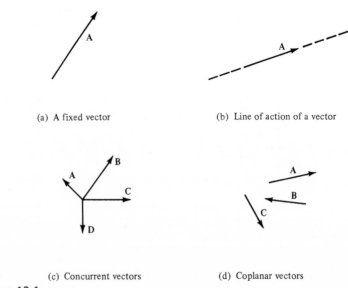

(a) A fixed vector   (b) Line of action of a vector

(c) Concurrent vectors   (d) Coplanar vectors

Figure 12.1

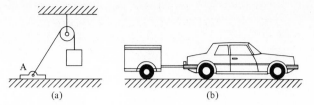

Figure 12.2

actions pass through a common point, as shown in Figure 12.1(c). *Coplanar* vectors act in a common plane, as represented in Figure 12.1(d).

A *force* is a push or pull of specific magnitude in a specific direction and may be represented by a vector, since the force has both magnitude and direction. Two examples of physical situations in which forces can be represented as vectors are shown in Figure 12.2. In Figure 12.2(a), the force exerted upon support A by the cable can be represented by a vector, as shown in Figure 12.3(a). For Figure 12.2(b), the force exerted on the trailer by the car is represented by a vector, as shown in Figure 12.3(b). The direction and sense of each force are obvious from the vector. Usually the length of the vector is proportional to the magnitude of the force.

Another set of vectors representing forces is shown in Figure 12.4. Again, the direction and sense of each force are obvious. If the scale is as shown, force A is 30 N, force B is 25 N, and force C is 15 N.

Although we can represent a vector graphically by an arrow, we also need to represent it mathematically. This can be done in either *Cartesian* components of the vector or in polar vector form.

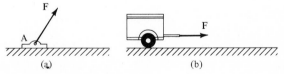

Figure 12.3 Vectors representing forces

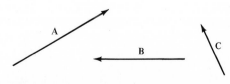

Scale: 1 mm = 1 N

Figure 12.4 Vectors representing forces

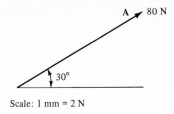

Scale: 1 mm = 2 N

Figure 12.5 Vector A

A boldface character is often used to represent a vector, such as **A** in Figure 12.5. In handwritten form a vector is often written as $\vec{A}$, a letter with an arrow over it, or $\underline{A}$, a letter underlined.

It is convenient to represent a vector in terms of its Cartesian or rectangular components, which in the $x - y$ plane are its components in the x- and y-directions. This is shown in Figures 12.5 and 12.6. A_x is the component of the vector in the x-direction, and A_y is the component of the vector in the y-direction.

In polar vector form the vector, **A**, is written in the form

$$\mathbf{A} = A \,\underline{/\theta}$$

where A is the scalar magnitude of the vector and the angle, θ, is the angle that the vector makes with the positive x-axis measured counterclockwise. The following vector form conversions will make the two mathematical representations of vectors easier to understand.

The vector in Figure 12.5 has a magnitude of 80 N in the direction shown. In polar vector form, $\mathbf{A} = 80\text{ N }\underline{/30°}$. This force vector can be resolved into its Cartesian, or rectangular, components in the x- and y-directions. These components are depicted graphically in Figure 12.6 as A_x and A_y.

The values of A_x and A_y can be determined as

$$A_x = A \cos 30° = 80 \cos 30° = 69.3 \text{ N}$$

$$A_y = A \sin 30° = 80 \sin 30° = 40.0 \text{ N}$$

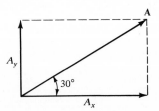

Figure 12.6 Rectangular components of Vector A

Resolution of a Vector into Cartesian Components

To resolve a vector into its Cartesian or rectangular components in the x- and y-directions, these equations are always correct.

$$A_x = A \cos \theta$$

(12.1)

$$A_y = A \sin \theta$$

where θ is the angle that the vector makes with the positive x-axis measured counterclockwise, and A is the magnitude of the vector. Another representation often used for the magnitude of the vector is $|\mathbf{A}|$.

Addition of Cartesian Components

If the Cartesian components of a vector are known, it is often necessary to determine the magnitude and direction of the vector. The magnitude of the vector is easily determined by means of the Pythagorean theorem.

$$|\mathbf{A}| = \sqrt{A_x^2 + A_y^2}.$$

To determine the angle θ for the direction of the vector, a sketch should be made of the vector. This is necessary because calculators usually determine only angles less than or equal to 90°. The angle θ can be determined by trigonometry, as shown in the following examples.

Example 12.1: Express the forces in Figure 12.7 in polar vector form and resolve the forces into their Cartesian or rectangular components.

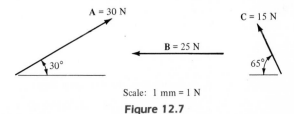

Scale: 1 mm = 1 N

Figure 12.7

Solution: The angles θ are depicted in Figure 12.8 measured counterclockwise from the positive x-axis.

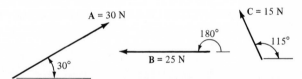

Figure 12.8

Therefore, in polar form,

$$\mathbf{A} = 30 \text{ N } \underline{/30°}$$

$$\mathbf{B} = 25 \text{ N } \underline{/180°}$$

$$\mathbf{C} = 15 \text{ N } \underline{/115°}$$

The rectangular components are depicted in Figure 12.9 and calculated below:

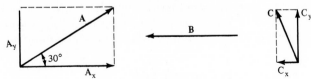

Figure 12.9

$$A_x = A \cos 30° = 30 \cos 30° = 25.98 \text{ N}$$

$$A_y = A \sin 30° = 30 \sin 30° = 15.00 \text{ N}$$

$$B_x = -B = -25 \text{ N}$$

$$B_y = 0$$

$$C_x = C \cos 115° = 15 \cos 115° = -6.34 \text{ N}$$

$$C_y = C \sin 115° = 15 \sin 115° = 13.59 \text{ N}$$

Example 12.2: A force has rectangular components

$$F_x = 13.5 \text{ N}$$

$$F_y = -17.2 \text{ N}$$

Express **F** in polar vector form.

Solution: A graphical description is shown in Figure 12.10.

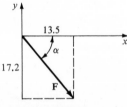

Scale: 1 mm = 1 N

Figure 12.10

The magnitude of **F** is

$$|\mathbf{F}| = \sqrt{(13.5)^2 + (17.2)^2} = 21.9 \text{ N}$$

The simplest angle to determine is α, shown in Figure 12.10.

$$\alpha = \tan^{-1}\left(\frac{-17.2}{13.5}\right) = -51.9°$$

Therefore the angle that **F** makes with the positive x-axis measured counter-clockwise is

$$\theta = 360° - 51.9° = 308.1°$$

$$\mathbf{F} = 21.9 \text{ N } /308.1°$$

Example 12.3: A force is given in polar vector form as

$$\mathbf{R} = 35 \text{ N } /210°$$

Determine the Cartesian components of **R**.

Solution: A graphical representation is shown in Figure 12.11.

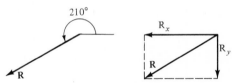

Figure 12.11

Using Equation 12.1,

$$R_x = 35 \cos(210°) = -30.3 \text{ N}$$

$$R_y = 35 \sin(210°) = -17.5 \text{ N}$$

Problems p12.1–p12.10

▲ 12.2 Resultant of Concurrent, Coplanar Forces

Several forces may act on a body or at a point simultaneously, and it is often necessary to determine the resultant of these forces. The *resultant* of two or more forces is the single force that would produce the same effect on a body as the forces it replaces. Since the resultant is the vector sum of the forces, the forces must be added vectorially. Two vectors can be added using the parallelogram law of vector addition, but if more than two concurrent vectors are to be added, it is simpler to add the forces using the Cartesian vector form.

To add two vectors to determine their resultant using the *parallelogram law of vector addition,* the vectors are joined at their tails, as shown in Figure 12.12(a). This forms two adjacent sides of a parallelogram. The resultant, **R**, is the line from the tails of **A** and **B** to the opposite corner of the parallelogram, as shown in Figure 12.12(a).

Another way of depicting this addition is by the triangular construction shown in Figure 12.12(b). **A** and **B** are joined tip-to-tail. **R** is the vector from the tail of **B** to the tip of **A**.

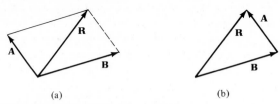

(a)   (b)

Figure 12.12 Parallelogram law of vector addition

Example 12.4: Two cables are exerting forces on a pin, as shown in Figure 12.13. Determine the resultant of the forces.

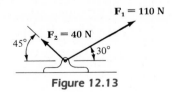

Figure 12.13

Solution: The parallelogram law of vector addition may be used.
The forces F_1 and F_2 are joined tail-to-tail to form adjacent sides of a parallelogram, as shown in Figure 12.14(a). The resultant, F_R, is the diagonal of the parallelogram from the tails of F_1 and F_2. The forces may also be drawn tail-to-head to form a triangle, shown in Figure 12.14(b). The resultant is the third side of the triangle.

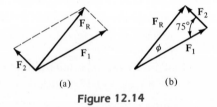

(a)   (b)

Figure 12.14

In Figure 12.14(b), the angle between $\mathbf{F}_1$ and $\mathbf{F}_2$ can be determined by geometry to be $75°$, as shown in Figure 12.15.

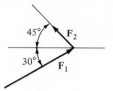

Figure 12.15

The law of cosines can be used to determine the magnitude of $\mathbf{F}_R$:

$$|\mathbf{F}_R| = \sqrt{(110)^2 + (40)^2 - 2(110)(40)\cos 75°}$$

$$|\mathbf{F}_R| = 106.9 \text{ N}$$

The law of sines can be used to determine the angle ϕ:

$$\frac{40}{\sin \phi} = \frac{106.9}{\sin 75°}$$

$$\phi = 21.2°$$

The angle, θ, that $\mathbf{F}_R$ makes with the positive x-axis, measured counterclockwise, is

$$\theta = 30° + 21.2° = 51.2°$$

In polar form:

$$\mathbf{F} = 106.9 \text{ N } \underline{/51.2°}$$

To obtain the Cartesian components of the force resultant, use Equation 12.1.

$$F_x = 106.9 \cos(51.2°) = 67.0 \text{ N}$$

$$F_y = 106.9 \sin(51.2°) = 83.3 \text{ N}$$

It is also possible to express the two forces, $\mathbf{F}_1$ and $\mathbf{F}_2$, in their Cartesian components for addition.

$$F_{1x} = 110 \cos 30° = 95.3$$

$$F_{1y} = 110 \sin 30° = 55.0$$

$$F_{2x} = 40 \cos 135° = -28.3$$

$$F_{2y} = 40 \sin 135° = 28.3$$

$$F_x = F_{1x} + F_{2x} = 95.3 - 28.3 = 67.0 \text{ N}$$

$$F_y = F_{1y} + F_{2y} = 55.0 + 28.3 = 83.3 \text{ N}$$

Example 12.5: Determine the resultant of the concurrent coplanar force system in Figure 12.16.

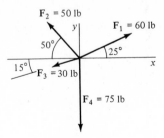

Figure 12.16

Solution: The forces could be added using the parallelogram law of addition, but this would be more time-consuming than using the Cartesian components. Using the Cartesian components, the solution is as follows:

$$F_{1x} = 60 \cos 25° = 54.4$$

$$F_{1y} = 60 \sin 25° = 25.4$$

$$F_{2x} = 50 \cos 130° = -32.1$$

$$F_{2y} = 50 \sin 130° = 38.3$$

$$F_{3x} = 30 \cos 195° = -29.0$$

$$F_{3y} = 30 \sin 195° = -7.8$$

$$F_{4x} = 0.0$$

$$F_{4y} = -75.0$$

$$F_{Rx} = F_{1x} + F_{2x} + F_{3x} + F_{4x}$$
$$= 54.4 - 32.1 - 29.0$$
$$= -6.7 \text{ lb}$$

$$F_{Ry} = F_{1y} + F_{2y} + F_{3y} + F_{4y}$$
$$= 25.4 + 38.3 - 7.8 - 75.0$$
$$= -19.1 \text{ lb}$$

The resultant is depicted graphically in Figure 12.17.

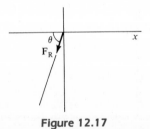

Figure 12.17

To convert into polar form:

$$|\mathbf{F_R}| = \sqrt{(6.7)^2 + (19.1)^2} = 20.2 \text{ lb}$$

$$\theta = \tan^{-1}\left(\frac{19.1}{6.7}\right) + 180° = 70.7° + 180° = 250.7°$$

$$\mathbf{F} = 20.2 \text{ lb } \underline{/250.7°}$$

Supplementary Example 12.12
Problems p12.11–p12.22

▲ 12.3 Moments Caused by Forces

A force is sometimes used to cause a body to turn, as depicted by the wrench in Figure 12.18. In this case, because of the direction of the force, **F**, the wrench tends to turn counterclockwise about point A. This tendency to turn or rotate is caused by the *moment* of the force about point A. The magnitude of the moment of a force about a point is the magnitude of the force times the perpendicular distance from the line of action of the force to the point. In Figure 12.18 the moment about point A is Fl. The moment will be referred to by its magnitude, a scalar quantity, and in Figure 12.18, it is the magnitude of the vector, $|\mathbf{F}|$, or simply, F, times the perpendicular distance from the line of action of **F** to the point A, which is the distance, l. The sign convention for moments of forces is arbitrary, but in this text we will designate counterclockwise moments as positive and clockwise moments as negative.

The moment of the force about point A in Figure 12.18 can be changed by moving the point of action of the force, as shown in Figure 12.19. The moment about point A is now Fl_1 and, of course, will be smaller if **F** remains constant. The moment can also be changed by changing the direction of the force, as shown in Figure 12.20.

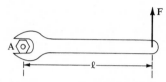

Figure 12.18

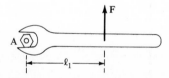

Figure 12.19

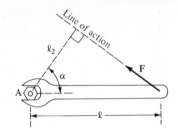

Figure 12.20

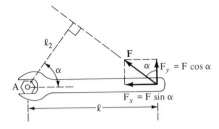

Figure 12.21

Note that in Figure 12.20, the line of action of the force is not the same as it was in the two preceding figures. The moment about A will be changed because the perpendicular distance from the line of action of the force to the point of rotation has changed. The moment about A is now Fl_2 or $Fl \cos \alpha$.

An alternative way of computing the moment about A caused by the force shown in Figure 12.20 is to resolve the force into its components, which are perpendicular to and parallel to the line from the point of the force to point A. As shown in Figure 12.21, the components in this case are F_x and F_y. F_x will not cause a moment about point A because its line of action passes directly through the point, but the moment caused by F_y about A is $F_y l = F \cos \alpha (l)$, which, of course, is the same result determined from Figure 12.20.

Example 12.6: Determine the moment about point B caused by the forces $\mathbf{F}_A$ and $\mathbf{F}_c$ in Figure 12.22.

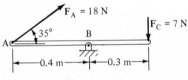

Figure 12.22

Solution: The first step is to resolve $\mathbf{F}_A$ into its components perpendicular to and parallel to the line from the point of the force, A, to point B.

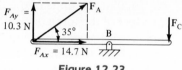

Figure 12.23

$$F_{A_x} = F_A \cos 35° = 18 \cos 35° = 14.7$$

$$F_{A_y} = F_A \sin 35° = 18 \sin 35° = 10.3$$

F_{A_x} will not cause a moment about point B, since its line of action is through B. F_{A_y} and F_c will both cause moments about point B that are clockwise and, thus, negative.

$$M_B = -(10.3 \text{ N})(0.4 \text{ m}) - (7.0 \text{ N})(0.3 \text{ m})$$

$$M_B = -6.2 \text{ N} \cdot \text{m}$$

Comment: The value of the moment is negative which means that it is clockwise. The units of N · m are dimensionally correct, since a moment is force times distance.

Although the examples so far have included only concentrated forces, that is, forces at a point, it is sometimes more realistic to model a force system as a uniformly distributed load. For example, the weight of the box in Figure 12.24(a) resting on the floor is to be modeled as a force in the x-y plane. If the mass of the box is uniformly distributed, then the weight of the box will also have to be uniformly distributed. Although it can be modeled as a concentrated force of 300 N in the middle of the box, as in Figure 12.24(b), which is sufficient for some circumstances, a more realistic model is as a force uniformly distributed over the length of the box, as shown in Figure 12.24(c).

$$w = \frac{300 \text{ N}}{2 \text{ m}} = 150 \frac{\text{N}}{\text{m}}$$

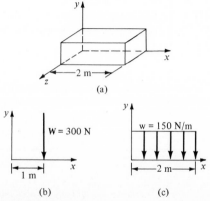

Figure 12.24 Uniformly distributed load

Notice that the units of the distributed force are force per unit length. The product of the force distribution, w, times the length over which it acts, l, is equal to the total force. A uniformly distributed force may be replaced by an equivalent concentrated force acting at the center of the length. It is easy to determine the moment caused by a uniformly distributed force if it is replaced by its equivalent concentrated force.

Example 12.7: Determine the moment about point B caused by the force system in Figure 12.25(a).

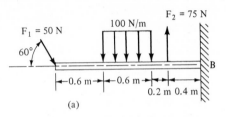

(a)

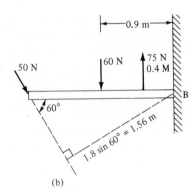

(b)

Figure 12.25

Solution: The first step is to replace the uniformly distributed load by its equivalent concentrated load at the center of the uniform distribution

$$F = (100 \text{ N/m})(0.6 \text{ m}) = 60 \text{ N}$$

The perpendicular distance between the line of action of $\mathbf{F}_1$ and point B is calculated as shown in Figure 12.25(b). The moment is now computed:

$$M_B = (50)(1.56) + (60)(0.9) - (75)(0.4)$$

$$M_B = 102 \text{ N} \cdot \text{m}$$

Problems p12.23 – p12.30

TABLE 12.1 Supports or Connections for a Rigid Body in a Plane

Connection Type and Sketch	Force or Reaction at Connection	Description
Roller (no friction)	R_1	A force always perpendicular to the surface on which the roller can roll.
Pin or hinge	R_2 R_1	The connection at the pin can rotate. A force through the pin can be in any direction. Usually the unknown reactions are depicted in the Cartesian coordinate directions.
Fixed	R_2 M_1 R_1	The fixed connection cannot move. Therefore, in addition to a force, there may be a moment at the fixed support.
Smooth contacting surfaces (no friction)	R_1	Similar to a roller. The reaction is perpendicular to the flat surface at the point of contact.
Cable		The cable is flexible and inextensible. The force must be tension along the cable.

▲ 12.4 Free-Body Diagrams

A free-body diagram of a rigid body is a sketch of a rigid body showing the external forces and moments that act on it. To determine the internal forces in a rigid body, it is first necessary to determine the external forces. Even though many of the external forces acting on a body are known, often one or more other forces may be unknown. These unknowns are usually the forces at *supports* or *connections*. Unless a body is floating freely in the air, it has supports and/or connections. To draw a correct free-body diagram, it is first necessary to determine the forces at the supports or connections. There are standard notations for depicting the supports or connections, and Table 12.1 shows some of the most common ones, those used in this text. The support or connection is depicted in its common notation in column 1; the possible

Illustration 12.1 Concrete columns are commonly used to support loads in bridges.

reactions, forces, and/or moments at the support or connection are shown in column 2; and a written description is provided in the table in column 3.

Example 12.8: Sketch the free-body diagram for the rigid body in Figure 12.26.

$F_1 = 60$ lb

30°

$M_1 = 89$ in·lb

Figure 12.26

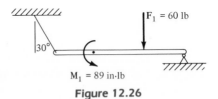

R_1

30°

60 lb

R_2

89 in·lb

R_3

Figure 12.27 Free-body diagram

Solution: There are two known loads on the rigid body, the force, F_1, and the moment, M_1. There is a cable connected to the left end of the body and a pin connection at the right end. Figure 12.27 depicts all external forces and reactions that are acting on the rigid body.

Example 12.9: Sketch a free-body diagram of the rigid body depicted in Figure 12.28.

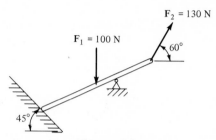

Figure 12.28

Solution: The external forces are F_1 and F_2. The connections are a smooth contacting surface at the left end and a pin near the middle of the body. The correct free-body diagram is shown in Figure 12.29.

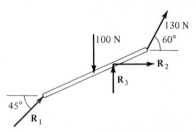

Figure 12.29 Free-body diagram

Supplementary Examples 12.13 – 12.15
Problems p12.31 – p12.38

▲ 12.5 Equations of Equilibrium in a Plane

Newton's first law of motion defines static equilibrium as follows:

A particle continues in its state of rest or uniform motion in a straight line if there is no unbalanced force acting on it.

For a rigid body, the result of static equilibrium is that the sum of the external forces acting on the body must be equal to zero and that the sum of the moment about any point in the plane must be equal to zero. For a rigid body in a plane, using the x- and y- Cartesian coordinates, the requirement may be stated mathematically as scalar equations:

$$\Sigma F_x = 0$$

$$\Sigma F_y = 0$$

$$\Sigma M = 0$$

Because these equations must be satisfied for any body in static equilibrium, the unknown reactions may often be found by using the equations. The steps to be taken to determine the reactions are:

1. Sketch a correct free-body diagram.
2. Apply the equations of static equilibrium in a plane, and solve for the unknown reactions.

It is possible for some systems to have too many unknown reactions to be able to solve for them; that is, they are indeterminant systems; however, we will not deal with such problems in this text.

Example 12.10: Determine the unknown reactions on the body shown in Figure 12.30.

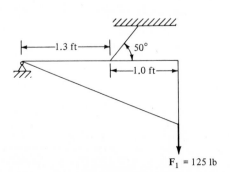

Figure 12.30

Solution: The free-body diagram is shown in Figure 12.31. The equations of equilibrium may now be used:

$$\Sigma F_x = 0$$

$$R_2 + R_3 \cos(50°) = 0$$

$$R_2 = -R_3 \cos(50°) \tag{12.2}$$

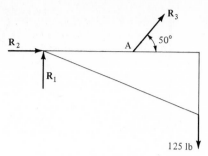

Figure 12.31 Free-body diagram

$\Sigma F_y = 0$

$R_1 + R_3 \sin(50°) - 125 = 0$

$R_1 = 125 - R_3 \sin(50°)$ (12.3)

It is convenient to take the moments about point A because R_3 will be eliminated from the moment equation, since R_3 passes through point A and thus cannot cause any moment about it. However, any point that is desired can be chosen for writing the moment equation.

$$\Sigma M_A = 0$$

$$-R_1 (1.3) - (125)(1.0) = 0$$

$$R_1 = -96.2 \text{ lb}$$

Rearranging Equation 12.3,

$$R_3 \sin(50°) = 125 - R_1$$

$$R_3 = \frac{125 - (-96.2)}{\sin(50°)}$$

$$R_3 = 288.8 \text{ lb}$$

From Equation 12.2,

$$R_2 = -(288.8) \cos(50°)$$

$$R_2 = -185.6 \text{ lb}$$

Comments: The values determined for R_1 and R_2 are negative. This means that they are actually in the opposite direction than we assumed in the free-body diagram, Figure 12.31. Thus, it does not matter in what direction the unknown reactions are assumed in the free-body diagram, because the resulting answers will indicate the correct direction.

Example 12.11: Determine the unknown reactions on the body shown in Figure 12.32.

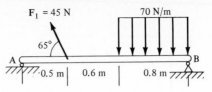

Figure 12.32

Solution: The correct free-body diagram is shown in Figure 12.33.

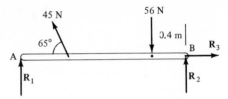

Figure 12.33 Free-body diagram

Now the equations of equilibrium may be applied:

$\Sigma F_x = 0$

$R_3 - (45) \cos(65°) = 0$

$R_3 = 19 \text{ N}$

$\Sigma F_y = 0$

$R_1 + R_2 + (45) \sin(65°) - 56 = 0$

$R_1 + R_2 = 15.2$ \hfill (12.4)

It would be convenient to take moments about point B because R_2 does not cause a moment about B and thus will not be an unknown in the equation. However, remember that the sum of the moments about any point in the plane must be zero, so any point may be chosen. Using the sign convention that moments counterclockwise are positive,

$$\Sigma M_B = 0$$

$$-R_1 (1.9) - (45) \sin(65°)(1.4) + (56)(0.4) = 0$$

$$R_1 = -18.3 \text{ N}$$

Using the previous Equation 12.4,

$$-18.3 + R_2 = 15.2$$

$$R_2 = 33.5 \text{ N}$$

Supplementary Examples 12.13–12.15
Problems p12.39–p12.54

● CHAPTER SUMMARY

This chapter introduced the concept of static forces acting on rigid bodies, described vectors representing forces, and explained concurrent coplanar forces. We also discussed supports and connections for rigid bodies and the important concept of the free-body diagram.

Structures with external forces and supports and connections were analyzed using the equations of static equilibrium in a plane.

Supplementary Examples

Example 12.12: Find the resultant of the concurrent, coplanar forces **A**, **B**, and **C**.

$$\mathbf{A} = 25 \text{ N } \underline{/260°}$$

$$\mathbf{B} = 37 \text{ N } \underline{/20°}$$

$$\mathbf{C} = 18 \text{ N } \underline{/180°}$$

Solution: Because this is a set of three concurrent, coplanar forces, the resultant should be found by expressing the forces as Cartesian components.

$$A_x = 25 \cos 260° = -4.34$$

$$A_y = 25 \sin 260° = -24.62$$

$$B_x = 37 \cos 20° = 34.77$$

$$B_y = 37 \sin 20° = 12.65$$

$$C_x = 18 \cos 180° = 18.00$$

$$C_y = 18 \sin 180° = 0.00$$

The resultant components are the sum of the x-components and the sum of the y-components.

$$R_x = -4.34 + 34.77 + 18.00$$
$$= 12.43 \text{ N}$$

$$R_y = -24.62 + 12.65$$
$$= -11.97 \text{ N}$$

A sketch of **R** is shown in Figure 12.34:

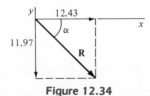

Figure 12.34

$$\alpha = \tan^{-1}\left(\frac{-11.97}{12.43}\right) = -43.92°$$

Therefore the angle θ is $360° - 43.92° = 316.08°$

$$|\mathbf{R}| = \sqrt{(12.43)^2 + (11.97)^2} = 17.26$$

Thus,

$$\mathbf{R} = 17.26 \text{ N } \underline{/316.08°}$$

Example 12.13:

Draw a free-body diagram of the bar shown in Figure 12.35, and determine the reactions at the support.

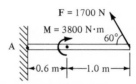

F = 1700 N

M = 3800 N·m

60°

A

0.6 m — 1.0 m

Figure 12.35

Solution: $\mathbf{F}$ is resolved into its x- and y-components:

$$F_x = -1700 \cos 60° = -850$$

$$F_y = 1700 \sin 60° = 1472$$

The free-body diagram is shown in Figure 12.36.

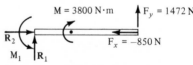

M = 3800 N·m $F_y = 1472$ N

R_2 $F_x = -850$ N

M_1 R_1

Figure 12.36

Applying the equations of equilibrium,

$$\Sigma F_x = 0$$

$$R_2 - 850 = 0$$

$$R_2 = 850 \text{ N}$$

$$\Sigma F_y = 0$$

$$R_1 + 1472 = 0$$

$$R_1 = -1472 \text{ N}$$

Taking the moments about point A,

$$\Sigma M_A = 0$$

$$(1472)(1.6) - 3800 + M_1 = 0$$

$$M_1 = 1444.8 \text{ N} \cdot \text{m}$$

Example 12.14:

For the body shown in Figure 12.37, draw the free-body diagram, and determine the reactions at the supports.

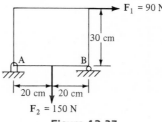

Figure 12.37

Solution: The free-body diagram is shown in Figure 12.38

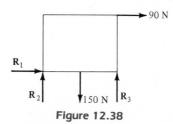

Figure 12.38

Applying the equations of equilibrium:

$$\Sigma F_x = 0$$

$$R_1 + 90 = 0$$

$$R_1 = -90 \text{ N}$$

$$\Sigma F_y = 0$$

$$R_2 + R_3 - 150 = 0$$

$$R_2 + R_3 = 150 \tag{12.5}$$

$\Sigma M_A = 0$

$-(90)(0.3) + R_3(0.4) - (150)(0.2) = 0$

$R_3 = 142.5$ N

From Equation 12.5,

$$R_2 = 7.5 \text{ N}$$

Example 12.15:
Draw the free-body diagram and determine the reactions at the supports for the body in Figure 12.39.

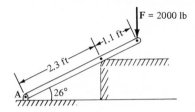

Figure 12.39

Solution: The free-body is shown in Figure 12.40:

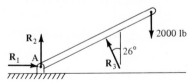

Figure 12.40

Applying the equations of equilibrium,

$\Sigma F_x = 0$

$R_1 - R_3 \sin 26° = 0$

$R_1 = 0.44 R_3$ \hfill (12.6)

$\Sigma F_y = 0$

$R_2 - 2000 + R_3 \cos 26° = 0$

$R_2 = 2000 - R_3 \cos 26°$ \hfill (12.7)

$\Sigma M_A = 0$

$(-2000)(3.4) \cos 26° + R_3(2.3) = 0$

$R_3 = 2657$ lb

From Equation 12.6,

$$R_1 = 1169 \text{ lb}$$

From Equation 12.7,

$$R_2 = -388 \text{ lb}$$

Comment: R_2 is negative, which means that the force is in the direction opposite to what we assumed.

▲ Problems

p12.1–p12.4   Express the following forces in polar vector form and then in terms of their Cartesian components in the x- and y-directions.

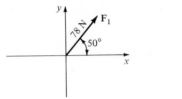

Figure p12.1

Figure p12.2

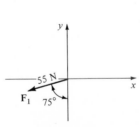

Figure p12.3

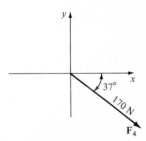

Figure p12.4

p12.5–p12.10   Given the Cartesian components of the forces, determine the polar vector form.

p12.5 $A_x = 36.5 \text{ N}, A_y = 29.4 \text{ N}$
p12.6 $B_x = -29.0 \text{ N}, B_y = 82.5 \text{ N}$
p12.7 $C_x = 55.5 \text{ N}, C_y = -36.6 \text{ N}$
p12.8 $F_x = -62.4 \text{ N}, F_y = -37.9 \text{ N}$
p12.9 $F_x = 145.78 \text{ N}, F_y = 88.36 \text{ N}$
p12.10 $A_x = -44 \text{ N}, A_y = 25 \text{ N}$

p12.11–p12.16   Add the following concurrent vectors, expressing the resultant in polar vector form:

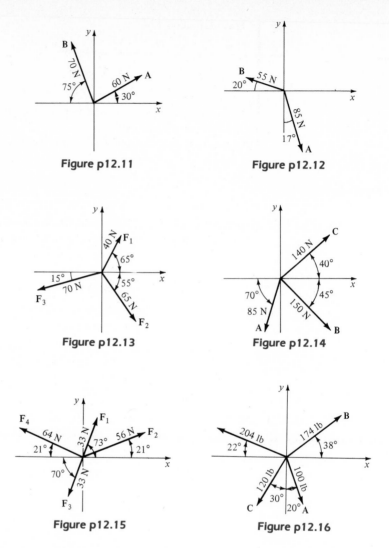

Figure p12.11

Figure p12.12

Figure p12.13

Figure p12.14

Figure p12.15

Figure p12.16

p12.17–p12.22 Add the following concurrent vectors, expressing the resultant in polar vector form:

p12.17 $A_x = 66.0$ N, $A_y = 82.2$ N
$B_x = 32.4$ N, $B_y = -18.4$ N

p12.18 $A_x = -21.8$ N, $A_y = -46.4$ N
$C_x = -45.8$ N, $C_y = 72.7$ N
$D_x = 33.3$ N, $D_y = 61.5$ N

p12.19 $F_{1x} = 159.6$ N, $F_{1y} = -36.8$ N
$F_{2x} = -106.0$ N, $F_{2y} = 175.6$ N
$F_{3x} = 47.5$ N, $F_{3y} = 155.7$ N
$F_{4x} = -144.0$ N, $F_{4y} = 46.3$ N

p12.20 $A = 140$ N $\underline{/47°}$
         $B = 78$ N $\underline{/125°}$
         $C = 37$ N $\underline{/227°}$

p12.21 $F_1 = 36.6$ N $\underline{/356°}$, $F_3 = 21.4$ N $\underline{/58°}$,
         $F_2 = 16.7$ N $\underline{/116°}$, $F_4 = 5.8$ N $\underline{/22°}$

p12.22 $F_1 = 150$ N $\underline{/30°}$, $F_3 = 57$ N $\underline{/257°}$,
         $F_2 = 87$ N $\underline{/69°}$, $F_4 = 194$ N $\underline{/118°}$

p12.23–p12.30   For each of the following force systems, determine the moment about point A caused by the forces:

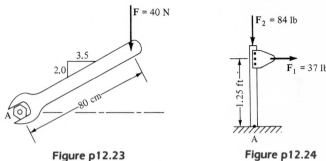

Figure p12.23   Figure p12.24

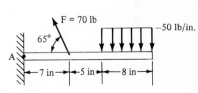

Figure p12.25   Figure p12.26

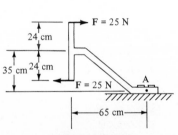

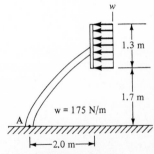

Figure p12.27   Figure p12.28

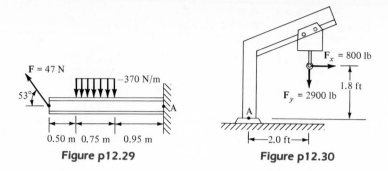

Figure p12.29   Figure p12.30

p12.31–p12.38   Sketch the correct free-body diagram for the following bodies, labeling all forces, including the unknown forces at the supports and connections:

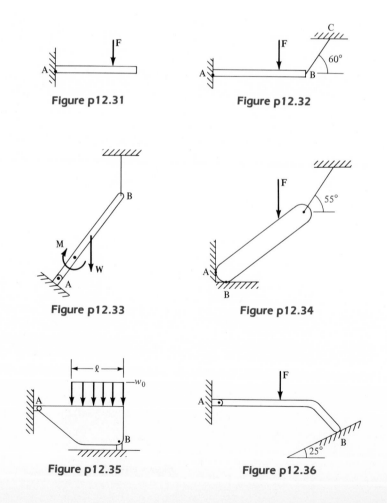

Figure p12.31   Figure p12.32

Figure p12.33   Figure p12.34

Figure p12.35   Figure p12.36

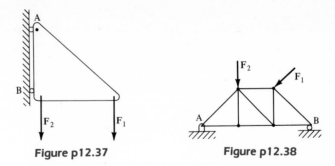

Figure p12.37

Figure p12.38

p12.39–p12.46   Determine the unknown reactions for the following bodies:

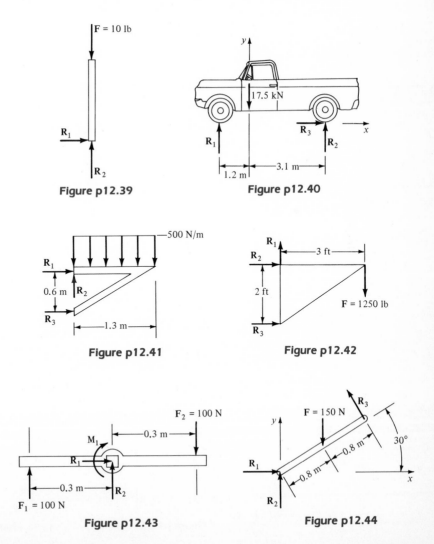

Figure p12.39

Figure p12.40

Figure p12.41

Figure p12.42

Figure p12.43

Figure p12.44

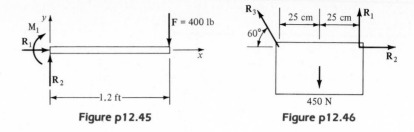

Figure p12.45

Figure p12.46

p12.47–p12.54 For the following bodies, determine the forces and/or moments at the supports or connections:

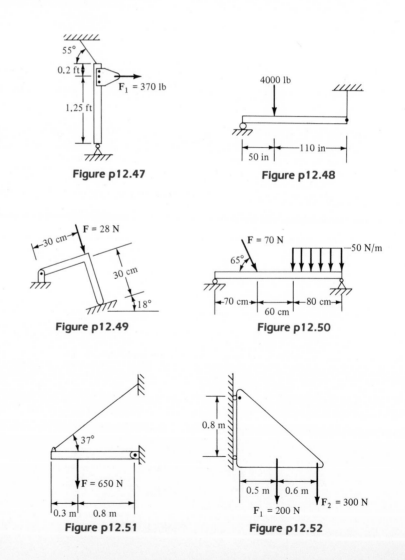

Figure p12.47

Figure p12.48

Figure p12.49

Figure p12.50

Figure p12.51

Figure p12.52

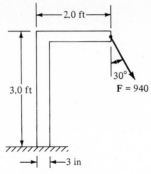

Figure p12.53

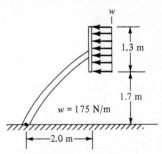

Figure p12.54

CHAPTER 13

Communication*

Communication skills distinguish the true professional from the competent technician: a professional can explain what he or she does, whereas a technician can only do. Effectiveness as an engineer is determined not only by engineering expertise but also by an ability to communicate engineering knowledge to those who need it. Indeed, various surveys have shown that engineers spend from one-fourth to one-half of their time preparing written and/or oral presentations. This chapter discusses the communication skills required of engineers and the techniques that can be used to develop those skills.

Objective: The objective of this chapter is to introduce you to the important components of engineering communication.

Criteria: After you have completed this chapter, you should be able to do the following:

- **13.1** Identify and/or list engineers' purposes for communicating in writing.
- **13.2** Identify and/or list the types of communications that engineers use.
- **13.3** Describe the various elements in the format of a technical writing assignment and categorize these elements as part of the front matter, the body, or the back matter.
- **13.4** List and briefly discuss the items to consider in order to make an effective oral presentation.
- **13.5** List the characteristics of an appropriate audiovisual aid.

---

* Portions of this chapter were contributed by Dr. Lawrence Johnson of the University of Texas at El Paso. Information was also provided by the Water Pollution Control Federation.

▲ 13.1 Purposes of Engineering Communications

Whenever an engineer is asked to design something, the first step in the overall process is determining what the design is expected to do. Unfortunately, when faced with a writing project, too few people ask themselves, "What's it supposed to do?" Instead, they just start writing and hope that their readers will somehow grasp the purpose of their communication. But that is not only poor engineering, it is poor writing as well.

To answer the question of what something is supposed to do, a good engineer looks at what are commonly seen as the three possible goals of any communication:

1. to provide information.
2. to prove a point.
3. to convince someone to do something.

Although no communication is limited to a single purpose, we can identify one purpose as the primary one and the others as secondary. For example, each year the president gives his "State of the Union" address to the nation. That speech is ostensibly informative: The president is reporting to the voters on events of the last year. At the same time, however, he is

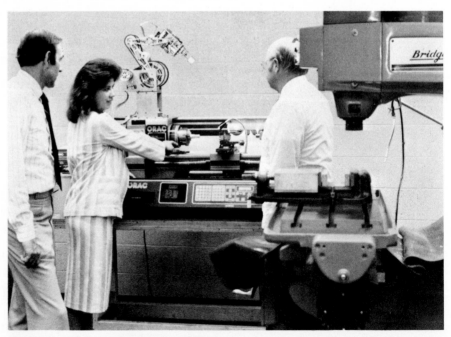

Illustration 13.1 Communication skills are very important to all aspects of engineering

arguing that his administration handled those events properly, and thus he is attempting to persuade the voters to support his policies and, indirectly, is praising himself for a job well done. The structure of such a speech is that of an informative communication, even though it also uses, at various points, techniques of argumentation, persuasion, and praise. We shall discuss the major characteristics of each of these types of communication.

Informational Communications

Effective informational communications emphasize completeness: The writer provides all the data available so that the reader will have the maximum amount of information possible on which to base any decisions. Those decisions, however, are largely left to the reader.

The structure of informational communications stresses the systematic display of the data: Using the structural pattern that best fits the material, the writer lays out the data in a way that facilitates the readers' access to and assimilation of those data. Examples of informational communications are progress reports, inspection reports, and laboratory reports.

Argumentative Communications

In effective argumentative communications, the engineer has already drawn conclusions based on extensive research and evaluation and thus selects those data from that work that can logically demonstrate those conclusions. Although additional data are often supplied, they are relegated to tables and appendices where the reader who wants more information can find them.

Structured differently from informational communications, argumentative communications state what the paper, each of its sections, and each of its paragraphs will prove and then incorporate the relevant data into statements supporting the argument. Examples of argumentative reports are feasibility studies, recommendation reports, and journal articles.

Persuasive Communications

Persuasive communications do much more than present sound engineering information. Although engineering information is central to almost any technical presentation, the values that shape that information and require special attention from the engineer are those of the reader, who may be skeptical about the engineer's judgment, motivation, or cost consciousness. Through persuasive techniques, then, the engineer establishes the reader's confidence in what has been presented. Examples of persuasive communications are technical proposals and personnel evaluations.

Problems p13.1 – p13.8

▲ 13.2 Types of Engineering Communications

These three most common reasons for engineering communications—information, argument, and persuasion—can be categorized according to the type of communication involved. The most common types of communications with which engineers are associated are lab and field notebooks, memos, executive summaries, progress reports, technical reports, technical papers, and proposals.

Lab and field notebooks are essentially informal records of data or results obtained as part of an engineering investigation. Such notebooks are typical, for example, in research laboratories and in field work such as surveying and inspection. Engineers' daily activity logs (required by some companies) are also included in this category.

Memos (an abbreviation for memoranda) are informal written communications that are directed mainly to an individual or a group of people within an organization. A memo must specify its receiver, sender, subject, and date. A sample format is shown in Figure 13.1.

An *executive summary* is a short overview (generally fewer than two pages) of a complete report. Its purpose is to give the reader enough information to understand the report's main findings. It is generally intended for readers (either technical or nontechnical) who are high enough in an organization that they must know the thrust of a report but who generally do not have the time to read it all. The main focus of a summary should be the report's recommendations, with one or two lines devoted to its purpose, scope, methods, and findings.

```
                    INTEROFFICE MEMORANDUM



    Date:       August 19, 1992

    To:         Member of Engineering Design Group

    From:       Dolores Diaz, Chief Engineer

    Subject:    Design Group Meeting



         Please plan to meet at 3:00 on Wednesday, August 26, 1992
    in the west conference room of Building 26.  Bring your
    suggestions for alterations to the main engine.
```

Figure 13.1 *Sample format of a memo*

Progress reports are periodic reports (typically, monthly, quarterly, or annual) that discuss the status of a project that has not yet been completed. They tell their readers what has been accomplished, what has yet to be completed, and any other details that may be of interest (unexpected difficulties, schedule changes, budget difficulties, and the like).

Technical reports form the backbone of engineering communications, in that the end product of all engineering projects is the final report. Technical reports thus are authoritative presentations of all of the information that is relevant to the project of interest. The format for technical reports is discussed in the next section of this chapter.

Technical papers are the primary means for presenting research results and state-of-the-art designs. Technical papers are essentially shortened versions of technical reports and frequently appear in professional journals and at technical conferences.

Proposals are communications that are intended to persuade an interested client to undertake a particular course of action. Engineers often prepare proposals to submit to governmental agencies (local, state, and federal) in order to obtain funding for applied research and development projects.

Problems p13.9 – p13.16

▲ 13.3 The Technical Report

When an engineer is familiar with and can use conventional formats, materials, and techniques in a report, there is a significant increase in both the efficiency and the effectiveness of the report. Conventional formats ensure that the engineer addresses all issues relevant to such reports. Conventional materials — standard nomenclature, notations, tables, and citations — increase the report's clarity and completeness and help the readers find the information they need. More importantly for the engineer, the conventional techniques for reporting technical information can both speed up the preparation of such reports and increase their effectiveness.

Just as conventional circuit designs vary in detail from manufacturer to manufacturer, so reporting conventions will vary in one detail or another from organization to organization. Nonetheless, every formal engineering report will have the following elements:

1. A set of introductory materials (commonly referred to as *front matter*), which may include a preface, letter of transmittal, title page, table of contents, list of tables and illustrations, and a descriptive or informative abstract.
2. The *body* of the report, which usually contains an introduction, the report itself, and the conclusion of the report, in the form of findings, conclusions, and recommendations.

3. The *back matter* which contains supplementary information in the form of graphs, tables, appendices, annexes, footnotes, and bibliographies.

Front Matter

A *preface* and a *letter of transmittal* serve the same function, and so it is usually not necessary to use both. A letter of transmittal is found either at the front of the report or clipped to the cover and is addressed to a single person or group; a preface provides the same information to a more general audience. Both a letter of transmittal and a preface should be brief and yet

```
                        STONE CONSULTANTS, INC.



                                            March 26, 1992



    Ms. Jane A. Smith Purchasing Supervisor
    ABC Company
    P. O. Box 22046
    El Paso, TX 79968

    Dear Ms. Smith:

         Enclosed is one copy of the Consulting Agreement which
    provides $20 451 support of the project entitled "Field and
    Modeling Studies of Land Disposal of Cadmium-laden Industrial
    Wastewater Sludge" to be directed by Dr. J. R. Gomez for the
    period April 1, 1992 through May 31, 1993.  I have signed all
    copies of the document on behalf of Stone Consultants, Inc.

         We have retained one fully executed copy of the document
    for our official company records.

                                   Sincerely yours,



                                   Edward Parker
                                   President


    EP:aga
```

Figure 13.2 Sample letter of transmittal

```
                      Table of Contents

      I.   Abstract                              page 1

     II.   Introduction                               2
           A. Purpose                                 2
           B. Background                               3

    III.   Procedure                                  4

     IV.   Presentation of Solution                   6
           A. Feed mechanism                          6
           B. Cutting mechanism                       8
           C. Control system                         11

      V.   Conclusions                               14

     VI.   Appendices                               15
           A. Machine drawings                       15
           B. Operating manual                       19
           C. Maintenance manual                     21
           D. Draft parts manual                     24
```

Figure 13.3 Sample table of contents

outline for the reader the subject, purpose, and context of the accompanying report. Although a particular organization may specify additional information that should be included in a letter of transmittal or a preface, you should be brief and not introduce any additional information unless it is absolutely necessary. Figure 13.2 is an example of a letter of transmittal.

The same principles apply to the construction of a *title page*. Although an organization's established conventions may specify additional information as a standard part of such title pages, the minimum essential information is what the reader needs to identify the report and distinguish it from other reports: usually the title of the report (but not necessarily its subtitle), its date, and the name of the individual (or organization) responsible for the report. The inclusion of any other information should either be an organizational specification—many firms, for example, require that the title page include the name of the firm for whom the report was prepared—or, if necessary, a contract number or a proprietary or security notice. To make a title page clear and useful, include on it only what you must and not everything you would like.

A *table of contents* is often useful, but it can also be distracting. Properly used, a table of contents can help the reader find information rapidly and offer an overview of the topics that the report covers, its organizational logic, and the approximate weight given to each topic. If a table of contents does not serve these functions (and if there is no organizational requirement for such a table), then it is only a distraction and should be omitted. Figure 13.3 shows a sample table of contents.

A *list of tables, illustrations,* or *figures* is often included as part of the report's introductory material, separate from the table of contents. Tables and figures are usually listed separately because they are two entirely different types of nontext material that provide two types of information; separate listings also allow the reader to determine what information is provided graphically and what is available in the more precise form of tables. Again, you must first ask yourself if either of these listings is actually needed. If there are only a few tables or figures, there is usually no reason for such a listing. If, on the other hand, there are many tables or figures or if the information they contain is of special interest to the reader, then listing them is appropriate. A sample list of tables is shown in Figure 13.4.

List of Tables

Appendix Tables

Figure 13.4 Sample list of tables

Abstract

A method is presented which can reduce significantly the size of eigenvalue problems necessary for accurate Rayleigh-Ritz solutions in vibration and buckling problems. Instead of carrying more and more terms in the assumed solution, this method selects terms which are most significant to the eigenvalues of interest. Only the significant terms are used in the eigenvalue problem that is to be solved. The significant terms are chosen by using a Taylor's series approximation of the eigenvalues. The Taylor's series is discussed, the method is explained, and examples of applications of the method are shown which indicate its effectiveness.

Figure 13.5 *Sample descriptive abstract*

The final element in the introductory material is an *abstract*. An abstract may either be descriptive or informative. Both kinds give the reader additional information about the report: the *descriptive abstract* outlines the major topics addressed in the report, and the *informative abstract* recapitulates the central points of information in the report. Descriptive abstracts are almost always short and succinct and provide no information beyond an enumeration of the topics covered by the report. A descriptive abstract enables the reader to determine whether or not the report is of potential value because it treats a topic of interest; it does not, however, give any information about that or any other topic. A descriptive abstract is roughly analogous to a table of contents without the page numbers and is often used in lieu of a table of contents, especially in shorter reports. Regardless of the report's length, its contents can usually be outlined in a descriptive abstract of ten or fewer lines. Informative abstracts summarize key information. They should state the issues addressed, the methodologies used, and the major findings. In some cases, the main recommendations also are included. Though journals and some organizations limit an abstract to several hundred words, the length of an informative abstract for an engineering report will usually be no more than 5 to 10 percent of the length of the report itself. In preparing either type of abstract, it is important to remember that you are now writing about the report, and not about the engineering problems and solutions addressed in that report. Your task is to tell the reader the contents of the report. A sample of a descriptive abstract is shown in Figure 13.5.

The Body of a Report

The body of a technical report consists of the following:

1. An introduction, which first defines for a reader the report's subject, purpose, and scope and then describes its general design.
2. The core report, consisting of conventional informative, demonstrative, and persuasive structures that convey all the engineering data relevant to the report's subject, supportive of the report's purpose and commensurate with its scope.
3. The conclusion of the report, which may simply summarize the report's major findings or make recommendations based on those findings.

The *introduction* tells the readers the report's subject, purpose, scope, and plan of development. The *subject* of the report should be announced as soon as possible, preferably in the first sentence. A simple statement such as

> This report evaluates the proposed design changes developed by Stone Consultants in their study dated June 13, 1985.

is not exciting, but it is specific, and the reader knows immediately what the report is going to address. Of course, the report writer can describe more precisely in the introduction what the report covers:

> This report addresses the changes recommended by Stone Consultants in the proposed offshore pumping facilities, the terminal transfer points, the pumping stations, the terminal manifolding, and the intraterminal flood and transfer pump systems.

Although such elaboration is not strictly necessary, it is often greatly appreciated by the reader, who may have forgotten exactly what Stone Consultants proposed six months ago.

Each report has a specific *purpose* that should be stated early in the introduction. Such a statement can be a simple reference to a key event that led to the report; for example,

> This report is prepared in response to your request of July 17.

More often, however, it restates the original charge to the engineers who did the evaluation:

> This report, in response to your request of July 17, evaluates the mechanical soundness of the alternative designs recommended by Stone Consultants, their impact on the mean flow rates in the system over a three-year operational period, and comparative maintenance requirements against the original design.

Such a statement of purpose tells the reader why the report was written, identifies the issues that will be addressed, and states the order in which they will be treated.

The purpose of an engineering report is further clarified by a statement of its *scope*, that is, what it will and will not address. A scope statement may describe the audience for whom the report is intended and the type of work done and often mentions procedures that were beyond the scope of the work. For example:

> This report was prepared for review by the Operational Analysis Section and action by the Contracts Branch. The evaluation of the mechanical soundness of the alternative designs was conducted according to API procedures; no field testing was possible because of the unique designs involved. Mean flow rates were calculated by means of those computer simulations currently available to the company and developed from the operation of our existing systems. Comparative maintenance requirements were established for both systems, using historical data for equipment evidencing similar design features and operating parameters.

Finally, before reaching the body of the report, the writer may prepare the reader for what is to follow, by giving a preview of the report's *structure*. Many experienced readers, pressed for time, will skip large chunks of text in lengthy reports and go straight to what they consider to be, for them, the "meat." Thus it is useful for an engineer to tell such readers where the "meat" is located in a particular report. For example:

> This report will first review the original system designs, noting, where appropriate, Stone Consultants' criticism of those designs. Each modification proposed by Stone Consultants will be described, beginning with the offshore pumping facilities, proceeding through the terminal transfer points, the pumping stations, and the terminal manifolding, and concluding with the intraterminal flood and transfer pump systems. The evaluation of each modification will describe the evaluation criteria and procedures, followed by major findings in each instance; detailed test data can be found in Appendices A through F. Finally, after the major problems with the consultants' recommendations have been identified, the report will conclude with a proposed plan for the implementation of those system modifications that this study proved to be feasible.

A report's statement of its subject, purpose, scope, and plan of development is usually prepared only after the body of the report has been designed and is in its final draft. Although good writers may be tired of the whole project by that point, they recognize that these points, more than anything else, shape the reader's initial response to the whole report and thus deserve special care.

The core of a report states what the engineer did and why. The core of many reports begins with a brief background statement, or a straight chronological narrative of the events leading to the request for the engineering work covered in the report. It should specify dates, names of key individuals, and other critical data.

The bulk of an engineering report, however, describes the work done and provides the engineering data that justify the engineers' conclusions and recommendations. This portion of the report is easy to organize if the engineer first lists, in chronological order, the major engineering procedures carried out in regard to each issue. This chronological narration is the minimum information required in an engineering report. Some audiences, however, may require more information than can be provided in a series of statements describing what was done, for example, why a particular procedure was employed, especially when that procedure is not normally employed in such situations. Readers also often want to know exactly what devices, techniques, and equipment were used in each step of the engineering analysis.

In general, an engineering analysis must anticipate the five following questions:

1. *What* steps did the engineer take to address the issue?
2. *When* or in what order were those steps taken?
3. *Why* was each step taken?
4. *How* was each step executed?
5. *What* were the results of each step?

The answers to such questions may be implicit in the report, but a good writer will anticipate such questions and make sure that the answers are given in the text.

An effective report carefully distinguishes among its findings, recommendations, and concluding summary. A report's *findings* are the facts established by the engineering analysis described in the report. The engineer should place his or her conclusions at or near the end of the report, describing concisely and clearly the relationship among various conclusions and highlighting those findings critical to decisions based on the report.

```
                    Recommendations

     The following recommendations are made in light of the
time and budgetary constraints discussed in section 3.2 of this
report.

     1. The accuracy of the flow meters from each pump should
        be checked as soon as possible.

     2. The running times per day for each pump should be
        determined before the automatic controllers are
        installed.

     3. Bids for various size bowl assemblies should be
        solicited so that decisions can be made regarding
        which should be replaced.

     4. Until the computer-assisted control system is fully
        functional, the tables presented in section 6.4 of this
        report should be used for pump selection.
```

Figure 13.6 *Sample technical report recommendations*

Summary

Any of the five methods of wastewater disposal discussed above are acceptable methods for the disposal of effluent from a secondary wastewater treatment plant. However, each method must be properly evaluated and the system properly constructed and operated to prevent pollution of other natural resources. Procedures for estimating the costs of disposal by subsurface injection and evaporation pond have been developed in this study. The procedures and cost calculations for the suggested methods are discussed in Section III.

Figure 13.7 Sample summary

Findings, however, are distinct from *recommendations*. A recommendation is a conclusion drawn from the findings that is open to debate. Whereas an engineer's findings are not (or at least should not be) debatable, recommendations are options that should be carefully considered by the reader but can be rejected. A recommendation usually describes a course of action, the conditions under which the action should be taken, who or what should take the action, and the engineering evidence that supports such an action. Figure 13.6 shows a sample of recommendations from a technical report.

The *summary* is a brief restatement of the problems, the work done, and the findings. A summary gives the writer one last opportunity to call the reader's attention to those main points. It is not a place to introduce new information. In reports accompanied by an abstract or an executive summary, a concluding summary is often redundant and can often be omitted. Figure 13.7 shows a sample summary.

Back Matter

The core of every engineering report should be able to stand on its own merits, but there are a number of devices that can further enhance its clarity, completeness, and usefulness. These include a variety of documentation, tables and graphics, and other apparatus. Used intelligently, they can aid the reader in finding information, offer additional information without clogging up the text, and give additional credibility to the report.

Documenting your facts, the validity of your procedures, and the soundness of the principles you use in your engineering analysis will strengthen the credibility of your report. Such documentation usually is an informal or formal citation of an established authority on the subject. Informal documentation is usually a simple reference to such an authority without further information about that authority; for example, a writer might simply note that measurements were made in compliance with API standards, confident that the reader knows what API is and appreciates the standardization implied in that citation.

More formal documentation consists of a bibliographic citation in the text, followed by a footnote or end note. It is almost impossible to provide too much documentation for an engineering report. At the same time, the potential importance of such documentation to a reader requires that you make sure that the citation is accurate and in the appropriate bibliographical format used in your discipline. Figure 13.8 shows a sample bibliography.

Tables are not graphic devices, and graphic devices should not pretend to be tables. Tables offer the reader access to data supporting a particular point. Graphs cannot even come close to achieving the precision of a table, but they can visually represent the data in a form that is both immediate and memorable. For specific information, then, readers will turn to tables; for the pattern of that information, they will look for a graph.

Finally, for that information you would like to provide but cannot include in the text itself, you should use appendices, separate sections added at the end of your report. Appendices usually are small, self-contained reports and should be constructed according to the same principles as is the report itself. Do not expect that many will read them but that those who do will be interested in the information they contain and thus will look for the same quality of work found in the report itself.

The body of a report provides information that is essential to all of the readers. The supporting devices—documentation, graphics, tables, and appendices—allow the writer to respond to less universal needs. In designing the report, an accurate assessment of both the purpose and varied needs of the audience can lead to an effectively designed report that puts information where it best reaches the right audience.

Problems p13.17–p13.32

▲ 13.4 Oral Presentations

Communication is the art of being understood through the transfer of ideas from one mind to another. Because a speaker cannot simply transfer his ideas from his brain to that of the listener, he must present his ideas in such a

Bibliography

1. Conway, H. D., Becker, E. C. H., and Dubil, J. F.,
    "Vibration Frequencies of Tapered Bars and Circular
    Plates," Journal of Applied Mechanics, ASME, Vol. 31,
    June 1964, pp. 329-331.

2. Conway, H. D., Becker, E. C. H., and Dubil, J. F.,
    "Vibration Frequencies of Truncated-Cone and Wedge
    Beams," Journal of Applied Mechanics, ASME, Vol. 32,
    Dec. 1965, pp. 931-934.

3. Gorman, D. J., Free Vibration Analysis of Beams and
    Shafts, John Wiley & Sons, New York, 1975.

4. Goel, R. P., "Transverse Vibrations of Tapered
    Beams," Journal of Sound and Vibration, Vol 47, No.1,
    1976, pp. 1-7.

5. Downs, B., "Transverse Vibrations of Cantilever Beams
    Having Unequal Breadth and Depth Tapers," Journal of
    Applied Mechanics, ASME, Vol. 44, Dec. 1977,
    pp. 737-742.

6. Mabie, H. H., and Rogers, C. B., "Transverse
    Vibrations of Double-Tapered Cantilever Beams With
    End Support and With End Mass," Journal of Acoustical
    Society of America, Vol. 55, May 1974, pp. 986-991.

7. Laura, P. A. A., Pombo, J. L., and Susemihl, E. A.,
    "A Note on the Vibrations of a Clamped-Free Beam With
    a Mass at the Free End," Journal of Sound and
    Vibration, Vol. 37, No.2, 1974, pp. 161-168.

8. Lee, T. W., "Transverse Vibrations of a Tapered Beam
    Carrying a Concentrated Mass," Journal of Applied
    Mechanics, ASME, Vol. 43, June 1976, pp. 366-367.

9. Lau, J. H., "Vibration Frequencies of Tapered Bars
    With End Mass," Journal of Applied Mechanics, Vol.
    51, March 1984, pp. 179-181.

10. Rutenberg, A., "Vibrations Frequencies for a Uniform
    Cantilever With a Rotational Constraint at a Point,"
    Journal of Applied Mechanics, ASME, Vol. 45, June
    1978, pp. 422-423.

Figure 13.8 *Sample bibliography*

way that meanings are stirred in the mind of the listener. This can best be
accomplished by means of the following:

1. Identify the goal of your presentation as principally informative,
argumentative, or persuasive, and then select the material that will help
achieve that end.

2. Analyze your audience and structure your presentation so that the
material you present will increase your listeners' knowledge. A speech

about radioactive waste disposal would obviously not be as technical when it is presented to the Lions Club as when it is presented to the American Society of Mechanical Engineers.

3. Keep it short. The normal span of listening attention is between twenty and forty minutes. Generally, then, a twenty-minute talk is better than a thirty-minute talk. It is better to stop talking while the audience wants to hear more than after it wishes the speaker would stop. A sample outline for a thirty-minute talk is shown in Figure 13.9.

4. Use simple, clear, precise, and appropriate terminology. Do not let hackneyed expressions dull your communication or overly technical language obscure your message.

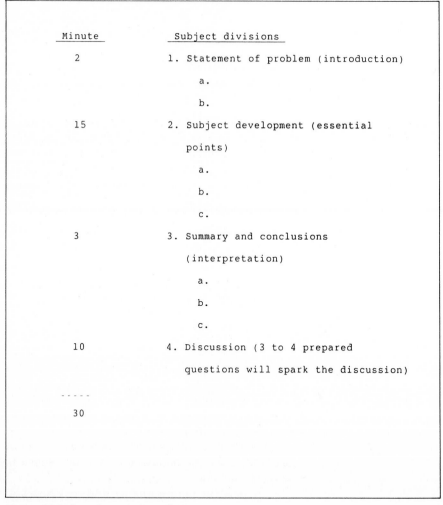

```
        Minute                 Subject divisions

          2              1. Statement of problem (introduction)

                             a.

                             b.

         15              2. Subject development (essential

                             points)

                             a.

                             b.

                             c.

          3              3. Summary and conclusions

                             (interpretation)

                             a.

                             b.

                             c.

         10              4. Discussion (3 to 4 prepared

                             questions will spark the discussion)

          - - - - -

         30
```

Figure 13.9 *Sample speech outline*

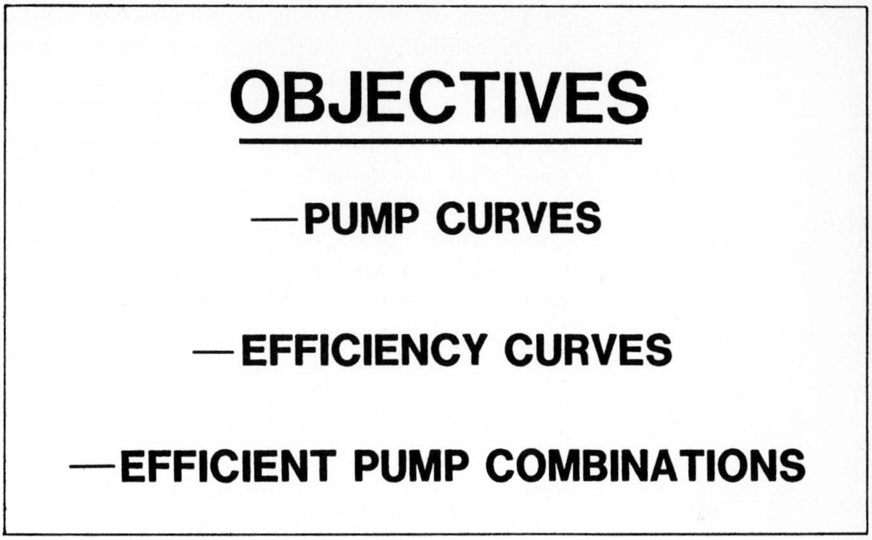

OBJECTIVES

—PUMP CURVES

—EFFICIENCY CURVES

—EFFICIENT PUMP COMBINATIONS

Figure 13.10 *Slide containing key words*

Poor: The foregoing experiments are favorable indications that molecules of the compound in the process of being studied did not under these conditions undergo a type of linkage that might be called cross-linking.

Better: There was no evidence of cross-linking.

Poor: Since the anticipated student body will consist of approximately 50 in each course, it will be mandatory that we utilize the auditorium for these courses.

Better: Since we anticipate classes of approximately 50, we need the auditorium.

Poor:	*Better:*
manual implements	tools
monetary funds	money
fatal termination	death

5. Use visual aids. There is almost no technical presentation that could not be improved through the use of slides, models, or other visual aids. Besides the obvious slides of experimental setups, construction sites, equipment used, graphs, and bar charts, slides containing key words about the objectives, procedures, results, and conclusions can help keep the audience alert and attuned to your talk, as well as enforce your main points. Figure 13.10 is a sample of a slide containing key words.

6. Speak extemporaneously. Of the four basic methods of speaking (impromptu, reading, memorization, and extemporaneous), extemporaneous is by far the preferred method for most engineering presentations. This method requires the speaker to be familiar with his or her material and well

prepared, without having to memorize or read the speech. Visual aids can be very effective guideposts for extemporaneous presentations.

7. Speak up. Speaking up is speaking with heartiness and vitality. It requires opening your mouth. The almost universal characteristic of American speech is mumbling. The mumbler slurs over syllables (not to be confused with unaccented syllables) and comes up with such words as "reely" (two syllables) for "really" (three syllables), "intersting" (three syllables) for "interesting" (four syllables), "partickler" (three syllables) for "particular" (four syllables). Mumbling and poor enunciation are not synonymous, but they produce the same result — ineffective communication.

8. Look interested. You cannot expect your audience to be interested if you are not — or do not seem to be. Rehearse before a mirror. Observe the expression the audience will see, and decide honestly whether you find it stimulating.

9. Do not read from stapled pages, if you must read from a text. By the time your eyes have reached the last line of the page, you will have lowered your head and will be presenting the top of your head to your listeners. But if the pages are separated, you can move the page upward as you read and keep your face in your listeners' view.

10. Look at your audience. Try to take in every person in the room. Do not stare at one or a few, at one corner of the room, or at one spot on the ceiling. Make each person feel that you are communicating with him or her.

Illustration 13.2 In a conference with others, an engineer must use effective oral communication

11. Gestures are unnecessary unless they are spontaneous and natural. Vitality and enthusiasm expressed in your face can hold your listeners' attention. However, gestures, if spontaneous, and movement, if meaningful, add to the dynamics of an oral presentation, provided that they do not follow a pattern. Any set pattern may turn your listeners into watchers. Movement, such as stepping to the side of the lectern, can often achieve a change of pace. Approaching the first rows of your audience can establish "eye contact" and build audience rapport. But movement, just for its own sake, can be distracting and annoying.

12. Time your speech and rehearse it. You can speak within your time limit if you organize and rehearse it for the limit. The average rate of speaking is 100 to 150 words a minute. If necessary, you can speak more rapidly and be understood — if you speak up and enunciate distinctly. If you must read your speech, write in short paragraphs, double spacing the lines and triple spacing the paragraphs. If you find it necessary to "cut" as you approach your time limit, it is easier to omit a short paragraph than to skip lines in a paragraph.

13. If your talk is to be followed by discussion, prepare three or four pertinent questions. See that these questions are placed in the hands of persons who will ask them. They will catalyze the discussion and lead it into the channels you regard as the most important. As icebreakers, they will also open the way for other questions.

14. Never distribute material while you are talking. Your audience cannot simultaneously inspect "samples" and listen.

15. Pause and change pace. Do not feel that you must fill every instant of your time before an audience with sound. Occasional pauses can be used to emphasize, to introduce a new topic, to vary voice inflection, or to initiate a change of speaking pace.

16. If speaking into a stationary microphone, your voice will be least distorted if your lips are six to twelve inches from the mike.

17. A relaxed, at-ease posture is desirable. Poise communicates itself to the audience. But it is better to be visibly nervous than to assume an overrelaxed, lounging posture that may offend the audience. Stand erect. Let your posture indicate respect for your listeners. They, in turn, will respect you.

18. Rehearse, rehearse, rehearse.

Problems p13.33 – p13.41

▲ 13.5 Preparation of Visual Aids

Visual communication — the one picture that equals ten thousand words — is practically a standard accessory today to an oral presentation. People understand more readily and retain longer what they see than what they hear.

Visual aids, properly used, should perform several important jobs:

1. They should amplify and illustrate not the *words* but the *ideas* of the speaker.
2. They should add the extra dimension of visual imagery so as to make the ideas more easily understood and remembered.
3. They should perform these jobs without intruding on the message.

A good visual illustration (chart, graph, diagram, map, picture) makes its point quickly. It supplements the speaker's remarks by communicating in seconds, pictorially, what would take minutes to relate. It shows relationships, makes comparisons, and details patterns of flow, motion, or sequence. It gives figure information rather than merely converting a set of figures into a drawing. It is clearly visible and easily read by the listener in the last row. Just a little thought and care in preparing visual aids can add immeasurably to the overall quality of your presentation and the effectiveness of the information to be conveyed. The appropriate guidelines for preparing slides are few and simple:

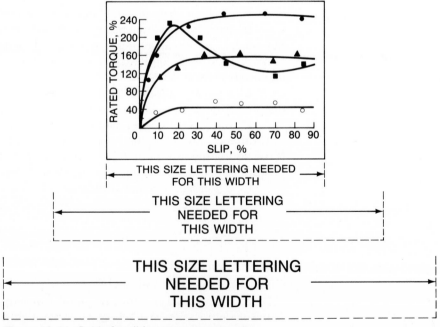

Figure 13.11 Guide for slide copy arrangement

Width of original figures, in.	Pen No.	Actual size lettering, template No., and symbols	Line weights
2 1/8	0	80 ▲■●	BORDER ——————— CURVE ——————— GRID ———————
4¼	1	175 ▲■●	BORDER ——————— CURVE ——————— GRID ——————
6½	2	240 ▲■●	BORDER ——————— CURVE ———— GRID ————————

Figure 13.12 *Guide for line weights*

1. Prepare rough sketches of your slides immediately after you prepare the first draft of your paper, and refer to the sketches as you revise the draft. In this way you can make sure that the slides support the points you are making in your paper.
2. Make sure that the lettering on your slides is legible. Figures 13.11 and 13.12 provide some guidelines that will ensure maximum visibility by the audience.
3. Since the size of a 35-mm slide is 24-mm high by 36-mm wide, it is best to prepare the printed material in the ratio of one to one and one-half so that most of the slide will be filled with material rather than large empty spaces. In general, vertical slides should be avoided because of projection readjustment requirements on the screen.
4. Never present a slide of a construction drawing or a blueprint. They invariably contain too much detail that will only confuse and frustrate the audience.
5. If a flow sheet is required to depict a system, do not photograph it. Redraw it and include only those elements needed to define the system.
6. If at all possible, do not present tables of data—charts or graphs are the most effective way to depict the effect of process parameters or experi-

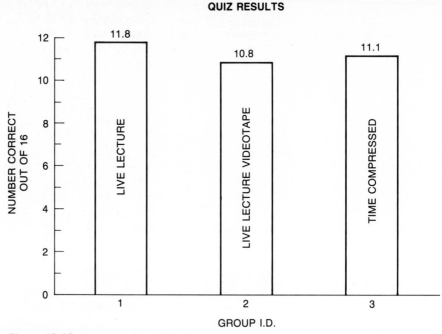

Figure 13.13 Example of an effective slide

mental variables. If tabular data must be shown, make sure they can be read easily in the short time that slide will be projected. *Rule of thumb:* limit tables to a *maximum* of four rows and four columns, Figure 13.13 is an example of an effective graph for a slide.

7. Generally, no more than two curves should be included on the same slide. Figure 13.14 shows a simple curve for a slide.

8. Though clarity and simplicity are far more important than aesthetics, color will add to the overall impression of your presentation. Contrasting colors should be used. (Red, white, and yellow is a particularly effective color combination.)

9. Always conduct a test run of your slides well in advance of your presentation. If the detail you wish to present cannot be seen or read at 100 feet when projected on a 6-foot screen, you will have to redraw the slide. If this large a room is not available, test for readability at 50 feet on a 3-foot screen. Always remember—the minute you have to resort to such comments as "You probably can't read this, but," or "The only important data are in column 6, row 10 . . . ," you have begun to alienate your audience.

Problems p13.42–p13.46

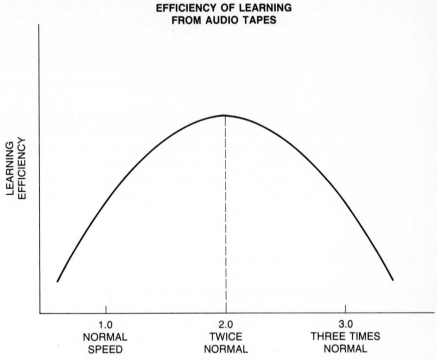

Figure 13.14 Example of a simple curve for a slide

● CHAPTER SUMMARY

This chapter stressed the importance of communication to engineers. We enumerated and defined the types and purposes of written communication that engineers are likely to use, and we discussed the format of technical reports and their contents. Finally, we considered various techniques of oral presentations and the preparation of effective visual aids.

▲ Problems

p13.1   List the three possible goals of any communication.

p13.2   Provide two examples of informational communications.

p13.3   What is the primary difference between informational and argumentative communications with respect to handling of the data?

p13.4   Provide two examples of an argumentative communication.

p13.5   Provide two examples of a persuasive communication.

p13.6   To confirm the communication demands placed on engineers, interview two or more engineers who have been in the field for five years or more. In those interviews,
(a) Establish how much time each engineer spends doing engineering and how much time is spent communicating; and
(b) Identify at least three groups of people with whom each engineer communicates.

p13.7   Read an article in *Scientific American* or other technical journal and identify one informational and one argumentative statement.

p13.8   Obtain from a researcher a copy of a successful unsolicited proposal and identify two persuasive sentences.

p13.9   What four items must be included in a memo?

p13.10   Obtain a memo from an engineering faculty member and identify the four items that all memos contain.

p13.11   In general, what is the length of an executive summary?

p13.12   State what is meant by a progress report and list at least three items that would be included in one.

p13.13   Professional journals constitute the primary outlet for what type of engineering communication?

p13.14   What type of engineering communication is intended to persuade a potential client to undertake a particular course of action?

p13.15   What is the purpose of a lab notebook?

p13.16   List the primary purpose (as stated in section 13.1) for each of the following types of engineering communications:
(a) memo   (b) technical paper   (c) proposal
(d) progress report   (e) executive summary

p13.17   Identify the three elements that are included in every formal engineering report.

p13.18   List five items that may be included in the front matter of a formal report.

p13.19   What is the major difference between findings and recommendations?

p13.20   What information is usually contained on the title page of a formal report?

p13.21   List three of the functions that a table of contents should serve.

p13.22   What are the major differences between descriptive and informative abstracts?

p13.23   What is the length of a typical descriptive abstract? A typical informative abstract?

p13.24   What are the three main parts of the body of a technical report?

p13.25   What is the purpose of the introduction in the body of a formal report?

p13.26   What five questions should the writer anticipate in the write-up of a formal report?

p13.27   List at least three items which may be included in the back matter of a formal report.

p13.28   What is the difference between formal and informal documentation?

p13.29   What is an appendix and what is its purpose?

p13.30 To identify techniques of informative writing, analyze two news stories to identify the "Who, What, Where, Why, When, and How" questions.

p13.31 Using an engineering report that has, at a minimum, a title page, a table of contents, a list of tables or illustrations, and an abstract, answer the following questions:
   (a) From the title page alone, what information do you have?
   (b) From the title page, the table of contents, and the list of tables or illustrations, what information do you have?

p13.32 Which of the following statements are probably findings and which are recommendations? Why do you think so?
   (a) An increase in ultrasonic intensity is more effective in sterilization than an increase in the duration of exposure.
   (b) To increase the effectiveness of sterilization, ultrasonic intensity should be increased.
   (c) Well flow rates could be increased by as much as 10% by purchasing a new line of pumps.
   (d) The variation in data accuracy may result from either operator error or inadequate metering systems.

p13.33 What are the four basic speaking methods for making oral presentations?

p13.34 What is meant by extemporaneous speaking?

p13.35 What is the normal attention span of a listener?

p13.36 If a speech must be read, why is it best not to read from stapled pages?

p13.37 Why should gestures made during oral presentations not follow a pattern?

p13.38 What is the advantage of writing a speech using short paragraphs?

p13.39 Why is it a good idea to prepare three or four questions and place them in the hands of people in the audience of your oral presentation?

p13.40 How is voice distortion best avoided when speaking into a microphone?

p13.41 Why is it important for a speaker to stand erect during an oral presentation?

p13.42 List three important functions of an effective visual aid.

p13.43 In preparing 35-mm slides, why should the printed material be kept in a $1 : 1\frac{1}{2}$ ratio?

p13.44 Why should vertical slides be avoided?

p13.45 What is the maximum number of rows and columns that should be included in a slide?

p13.46 An effective slide is generally limited to how many curves?

Appendix A

Engineering Mathematics

All engineers are expected to have reasonably well developed skills in mathematics and the physical sciences. Mathematics enables the precise description and logical organization of a specific problem and provides the analytic tools that facilitate a solution. This appendix reviews some of the more important mathematical skills needed for engineering.

Objective: The objective of this appendix is to review certain basic mathematical concepts that are widely used in engineering computations.

Criteria: After you have completed this appendix you should be able to do the following:

- **A.1** Indicate the meaning of each of the symbols shown in Table A.1.
- **A.2** Add, subtract, multiply, or divide numbers raised to integer, fractional, or zero exponents, given the numbers.
- **A.3** Convert a given logarithmic function into an exponential function and vice versa, calculate the product and quotient of two numbers using their logarithms, and calculate the value of a number raised to any power using logarithms.
- **A.4** Sketch and/or evaluate each of the following for given values of m and x:

$$y = e^{mx}, \quad y = e^{-mx}, \quad y = \log x, \quad y = x^m$$

TABLE A.1 Some Commonly Used Mathematical Symbols

+	plus	$-$	minus
$\pm$	plus or minus	$\times, \cdot, ()()$	times
$/, \div$	divided by	:	ratio
=	equals	$\neq$	not equal
$\approx$	approximately equal	$\equiv$	identically equal
>	greater than	<	less than
$\geq$	greater than or equal to	$\leq$	less than or equal to
$\gg$	much greater than	$\ll$	much less than
$\rightarrow$	approaches	$\propto$	proportional to
∞	infinity	$|n|$	absolute value of n
$\sqrt{\ }$	square root	$\sqrt[n]{\ }$	nth root
$\angle$	angle	$\parallel$	parallel
$\perp$	perpendicular	$\triangle$	triangle
$\square$	square	$\square$	rectangle
$\square$	parallelogram	$\bigcirc$	circle
$\overline{AB}$	line segment	$\overarc{AB}$	arc
$\sim$	similar	$\cong$	congruent
$\therefore$	therefore	$\circ$	degree
$'$	minute	$''$	second
Σ	summation	Π	product
( )	parentheses	[ ]	brackets
{ }	braces	!	factorial
$|A|$	determinant of $\mathbf{A}$	$\mathbf{A}$	matrix
$\mathbf{V}$	vector	$\mathbf{A} \times \mathbf{B}$	vector cross product
$\mathbf{A} \cdot \mathbf{B}$	vector dot product	$\mathbf{A}^ت$	matrix transpose
$\mathbf{A}^*$	vector complex conjugate		

▲ A.1 Mathematical Symbols

Much of problem solving is organizing ideas and information for subsequent manipulation. One might expect that often there is a lack of information, but this may not be the case. Typically, one is overwhelmed with data, and so the real problem is to determine the interrelationships among the various pieces of information and what is important. Mathematics provides both a logical approach to problem solving and the appropriate symbols and related concepts to express concisely various ideas or information. Table A.1 summarizes many of the symbols commonly used in engineering mathematics to express and develop concepts and relationships.

TABLE A.2 Laws of Exponents

$$a^m a^n = a^{m+n}$$
$$(a^m)^n = a^{mn}$$
$$(ab)^n = a^n b^n$$
$$\left(\frac{a}{b}\right)^n = \frac{a^n}{b^n} \qquad \text{where } b \neq 0$$
$$\frac{a^m}{a^n} = a^{m-n} = \frac{1}{a^{n-m}} \qquad \text{where } a \neq 0$$
$$a^{-n} = \frac{1}{a^n} \qquad \text{where } a \neq 0$$
$$a^0 = 1$$
$$\sqrt[n]{a} = b \text{ means } b^n = a$$
$$a^{1/n} = \sqrt[n]{a}$$
$$a^{m/n} = \sqrt[n]{a^m} = (\sqrt[n]{a})^m$$

▲ A.2 Exponents

The numbers that engineers and scientists work with vary over many orders of magnitude, and a number of fundamental laws state the relationships that are best expressed using exponents. For these reasons, a basic understanding of exponential expressions is desirable. This section will review the rules that govern permitted arithmetic operations on such expressions. Table A.2 summarizes these rules. We shall review the most important implications of the equations in Table A.2.

Numbers raised to powers can be added or subtracted only if the powers are the same. Thus, the following expression cannot be correctly evaluated in the manner suggested:

$$2^3 + 2^4 \neq 2^7 \quad \text{or} \quad 4^7$$

This expression can be evaluated by converting both numbers into forms containing the same exponential powers. This is done as follows:

$$2^3 + 2^4 = 1 \times 2^3 + 2 \times 2^3$$
$$= 3 \times 2^3$$
$$= 3 \times 8$$
$$= 24$$

An alternative way to evaluate such expressions is to convert both numbers directly into their decimal equivalents, as follows:

$$2^3 + 2^4 = 8 + 16$$
$$= 24$$

Similarly, numbers expressed with powers of 10 (i.e., scientific notation) cannot be added or subtracted directly, unless the powers of 10 are the same. For example,

$$(2.34 \times 10^3) + (1.63 \times 10^3) = 3.97 \times 10^3$$

When the powers of 10 are different, the numbers involved must be changed so that the powers of 10 are the same, or the numbers must be converted into their decimal equivalents before they are added or subtracted. Thus,

$$(1.31 \times 10^2) + (2.200 \times 10^3) = (1.31 \times 10^2) + (22.00 \times 10^2)$$
$$= 23.31 \times 10^2$$
$$= 2331$$

The same result is obtained by direct conversion into the decimal equivalents, which results in

$$(1.31 \times 10^2) + (2.200 \times 10^3) = 131 + 2200$$
$$= 2331$$

When numbers raised to powers are multiplied or divided, the exponents are added or subtracted, respectively. In general form,

$$(x^a)(x^b) = x^{a+b} \tag{A.1}$$

$$\frac{x^a}{x^b} = x^{a-b} \tag{A.2}$$

Equations A.1 and A.2 apply whether the exponents are positive, negative, or fractions. The following expressions illustrate applications requiring these equations:

$$(3^4)(3^3) = 3^{4+3} = 3^7$$

$$(8^{3.5})(8^{-0.4}) = 8^{3.5-0.4} = 8^{3.1}$$

$$\frac{5^{-3}}{5^{-7}} = 5^{-3-(-7)} = 5^4$$

When numbers raised to powers are themselves raised to powers, the powers are multiplied. Again, this is true for positive, negative, or fractional powers. In general form,

$$(x^a)^b = x^{ab} \tag{A.3}$$

Thus, from Equation A.3,

$$(2^3)^4 = 2^{(3)(4)} = 2^{12}$$

$$(7^{-2})^5 = 7^{(-2)(5)} = 7^{-10} \quad \text{or,}$$

$$[(6^{0.3})^4]^2 = 6^{(0.3)(4)(2)} = 6^{2.4}$$

These rules governing exponents may be applied more than once and in different orders to simplify a specific expression. The following example illustrates how this is done:

Example A.1: Simplify the following expressions, including eliminating negative exponents:

(a) $(2x^4y^2)(4xy^3)$

(b) $(2x^3y^4)^2$

(c) $\dfrac{(2x^3)}{y}\left(\dfrac{y^2}{x^3}\right)^4$

(d) $(x^{-2}y^4)^{-3}$

(e) $\dfrac{4x^4y^{-5}}{2x^{-2}y^3}$

Solution

(a) $(2x^4y^2)(4xy^3)$

$= (2)(4)x^4xy^2y^3$

$= 8x^5y^5$

(b) $(2x^3y^4)^2$

$= (2^2)(x^3)^2(y^4)^2$

$= 4x^6y^8$

(c) $\dfrac{(2x^3)}{y}\left(\dfrac{y^2}{x^3}\right)^4$

$= \dfrac{2x^3}{y}\dfrac{y^8}{x^{12}}$

$= 2x^3x^{-12}y^{-1}y^8$

$= \dfrac{2y^7}{x^9}$

(d) $(x^{-2}y^4)^{-3}$

$= \left(\dfrac{y^4}{x^2}\right)^{-3}$

$= \dfrac{y^{-12}}{x^{-6}}$

$= \dfrac{x^6}{y^{12}}$

(e) $\dfrac{4x^4y^{-5}}{2x^{-2}y^3}$

$= \dfrac{2x^4x^2}{y^3y^5}$

$= \dfrac{2x^6}{y^8}$

This example illustrated the manipulation of algebraic expressions containing only integer exponents. Fractional exponents are also permissible. If a and b are nonnegative real numbers and n is a positive integer, or if a and b are both negative and n is an odd positive integer, then

$$\sqrt[n]{a} = b \quad \text{and} \quad b^n = a$$

The number $\sqrt[n]{a}$ is called the principal *nth root* of a. The symbol $\sqrt[n]{a}$ is called a *radical*, and the number a is called the *radicand*; n is said to be the *index of the radical*, and $\sqrt{\ }$ is called the *radical sign*. If n is a positive integer and a is a real number, then

$$a^{1/n} = \sqrt[n]{a}$$

provided that $\sqrt[n]{a}$ is a real number. Furthermore, if m/n is a rational number and n is positive, then

$$a^{m/n} = (\sqrt[n]{a})^m = \sqrt[n]{a^m}$$

Manipulations involving fractional exponents are illustrated in the following example:

Example A.2: Simplify the following expressions:
(a) $(-27)^{4/3}(16)^{-3/2}$
(b) $(8^2 2^3)^{1/3}$
(c) $(27)^{2/3} + (32)^{3/5}$
(d) $(27)^{-2/3} + (32)^{-3/5}$

Solution
(a) $(-27)^{4/3}(16)^{-3/2}$
$= (\sqrt[3]{-27})^4(\sqrt[2]{16})^{-3}$
$= (-3)^4(4)^{-3}$
$= \dfrac{81}{64}$

(b) $(8^2 2^3)^{1/3}$
$= 8^{2/3}2^{3/3}$
$= (\sqrt[3]{8})^2(2)$
$= (2)^2(2) = 8$

(c) $(27)^{2/3} + (32)^{3/5}$
$= (\sqrt[3]{27})^2 + (\sqrt[5]{32})^3$
$= 3^2 + 2^3$
$= 9 + 8$
$= 17$

(d) $(27)^{-2/3} + (32)^{-3/5}$

$$= \frac{1}{(\sqrt[3]{27})^2} + \frac{1}{(\sqrt[5]{32})^3}$$

$$= \frac{1}{9} + \frac{1}{8}$$

$$= 0.1111 + 0.1250$$

$$= 0.2361$$

Problems pA.1–pA.9

▲ A.3 Logarithms

It can be shown that every positive real number N can be expressed as a power of a given positive number b, if b is not equal to 1. Symbolically, this can be stated as

$$p = \log_b N \tag{A.4}$$

or

$$N = b^p \tag{A.5}$$

where N is the positive real number, b is the base, and p is the power. Logarithms are very useful for certain classes of engineering problems. Suppose you want to show how some quantity changes as a function of light intensity. The experiment might start by using a light intensity equivalent to that available on a starlit night with no moon. Increasing the light intensity by perhaps 10 percent would make very little difference; the human eye would have trouble detecting such a small change. But suppose the light intensity were instead doubled. The human eye would still perceive the scene as very dark, although the actual light intensity would be twice what it initially was. Consider how many times the light intensity would have to be doubled to reach an intensity approaching that of a bright summer day. Suppose that the data obtained from such an experiment are to be plotted as a function of light intensity. If a normal linear plot of the information were to be made, each new data point would be located twice as far from the origin as the previous point was. An experiment that required doubling the abscissa a large number of times would obviously produce a very large graph. However, the abscissa of the graph could be substantially shortened or compressed by choosing an appropriate base and plotting the logarithm of the data rather than the data itself. Logarithms thus provide a convenient way of compressing data into numbers that are easier to manipulate. Although logarithms may initially seem to be a clumsy or at least an inefficient way of representing numbers, they are very convenient, because many physical processes are logarithmic in nature. Human sight and hearing are examples of logarithmic processes. Without the logarithmic or "compressing" effect, our senses of sight and hearing would be much less useful to us. Any positive real number not equal to one can be used as a base for logarithms. In practice, two bases are commonly used. Logarithms using base 10 are typically called *common* or *Briggsian logarithms,* and the notation, "log," really implies $\log_{10}$ (log to the base 10). A second commonly used base is $e = 2.71828$. Logarithms utilizing this base are called *natural* or *Naperian logarithms.* This form is normally indicated by writing "ln." The desirability of using logs of quantities in certain situations instead of the quantities themselves is illustrated in Example A.3 and the accompanying Table A.3.

Example A.3: Develop a table that shows the light intensities for a variety of lighting conditions. Include in the table the log and ln of the light intensities and note how the size of the numbers is affected by use of the logarithmic functions.

TABLE A.3 Sources of Light and Corresponding Photometric Brightness

source	luminance (foot lamberts)	log of luminance	ln of luminance
atomic fission bomb	6×10^{11}	11.78	27.12
lightning flash	2×10^{10}	10.30	23.72
sun	4.7×10^8	8.67	19.97
carbon arc	4.7×10^6	6.67	15.36
tungsten filament lamp	2.6×10^6	6.42	14.77
clear blue sky	2300	3.36	7.74
fluorescent lamp	2000	3.30	7.6
bright spot on moon	730	2.86	6.59

Comment: Notice how the range of the numbers used to describe luminance has been dramatically decreased by the use of logarithms. The original numbers ranged from 730 to 600 000 000 000, but their logs range from 2.86 to 11.78. Since all of the logarithms of the numbers are roughly the same size, tasks like plotting are simplified, and errors are easier to detect.

Multiplication and Division Using Logarithms

Numbers can be multiplied and divided using logarithms, and before the widespread availability of hand-held calculators, this was a common manual solution procedure. The multiplication of two numbers using logarithms is illustrated in Example A.4.

Example A.4: Find the product of the following two numbers using logarithms:

$$(93.5)(471)$$

Solution: Numbers are multiplied by adding their logarithms, as indicated in the following general equation:

$$\log_{10} A = \log_{10} A + \log_{10} B \qquad (A.6)$$
$$= \log_{10}(93.5) + \log_{10}(471)$$
$$= 1.9708 + 2.6730$$
$$= 4.6438$$

The result is the $\log_{10}$ of the answer. The answer itself is obtained by taking the antilog of 4.6438:

$$(93.5)(471) = \text{antilog } 4.6438$$
$$= 10^{4.6438}$$
$$= 44\ 035$$

Comment: The actual product of 93.5 times 471 is 44 038.5. The small error is due to maintaining only a four-place accuracy when computing the logarithms.

A second example illustrates the computation of a quotient of two numbers using logarithms.

Example A.5: Compute 2096/14.85 using logarithms.

Solution: Numbers are divided by subtracting their logarithms.

$$\log \frac{A}{B} = \log A - \log B \qquad (A.7)$$

$$\log \frac{2096}{14.85} = \log 2096 - \log 14.85$$
$$= 3.3214 - 1.1717$$
$$= 2.1497$$

and

$$\frac{A}{B} = \text{antilog } 2.1497$$
$$= 141.16$$

Comment: The actual value is 141.1448. The small error, again, was introduced by rounding.

Computing Powers of a Number Using Logarithms

Logarithms also make it easier to raise a number to a power. An example illustrates the process.

Example A.6: Compute $(25.42)^{2.55}$ using logarithms.

Solution: Numbers may be raised to powers according to the following equation:

$$\log N^p = p \log N \tag{A.8}$$

$$
\begin{aligned}
\log(25.42)^{2.55} &= 2.55 \log 25.42 \\
&= 2.55(1.4052) \\
&= 3.5833
\end{aligned}
$$

$$
\begin{aligned}
(25.42)^{2.55} &= \text{antilog } 3.5833 \\
&= 3830
\end{aligned}
$$

The most common uses of logarithms are summarized in Table A.4.

Change of Base of Logarithms

Occasionally, it is necessary to convert logarithmic information expressed using one base into equivalent information using a second base. The following equation facilitates this conversion:

$$\log_b u = \frac{\log_a u}{\log_a b} \tag{A.9}$$

A special case of Equation A.9 is obtained by letting $u = a$. The result follows:

$$\log_b a = \frac{1}{\log_a b}$$

Several examples illustrate how these equations may be used.

Example A.7: The $\log_{10}$ of the luminance of a fluorescent lamp is 3.30. Find the luminance of this lamp expressed as a natural logarithm.

Solution:

$$\log_b u = \frac{\log_a u}{\log_a b}$$

$$
\begin{aligned}
\ln u &= \frac{\log_{10} u}{\log_{10} e} \\
&= \frac{3.30}{0.4343} \\
&= 7.598
\end{aligned}
$$

TABLE A.4 Laws of Logarithms

$\log(AB) = \log A + \log B$	$\ln(AB) = \ln A + \ln B$
$\log A/B = \log A - \log B$	$\ln A/B = \ln A - \ln B$
$\log N^p = p \log N$	$\ln N^p = p \ln N$

Example A.8: Find $\log_{10} 1024$.

Solution: Since $2^{10} = 1024$ it follows that $\log_2 1024 = 10$.

$$\log_b u = \frac{\log_a u}{\log_a b}$$

$$\log_{10} 1024 = \frac{\log_2 1024}{\log_2 10}$$

$$= \frac{10}{3.3222}$$

$$= 3.0101$$

Comment: $\log_2 10$ is found as follows:

$$2^x = 10$$

$$\ln 2^x = \ln 10$$

$$x \ln 2 = \ln 10$$

$$x = \frac{\ln 10}{\ln 2}$$

$$= \frac{2.3026}{0.6931}$$

$$= 3.3222$$

and

$$\log_2 10 = 3.3222$$

Example A.9: Verify that

$$\log_2 4 = \frac{1}{\log_4 2}$$

Solution: We know that $2^2 = 4$ and $\sqrt{4} = 2$, and so the required logarithmic values are easily found, as follows:

$$\log_2 4 = 2$$

and

$$\log_4 2 = \frac{1}{2}$$

so

$$2 = \frac{1}{\frac{1}{2}} = 2$$

Problems pA.10 – pA.24

▲ A.4 Exponential and Logarithmic Functions

An exponential function has the form

$$f(x) = a^x \tag{A.10}$$

where a is a positive real number. The graph of $y = a^x$ will assume one of two characteristic forms, depending on the value of a. The two possibilities are shown in Figure A.1.

Many naturally occurring phenomena are modeled using exponential equations of the form

$$y = c\, a^{kx} \tag{A.11}$$

where a is often replaced by e (the base for natural logarithms) yielding a general equation of the form

$$y = c\, e^{kx} \tag{A.12}$$

An example of such a process is radioactive decay, in which the number of particles remaining at time t is n if n_0 particles are available at time $t = 0$, and T is a constant describing the particular process. The equation for the number of particles remaining at any point in time is

$$n = n_0\, e^{-t/T} \tag{A.13}$$

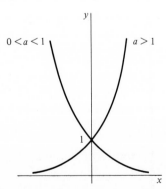

Figure A.1 Characteristic shapes of $y = a^x$

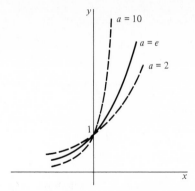

Figure A.2 Graphs of $y = a^x$ for various commonly used values for a

The choice of a in Equation A.11 for a particular application has some effect on the resulting graph, but the characteristic shape of the plot is not altered. Figure A.2 shows how various values of a affect the resulting graph.

An exponential equation is one in which the unknown appears in the exponent. Simple exponential equations involving terms with products can generally be solved by performing appropriate algebraic manipulations on the logarithm of both sides of the equation. An example illustrates this process.

Example A.10: Solve the following equation for x:

$$6(3^x) = 42$$

Solution:

$$\log 6(3^x) = \log 42$$

$$\log 6 + \log 3^x = \log 42$$

$$x \log 3 = \log 42 - \log 6$$

$$x = \frac{\log 42 - \log 6}{\log 3}$$

$$= \frac{1.6232 - 0.7782}{0.4771}$$

$$= 1.7711$$

The inverse of an exponential function is called a *logarithmic function* and has the general form

$$f(x) = \log_a x \tag{A.14}$$

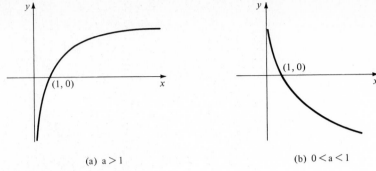

(a) $a > 1$ (b) $0 < a < 1$

Figure A.3 Graphs of $y = \log_a x$

where a is positive and not equal to 1. The characteristic shapes of logarithmic functions of the form $y = \log_a x$ are shown in Figure A.3.

An equation is said to be logarithmic if it contains the logarithm of an unknown. Such equations may be solved numerically or by using the laws of logarithms, in addition to those rules normally used in solving equations. Examples A.11 through A.14 illustrate the solutions of logarithmic and exponential equations.

Example A.11: Solve $5 \log(x + 1) = 10$ for x.

Solution:
$$5 \log(x + 1) = 10$$
$$\log(x + 1) = 2$$
$$\text{antilog}(\log(x + 1)) = \text{antilog}(2)$$
$$x + 1 = 100$$
$$x = 99$$

Example A.12: Solve $3 \log x - \log x = 10$ for x.

Solution:
$$3 \log x - \log x = 10$$
$$2 \log x = 10$$
$$\log x = 5$$
$$\text{antilog}(\log x) = \text{antilog}(5)$$
$$x = \text{antilog } 5$$
$$= 10^5$$

Example A.13: Suppose it is known that the number of bacteria in a certain culture double each hour. Find a mathematical relationship that allows the number of bacteria, n, to be computed at any point in time if the number of bacteria at time $t = 0$ is n_0.

Solution: The requirement of doubling implies raising 2 to an appropriate power. The required relationship is

$$n = n_0 \, 2^t$$

where $t = $ hours.

Example A.14: Suppose the initial and final number of bacteria is known in Example A.13. Find an expression for t, the time required to produce the given number of bacteria from those initially available.

Solution: The result of Example A.13 is solved for t as follows:

$$n = n_0 \, 2^t$$
$$2^t = n/n_0$$
$$\log_2 2^t = \log_2 n/n_0$$
$$t = \log_2 n/n_0$$

Problems pA.25 – pA.34

CHAPTER SUMMARY

Various symbols are used in engineering, mathematics, and the sciences. These symbols make the communication of ideas much more concise and facilitate the analysis and solution of problems. Although different authors and various engineering disciplines may use a specific symbol to represent different quantities, there are many symbols that have commonly understood meanings. Some of the most widely used symbols were presented in Table A.1.

In the past, logarithms and the mechanics of performing various logarithmic calculations were extensively studied by engineering students. But hand-held calculators and personal computers have greatly diminished the need to know the details of the manipulative aspects of these processes. However, logarithmic and exponential functions are often encountered in engineering systems, and familiarity with the properties of these functions is important. We examined the characteristic shapes of the various exponential and logarithmic functions. These functions are particularly useful when dealing with data values that range over several orders of magnitude.

▲ Problems

pA.1   Compute $4^3 + 3^4$.

pA.2   Compute $1.0356 \times 10^5 + 9.872 \times 10^3$.

pA.3   Compute $1.0 - 1.0\ E^{-1.0}$.

pA.4   Compute $(2^3)^{-4}$.

pA.5   Compute $(6)^{-4/3}$.

pA.6   Simplify

$$(3x^{1/2}y^3)^{1/4}(2x^2y^{-1/3})^{1/2}$$

pA.7   Simplify

$$(3)(2)^{1/2}(8)^{2/3} + (27)^{1/3}(1/8)^{1/3}$$

pA.8   Simplify

$$\frac{4a^{1/2}b^{4/3}}{3a^3b^{-1/2}}$$

pA.9   Simplify

$$\frac{(2a^3)(2b^2)(a^{-1/2})^2}{2a^2b^3}$$

pA.10   Compute 1000 times 100 using logs.

pA.11   Repeat pA.10 using natural logarithms.

pA.12   Compute 475 times 253 using logs.

pA.13   Compute 2000 times 10 572 using logarithms.

pA.14   Compute 0.0014 times 0.0025 using logs.

pA.15   Compute 1000 divided by 10 using logs.

pA.16   Compute 1000 divided by 10 using natural logarithms.

pA.17   Compute 250 divided by 475 using logs.

pA.18   Compute 0.0012 divided by 10 500 using logs.

pA.19   Compute 0.0012 divided by 10 500 using natural logarithms.

pA.20   Compute 2.71828 divided by 8.15484 using natural logarithms.

pA.21   Compute 2^2 using logs.

pA.22   Compute $65\ 536^{1/8}$ using logs.

pA.23   Compute 2^{21} using logs.

pA.24   Compute $525^{17.25}$ using logs.

pA.25   Sketch graphs of $y = 1^x$, $y = 2^x$, $y = e^x$, $y = 10^x$ on the same sheet of paper.

pA.26   Sketch graphs of $y = \log_2 x$, $y = \ln x$, $y = \log_3 x$, and $y = \log 10^x$ on the same sheet of paper.

pA.27   The charge Q on a capacitor that is discharging from some initial charge Q_0 is given by

$$Q = Q_0 e^{-kt}$$

where k is a constant and t is time. Solve the equation for t.

pA.28   Solve the following equation:

$$\log(3x - 2) - \log(2x - 4) = \log 6$$

pA.29   Solve

$$\log 2^x - \log 2^{-x} = 6$$

pA.30   Solve $2(5^{3x}) = 4$

pA.31   Solve $\log(x + 3) - \log(2x + 1) = \log(1/x)$.

pA.32   Solve $\log(\log x) = \log 5$

pA.33   Solve $\log \sqrt[3]{x^2 - 1} = 2$.

pA.34   Solve $2^{4x-1} = 3^{x+2}$.

Appendix B

Selected Review of Trigonometry

A thorough understanding of certain concepts from algebra and trigonometry is a prerequisite to mastery of more advanced engineering courses, such as statics, dynamics, and fluid mechanics. In this appendix, we shall discuss selected topics from high school mathematics courses that are important to additional engineering study and have been found to cause many students difficulty. Examples and problems are provided for those who wish to review these concepts more extensively.

Objective: The objective of this appendix is to review elementary mathematics topics necessary to understand the material presented in this text.

Criteria: After you have completed this Appendix you should be able to do the following:

- **B.1** Sketch solutions to inequality statements using the real number line.
- **B.2** Plot points on a Cartesian coordinate system for given ordered pairs of numbers.
- **B.3** Compute distances between specified points in a Cartesian coordinate system.
- **B.4** Draw and measure angles using degrees; degrees, minutes, and seconds; and radians for angle measurements. Convert from radians into degrees and conversely.
- **B.5** Define the trigonometric functions: sine, cosine, tangent, cotangent, secant, and cosecant in terms of the sides of a right triangle.
- **B.6** Define the inverse trigonometric functions.
- **B.7** Sketch a graph of each of the trigonometric functions.
- **B.8** Solve a right triangle for any specified unknown.
- **B.9** Solve any general triangle for a stated unknown using the law of sines and/or the law of cosines.

■ **B.10** Given a set of points consisting of abscissa and ordinate values, compute, using linear interpolation, the approximate ordinate value of a new point whose abscissa is specified.

▲ B.1 Number Line and Solution of Inequalities

A useful concept is that of a number line because it allows a set or subset of real numbers to be displayed in graphical form. Figure B.1 shows such a line. By convention, the positive direction is displayed to the right, and the negative direction is displayed to the left. One use of number lines is to display inequalities. Examples B.1 and B.2 show how this is done.

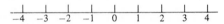

Figure B.1 Number line

Example B.1: Sketch on a number line the permitted values for x in the following inequality:

$$x \le -3 \quad \text{or} \quad x > 2$$

Solution: One subset of the permitted values is all points that are less than or equal to -3. These points are indicated by the line pointing to the left in Figure B.2. The second subset includes all points with a value greater than 2, but the point at $+2$ itself is excluded. The arrow pointing to the right in the figure represents this subset of points. Taken together, both arrows indicate the set of points that satisfies the inequality.

Figure B.2 Number line showing solutions for $x \le -3$ or $x > 2$

Example B.2: Sketch on a number line the permitted values for x in the following inequality:

$$-4 \le x < 3$$

Solution: The permitted points must lie between -4 and $+3$. The point at -4 is included in the set, but the point at $+3$ is not. Figure B.3 shows this set graphically.

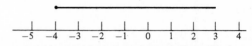

Figure B.3 Number line showing solutions for $4 \leq x < 3$

Problem pB.1

▲ B.2 Rectangular (Cartesian) Coordinate System

The horizontal axis is the x-axis, or abscissa, and the vertical axis is the y-axis, or ordinate. The two axes divide the plane into four quadrants numbered as shown in Figure B.4. Independent variables are usually plotted along the x-axis, and dependent variables are plotted along the y-axis. When ordered pairs representing points in the plane are given, the order is always the x-coordinate followed by the y-coordinate (x,y). The use of a Cartesian coordinate system for displaying an ordered pair of numbers as a point is shown in Example B.3.

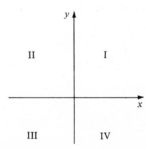

Figure B.4 Rectangular or Cartesian coordinate system

Example B.3: Plot the following points on a Cartesian coordinate system:

$$(2,1), \ (-3,-4), \ (-3,+2), \ (2,-3)$$

Solution: The ordered pair of numbers is given in the order x, or abscissa, followed by y, or ordinate. The ordered pairs are plotted as points in Figure B.5.

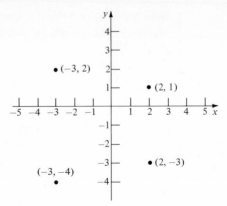

Figure B.5 Plotting ordered pairs of numbers as points in rectangular coordinates

Problem pB.2

▲ B.3 Computation of Distance

The simplest form of the distance formula is based on the Pythagorean theorem, which states that for a right triangle

$$c^2 = a^2 + b^2 \tag{B.1}$$

where c is the hypotenuse of the triangle and a and b are its remaining sides. A more general equation is based on the same idea but uses differences of coordinates to represent horizontal and vertical distances:

$$\text{distance} = \sqrt{(x_2 - x_1)^2 + (y_2 - y_1)^2} \tag{B.2}$$

where (x_1, y_1) and (x_2, y_2) form the end points of a line segment whose distance or length is to be determined. These ideas are shown graphically in Figure B.6.

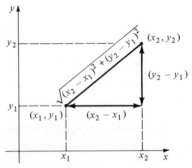

Figure B.6 Distance between two points

Example B.4: Compute the distance between the points $(-2,-4)$ and $(2,5)$.

Solution: Let $(x_1,y_1) = (-2,-4)$ and $(x_2,y_2) = (2,5)$. Using Equation B.2,

$$
\begin{aligned}
\text{distance} &= \sqrt{(x_2 - x_1)^2 + (y_2 - y_1)^2} \\
&= \sqrt{(2 - (-2))^2 + (5 - (-4))^2} \\
&= \sqrt{4^2 + 9^2} \\
&= \sqrt{16 + 81} = \sqrt{97} \\
&= 9.85
\end{aligned}
$$

Problem pB.3

▲ B.4 Measurement of Angles

Angles are formed by rotating a half line (or ray) in a plane about one of its end points (vertex). An arbitrary angle is shown in Figure B.7(a), and an angle in the "standard position" is shown in Figure B.7(b). Note that in the standard position, positive angles are measured counterclockwise from the positive x-axis. A unit circle $(x^2 + y^2 = 1)$ is shown in Figure B.8. The angle generated by one complete counterclockwise rotation of the initial side is

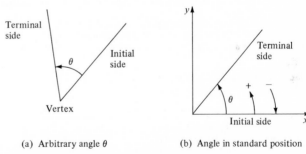

(a) Arbitrary angle θ (b) Angle in standard position

Figure B.7 Generation and display of angles

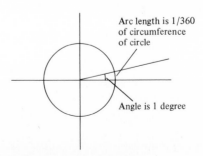

Figure B.8 Unit circle used to define one degree

assigned the value 360°. A degree is 1/360 of the above rotation or can equivalently be viewed as the central angle subtended by an arc whose length is 1/360 of the circle's circumference. A degree may be subdivided into 60 minutes (60′), and a minute may be further divided into 60 seconds (60″). Thus

$$360° = 1 \text{ revolution}$$

$$1° = 60′$$

$$1′ = 60″$$

Often degrees, minutes, and seconds are converted into fractions of degrees, by means of the following formula:

$$\text{angle(degrees)} = \text{degrees} + \frac{\text{minutes}}{60} + \frac{\text{seconds}}{3600} \qquad \text{(B.3)}$$

Figure B.9 shows an angle θ in standard position with a circle having a radius r. If s is the length of the arc, AB, then the angle θ measured in radians will be given by

$$\theta = \frac{s}{r} \qquad \text{(B.4)}$$

If θ is an angle produced by one complete rotation in the counterclockwise direction (360°), then $s = 2\pi r$, which is the circumference of the circle and

$$\theta = \frac{s}{r} = \frac{2\pi r}{r} = 2\pi \text{ radians} \qquad \text{(B.5)}$$

so

$$360° = 2\pi \text{ radians and}$$

$$1° = \pi/180 = 0.017\ 45 \text{ radians} \qquad \text{(B.6)}$$

When $s = r$,

$$\theta = 1 \text{ radian} = 180°/\pi = 57.2958° \qquad \text{(B.7)}$$

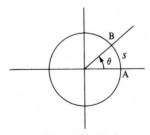

Figure B.9 Circle used to define radian measure

TABLE B.1 Degrees and Corresponding Radian Measure for Some Common Angles

Degrees	Radians	Radians
0	0	0
15	0.2618	$\pi/12$
30	0.5236	$\pi/6$
45	0.7854	$\pi/4$
60	1.0472	$\pi/3$
75	1.3090	$5\pi/12$
90	1.5708	$\pi/2$
120	2.0944	$2\pi/3$
150	2.6180	$5\pi/6$
180	3.1416	π
270	4.7124	$3\pi/2$
360	6.2832	2π

Table B.1 contains some commonly used angles expressed in both degrees and radians.

Example B.5: Convert 32 degrees, 57 minutes, and 25 seconds $(32°, 57', 25'')$ into an angle expressed in degrees and decimal fractions.

Solution: The conversion is readily accomplished using Equation B.3.

$$\text{angle (degrees)} = \text{degrees} + \frac{\text{minutes}}{60} + \frac{\text{seconds}}{3600}$$

$$\text{angle (degrees)} = 32 + \frac{57}{60} + \frac{25}{3600}$$

$$= 32 + 0.95 + 0.006\ 94$$

$$= 32.956\ 94°$$

Example B.6: Show, on a sketch, an angle of $+120$ degrees. Convert this angle into radian measure.

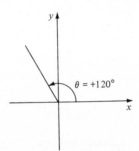

Figure B.10 Graph of $+120°$ angle

Solution: Positive angles are by convention measured in a counterclockwise direction from the positive x-axis. The desired angle is shown in Figure B.10. This angle can be converted into radians by using Equation B.6, as follows:

$$\theta = (120 \text{ degrees}) (0.017\ 45 \text{ radians/degree})$$
$$= 2.094 \text{ radians}$$

Example B.7: Show, on a sketch, an angle of -7 radians.

Solution: Since the angle is negative, the corresponding rotation must be clockwise. One complete revolution is 2π, or approximately 6.283 radians. Thus, the required angle goes more than "once around." The rotation in excess of one revolution is

$$-7 - (-6.283) = -0.717 \text{ radians}$$

At this point, for purposes of sketching, it is convenient to convert the angles in radian measure into the corresponding angles expressed in degrees.

$$-7 \text{ radians} \left(\frac{1 \text{ degree}}{0.017\ 45 \text{ radians}} \right) = -401.15 \text{ degrees}$$

$$-0.717 \text{ radians} \left(\frac{1 \text{ degree}}{0.017\ 45 \text{ radians}} \right) = -41.09 \text{ degrees}$$

The desired angles are shown in Figure B.11.

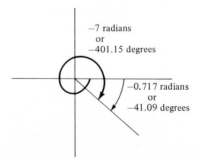

Figure B.11 Sketch of angle of -7 radians

Problems pB.4 – pB.9

▲ B.5 Trigonometric Functions and Triangles

Triangles are three-sided figures that are completely known when three sides and three angles are specified. Figure B.12 shows a notational scheme that is often used. Small letters represent the lengths of the triangle's sides, and capital letters represent the angles. A specific triangle side is always opposite its corresponding angle. Thus, side a is opposite angle A.

Definitions of Trigonometric Functions

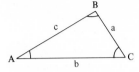

Figure B.12 General triangle

If angle C of Figure B.12 is made equal to $90°$, then the resulting triangle is said to be a right triangle. Such a triangle is shown in Figure B.13. Note that special names are attached to sides a, b, and c. The various trigonometric functions are defined as ratios of one side to another. These definitions are as follows:

$$\sin A = \frac{\text{side opposite } A}{\text{hypotenuse}} = \frac{a}{c} \tag{B.8}$$

$$\cos A = \frac{\text{side adjacent } A}{\text{hypotenuse}} = \frac{b}{c} \tag{B.9}$$

$$\tan A = \frac{\text{side opposite } A}{\text{side adjacent } A} = \frac{a}{b} \tag{B.10}$$

$$\csc A = \frac{\text{hypotenuse}}{\text{side opposite } A} = \frac{c}{a} \tag{B.11}$$

$$\sec A = \frac{\text{hypotenuse}}{\text{side adjacent } A} = \frac{c}{b} \tag{B.12}$$

$$\cot A = \frac{\text{side adjacent } A}{\text{side opposite } A} = \frac{b}{a} \tag{B.13}$$

▲ B.6 Inverse Trigonometric Functions

Equations B.8 through B.13 are useful for determining the ratios of the various sides of a triangle if a specific angle is known. Often the reverse process is also necessary (i.e., two sides of the triangle are known, and the

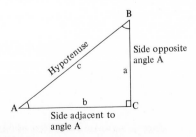

Figure B.13 Right triangle

corresponding angle is desired). A second set of functions called the *inverse trigonometric functions* permits this calculation. These functions are denoted by a prefix "arc" or, equivalently, by a superscript (-1) attached to the corresponding trigonometric function. The definitions of these functions are as follows:

$$A = \sin^{-1}\frac{a}{c} \text{ for } -1 \le \frac{a}{c} \le 1 \text{ and } -\pi/2 \le A \le \pi/2 \tag{B.14}$$

$$A = \cos^{-1}\frac{b}{c} \text{ for } -1 \le \frac{b}{c} \le 1 \text{ and } 0 \le A \le \pi \tag{B.15}$$

$$A = \tan^{-1}\frac{a}{b} \text{ for } \frac{a}{b} \text{ real and } -\pi/2 < A < \pi/2 \tag{B.16}$$

$$A = \cot^{-1}\frac{b}{a} \text{ for } \frac{b}{a} \text{ real and } 0 < A < \pi \tag{B.17}$$

$$A = \sec^{-1}\frac{c}{b} \text{ for } \left|\frac{c}{b}\right| \ge 1 \text{ and } 0 \le A \le \pi, A \ne \pi/2 \tag{B.18}$$

$$A = \csc^{-1}\frac{c}{a} \text{ for } \left|\frac{c}{a}\right| \ge 1 \text{ and } -\pi/2 \le A \le \pi/2, A \ne 0 \tag{B.19}$$

▲ B.7 Graphs of Trigonometric Functions

Figure B.14 shows the graphs of the various trigonometric functions. The shapes of the sine and cosine functions are easily recalled by noting that they are periodic and look like a continuous wave. The horizontal displacement of the wave is established by remembering that $\sin 0° = 0$ and $\cos 0° = 1$. The shapes of the four remaining graphs may be remembered by relating them to the sine and cosine functions. The following equations show these relationships:

$$\tan \theta = \frac{\sin \theta}{\cos \theta}$$

$$\cot \theta = \frac{\cos \theta}{\sin \theta}$$

$$\csc \theta = 1/\sin \theta$$
$$\sec \theta = 1/\cos \theta$$

The values of θ that cause the denominators of these expressions to become zero are convenient for recalling the shapes of each graph, as the resulting function approaches positive or negative infinity at these points.

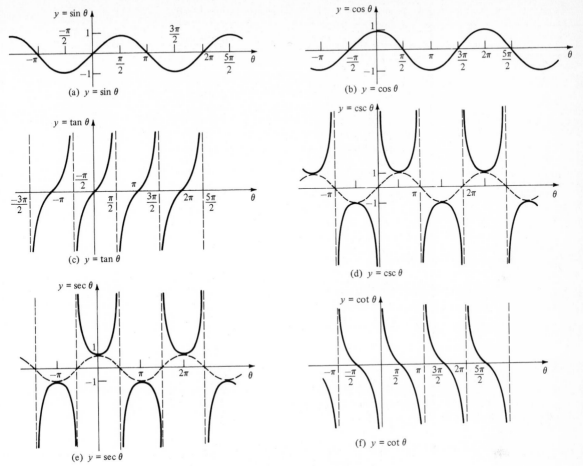

$y = \sin\theta$

(a) $y = \sin\theta$

$y = \cos\theta$

(b) $y = \cos\theta$

$y = \tan\theta$

(c) $y = \tan\theta$

$y = \csc\theta$

(d) $y = \csc\theta$

$y = \sec\theta$

(e) $y = \sec\theta$

$y = \cot\theta$

(f) $y = \cot\theta$

Figure B.14 Graphs of trigonometric functions

▲ B.8 Solution of Right Triangles

The Pythagorean theorem (Equation B.1) and the definitions of the various trigonometric functions and their inverses (Equations B.8 through B.19) allow the solution of many problems involving right triangles. Because one angle is already known to be $90°$, all three sides and the other two angles of any right triangle can be determined if either two sides are specified or one of the acute angles and one side is given. Examples B.8 and B.9 show in greater detail how this is done.

Example B.8: Find the unknown side and angles for the triangle shown in Figure B.15.

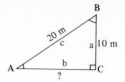

Figure B.15 Triangle used in Example B.8

Solution: Since two sides are already known, the third side can be computed using the Pythagorean theorem (Equation B.1).

$$c^2 = a^2 + b^2$$
$$b^2 = c^2 - a^2$$
$$b = \sqrt{c^2 - a^2}$$
$$= \sqrt{20^2 - 10^2}$$
$$= 17.32 \text{ m}$$

Also,

$$\cos A = b/c$$
$$= \frac{17.32}{20}$$
$$= 0.866$$

$$A = \cos^{-1}(0.866)$$
$$= 30°$$

The final angle is determined by recalling that the sum of the angles in a triangle must equal 180°.

$$A + B + C = 180° \qquad\qquad \text{(B.20)}$$
$$B = 180° - A - C$$
$$= 180° - 30° - 90°$$
$$= 60°$$

Example B.9: Solve the triangle shown in Figure B.16.

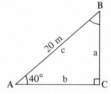

Figure B.16 Triangle used in Example B.9

Solution: The unknowns are now B, a, and b. B is again easily found, since the three angles must sum to 180°.

$$A + B + C = 180°$$

$$B = 180° - A - C$$
$$= 180° - 40° - 90°$$
$$= 50°$$

Sides a and b must be found and can be solved using the sin or cos functions:

$$\cos B = \frac{a}{c}$$

$$a = c \cos B$$
$$= 20 \cos 50$$
$$= 20\,(0.6428)$$
$$= 12.86 \text{ m}$$

$$\cos A = \frac{b}{c}$$

$$b = c \cos A$$
$$= 20 \cos 40°$$
$$= 20\,(0.766)$$
$$= 15.32 \text{ m}$$

Supplementary Example pB.15
Problem pB.10

▲ B.9 Solution of General Triangles

Law of Sines

The law of sines applies to any triangle, including right triangles. It is used to solve a triangle when either of the following conditions exists:

1. Two angles and one side of the triangle are given.
2. Two sides and the angle opposite one of them are given.

The law of sines for any triangle ABC is given by

$$\frac{a}{\sin A} = \frac{b}{\sin B} = \frac{c}{\sin C} \tag{B.21}$$

The following examples illustrate how this law is used to solve general triangles:

Example B.10: Solve the triangle of Figure B.17.

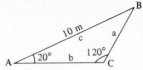

Figure B.17 Triangle used for Example B.10

Solution: Angle B can easily be found, since the angles must sum to $180°$.

$$A + B + C = 180°$$

$$B = 180° - 20° - 120°$$
$$= 40°$$

Side b is now found as follows:

$$\frac{b}{\sin B} = \frac{c}{\sin C}$$

$$b = c\,\frac{\sin B}{\sin C}$$

$$= 10\,\frac{\sin 40°}{\sin 120°}$$

$$= 10\,\frac{(0.6428)}{(0.8660)}$$

$$= 7.422 \text{ m}$$

Side a is found in a similar manner:

$$\frac{a}{\sin A} = \frac{c}{\sin C}$$

$$a = c\,\frac{\sin A}{\sin C}$$

$$= 10\,\frac{\sin 20°}{\sin 120°}$$

$$= 10\,\frac{(0.3420)}{(0.8660)}$$

$$= 3.949 \text{ m}$$

Example B.11: Solve the triangle of Figure B.18.

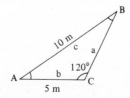

Figure B.18 Triangle used for Example B.11

Solution: This triangle represents the second case for which the law of sines is used to find the solution. The three knowns are C, c, and b, and so the next step is to find B, as follows:

$$\frac{b}{\sin B} = \frac{c}{\sin C}$$

$$\sin B = \frac{b}{c}\sin C$$

$$B = \sin^{-1}\left(\frac{b}{c}\sin C\right)$$

$$= \sin^{-1}\left(\frac{5}{10}\sin 120°\right)$$

$$= \sin^{-1}\left(\frac{5}{10}(0.8660)\right)$$

$$= \sin^{-1} 0.4330$$

$$= 25.66°$$

Two angles are now known, and so the third can easily be found:

$$A + B + C = 180°$$

$$A = 180° - B - C$$

$$= 180° - 25.66° - 120°$$

$$= 34.34°$$

The final unknown is side a:

$$\frac{a}{\sin A} = \frac{c}{\sin C}$$

$$a = c\,\frac{\sin A}{\sin C}$$

$$= 10\,\frac{\sin 34.34°}{\sin 120°}$$

$$= 10\,\frac{(0.5641)}{(0.8660)}$$

$$= 6.51 \text{ m}$$

Law of Cosines

The law of cosines also applies to any general triangle, including right triangles. It is used to solve a triangle when either of the following conditions exists:

1. Two sides and the included angle of a triangle are given.
2. Three sides of a triangle are given.

The law of cosines for any triangle ABC is given by

$$a^2 = b^2 + c^2 - 2bc \cos A \tag{B.22}$$

$$b^2 = a^2 + c^2 - 2ac \cos B \tag{B.23}$$

$$c^2 = a^2 + b^2 - 2ab \cos C \tag{B.24}$$

The following examples show the use of this law:

Example B.12: Solve the triangle shown in Figure B.19.

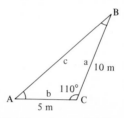

Figure B.19 Triangle used in Example B.12

Solution: The unknowns are A, B, and c. This problem is case 1 of the law of cosines. The third side, side c, can be found as follows:

$$
\begin{aligned}
c^2 &= a^2 + b^2 - 2ab \cos C \\
&= (10)^2 + (5)^2 - 2(10)(5) \cos 110° \\
&= 100 + 25 - 100(-0.3420) \\
&= 159.2
\end{aligned}
$$

$$c = \sqrt{159.2} = 12.62 \text{ m}$$

Angle A can now be determined as follows:

$$a^2 = b^2 + c^2 - 2bc \cos A$$

$$2bc \cos A = b^2 + c^2 - a^2$$

$$\cos A = \frac{b^2 + c^2 - a^2}{2bc}$$

$$
\begin{aligned}
A &= \cos^{-1}\left(\frac{b^2 + c^2 - a^2}{2bc}\right) \\
&= \cos^{-1}\left(\frac{(5)^2 + (12.62)^2 - (10)^2}{2(5)(12.62)}\right) \\
&= \cos^{-1}\left(\frac{25 + 159.2 - 100}{126.2}\right) \\
&= \cos^{-1} 0.6672 \\
&= 48.15°
\end{aligned}
$$

The last angle is obtained from Equation B.20.

$$A + B + C = 180°$$

$$
\begin{aligned}
B &= 180° - A - C \\
&= 180° - 48.15° - 110° \\
&= 21.85°
\end{aligned}
$$

Example B.13: Solve the triangle shown in Figure B.20.

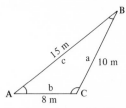

Figure B.20 Triangle used in Example B.13

Solution: This example represents the situation found in case 2 of the law of cosines. The three angles, A, B, C, are the unknowns and are found as follows:

$$a^2 = b^2 + c^2 - 2bc \cos A$$

$$2bc \cos A = b^2 + c^2 - a^2$$

$$\cos A = \frac{b^2 + c^2 - a^2}{2bc}$$

$$
\begin{aligned}
A &= \cos^{-1}\left(\frac{b^2 + c^2 - a^2}{2bc}\right) \\
&= \cos^{-1}\left(\frac{(8)^2 + (15)^2 - (10)^2}{2(8)(15)}\right) \\
&= \cos^{-1}\left(\frac{64 + 225 - 100}{240}\right) \\
&= \cos^{-1}(0.7875) \\
&= 38.05°
\end{aligned}
$$

Angle B is found as follows:

$$b^2 = a^2 + c^2 - 2ac \cos B$$

$$\cos B = \frac{a^2 + c^2 - b^2}{2ac}$$

$$
\begin{aligned}
&= \cos^{-1}\left(\frac{(10)^2 + (15)^2 - (8)^2}{2(10)(15)}\right) \\
&= \cos^{-1}\left(\frac{100 + 225 - 64}{300}\right) \\
&= \cos^{-1}(0.8700) \\
&= 29.54°
\end{aligned}
$$

The last angle C is found using a similar procedure:

$$c^2 = a^2 + b^2 - 2ab \cos C$$

$$\cos C = \frac{a^2 + b^2 - c^2}{2ab}$$

$$C = \cos^{-1}\left(\frac{a^2 + b^2 - c^2}{2ab}\right)$$

$$= \cos^{-1}\left(\frac{(10)^2 + (8)^2 - (15)^2}{2(10)(8)}\right)$$

$$= \cos^{-1}\left(\frac{100 + 64 - 225}{160}\right)$$

$$= \cos^{-1}(-0.3813)$$

$$= 112.41°$$

These answers may be tested for validity because they must add to $180°$.

$$A + B + C = 38.05° + 29.54° + 112.41°$$
$$= 180.00°$$

Table B.2 provides the appropriate solution method for various given conditions.

Supplementary Example B.16
Problem pB.11

TABLE B.2 Solution of General Triangles

Data Given	Solution Method	Existence of Solution
Two angles and one side.	Law of sines	Unique solution.
Two sides and the angle opposite one of them.	Law of sines	Ambiguous case: 1. No solution. 2. One unique solution. 3. Two possible solutions.
Two sides and the included angle.	Law of cosines	Unique solution.
Three sides.	Law of cosines.	Unique solution unless sum of any two sides is less than third side.
Three angles.		No unique solution.

▲ B.10 Linear Interpolation

Much of the information that engineers use comes in the form of tables. Such information may be obtained from experiments or digital computers that supply a series of points rather than an equation as the solution to a specific

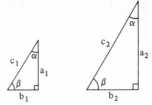

Figure B.21 Two similar triangles

problem. The subsequent usage of such information often requires estimating a value for a particular quantity not contained in the available table. One such estimation technique is called *linear interpolation* and is based on relationships between similar right triangles. Two right triangles are said to be similar if their angles are the same. A consequence is that the corresponding sides are then known to be proportional. Two similar triangles are shown in Figure B.21.

The following relations must always be true for similar triangles:

$$\frac{a_1}{a_2} = \frac{b_1}{b_2} = \frac{c_1}{c_2} \tag{B.25}$$

Example B. 14 shows how the properties of similar triangles can be used to estimate unstated values.

Example B.14: The freezing point of a certain salt solution was measured for various concentrations of salt. The resulting values are shown in Table B.3. Using linear interpolation, estimate the freezing point of a 7.0 percent salt solution.

TABLE B.3   Concentrations of Salt and Corresponding Freezing Points

Salt Concentration (percent)	Freezing Point (degrees C)
0	0.0
5	−2.8
10	−6.0
15	−10.0
20	−15.0

The freezing temperatures for various concentrations are plotted in Figure B.22.

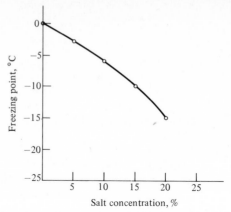

Figure B.22 Freezing point of salt solution as concentration is changed

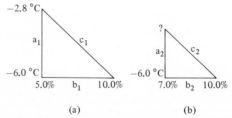

Figure B.23 Similar triangles used for linear interpolation

Solution: The required freezing point corresponding to a concentration of 7.0 percent falls between known values of $-2.8°C$ at 5 percent and $-6.0°C$ at 10 percent. The adjacent values of 5 percent and 10 percent are used to form a triangle, as shown in Figure B.23a. A second triangle similar to the first is also constructed. The height of this second triangle is the unknown but can be found by using ratios of the sides of the similar triangles. Since the values for a_1, b_1, and b_2 are readily computed, the following variation of Equation B.25 is selected:

$$\frac{a_2}{a_1} = \frac{b_2}{b_1} \tag{B.26}$$

$$a_2 = \frac{b_2\, a_1}{b_1}$$

$$= \frac{(10\% - 7\%)}{(10\% - 5\%)}\,(-6.0° - (-2.8°))$$

$$= \frac{3}{5}(-3.2°)$$

$$= -1.92°$$

This intermediate result corresponds to the height of the second triangle. The required value is obtained by adding this temperature to $-6.0°C$, corresponding to the freezing point of a 10 percent concentration. This is accomplished as follows:

$$T_{7.0\%} = -6.0 + 1.92$$
$$= -4.08\,^\circ\mathrm{C}$$

Comment: The graph shown in Figure B.22 indicates that the functional relationship is not linear (the curve is not a straight line). The technique, however, replaces the actual curve with a straight line drawn between the two known adjacent points and uses this line as an approximation of the actual curve. The computed point ($-4.08\,^\circ\mathrm{C}$) actually falls on the straight line and not on the curve. An error is introduced by doing this. If the actual curve differs substantially from a straight line in the region of the needed approximation, other, more complex techniques may be used that yield greater accuracy. For most purposes, when the given points are reasonably close together, linear interpolation provides sufficient accuracy.

Supplementary Example B.17
Problems pB.12–pB.15

● CHAPTER SUMMARY

This chapter reviewed selected topics from high school mathematics that are widely used in engineering computations. If any of the topics were unfamiliar and difficult to understand, a more thorough review may be needed. It is important to understand the mathematics involved lest the complexities of most engineering problems, coupled with uncertainties concerning the involved mathematical operations, lead to confusion.

Supplementary Examples

Example B.15: A certain rocket is known to rise vertically during the first few seconds of flight. An observer is located 2 km from the launch site and notes that at 3 s after launch, the angle of elevation from horizontal is 7.5°. Four seconds later the angle of elevation is 65.3°. What distance has the rocket traveled between the two observations?

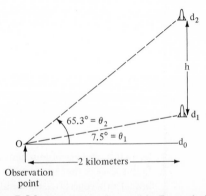

Figure B.24 *Right triangle used in Example B.15*

Solution: Figure B.24 shows the geometry of the problem. The two observations provide sufficient information to solve the two right triangles. The distance d_1d_2 is first determined using triangle d_0,d_1,O. The adjacent side and the angle at O are known, and the opposite side is needed.

$$\tan \theta_1 = \frac{d_0d_1}{Od_0}$$

$$d_0d_1 = Od_0 \tan \theta_1$$
$$= 2 \tan 7.5°$$
$$= 2(0.1316)$$
$$= 0.2632 \text{ km}$$

The second triangle (O, d_0, d_2) also must be solved:

$$\tan \theta_2 = \frac{d_0d_2}{Od_0}$$

$$d_0d_2 = Od_0 \tan \theta_2$$
$$= 2 \tan 65.3°$$
$$= 2(2.1741)$$
$$= 4.3483$$

The distance d_2d_1 is found as follows:

$$d_2d_1 = d_2d_0 - d_1d_0$$
$$= 4.3483 - 0.2632$$
$$= 4.08 \text{ km}$$

Example B.16: A lighthouse 50-m high sits on the top of a cliff. A ship is observed from the top of the lighthouse at an angle of depression of 30°. The same ship is observed from the base of the lighthouse at an angle of depression of 18°. How far away from the base of the lighthouse is the ship? How high is the cliff that the lighthouse sits on?

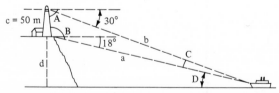

Figure B.25 Ship and lighthouse used in Example B.16

Solution: The problem geometry is shown in Figure B.25. Examination of this figure shows that two angles and the included side can be readily found. The law of sines can be used to solve this problem. Angles A and B are computed as follows:

$$A = 90° - 30° = 60°$$

$$B = 90° + 18° = 108°$$

$$C = 180° - A - B$$
$$= 180° - 168°$$
$$= 12°$$

Side a is required and found as follows:

$$\frac{a}{\sin A} = \frac{c}{\sin C}$$

$$a = \frac{\sin A}{\sin C} c$$

$$a = \frac{\sin 60°}{\sin 12°} (50)$$

$$= \frac{0.866}{0.2079} (50)$$

$$= 208.27 \text{ m}$$

The height of the cliff, d, is now computed. Angle D must be 18°. The cliff, the water surface, and side a form a right triangle.

$$\sin D = d/a$$
$$d = a \sin D$$
$$= 208.27 \, (\sin 18°)$$
$$= 208.27 \, (0.3090)$$
$$= 64.36 \text{ m}$$

Example B.17: Flow rates measured on the first day of the month for a certain stream are provided in the following table. Estimate the August 1 and June 10 flow rates using linear methods.

flow rate m³/s	150	170	200	350	380	370	330	280
month	Dec	Jan	Feb	Mar	Apr	May	Jun	Jul

Solution: This problem requires an estimate of a value beyond the end of the currently available data. This process is called *extrapolation,* and it is similar in form to *interpolation,* in which known values on either side of the desired one are available. The given points are approximately 30 days apart, and because the required point is 30 days beyond the last given point, the computations are particularly simple. From June to July, the flow rate decreased from 330 to 280 m³/s, which is 50 m³/s. If linear techniques are used and based on the last known data, this same decrease should occur from July to August. Basing the estimate on this assumption leads to

$$\text{flow rate}_{Aug} = 280 - 50 = 230 \text{ m}^3/\text{s}$$

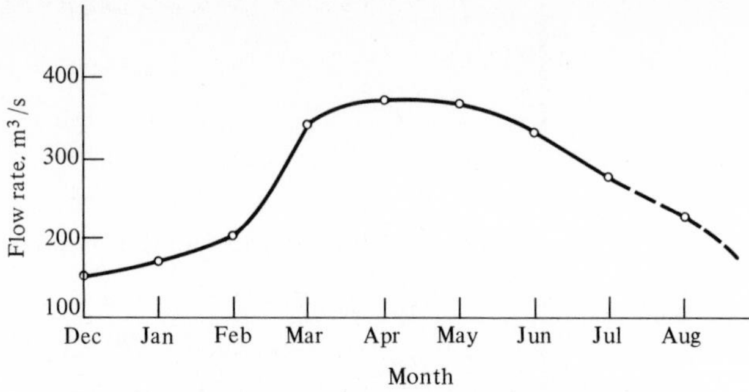

Figure B.26 Monthly flow rates for Example B.17.

The resulting graph of stream flow rate is shown in Figure B.26. There are many other ways to estimate the flow rate. Suppose the average decrease for the last two months is used. The result is

$$\text{flow rate}_{\text{Aug}} = 280 - \left(\frac{(370 - 330) + (330 - 280)}{2}\right)$$

$$= 280 - 45$$
$$= 235 \text{ m}^3/\text{s}$$

The flow rate on June 10 is next estimated. The flow rate in June fell from 330 to 280 m³/s. This is 50 m³/s in 30 days. A proportionality relationship can be established as follows:

$$\frac{10 \text{ days}}{30 \text{ days}} = \frac{x}{50}$$

$$x = \frac{10}{30}(50)$$

$$= 17 \text{ m}^3/\text{s}$$

This is the expected change in 10 days. The flow rate on June 10 is then

$$\text{flow rate}_{\text{June 10}} = 330 - 17$$
$$= 313 \text{ m}^3/\text{s}.$$

▲ Problems

pB.1   Sketch, on a number line, the solution to the following inequalities:
(a) $-2 < x < 4$ (b) $x > 2$ and $x \leq 4$
(c) $x > -3$ and $x < 5$ (d) $x < -1$ or $x \geq 2$
(e) $x \leq 2$ and $x \geq 2$ (f) $x \leq 1$ or $x \geq 2$

pB.2 Plot the following points on a Cartesian coordinate system:

(a) (2,4) (b) (−1,−2) (c) (−2,−3) (d) (−2,3)
(e) (3,2) (f) (−2,2) (g) (2,−4) (h) (1,−2)
(i) (−2,−4) (j) (2,+4)

pB.3 Determine the distances between the following pairs of points:

(a) (1,1) − (2,1) (b) (1,2) − (2,4)
(c) (1,−5) − (2,6) (d) (1,4) − (−1,−4)
(e) (−3,−2) − (2,3) (f) (6,1) − (1,6)

pB.4 Convert 32° 40′ 25″ into degrees.

pB.5 Convert 32.461 degrees into degrees, minutes, and seconds.

pB.6 Convert each of the following angles expressed in degrees to its equivalent expressed in radians:

(a) 45° (b) −135° (c) 720° (d) 135°
(e) 250° (f) 114.516° (g) −270° (h) −60°

pB.7 Find the angle subtended by an arc having a length of 7.5 cm on the circumference of a disk having a 5-cm radius.

pB.8 Convert the following into equivalent angular measurements expressed in degrees.

(a) $\pi/10$ (b) $2\pi/7$ (c) $5\pi/7$
(d) $10\pi/4$ (e) $-5\pi/3$ (f) 5π

pB.9 Sketch each of the following angles:

(a) −75° (b) −315°
(c) $\pi/4$ radians (d) -6π radians
(e) +260° (f) −100°
(g) $+3\pi/4$ radians (h) $-2\pi/7$ radians

pB.10 Fill in the following table, supplying all unknown values. If a unique value does not exist, so indicate. Figure pB.10 shows how a, b, c, A, B, and C are defined.

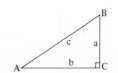

Figure pB.10 Right triangle

a	b	c	A	B	C	Does a unique solution exist?
(meters)			(degrees)			
		10	30		90	
5			15		90	
	20			60	90	
		20			90	
5	10				90	
2	3	3.6			90	
			30	60	90	

pB.11   Fill in the following table, supplying all unknown values. If a unique solution does not exist, so indicate. The various quantities are defined in Figure pB.11.

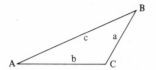

Figure pB.11 General triangle

a	b	c	A	B	C	Does a unique solution exist?
(meters)	(meters)	(meters)	(degrees)	(degrees)	(degrees)	
10			50	80		
10	20		40			
		10		120	130	
5		10			50	
20	15				30	
10	20	30				
			50	70	60	
	10	15		45		
10	20			50		
60	40	20				

pB.12   Using the data from Table B.3, determine the freezing point of a 12-percent salt solution.

pB.13   The following table shows the voltage and current for a resistive heating element. Find the current that will flow when 95 volts are applied to the element.

v volts	80	90	100	110	120	130
i amps	10	22	30	35	38	40

pB.14   Estimate the current flow in the heating element of pB.13 if a voltage of 75 volts is applied.

pB.15   Using the table of pB.13, estimate the current flow for a voltage of 140 volts. Make your estimate using linear methods and the current values corresponding to 120 and 130 volts. Will your estimate be too high or too low?

Appendix C

Conversion Factors

To convert from	Multiply by	To obtain
acres	4.047×10^{-1}	hectares
acres	4.356×10^{4}	sq ft
acres	4.047×10^{3}	sq meters
acres	4.840×10^{3}	sq yards
acre-feet	4.356×10^{4}	cubic ft
ampere-hrs	3.600×10^{3}	coulombs
angstroms	3.937×10^{-9}	inches
atmospheres	7.6×10^{1}	cms of mercury at 0°C
atmospheres	3.39×10^{1}	ft of water at 4°C
atmospheres	2.992×10^{1}	in. of mercury at 0°C
atmospheres	1.013×10^{5}	pascals
atmospheres	1.47×10^{1}	pounds/sq. in
barrels (oil)	4.2×10^{1}	gallons (oil)
bars	1.45×10^{1}	pounds/sq. in
Btu	1.0550×10^{10}	ergs
Btu	7.7816×10^{2}	ft-pounds
Btu	3.927×10^{-4}	horsepower-hours
Btu	1.055×10^{3}	joules
Btu	2.928×10^{-4}	kilowatt-hours
Btu/hr	2.162×10^{-1}	ft-pounds/s
Btu/hr	3.929×10^{-4}	horsepower
Btu/hr	2.931×10^{-1}	watts
Btu/min	1.296×10^{1}	ft-pounds/s
Btu/min	2.356×10^{-2}	horsepower
Btu/min	1.757×10^{-2}	kilowatts
Btu/sq. ft/min	1.22×10^{-1}	watts/sq. in
bushels	1.2445	cubic ft
bushels	3.524×10^{-2}	cubic meters
centimeters	3.281×10^{-2}	ft
centimeters	3.937×10^{-1}	inches
centimeters	6.214×10^{-6}	miles

To convert from	Multiply by	To obtain
centimeters	3.937×10^2	mils
centimeter-grams	1.0×10^{-5}	meter-kg
cm of mercury	1.316×10^{-2}	atmospheres
cm of mercury	4.461×10^{-1}	ft. of water
cm of mercury	1.333×10^3	pascals
cm of mercury	2.785×10^1	pounds/sq. ft
cm of mercury	1.934×10^{-1}	pounds/sq. in
centimeters/s	1.969	ft/min
centimeters/s	3.281×10^{-2}	ft/s
centimeters/s	3.6×10^{-2}	kilometers/h
centimeters/s	2.237×10^{-2}	miles/h
coulombs	1.036×10^{-5}	faradays
coulombs/sq. in	1.550×10^3	coulombs/sq. m
cubic cm	3.531×10^{-5}	cubic ft
cubic cm	6.102×10^{-2}	cubic in
cubic cm	1.308×10^{-6}	cubic yards
cubic cm	2.642×10^{-4}	gallons (U.S. liquid)
cubic cm	1.0×10^{-3}	liters
cubic cm	1.057×10^{-3}	quarts (U.S. liquid)
cubic feet	1.728×10^3	cubic inches
cubic feet	2.832×10^{-2}	cubic meters
cubic feet	7.48052	gallons (U.S. liquid)
cubic feet	2.832×10^1	liters
cubic feet/min	1.247×10^{-1}	gallons/s
cubic feet/min	4.720×10^{-1}	liters/s
cubic feet/s	6.46317×10^{-1}	million gals/day
cubic feet/s	4.48831×10^2	gallons/min
cubic inches	5.787×10^{-4}	cubic ft
cubic inches	1.639×10^{-5}	cubic meters
cubic inches	4.329×10^{-3}	gallons
cubic inches	1.639×10^{-2}	liters
cubic meters	3.531×10^1	cubic ft
cubic meters	6.1023×10^4	cubic inches
cubic meters	2.642×10^2	gallons (U.S. liquid)
cubic meters	1.0×10^3	liters
cubic yards	2.7×10^1	cubic ft
cubic yards	7.646×10^{-1}	cubic meters
dynes/sq. cm	9.869×10^{-7}	atmospheres
dynes	1.0×10^{-5}	joules/meter (newtons)
dynes	2.248×10^{-6}	pounds-force
ergs	9.486×10^{-11}	Btu
ergs	7.376×10^{-8}	ft-pounds
ergs	1.0×10^{-7}	joules
ergs	2.773×10^{-14}	kilowatt-hrs
ergs/sec	1.341×10^{-10}	horsepower
faradays	9.649×10^4	coulombs
fathoms	1.8288	meters
feet	3.048×10^{-4}	kilometers
feet	3.048×10^{-1}	meters
feet	1.894×10^{-4}	miles
feet of water	8.826×10^{-1}	in. of mercury
feet of water	3.048×10^{-2}	kgs/sq. meter

To convert from	Multiply by	To obtain
feet of water	6.243×10^1	pounds/sq. ft
feet of water	4.335×10^{-1}	pounds/sq. in
feet/min	1.829×10^{-2}	km/hr
feet/min	3.048×10^{-1}	meters/min
feet/min	1.136×10^{-2}	miles/h
feet/s	1.097	km/h
feet/s	1.829×10^1	meters/min
feet/s	6.818×10^{-1}	miles/h
feet/s²	3.048×10^{-1}	meters/s²
foot-pounds	1.286×10^{-3}	Btu
foot-pounds	1.356×10^7	ergs
foot-pounds	1.356	joules
foot-pounds	1.383×10^{-1}	kg-m
foot-pounds	3.766×10^{-7}	kilowatt-h
foot-pounds/min	1.286×10^{-3}	Btu/min
foot-pounds/min	3.030×10^{-5}	horsepower
foot-pounds/min	2.260×10^{-5}	kilowatts
foot-pounds/s	4.6263	Btu/h
foot-pounds/s	1.818×10^{-3}	horsepower
foot-pounds/s	1.356×10^{-3}	kilowatts
furlongs	6.6×10^2	ft
gallons	1.337×10^{-1}	cubic ft
gallons	3.785×10^{-3}	cubic meters
gallons	3.785	liters
gallons/min	2.228×10^{-3}	cu. ft/s
grams	2.205×10^{-3}	pounds-mass
gram calories	3.9683×10^{-3}	Btu
gram calories	3.086	ft-pounds
hectares	2.471	acres
horsepower	4.244×10^1	btu/min
horsepower	3.3×10^4	ft-lb/min
horsepower	5.50×10^2	ft-lb/s
horsepower	7.457×10^{-1}	kilowatts
horsepower-hours	2.547×10^3	Btu
horsepower-hours	1.98×10^6	ft-lb
horsepower-hours	2.684×10^6	joules
inches	2.540	centimeters
inches	2.540×10^{-2}	meters
inches of mercury	4.912×10^{-1}	pounds/sq. in
inches of water	3.613×10^{-2}	pounds/sq. in
joules	9.486×10^{-4}	Btu
joules	7.736×10^{-1}	ft-pounds
joules/s	5.6907×10^{-2}	Btu/min
kilograms	2.2046	pounds-mass
kilograms	6.8522×10^{-2}	slugs
kilograms/cu m	6.243×10^{-2}	pound-mass/cu. ft.
kilogram-calories	3.968	Btu
kilogram-calories	4.183×10^3	joules
kilometers	3.281×10^3	ft
kilometers	6.214×10^{-1}	miles
kilometers/h	5.468×10^1	ft/min
kilometers/h	9.113×10^{-1}	ft/s

To convert from	Multiply by	To obtain
kilometers/h	6.214×10^{-1}	miles/h
kilowatts	1.341	horsepower
kilowatt hour	3.413×10^3	Btu
kilowatt hour	2.655×10^6	ft-lb
kilowatt hour	3.6×10^6	joules
liters	1.0×10^3	cubic cm
liters	3.531×10^{-2}	cubic ft
liters	6.102×10^1	cubic inches
liters	1.0×10^{-3}	cubic meters
liters	2.642×10^{-1}	gallons
liters/min	4.403×10^{-3}	gallons/s
liters/s	1.5850×10^1	gallons/min
lumen/sq. ft	1.0	ft candles
lux	9.29×10^{-2}	ft candles
meters	1.0×10^{10}	angstroms
meters	3.281	ft
meters	3.937×10^1	inches
meters	6.214×10^{-4}	miles
meters	1.094	yards
meters/min	6.0×10^{-2}	km/h
meters/min	3.728×10^{-2}	miles/h
meters/s	1.968×10^2	ft/min
meters/s	3.281	ft/s
meters/s	3.6	km/h
meters/s	2.237	miles/h
miles	5.280×10^3	ft
miles	1.609	kilometers
miles	1.609×10^3	meters
miles/h	8.8×10^1	ft/min
miles/h	1.467	ft/s
miles/h	1.6093	km/h
miles/h	2.682×10^1	meters/min
millimeters	3.937×10^{-2}	inches
million gals/day	1.54723	cu. ft/s
mils	8.333×10^{-5}	ft
newtons	1.0×10^5	dynes
ounces	6.25×10^{-2}	pounds
ounces (fluid)	2.957×10^{-2}	liters
pace	3.0×10^1	inches
pints (liquid)	1.25×10^{-1}	gallons
pints (liquid)	4.732×10^{-1}	liters
pounds-force	4.448×10^5	dynes
pounds-force	4.448	newtons
pounds-force	1.6×10^1	ounces
pounds-mass	4.5359×10^2	grams
pounds-mass	4.5359×10^{-1}	kilograms
pounds-mass	3.1081×10^{-2}	slugs
pounds-mass/cu ft	1.602×10^1	kg/cu m
pounds-mass/cu in	2.768×10^4	kg/cu m
pounds-force/sq ft	4.725×10^{-4}	atmospheres
pounds-force/sq ft	1.602×10^{-2}	ft of water
pounds-force/sq ft	1.414×10^{-2}	inches of mercury

To convert from	Multiply by	To obtain
pounds-force/sq ft	4.788	pascals
pounds-force/sq in	2.307	ft of water
pounds-force/sq in	2.036	inches of mercury
pounds-force/sq in	6.895×10^3	pascals
quarts (liquid)	3.342×10^{-2}	cubic ft
quarts (liquid)	9.463×10^{-1}	liters
radians	5.7296×10^1	degrees
radians/s	9.5493	revolutions/min
revolutions/min	1.047×10^{-1}	radians/s
rods	5.029	meters
rods	1.65×10^1	ft
rope	2.0×10^1	ft
slugs	1.459×10^1	kilograms
slugs	3.217×10^1	pounds-mass
square cm	1.076×10^{-3}	sq ft
square cm	1.550×10^{-1}	sq in
square feet	2.296×10^{-5}	acres
square feet	1.44×10^2	sq inches
square feet	9.29×10^{-2}	sq m
square feet	3.587×10^{-8}	sq miles
square meters	2.471×10^{-4}	acres
square meters	1.076×10^1	sq ft
square meters	1.55×10^3	sq inches
square meters	3.861×10^{-7}	sq miles
square miles	2.788×10^7	sq ft
square miles	2.590×10^6	sq meters
square yards	9.0	sq ft
square yards	8.361×10^{-1}	sq meters
tons (long)	2.24×10^3	pounds-force
tons (short)	2.0×10^3	pounds-force
watts	3.4129	Btu/h
watts	1.0×10^7	ergs/s
watts	4.427×10^1	ft-lb/min
watts	7.378×10^{-1}	ft-lb/s
watts	1.341×10^{-3}	horsepower
watt hours	3.413	Btu
watt hours	2.656×10^3	ft-pounds
yards	9.144×10^{-1}	meters

Appendix D

Atomic Weights of Elements (based on ^{12}C = 12.0000 AMU)

Name	Symbol	Atomic Number	Atomic Weight	Valence
Actinium	Ac	89	(227)*	—
Aluminum	Al	3	26.9815	3
Americium	Am	95	(243)	3, 4, 5, 6
Antimony	Sb	51	121.75	3, 5
Argon	Ar	18	39.948	0
Arsenic	As	33	74.9216	3, 5
Astatine	At	85	(210)	1, 3, 5, 7
Barium	Ba	56	137.34	2
Berkelium	Bk	97	(249)	3, 4
Beryllium	Be	4	9.0122	2
Bismuth	Bi	83	208.980	3, 5
Boron	B	5	10.811	3
Bromine	Br	35	79.904	1, 3, 5, 7
Cadmium	Cd	48	112.40	2
Calcium	Ca	20	40.08	2
Californium	Cf	98	(251)	—
Carbon	C	6	12.01115	2, 4
Cerium	Ce	58	140.12	3, 4
Cesium	Cs	55	132.905	1

* ( ) means most stable isotope.

Name	Symbol	Atomic Number	Atomic Weight	Valence
Chlorine	Cl	17	35.453	1, 3, 5, 7
Chromium	Cr	24	51.996	2, 3, 6
Cobalt	Co	27	58.9332	2, 3
Copper	Cu	29	63.546	1, 2
Curium	Cm	96	(247)	3
Dysprosium	Dy	66	162.50	3
Einsteinium	Es	99	(254)	—
Erbium	Er	68	167.26	3
Europium	Eu	63	151.96	2, 3
Fermium	Fm	100	(253)	—
Fluorine	F	9	18.9984	1
Francium	Fr	87	(223)	1
Gadolinium	Gd	64	157.25	3
Gallium	Ga	31	69.72	2, 3
Germanium	Ge	32	72.59	4
Gold, aurum	Au	79	196.967	1, 3
Hafnium	Hf	72	178.49	4
Helium	He	2	4.0026	0
Holmium	Ho	67	164.930	3
Hydrogen	H	1	1.00797	1
Indium	In	49	114.82	3
Iodine	I	53	126.9044	1, 3, 5, 7
Iridium	Ir	77	192.2	3, 4
Iron	Fe	26	55.847	2, 3
Krypton	Kr	36	83.80	0
Lanthanum	La	57	138.91	3
Lawrencium	Lr	103	(257)	—
Lead	Pb	82	207.19	2, 4
Lithium	Li	3	6.939	1
Lutetium	Lu	71	174.97	3
Magnesium	Mg	12	24.312	2
Manganese	Mn	25	54.9380	2, 3, 4, 6, 7
Mendelevium	Md	101	(256)	—
Mercury	Hg	80	200.59	1, 2
Molybdenum	Mo	42	95.94	3, 4, 6
Neodymium	Nd	60	144.24	3
Neon	Ne	10	20.183	0
Neptunium	Np	93	(237)	4, 5, 6
Nickel	NI	28	58.71	2, 3
Niobium	Nb	41	92.906	3, 5
Nitrogen	N	7	14.0067	3, 5
Nobelium	No	102	(254)	—
Osmium	Os	76	190.2	2, 3, 4, 8
Oxygen	O	8	15.9994	2
Palladium	Pd	46	106.4	2, 4, 6
Phosphorus	P	15	30.9738	3, 5
Platinum	Pt	78	195.09	2, 4
Plutonium	Pu	94	(242)	3, 4, 5, 6
Polonium	Po	84	(210)	—
Potassium	K	19	39.102	1
Praseodymium	Pr	59	140.907	3

Name	Symbol	Atomic Number	Atomic Weight	Valence
Promethium	Pm	61	(145)	3
Protactinium	Pa	91	(231)	—
Radium	Ra	88	(226)	2
Radon	Rn	86	(222)	0
Rhenium	Re	75	186.2	—
Rhodium	Rh	45	102.905	3
Rubidium	Rb	37	85.47	1
Ruthenium	Ru	44	101.07	3, 4, 6, 8
Samarium	Sm	62	150.35	2, 3
Scandium	Sc	21	44.956	3
Selenium	Se	34	78.96	2, 4, 6
Silicon	Si	14	28.085	4
Silver	Ag	47	107.868	1
Sodium	Na	11	22.9898	1
Strontium	Sr	38	87.62	2
Sulfur	S	16	32.064	2, 4, 6
Tantalum	Ta	73	180.948	5
Technetium	Te	43	(99)	6, 7
Tellurium	Te	52	127.60	2, 4, 6
Terbium	Tb	65	158.924	3
Thallium	Tl	81	204.37	1, 3
Thorium	Th	90	232.038	4
Thulium	Tm	69	168.934	3
Tin	Sn	50	118.69	2, 4
Titanium	Ti	22	47.90	3, 4
Tungsten	W	74	183.85	6
Uranium	U	92	238.03	4, 6
Vanadium	V	23	50.942	3, 5
Xenon	Xe	54	131.30	0
Ytterbium	Yb	70	173.04	2, 3
Yttrium	Y	39	88.905	3
Zinc	Zn	30	65.37	2
Zirconium	Zr	40	91.22	4

Appendix E

Answers to Selected Problems

Chapter 3

p3.2   (a) 4   (f) 5
       (b) 3   (g) 2 or 3
       (c) 2   (h) 3
       (d) 3   (i) 1, 2, 3, 4, or 5
       (e) 2

p3.4   (a) 6.938×10^1
       (b) 7.8634×10^4
       (c) 3.29×10^{-3}
       (d) 5.6930×10^2
       (e) 9.3700×10^{-2}
       (f) 2.963020×10^3

p3.6   (a) 463.1
       (b) 0.89316
       (c) 23.00
       (d) 0.00132966
       (e) 0.0051900
       (f) 7319.1
       (g) 0.050 020
       (h) 99 631

p3.8   Minimum voltage = 8.7
       Maximum voltage = 9.3

p3.10 53.7 − 54.3

p3.12 0.43 ± 0.05

p3.14 0.3

p3.16 23.82 mA

p3.18 (a) 108.2 psi
       (b) 256.1 psi
       (c) 27.6 psi
       (d) 5.1 psi

p3.20 (a) 64.32
       (b) 8937
       (c) 436.2
       (d) 550 000
       (e) 0.003 400
       (f) 0.091 68

p3.22 (a) 90   (c) 0.002
       (b) 50 000   (d) 0.1

p3.24 (a) 199.77
       (b) 21.9701
       (c) 5744.03

p3.26 (a) 1518   (c) 102.6119
       (b) 22.13 (d) 193.1557

p3.28 (a) 1.56   (c) 18.2
       (b) 8.6   (d) 0.13

p3.30 (a) 159.40
       (b) 42.27
       (c) 13.3

p3.32 1265

Chapter 4

p4.2 (a) $(3 \ 9 \ 1 \ . \ 4 + 2 \ 1 \ 8 \ . \ 5 \ ) \div 5 \ . \ 2 =$

(b) $3 \ 9 \ 1 \ . \ 4$ ENTER $2 \ 1 \ 8 \ . \ 5 + 5 \ . \ 2 \div$

p4.4 (a) $4 \ . \ 7 \ y^x \ 3 + 2 \ . \ 3 \ y^x \ 2 =$

(b) $4 \ . \ 7$ ENTER $3 \ y^x \ 2 \ . \ 3$ ENTER $2 \ y^x +$

p4.6 (a) $. \ 1 \ 3 \ 4 - 2 \ . \ 5 +/- e^x =$

(b) $. \ 1 \ 3 \ 4$ ENTER $2 \ . \ 5$ CHS $e^x -$

p4.8 (a) $1 \ 8 \ 4 \ . \ 7 \ 5 \div 6 \ . \ 5 \ 6 + 3 \ . \ 7 \ 5 \ y^x \ 2 \ . \ 4 \ 4 =$

(b) $1 \ 8 \ 4 \ . \ 7 \ 5$ ENTER $6 \ . \ 5 \ 6 \div 3 \ . \ 7 \ 5$ ENTER $2 \ . \ 4 \ 4 \ y^x +$

p4.10 (a) $2 \ . \ 6 \ 3$ X $(\ 1 \ . \ 3 \ 6 + 7 \ 2 \ . \ 8$ SIN $) =$

(b) $2 \ . \ 6 \ 3$ ENTER $1 \ . \ 3 \ 6$ ENTER $7 \ 2 \ . \ 8$ SIN $+$ X

p4.12 (a) $(\ 3 \ . \ 4 \ e^x + 1 \ 2 \ 6$ TAN $) \div (\ 2 \ . \ 4 \ e^x - 2 \ 9 \ 4$ SIN $) =$

(b) $3 \ . \ 4 \ e^x \ 1 \ 2 \ 6$ TAN $+ 2 \ . \ 4 \ e^x \ 2 \ 9 \ 4$ SIN $- \div$

p4.14 (a) $(\ . \ 3 \ 5 \ 6 + 2 \ . \ 2$ X $. \ 2 \ 8 \ 4 - 1 \ . \ 8 \ 3$ X $. \ 5 \ 4 \ ) \div (\ 1 \ . \ 3$
    $3 + . \ 3 \ 2$ SIN $x^2 \ ) =$

(b) $. \ 3 \ 5 \ 6$ ENTER $2 \ . \ 2$ ENTER $. \ 2 \ 8 \ 4$ X $+ 1 \ . \ 8 \ 3$ ENTER $.$
    $5 \ 4$ X $- 1 \ . \ 3 \ 3$ ENTER $. \ 3 \ 2$ SIN $x^2 + \div$

p4.16 (a) $1 \ 0 \ 4$ X $(\ (\ 1 \ . \ 7 \ 3 + . \ 7 \ 2$ SIN $x^2 \ )$ LN $- . \ 2 \ 8 \ 4$ X $5 \ . \ 6$
    $2 \ 2 \ ) =$

(b) $1 \ . \ 7 \ 3$ ENTER $. \ 7 \ 2$ SIN $x^2 +$ LN $. \ 2 \ 8 \ 4$ ENTER $5 \ . \ 6 \ 2 \ 2$
    X $- 1 \ 0 \ 4$ X

p4.18 162.866 667

p4.20 1187.120

p4.22 0.630 897

p4.24 92 978 087.21

p4.26 27.840 763

p4.28 1826.201 565

p4.30 4295.499 653

p4.32 6.145 115

p4.34 0.331 496

Chapter 5

p5.2 (a) 167°F
(b) 626.7°R
(c) 348.2 K

p5.4 (a) 100°C   (c) 1059.7°R
(b) 153.2 K   (d) 1800°R

p5.6 M/F^2

p5.8 dimensionless

p5.10 ft-lb

p5.12 $lb \cdot s^2/ft$

p5.14 (a) M (d) L^3
(b) F (e) L/T
(c) L^2 (f) dimensionless

p5.16 (a) length = m, time = s,
      force = kg·m/s² or N,
      mass = kg
(b) length = ft, time = s,
      force = lb, mass = lb_m

p5.18 (a) 1.1 mm
(b) 1 cm
(c) 5.165 Mm
(d) 2.5 μm
(e) 7.32 N
(f) 2.1 dm
(g) 7.4 μm

p5.20 (a) 18 s
     (b) 75 m
     (c) 4 m/h
     (d) 6 A
     (e) 9 mm or nine millimeters
     (f) 7 N · m or seven newton-meters

p5.22 (a) 1500 in   (c) 3 m^3
     (b) 6366 m^3 (d) 161 hp

p5.24 1.2 m/s

p5.26 1.9 m^3

p5.28 $185

p5.30 36 tons

Chapter 6

p6.2 slope = 1.5, y-intercept = -2

p6.4 $x = 1$

p6.6 $y = 0.1875x + 0.6875$

p6.8 $x = 5, y = 3$

p6.10 $k = -4, t = 7$

p6.12 $x = 4, y = -3, z = 7$

p6.14 $x = -1, 5$

p6.16 $x = 0, 0, 1, 3$

p6.18 $x = 1.5130$

p6.20 $x = 0.3868$

Chapter 7

p7.26 one answer is $T = 0.97t - 21$

p7.28 one cycle

p7.30 two cycles

p7.32 one cycle

p7.38 one answer is $V = 470 \, e^{-0.39t}$

p7.40 one answer is $v = 1120 \, e^{-36t}$

p7.44 one answer is $C = 5.67 \, T^{-0.77}$

p7.46 one answer is $d = 0.77 \, F^{0.40}$

Chapter 8

p8.2 (a) 1.75, use 2
    (b) 3.5
    (c) $3.5 - 5.5$
    (d) $3.5 - 5.5 = 6$
         $5.5 - 7.5 = 6$
         $7.5 - 9.5 = 3$
         $9.5 - 11.5 = 2$

p8.4 (a) 3   (b) $9 - 12$

p8.6 $0 - 5 = 3, 5 - 10 = 12,$
    $10 - 15 = 23, 15 - 20 = 25$

p8.8 (a) 14   (b) 18   (c) 13

p8.10 (a) 16   (b) 10   (c) 64%

p8.12 (a) 5.6   (b) 5   (c) 3

p8.14 (a) 390   (b) 400   (c) 500

p8.16 (a) 5.4   (b) 5   (c) 5

p8.18 s = 2.55

p8.20 s = 2.69

p8.22 Set 1 much narrower and higher than set 2

p8.24 (a) 1.0   (b) 0   (c) -2.0

p8.26 (a) 89.5   (c) 66
     (b) 78   (d) 51

p8.28 (a) 1250
     (b) 400
     (c) 398

p8.30 $r = 0.62$

p8.32 $\Sigma x^2 = 210, \Sigma xy = 138,$
    $(\Sigma y)^2 = 361, n\Sigma y^2 = 465$

p8.34 (a) liters pumped/h
     (b) $\Sigma xy = 439$
     (c) $r = 0.99$

p8.36 $y = 3.48 + 0.0968(x - 33.8)$

p8.38 $y = 68.6 + 2.71(x - 28.3)$

Chapter 9

p9.2 0, 1, 2, 3, 4, 5, 6, 7, 8, 10, 11, 12, 13, 14, 15, 16, 17, 18, 20, 21, 22

p9.4 $1 \times 2^2 + 0 \times 2^1 + 1 \times 2^0 + 0 \times 2^{-1} + 1 \times 2^{-2} + 1 \times 2^{-3} + 1 \times 2^{-4}$

p9.6 (a) 45
(b) 423
(c) 158
(d) 2893
(e) 276

p9.8 No. Three bits are required for each octal digit in general.

p9.10

letter	ASCII	Binary
B	42_{16}	01000010
Y	59_{16}	01011001
T	54_{16}	01010100
E	45_{16}	01000101

p9.12 1000 0101 = 85

p9.16 The contents of a memory location is data and represents the value of a number, character etc. that is stored. The address of the data tells where in memory the information is stored.

p9.18 $2^{10} = 1024_{10}$. Memory locations would be numbered 0 to 1023_{10} relative to the start of the ROM

p9.24 total cost of order $514.50

p9.25 Ticket price of $3.40 produces maximum profit of $3,872.00

p9.30 Coordinates would be multiplied by appropriate sin and cos functions. This could be accomplished with a coordinate transformation matrix. The new data file would be the same size.

p9.32 (a) rectangular coordinates
(b) spherical coordinates
(c) spherical coordinates
(d) cylindrical coordinates

Chapter 10

p10.2 (a) Sulfur
(b) Tungsten
(c) Californium

p10.4 At wt = 35.458 AMU

p10.6 At wt = 20.18 AMU

p10.8 (a) H_2SO_4 (b) 98.07 g

p10.10 $CuSO_4$

p10.12 $C_3H_6O_2$

p10.14 312 g

p10.16 7.8×10^{23}

p10.18 25.44 moles

p10.20 172.8 g

p10.22 (a) 111 g
(b) 366.3 g
(c) 183.2 g

p10.24 10 mL

p10.26 (a) 0.2 N
(b) 0.4 M
(c) 39.2 g

p10.28 1.4 L

p10.30 101.6°F

p10.32 1119°C

p10.34 (a) Arsenic
(b) 33
(c) 35

p10.36 (a) Lead
(b) 82
(c) 214

p10.38 (a) 1.78 min
(b) 7.89 min
(c) 20.3 min

p10.40 3.25 years

Chapter 11

p11.2 6 volts

p11.4 30 ohms

p11.6 Ohm's law is not sufficient.

p11.8 14 ohms

p11.10 Total resistance increases and slope of resulting plot decreases.

p11.12 $R_{\text{TOTAL}} = 1.479$ ohms

p11.14 Total resistance decreases and slope of resulting plot increases.

p11.16 $R_{\text{TOTAL}} = 14.76$ ohms

p11.18 19.88 volts

Chapter 12

p12.2 110 N $\underline{/145°}$, $F_x = -90.1$ N, $F_y = 63.1$ N

p12.4 170 N $\underline{/323°}$, $F_x = 136$ N, $F_y = -102$ N

p12.6 87.4 N $\underline{/109°}$

p12.8 73.0 N $\underline{/211°}$

p12.10 51 N $\underline{/150°}$

p12.12 68 N $\underline{/246°}$

p12.14 208 N $\underline{/332°}$

p12.16 79.1 lb $\underline{/190°}$

p12.18 94.3 N $\underline{/111°}$

p12.20 142 N $\underline{/79.6°}$

p12.22 278 N $\underline{/78.1°}$

p12.24 -46.25 ft · lb

p12.26 -5956 in · lb

p12.28 534.6 N · m

p12.30 7240 ft · lb

p12.40 $R_1 = 12.6$ kN, $R_2 = 4.9$ kN, $R_3 = 0$

p12.42 $R_1 = 1250$ lb, $R_2 = -1875$ lb, $R_3 = 1875$ lb

p12.44 $R_1 = 32.5$ N, $R_2 = 93.7$ N, $R_3 = 65.0$ N

p12.46 $R_1 = 225$ N, $R_2 = 130$ N, $R_3 = 260$ N

p12.48 at left support: $R_y = 2750$ lb
tension in cable:
$T = 1250$ lb

p12.50 at left support: $R_y = 49.9$ N
at right support:
$R_x = -29.6$ N,
$R_y = 53.5$ N

p12.52 at upper support:
$R_x = -538$ N, $R_y = 500$ N
at lower support:
$R_x = 538$ N

p12.54 $R_x = 228$ N, $R_y = 0$,
$M = -535$ N · m

Chapter 13

p13.2 progress reports, inspection reports, laboratory reports

p13.4 feasibility studies, recommendation reports, journal articles

p13.12 progress reports relate the status of an incomplete project; should include what has been accomplished, what has been completed, unexpected difficulties, schedule changes, budget difficulties, etc.

p13.14 proposal

p13.16 (a) informational
(b) argumentative
(c) persuasive
(d) informational
(e) informational

p13.18 preface, letter of transmittal, title page, table of contents, list of tables or illustrations, abstract

p13.20 title of report, date, name of individual responsible for report

p13.22 Descriptive abstracts provide no information beyond an enumeration of topics covered while informative abstracts summarize key information.

p13.24 introduction, core report, conclusion of report

p13.26 what steps taken, when

taken, why, how executed, results

p13.28 Informal is usually a simple reference to an established authority while formal consists of a bibliographic reference in the text and a footnote or end note.

p13.32 (a) finding
(b) recommendation
(c) finding
(d) finding

p13.34 presentation of material without resorting to memorization or use of notes

p13.36 Stapled pages require the reader to lower his head too much.

p13.38 It is easier to skip parts of material when time limit is near.

p13.40 Place lips 6 to 12 inches from the microphone.

p13.42 amplify and illustrate ideas, add visual imagery to make ideas more easily understood, not intrude on message

p13.44 They may not fit on the projection screen.

p13.46 two

Appendix A

pA.2 1.13432×10^5
pA.4 0.0002441
pA.6 $1.861\ x^{9/8} y^{5/24}$
pA.8 $1.3333\ b^{11/6}/a^{5/2}$
pA.10 10^5
pA.12 120175
pA.14 0.0000035
pA.16 100
pA.18 1.1428×10^{-7}
pA.20 0.33333

pA.22 4
pA.24 8.3704×10^{46}
pA.28 $x = 2.44$
pA.30 $x = 0.14356$
pA.32 $x = 10^5$
pA.34 $x = 1.7266$

Appendix B

pB.4 32.6736°
pB.6 (a) 0.7853 radians
(b) −2.3558 radians
(c) 12.564 radians
(d) 2.3558 radians
(e) 4.3625 radians
(f) 1.9983 radians
(g) −4.7115 radians
(h) −1.047 radians

pB.8 (a) 18.00°
(b) 51.43°
(c) 128.6°
(d) 450.0°
(e) −300.0°
(f) 900.0°

pB.10

	a	b	c
1	5.00	8.66	10.0
2	5.0	18.66	19.32
3	11.54	20.0	23.1
4			20.0
5	5.0	10.0	11.18
6	2.0	3.0	3.6
7			

	A	B	C	Existence of Solution
1	30	60	90	yes
2	15	75	90	yes
3	30	60	90	yes
4				no
5	26.56	63.44	90	yes
6	33.69	56.31	90	yes
7	30	60	90	no

pB.12 −7.6°
pB.14 5.835 A

Index

B

C

D

Table of Symbols

Roman letters, capital:

A   cross-sectional area; uniform series of cash flows

C_o initial concentration

C_t concentration at time t

E   modulus of elasticity

F   future worth, force

F   force

F_x force component in x direction

F_y force component in y direction

I   current

K   kinetic energy

L   length

M   mass; molarity; moment

N   factor of safety

P   pressure; power; force; present worth

P_a absolute pressure

P_g gage pressure

Q   shear force; heat; volumetric flow rate

$\dot{Q}$ heat per unit time

R   hydraulic radius

R   reaction force

R_x reaction force component in x direction

R_y reaction force component in y direction

S   slope of energy grade line

T   time

U   work, internal energy

U   unit matrix

V   voltage; volume; potential energy; velocity

W   weight; work

W   weight

$\dot{W}$ work per unit time

Roman letters, lower case:

a   acceleration

a   acceleration

a_x acceleration component in x direction

a_y acceleration component in y direction

b   the y-intercept

c   specific heat

d   diameter

$\mathbf{f}_f$ frictional force

g   acceleration due to gravity, 32.2 ft/s^2 or 9.81 m/s^2

h   height

h_c depth to centroid

i $\sqrt{-1}$; interest rate

i   unit vector in x direction

j   unit vector in y direction

l   length

l_o initial length

m   mass; slope of line

n   coefficient of roughness; number of interest periods

r   correlation coefficient; radius

s   standard deviation

v   velocity

v   velocity

w   weight per unit length

Formulas

circumference of circle $= 2\pi r$

area of circle $= \pi r^2$

surface area of sphere $= 4\pi r^2$

volume of sphere $= (4/3)\pi r^3$

area of rectangle $= ab$

length of arc $= \pi r\Theta/180$, Θ in degrees

length of chord $= 2r \sin(0.5\ \Theta)$

area of ellipse $= \pi ab$

volume of pyramid $= 1/3$ area of base $\times$ altitude

volume of cylinder $= \pi r^2 h$

area of curved surface of a right cylinder $= 2\pi rh$

area of curved surface of a right cone $= \pi r \sqrt{r^2 + h^2}$

volume of a cone $= (1/3)\ \pi r^2 h$

lateral area of regular prism $=$ perimeter of right section $\times$ length

volume of regular prism $=$ area of base $\times$ altitude

volume of pyramid $= (1/3)$ area of base $\times$ altitude

quadratic equation: $x = \dfrac{-B \pm \sqrt{B^2 - 4AC}}{2A}$

Definitions and Values

density = mass/volume

specific weight = weight/volume

Pythagorean theorem: $a^2 + b^2 = c^2$

law of sines:

$$\frac{\sin A}{a} = \frac{\sin B}{b} = \frac{\sin C}{c}$$

law of cosines:

$$c^2 = a^2 + b^2 - 2ab \cos C$$

atmospheric pressure = 14.7 psi or 1.013×10^5 Pa

specific weight of water = 62.4 lb/ft³ or 8.33 lb/gal or 9800 N/m³

density of water = 62.4 lb_m/ft³ or 1.94 slug/ft³ or 1000 kg/m³

density of air = 1.225 kg/m³ or 0.07647 lb_m/ft³ or 0.002377 slug/ft³

acceleration due to gravity = 32.17 ft/s² or 9.81 m/s²

$\pi = 3.14159 \ldots$

$e = 2.71828 \ldots$

1 radian = 57.296°

Greek letters, capital:

Δ incremental change

Θ temperature

Σ summation

Ω Ohm

Greek letters, lower case:

γ specific weight

δ change in length

ϵ normal strain

μ arithmetic mean

η thermal efficiency

η_c Carnot efficiency

ρ density

σ normal stress

τ shear stress